THE ILLUSTRATED ENCYCLOPEDIA OF
BIRDS OF BRITAIN
EUROPE & AFRICA

THE ILLUSTRATED ENCYCLOPEDIA OF
BIRDS OF BRITAIN
EUROPE & AFRICA

DAVID ALDERTON

with illustrations by Peter Barrett

southwater

This edition is published by Southwater, an imprint of
Anness Publishing Ltd, Blaby Road, Wigston, Leicestershire LE18 4SE
Email: info@anness.com
Web: www.southwaterbooks.com; www.annesspublishing.com

If you like the images in this book and would like to investigate using
them for publishing, promotions or advertising, please visit our website
www.practicalpictures.com for more information.

Publisher: Joanna Lorenz
Editorial Director: Helen Sudell
Project Editors: Debra Mayhew and Catherine Stuart
Text Editor: Ian Woodward
Text and Jacket Design: Nigel Partridge
Chief Illustrator: Peter Barrett
Front Cover Photographs: little owl (main picture) supplied by
Dennis Avon; mute swan (montage, top-right) and blue tit (montage,
bottom-right) supplied by Ardea
Front Flap Photograph: red-crested touraco supplied by Dennis Avon
Additional Illustrations: see Picture Acknowledgements
Production Controller: Christine Ni

ETHICAL TRADING POLICY
At Anness Publishing we believe that business should be conducted in
an ethical and ecologically sustainable way, with respect for the
environment and a proper regard to the replacement of the natural
resources we employ.
As a publisher, we use a lot of wood pulp in high-quality paper for
printing, and that wood commonly comes from spruce trees. We are
therefore currently growing more than 750,000 trees in three Scottish
forest plantations. The forests we manage contain more than 3.5 times
the number of trees employed each year in making paper for the books
we manufacture.
Because of this ongoing ecological investment programme, you, as our
customer, can have the pleasure and reassurance of knowing that a
tree is being cultivated on your behalf to naturally replace the materials
used to make the book you are holding. For further information about
this scheme, go to www.annesspublishing.com/trees

Parts of this book have previously appeared in *The World Encyclopedia
of Birds and Birdwatching*

PUBLISHER'S NOTE
Although the advice and information in this book are believed to be
accurate and true at the time of going to press, neither the authors nor
the publisher can accept any legal responsibility or liability for any errors
or omissions that may have been made.

CONTENTS

THE DIRECTORY 64

The Avifauna of Great Britain, Europe and Africa 66

INTRODUCTION

Birds have been a source of fascination and inspiration to people since the dawn of history. Birds' mastery of the skies not only inspired humans to invent flying machines but also helped facilitate the development of modern aircraft, since aeroplane designers borrowed the aerodynamic features of birds to revolutionize inter-continental travel.

Birds have also influenced our cultures in a spiritual sense, as indicated, for example, by the thunderbird legends of the native North Americans and the phoenix featured in Egyptian mythology. In Europe also, birds have become significant in various festivals. The robin has become linked with Christmas, while the return of the common cuckoo (*Cuculus canorus*), from its African wintering grounds, is eagerly awaited as a sign of Spring. More unusually, the habit of nesting on rooftops favoured by white storks (*Ciconia ciconia*) enabled the parents of newborn babies to pretend to their curious children that the birds had carried them to the home.

It may seem surprising, but there are still new species of birds being discovered every year. Among the most recent is a new bald-headed parrot from the Mato Grosso region of Brazil, reported for the first time

Below: Birds have adapted to live, feed and breed in a wide range of different habitats. Here a puffin (Fratercula arctica) *is returning from a successful fishing trip at sea.*

Above: The ostrich (Struthio camelus) *is the largest bird in the world today, and can be found in open countryside, mainly in central and southern parts of Africa. Its call has been likened to a lion's roar.*

in July 2002. As an approximate guide, there are over 9,000 avian species present on Earth – a total far in excess of the number of mammals. There is virtually no environment on the planet where birds are not to be seen, even in the freezing tundra of the Arctic, where auks such as puffins (*Fratercula arctica*) nest in underground burrows or cliff faces to incubate eggs in one of the most inhospitable regions on Earth.

Birds have spread so widely over the surface of the planet not only because of their ability to fly, but also because they are often highly adaptable in their dietary habits. Birds eat a wide variety of foods, ranging from microsopic plankton to the carcasses of large mammals, as well as all types of vegetable matter and numerous invertebrates.

In recent years, human activities have continued to take their toll on avian populations around the world, and are now threatening the very survival of many species. On the bright side, however, more positive intervention is seeking to right these wrongs by using thorough research to promote the survival of diminished populations. The current efforts to rear and relocate young golden eagles (*Aquila chrysaetos*), discussed later under Endangered Species and Conservation, is an encouraging example of this new enlightenment.

Birdwatching has also benefited from new advances, and media such as the Internet now enable valuable

Below: Advanced photographic equipment has greatly aided the study of birds, enabling species such as this hoopoe (Upupa epops) to be observed in flight and even at the entrance to its nest.

information on new sightings to be relayed instantly. Undoubtedly, webcam opportunities to observe bird sites, even on another continent, will increase in the years ahead. The fact that we are able to spot birds in any locality helps to explain why it remains a popular pastime. No special equipment is necessarily required, although binoculars, sketchpads and similar items can add to your enjoyment and understanding of avian life.

This book is a celebration of birds that sets out to reveal the diversity in both their form and lifestyles. The second part features a directory of species which can be seen throughout Great Britain, Europe and Africa, and off the shores of these continents. Each bird is placed within the geographical context in which it is most likely to be seen. Even if you do not have the opportunity to visit the forests of the Congo, or the icy landscape of the northern Arctic, you can still marvel at the diversity of avian life, as portrayed in these pages.

HOW BIRDS LIVE

The most obvious thing that distinguishes all birds, from the tiny goldcrest *(Regulus regulus)*, which is Europe's smallest bird, to the gigantic African ostrich *(Struthio camelus)*, is the presence of feathers on their bodies. The need for birds' bodies to be lightweight so that they can fly with minimum effort has led to evolutionary changes in their anatomy, and yet the basic skeletal structure of all birds is remarkably similar, irrespective of size. It is evident that even the few groups of flightless birds, which include open country species like the ostrich, as well as Antarctic inhabitants such as penguins (Spheniscidae), are descended from ancestors that once possessed the power of flight, although these birds have since evolved along different lines to suit their habitat.

The other feature unique to birds is that all species reproduce by means of calcareous eggs. Actual breeding habits are very diverse, however. Some birds even transfer the task of incubation to other species, by laying in their nests, while other species create natural incubators that serve to hatch their chicks and carefully regulate the temperature inside.

There is even greater diversity in the feeding habits of birds, as reflected by differences in their bill structure and also in their digestive tracts. Birds' dietary preferences play a critical part in the survival of their habitat. For example, in tropical rainforests, many fruit-eating species help to disperse indigestible seeds through the forest, thus helping to ensure the natural regeneration of the vegetation.

The birds of tropical rainforests are often surprisingly hard to observe, betraying their presence more by their calls than by their bright colours. Birdwatching itself can develop into an absorbing pastime, offering an unparalleled insight into the natural world. The pages that follow offer practical tips on observing birds safely and successfully, and present detailed colour illustrations and in-depth profiles of distribution, habitat, size, nests and food, to help you identify a vast range of species.

Left: Black-headed gulls (Larus ridibundus). These noisy and conspicuous birds have highly adaptable and sociable natures, and may be seen in large groups. They have extended their range inland from coastal areas in recent years, thanks to a wider availability of food near to human habitations.

THE ORIGINS OF BIRDS

Vertebrates – first flying reptiles called pterosaurs, and later birds – took to the air about 190 million years ago. Adapting to an aerial existence marked a very significant step in vertebrate development, because of the need for a new method of locomotion, and a radically different body design.

The age of *Archaeopteryx*

Back in 1861, workers in a limestone quarry in Bavaria, southern Germany, unearthed a strange fossil that resembled a bird in appearance and was about the size of a modern crow, but also had teeth. The idea that the fossil was a bird was confirmed by the clear evidence of feathers impressed into the stone, as the presence of plumage is one of the characteristic distinguishing features of all birds. The 1860s were a time when the debate surrounding evolution was becoming fierce, and the discovery created huge interest, partly because it suggested that birds may have evolved from dinosaurs. It confirmed that birds had lived on Earth for at least 145 million years, existing even before the age of the dinosaurs came to a close in the Cretaceous period, about 65 million years ago. As the oldest-known bird, it was given the name *Archaeopteryx*, meaning "ancient wings".

Pterosaurs

A study of the anatomy of *Archaeopteryx*'s wings revealed that these early birds did not just glide but were capable of using their wings for active flight. Yet they were not the first

vertebrate creatures to have taken to the skies. Pterosaurs had already successfully developed approximately 190 million years ago, during the Jurassic period, and even co-existed with birds for a time. In fact, the remains of one of the later pterosaurs, called *Rhamphorhynchus*, have been found in the same limestone deposits in southern Germany where *Archaeopteryx* was discovered. The pterosaur's wings more closely resembled those of a bat than a bird, consisting simply of a membrane supported by a bony framework, rather than feathers overlying the skin.

Some types of pterosaurs developed huge wingspans, in excess of 7m (23ft), which enabled them to glide almost effortlessly over the surface of the world's oceans, much like albatrosses do today. It appears that they fed primarily on fish and other marine life, scooping their food out of the water in flight. Changes in climate probably doomed the pterosaurs, however, since increasingly turbulent weather patterns meant that gliding became difficult, and they could no longer fly with ease.

Right: An impression of how Archaeopteryx *may have looked. It is impossible to be sure of its coloration from its fossilized remains.*

Avian giants

In the period immediately after the extinction of the dinosaurs, some groups of birds increased rapidly in physical size, and in so doing, lost the ability to fly. Since their increased size meant that they could cover large distances on foot, and as they faced no predators, because large hunting mammals had not yet evolved, these large birds were relatively safe. In New Zealand, home of the large flightless moas, such giants thrived until the start of human settlement about a millennium ago. The exact date of the final extinction of the moas is not recorded, but the group had probably died out entirely by the middle of the 19th century.

Below: The largest species of moa would have dwarfed a man.

Below: All pterosaurs had a similar body shape with a narrow head, which may have been embellished with a crest of some sort. This may have been used for display purposes and also to reduce air resistance in flight. The wing structure of pterosaurs was very different from that of birds: their wings basically consisted of skin membranes, stretched out behind the forearms.

It was this large surface area that allowed them to glide with little effort, but becoming airborne in the first place required great effort. The lack of body covering over the skin also had the effect of causing greater heat loss from the body. In birds, the feathers provide insulation as well as assisting active flight.

Below: The chicks of the South American hoatzin (Opisthocomus hoazin) are unique in possessing claws on their wing tips, which enable them to climb trees. These claws disappear by the time the birds are old enough to fly.

The spread of birds

After the age of *Archaeopteryx*, it is thought that birds continued to radiate out over the globe and became increasingly specialized. Unfortunately, there is very little fossil evidence to help us understand their early history. This lack of fossils is partly due to the fact that the small carcasses of birds would have been eaten whole by scavengers, and partly because their lightweight, fragile skeletons would not have fossilized easily. In addition, most birds would not have been trapped and died under conditions that were favourable for fossilization.

By the end of the age of the dinosaurs, birds had become far more numerous. Many seabirds still possessed teeth in their jaws, reflecting their reptilian origins. These probably assisted them in catching fish and other aquatic creatures. It was at this stage that the ancestors of contemporary bird groups such as waterfowl and gulls started to emerge. Most of the forerunners of today's birds had evolved by the Oligocene epoch, some 38 million years ago.

Some groups of birds that existed in these times have since disappeared, notably the phororhacids, which ranged widely over South America and even into parts of the southern United States. These birds were fearsome predators, capable of growing to nearly 3m (10ft) in height. They were equipped with deadly beaks and talons, and probably hunted together in groups.

Recent finds

During the mid-1990s, the discovery of avian fossils in China that were apparently contemporary with those of *Archaeopteryx* aroused considerable interest. Like its German relative, *Confuciusornis* possessed claws on the tips of its wings, which probably helped these early birds to move around. Similar claws are seen today in hoatzin chicks. *Confuciusornis* resembled modern birds more closely than *Archaeopteryx* in one significant respect: it lacked teeth in its jaws. Further study of the recent fossil finds from this part of the world is required, however, as some may not be genuine.

THE SKELETON AND PARTS OF A BIRD

The bird's skeleton has evolved to be light yet robust, both characteristics that help with flight. To this end, certain bones, particularly in the skull, have become fused, while others are absent, along with the teeth. The result is that birds' bodies are lightweight compared to those of other vertebrates.

In order to be able to fly, a bird needs a lightweight body so that it can become airborne with minimal difficulty. It is not just teeth that are missing from the bird's skull, but the associated heavy jaw muscles as well. These have been replaced by a light, horn-covered bill that is adapted in shape to the bird's feeding habits. Some of the limb bones, such as the humerus in the shoulder, are hollow, which also cuts down on weight. At the rear of the body, the bones in the vertebral column have become fused, which gives greater stability as well as support for the tail feathers.

The avian skeleton

In birds, the most marked evidence of specialization can be seen in the legs. Their location is critical to enable a bird to maintain its balance. The legs are found close to the midline, set slightly back near the bird's centre of gravity. These limbs are powerful, helping to provide lift at take-off and absorb the impact of landing. Strong legs also allow most birds to hop over the ground with relative ease.

There are some differences in the skeleton between different groups of birds. For example, the atlas and axis bones at the start of the vertebral column are fused in the case of hornbills, but in no other family.

Feet and toes

Birds' feet vary in length, and are noticeably extended in waders, which helps them to distribute their weight more evenly. The four toes may be arranged either in a typical 3:1 perching grip, with three toes gripping the front of the perch and one behind, or in a 2:2 configuration, known as zygodactyl, which gives a surer grip. The zygodactyl grip is seen in relatively few groups of birds, notably parrots and toucans. Touracos have flexible toes so they can swap back and forth between these two options.

The zygodactyl arrangement of their toes helps some parrots to use their feet like hands for holding food. Birds generally have claws at the ends of their toes, which have developed into sharp talons in the case of birds of prey, helping them to catch their quarry even in flight. Many birds also use their claws for preening, and they can provide balance for birds that run or climb.

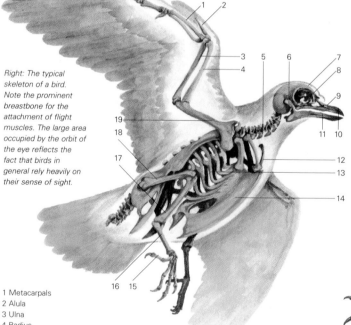

Right: The typical skeleton of a bird. Note the prominent breastbone for the attachment of flight muscles. The large area occupied by the orbit of the eye reflects the fact that birds in general rely heavily on their sense of sight.

1 Metacarpals
2 Alula
3 Ulna
4 Radius
5 Cervical vertebrae
6 Ear
7 Cranium
8 Eye socket
9 Nostril
10 Bill (upper mandible)
11 Bill (lower mandible)
12 Clavicle (wishbone)
13 Ribs
14 Sternum (breastbone)
15 Metatarsals
16 Tarsus
17 Tibia and Fibula
18 Femur
19 Humerus

Parrot

Above: Parrots use their feet for holding food, rather like human hands.

Bird of prey

Above: In birds of prey, the claws have become talons for grasping prey.

Wader

Above: Long toes make it easier for waders to walk over muddy ground or water plants.

Duck

Above: The webbed feet of ducks provide propulsion in water.

Above: The narrow bill of waders such as this curlew (Numenius arquata) enables these birds to probe for food in sandy or muddy areas.

Above: Birds of prey such as the golden eagle (Aquila chrysaetos) rely on a sharp bill with a hooked tip to tear their prey apart.

Above: Herons (Ardea) have strong, pointed bills, which they use like scissors to seize and hold slippery prey such as frogs.

Above: Flamingos (Phoenicopteridae) have bills that enable them to feed with their heads trailing backwards in the water.

Above: The grey parrot (Psittacus erithacus) has a strong bill for cracking nuts, further aided by a pointed tip on the upper part.

Above: Whale-headed storks (Balaeniceps rex) have large bills that allow them to scoop up quite large vertebrate prey.

Bills

The bills of birds vary quite widely in shape and size, and reflect their feeding habits. The design of the bill also has an impact on the force that it can generate. The bills of many larger parrots are especially strong, allowing them to crack hard nut shells. In addition, they can move their upper and lower bill independently, which produces a wider gape and, in turn, allows more pressure to be exerted.

Wings

A bird's wing is built around just three digits, which correspond to human fingers. In comparison, bats have five digits supporting their fleshy

membranes. The three digits of birds provide a robust structure. The power of the wings is further enhanced by the fusion of the wrist bones and the carpals to create the single bone known as the carpometacarpus, which runs along the edge of the wing.

At the front of the chest, the clavicles are joined together to form what in chickens is called the wishbone. The large, keel-shaped breastbone, or sternum, runs along the underside of the body. It is bound by the ribs to the backbone, which provides stability, especially during flight. In addition, the major flight muscles are located in the lower body when the bird is airborne.

Bizarrely built birds

Nature has resulted in a number of decidedly odd-looking birds, notably on the offshore islands of vast oceans where they evolved undisturbed by predators. One famous species has captured the human imagination for centuries. First recorded in 1601, the dodo (*Raphus cucullatus*) had been driven to extinction by 1690, although several living examples of this flightless pigeon were brought to Europe, and aroused great curiosity because of their ungainly appearance. Unfortunately, many of today's representations of dodos are the subject of some artistic licence, as there is not a complete surviving specimen in any museum in the world. Those on display at such institutions have been constructed with reference to contemporary accounts and artworks, and it has been noted by ornithologists that, while early European portraits capture the dodo's athleticism, later artworks increasingly depict the famous bird as fat, colourful and ungainly. This may, in part, suggest a preference for the absurd among the artists, but also that the captive dodos were fed an inappropriate diet. These portraits should not be viewed as a measure of strict anatomical accuracy.

Below: The most striking feature of the dodo was its long, hooked bill. As a flightless bird, its wings were little more than stubs which hung on each side of its plump body. Rather uniquely, it also seems to have possessed a short tail. The legs, by contrast, were thick and strong – a valuable support for its weight, and possibly also an aid to speed and agility when running through woodland.

FEATHERS

The presence of feathers is one of the main distinguishing characteristics that set birds apart from other groups of creatures on the planet. The number of feathers on a bird's body varies considerably – a swan may have as many as 25,000 feathers, for instance, while a tiny hummingbird has just 1,000 in all.

Aside from the bill, legs and feet, the entire body of the bird is covered in feathers. The plumage does not grow randomly over the bird's body, but develops along lines of so-called feather tracts, or pterylae. These are separated by bald areas known as apteria. The apteria are not conspicuous under normal circumstances, because the contour feathers overlap to cover the entire surface of the body. Plumage may also sometimes extend down over the legs and feet as well, in the case of birds from cold climates, providing extra insulation here.

Feathers are made of a tough protein called keratin, which is also found in our hair and nails. Birds have three main types of feathers: the body, or contour, feathers; the strong, elongated flight feathers on the wings, and the warm, wispy down feathers next to their skin.

A diet deficient in sulphur-containing amino acids, which are the basic building blocks of protein, will result in poor feathering, creating "nutritional barring" across the flight and tail feathers. Abnormal plumage coloration can also have nutritional causes in some cases. These changes are usually reversible if more favourable environmental conditions precede the next moult.

The functions of feathers

Plumage has a number of functions, not just relating to flight. It provides a barrier that retains warm air close to the bird's body and helps to maintain body temperature, which is higher in birds than mammals – typically between 41 and 43.5°C (106 and 110°F). The down feathering that lies close to the skin, and the overlying contour plumage, are vital for maintaining body warmth. Most birds have a small volume relative to their surface area, which can leave them vulnerable to hypothermia.

A special oil produced by the preen gland, located at the base of the tail, waterproofs the plumage. This oil, which is spread over the feathers as the bird preens itself, prevents water penetrating the feathers, which would cause the bird to become so

Below: Feathering is highly significant for display purposes in some species, particularly members of the Phasanidae family. The cock blue peafowl (Pavo cristatus) has a very elaborate train of feathers, which it fans open to deter rivals and attract mates.

Above: A bird's flight feathers are longer and more rigid than the contour feathers that cover the body, or the fluffy down feathers that lie next to the skin. The longest, or primary, flight feathers, which generate most thrust, are located along the outer rear edges of the wings. The tail feathers are often similar in shape to the flight feathers, with the longest being found in the centre. Splaying the tail feathers increases drag and so slows the bird down.

1 Primaries	9 Auricular region
2 Secondaries	(ear)
3 Axillaries	10 Nape
4 Rump	11 Back
5 Lateral tail feathers	12 Greater under-
6 Central tail feathers	wing coverts
7 Breast	13 Lesser under-
8 Cere	wing coverts

Above: The vulturine guineafowl (Acryllium vulturinum) is so called because of its bare head and neck, which is a feature of vultures, although it is not a carnivorous species itself.

waterlogged that it could no longer fly. The contour feathers that cover the body are also used for camouflage in many birds. Barring, in particular, breaks up the outline of the bird's body, helping to conceal it in its natural habitat.

The plumage has become modified in some cases, reflecting the individual lifestyle of the species concerned. Woodpeckers, for example, have tail feathers that are short and rather sharp at their tips, providing additional support for gripping onto the sides of trees. Vultures, on the other hand, have bare heads because plumage here would soon become stained and matted with blood when these birds fed on a carcass.

Social significance of plumage

Plumage can also be important in social interactions between birds. Many species have differences in their feathering that separate males from females, and often juveniles can also be distinguished by their plumage. Cock birds are usually more brightly coloured, which helps them to attract their mates, but this does not apply in every case. The difference between the sexes in terms of their plumage can be quite marked. Cock birds of a number

of species have feathers forming crests as well as magnificent tail plumes, which are seen to greatest effect in peacocks (*Pavo cristatus*), whose display is one of the most remarkable sights in the whole of the avian world.

Recent studies have confirmed that the birds that appear relatively dull in colour to our eyes, such as the hill mynah (*Gracula religiosa*) with its blackish plumage, are seen literally in a different light by other birds. They are able to visually perceive the ultraviolet component of light, which is normally invisible to us, making these seemingly dull birds appear greener. Ultraviolet coloration may also be significant in helping birds to choose their mates.

Moulting

Birds' feathering is maintained by preening, but it becomes frayed and worn over time. It is therefore replaced by new plumage during the process of moulting, when the old feathers are shed. Moulting is most often an annual event. However, many young birds shed their nest feathers before they are a year old.

Moulting may also be triggered by the onset of the breeding season in some species, as is the case in many whydahs and weavers. These birds resemble sparrows for much of the year, but their appearance is transformed at the onset of the breeding period. Whydah cock birds develop lengthy tail plumes, and the birds also become more strikingly coloured. Hormonal alterations in the body are important in triggering this process, with external factors such as changing day length also playing a part.

Right: The feather shaft holds the feather in place in the skin. The barbs run off the shaft at regular intervals, rather like the branches of a tree, and divide into smaller branches called barbules. These have tiny hooks attached to them that reinforce the structure of the flight feather, making it more rigid.

Iridescence
Some birds are not brightly coloured, but their plumage literally sparkles in the light, thanks to its structure, which creates an iridescent effect. One of the particular features of iridescence is that the colour of the plumage alters, depending on the angle at which it is viewed, often appearing quite dark, almost black from a side view. This phenomenon is particularly common in some groups of birds, notably members of the starling family (Sturnidae), hummingbirds (Trochilidae) and sunbirds (Nectarinidae), which are described as having metallic feathers as a result.

In some cases, the iridescent feathering is localized, while in others, it is widespread over most of the body. Green and blue iridescence is common, with reddish sheens being seen less often. Iridescence is especially common in cock birds, helping them to attract mates. In some cases, therefore, it is seen only in the breeding plumage, notably on the upperparts of the body and the wings rather than the underparts.

Below: Many cock sunbirds, such as this West African green-headed species (Nectarinia verticalis), display green or bluish iridescent plumage on the head.

Barb | Barbule | Shaft

FLIGHT

Some birds spend much of their lives in the air, whereas others will only fly as a last resort if threatened.
A few species are too heavy to take off at all. The mechanics of flight are similar in all birds, but flight
patterns vary significantly, which can help to identify the various groups in the air.

In most cases, the whole structure of the bird's body has evolved to facilitate flight. It is important for a bird's body weight to be relatively light, because this lessens the muscular effort required to keep it airborne. The powerful flight muscles, which provide the necessary lift, can account for up to a third of the bird's total body weight. They are attached to the breastbone, or sternum, in the midline of the body, and run along the sides of the body from the clavicle along the breastbone to the top of the legs.

Weight and flight
There is an upper weight limit of just over 18kg (40lb), above which birds would not be able to take off successfully. Some larger birds, notably pelicans and swans, need a run-up in order to gain sufficient momentum to lift off, particularly from water. Smaller birds can dart straight off a perch. Approaching the critical upper weight limit for flight, the male Kori bustard (*Ardeotis kori*) is the world's heaviest flying bird, although it prefers to run rather than fly because of the effort involved in becoming airborne.

Below: A typical take-off, as shown by a Harris's hawk (Parabuteo unicinctus).

Above: Birds such as the lammergeier or bearded vulture (Gypaetus barbatus) *can remain airborne with minimum expenditure of energy, by gliding rather than flying.*

Wing shape and beat
The shape of the wing is important for a bird's flying ability. Birds that remain airborne for much of their lives, such as albatrosses, have relatively long wings that allow them to glide with relatively little effort. The wandering albatross (*Diomedea exulans*) has the largest wingspan of any bird, measuring about 3.4m (11ft) from one wing tip to the other. Large, heavy birds such as griffon vultures (*Gyps fulvus*) may have difficulty in flying early in the day, before the land has warmed up. This is because at this stage, there is insufficient heat coming up from the ground to create the thermal air currents that help to keep them airborne. In common with other large birds of prey, griffon vultures seek out these rising columns of air, which provide uplift, and then circle around in them.

The number of wing beats varies dramatically between different species. Hummingbirds (Trochilidae), for example, beat their wings at a greater frequency than any other bird as they hover in front of flowers. Their wings move so fast – sometimes at over 200 beats per minute – that they appear as a total blur to our eyes. At the other extreme, heavy birds such as swans fly with slow, deliberate wing beats.

Lightening the load
It is not just the lightness of the bird's skeleton that helps it to fly. There have been evolutionary changes in the body organs too, most noticeably in the urinary system. Unlike mammals, birds do not have a bladder that fills with urine. Instead, their urine is greatly concentrated, in the form of uric acid, and passes out of the body with their faeces, appearing as a creamy-white, semi-solid component.

1. When resting, a bird typically has a relatively upright stance.

2. As it leans forwards for take-off, it raises its wings and starts to lift its legs.

3. Leaving its perch, the bird pushes off into the air, and opens its wings.

Above: Waterfowl such as this mallard (Anas platyrhynchos) have few difficulties becoming airborne from water, as their plumage is designed to prevent waterlogging.

Below: Some gulls (Laridae) *spend much of their lives on the wing, scanning the surface of the ocean for a sign of prey.*

The aerofoil principle

Once in flight, the shape of the wing is crucial in keeping the bird airborne. Viewed in cross-section from the side, a bird's wing resembles an aeroplane's wing, called an aerofoil, and in fact aeroplanes use the same technique as birds to fly.

The wing is curved across the top, so the movement of air is faster over this part of the wing compared with the lower surface. This produces reduced air pressure on top of the wing, which provides lift and makes it easier for the bird to stay in the air.

The long flight feathers at the rear edge of the wings help to provide the thrust and lift for flight. The tail feathers, too, can help the bird remain airborne. The kestrel (*Falco tinnunculus*), for example, having spotted prey on the ground, spreads its tail feathers to help it remain aloft while it hovers to target its prey.

A bird's wings move in a regular figure-of-eight movement while it is in flight. During the downstroke, the flight feathers join together to push powerfully against the air. The primary flight feathers bend backwards, which propels the bird forwards. As the wing moves upwards, the longer primary flight feathers move apart, which reduces air resistance. The secondary feathers further along the wing provide some slight propulsion. After that the cycle repeats itself.

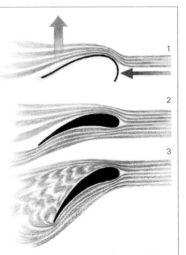

Above: The flow of air over a bird's wing varies according to the wing's position.
1. When the wing is stretched out horizontally, an area of low pressure is created above the wing, causing lift.
2. As the wing is tilted downwards, the flow of the air is disrupted, causing turbulence and loss of lift.
3. When the wing is angled downwards, lift slows, which results in stalling. The bird's speed slows as a consequence.

Flight patterns and formations

Different species of birds have various ways of flying, which can actually aid the birdwatcher in helping to identify them. For example, small birds such as tits (Paridae) and finches (Fringillidae) alternately flap their wings and fold them at their sides, adopting a streamlined shape, which helps to save energy. This produces a characteristic dipping flight. Larger birds such as ducks and geese (Anatidae) maintain a straighter course at an even height.

In some cases, it is not just the individual flying skills of a bird that can help it to stay airborne, but those of its fellows nearby. Birds flying in formation create a slipstream, which makes flying less effort for all the birds behind the leader. This formation is often used on long-distance journeys.

4. Powerful upward and downward sweeps of the wings propel the bird forwards.

5. When coming in to land, a bird lowers its legs and slows its wing movements.

6. Braking is achieved by a vertical landing posture, with the tail feathers spread.

LOCOMOTION

For most birds, flight is the main means of locomotion. However, the ability to move on the ground or in water can be vital, particularly when it comes to obtaining food. Some birds have even lost the ability to fly, relying instead on their swimming or running skills to escape predators and find food.

Not all birds possess the ability to fly, but this does not mean they are handicapped in their natural environment. Penguins may appear to be rather clumsy, shuffling around on land, but they are extremely well adapted to life in the water. Like other primarily aquatic birds, their webbed feet enable them to swim very effectively. Webbing is a common feature seen in aquatic birds. The skin folds linking the toes turn the foot into an effective paddle, allowing the bird to maximize its propulsive forward thrust by pushing against the water. On land, however, webbed feet do impose certain restrictions, because being linked together in this way means that the individual toes are not as flexible.

Aquatic locomotion
When penguins dive, their sleek, torpedo-shaped bodies allow them to swim fast underwater, reaching speeds equivalent to 40km/h (25mph). Their flippers, which evolved from wings,

Below: A group of king penguins (Aptenodytes patagonicus) leap in and out of the water as they swim along, in a form of movement known as porpoising.

help them to steer very effectively as they pursue fish, which form the basis of their diet. Like flying birds, penguins need effective wing muscles to control their movements, so their skeletal structure bears a close similarity to that of flying birds.

Flightless ducks and other aquatic birds, such as the Galapagos Island cormorant (*Nannopterum harrisi*), use a different method of locomotion: they rely entirely on their feet rather than their wings for propulsive power. Their skeletons differ from those of flying birds in that they lack the prominent keel on the sternum for the attachment of flight muscles.

Flightless land birds
A number of land birds have lost the ability to fly. Typically, they are birds that inhabit islands where, until the arrival of cats and rats brought by ships from Europe, they faced few predators. The arrival of predators has left them vulnerable, and many have since become extinct, including the dodo (*Raphus cucullatus*) – a large, flightless pigeon from the island of Mauritius in the Indian Ocean. Even larger in stature was the elephant bird

Above: Puffins (Fratercula arctica) are less agile on land than they are in the sea, and spend much of their life in the water. When swimming, they use their wings like flippers.

(*Aepyornis maximis*), a gigantic species found on Madagascar until as recently as 400 years ago. These birds would dwarf a modern ostrich in size, standing up to 3.15m (10ft) tall, and weighing perhaps as much as 454kg (1,000lb). Their eggs had a volume comparable to seven ostrich eggs, and measured over 30cm (12in) in length.

The moas (*Dinornis maximus*) of New Zealand were the most diverse group of flightless birds ever recorded, the last examples dying out in the 19th century, around the time of European settlement. There may have been as many as a dozen or more different species, and they filled the same sort of niche as grazing mammals, which were then absent from New Zealand.

In the absence of predatory mammals, the moas faced no significant threats to their survival until the first human settlers reached New Zealand. Their large size made them conspicuous, and, having evolved in an environment where they had been safe from persecution, they had lost their ability to fly. Moas were not even able to run fast, in contrast to modern flightless birds such as ostriches. Tragically, they were soon hunted to extinction.

Circulation

The circulatory system is vital in supporting the activities of both flighted and flightless birds, ensuring that their muscles are well supplied with oxygen. The heart acts as the pump, driving the blood around the body. The basic design of the heart is similar to that of a mammal, with the left side being highly developed because it does more work. Overall, the heart rate of birds is much more rapid than mammals of similar size, having been measured at 1,000 beats per minute in the case of canaries at rest. The heart beat rises dramatically during flight, but soon returns to normal when the bird touches down.

The respiratory system

Birds have lungs, located close to the vertebral column, but these do not expand and contract in the same way as those of mammals. Instead, birds rely on a series of air sacs that act rather like bellows, to suck

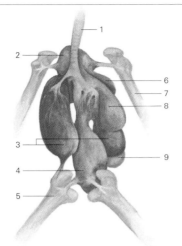

air through their respiratory system. In some cases, these link with the hollow limb bones, and thus help to meet the bird's high requirement for oxygen when flying. A bird's respiratory rate is a reflection of its body size, as well as its level of activity and lifestyle. Common starlings (*Sturnus vulgaris*), for example, typically breathe about 85 times every minute, whereas domestic chickens, which are more sedentary, have an equivalent respiratory rate of only about 20 breaths per minute.

1 Trachea
2 Interclavicular air sac
3 Lungs
4 Abdominal air sac
5 Femur (leg bone)
6 Cervical air sac
7 Humerus (wing bone)
8 Anterior thoracic air sac
9 Posterior thoracic air sac

Above: The ostrich (Struthio camelus) *is the only bird to have just two toes on each foot. This arrangement promotes stability when running, rather like a horse's hoof.*

Ratites

Not all flightless birds are helpless in the face of danger, however. The large, flightless birds known as ratites, including cassowaries, ostriches, emus and rheas, are particularly well able to defend themselves. Their strong legs are quite capable of inflicting lethal blows, especially in the case of the cassowaries (Casuariidae), found in parts of northern Australia, New Guinea and neighbouring islands. These birds have an elongated and deadly sharp claw on their innermost toe. If the cassowary is cornered and unable to run away, it lashes out with its legs and is quite capable of disembowelling a person with its

claws. The bird also has a hard, bony crest called a casque, which protects the top of its head.

The large ratites all share a similar shape, having bulky bodies, long legs and long, slender necks. Like all flightless birds, they do possess wings, which assist them in keeping their balance and may also be used for display purposes. Most birds have four toes on each foot, but ratites have no more than three toes, and less in some cases. Ostriches have just two toes on each foot. The fastest birds on land, they can run at speeds equivalent to 50km/h (31mph). The reduction in the number of toes may help these birds to run faster.

Emus (*Dromaius novaehollandiae*) have the most rudimentary wings of all ratites, which are not even used for display purposes. The rheas (Rheidae) of South America have the most prominent wings of the ratites. They cover the rump, but they do not enable these birds to fly, even when they are young.

Kiwis (Apterygidae) are also ratites, but they are much smaller birds with shorter legs. Unlike other ratites, they are not fast runners, but rely on camouflage and their nocturnal habits to conceal their presence from predators, rather than speed to escape.

Running in flighted birds

Some birds that are able to fly still prefer to use their running abilities to obtain food and escape danger. They include the roadrunners (*Geococcyx californianus*) of North America. With their short wings, these birds can fly clumsily, but prefer to use their strong legs to overtake and pounce on prey. In general, flying uses considerable energy compared to running or hopping. Many birds will elect to move swiftly over the ground to pounce on a food item or avoid an enemy if they judge that the situation does not warrant flight.

Above: The height and keen eyesight of ostriches means that they are hard to ambush in open country. Their pace allows them to escape from danger with little difficulty, while their long stride length when running enables them to cover large amounts of ground in a single step.

AVIAN SENSES

The keen senses of birds are vital to their survival, in particular helping them to find food, escape from enemies and find mates in the breeding season. Sight is the primary sense for most birds, but some species rely heavily on other senses to thrive in particular habitats.

All birds' senses are adapted to their environment, and the shape of their bodies can help to reflect which senses are most significant to them.

Sight and lifestyle

Most birds rely on their sense of sight to avoid danger, hunt for food and locate familiar surroundings. The importance of this sense is reflected by the size of their eyes, with those of

starlings (*Sturnus vulgaris*), for example, making up 15 per cent of the total head weight. The enlargement of the eyeballs and associated structures, notably the eye sockets in the skull, has altered the shape of the brain. In addition, the optic lobes in the brain, which are concerned with vision, are also enlarged, whereas the olfactory counterparts, responsible for smell, are poorly developed.

The structure of the eye also reveals much about a bird's habits. Birds of prey have large eyes in proportion to their head, and have correspondingly keen eyesight. Species that regularly hunt for prey underwater, such as penguins, can see well in the water. They have a muscle in each eye that reduces the diameter of the lens and increases its thickness on entering water, so that their eyes can adjust easily to seeing underwater. In addition, certain diving birds such as little auks (*Alle alle*) use a lens that forms part of the nictitating membrane, or third eyelid, which is normally hidden from sight. Underwater, when this membrane covers the eye, its convex shape serves as a lens, helping the bird to see in these surroundings.

Eye position

The positioning of the eyes on the head gives important clues to a bird's lifestyle. Most birds' eyes are set on the sides of the head. Owls, however, have flattened faces and forward-facing eyes that are critical to their hunting ability. These features allow owls to target their prey.

There are disadvantages, though – owls' eyes do not give a rounded view of the world, so they must turn their heads to see around them. It is not just the positioning of owls' eyes that is unusual. They are also able to hunt effectively in almost complete darkness. This is made possible in two

Above: Scavengers such as this lappet-faced vulture (Aegypius tracheliotus) have an acute sense of smell, and a huge beak that enables them to cut into the flesh of the carcass.

ways. First, their pupils are large, which maximizes the amount of light passing through to the retina behind the lens, where the image is formed. Second, the cells here consist mainly of rods rather than cones. While cones give good colour vision, rods function to create images when background illumination is low.

The positioning of the eyes of game birds such as woodcocks (*Scolopax rusticola*) allows them to spot danger from almost any angle. It is even possible for them to see a predator sneaking up from behind. Their only blind spot is just behind the head.

Smell

Very few birds have a sense of smell, but kiwis (Apterygidae) and vultures (forming part of the order Falciformes) are notable exceptions. Birds' nostrils are normally located above the bill, opening directly into the skull, but kiwis' nostrils are positioned right at the end of the long bill. They probably help these birds to locate earthworms

---

Field of vision

The positioning of a bird's eyes on its head affects its field of vision. The eyes of owls are positioned to face forwards, producing an overlapping image of the area in front known as binocular vision. This allows the owl to pinpoint its prey exactly, so that it can strike. In contrast, the eyes of birds that are likely to be preyed upon, such as woodcocks, are positioned on the sides of the head. This eye position gives a greatly reduced area of binocular vision, but it does give these birds practically all-round vision, enabling them to spot danger from all sides.

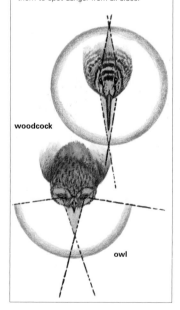

woodcock

owl

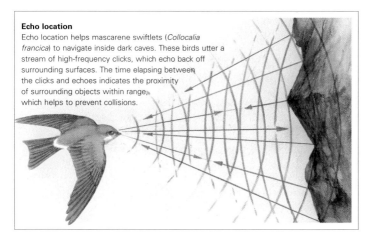

Echo location

Echo location helps mascarene swiftlets (*Collocalia francica*) to navigate inside dark caves. These birds utter a stream of high-frequency clicks, which echo back off surrounding surfaces. The time elapsing between the clicks and echoes indicates the proximity of surrounding objects within range, which helps to prevent collisions.

in the soil. Vultures have very keen eyesight, which helps them to spot dead animals on the ground from the air, but they also have a strong sense of smell, which helps when homing in on a distant carcass.

Taste
The senses of smell and taste are linked, and most birds also have correspondingly few taste buds in their mouths. The number of taste buds varies, with significant differences between groups of birds. Pigeons may have as few as 50 taste buds in their mouths, parrots as many as 400.

Birds' taste buds are located all around the mouth, rather than just on the tongue, as in mammals. The close

Below: Birds have good colour vision. It is this sense that enables sunbirds (Nectarinidae) to source nectar and pollen from these brightly-coloured red flowers.

links between smell and taste can lead vultures, which feed only on fresh carcasses, to reject decomposing meat. They may start to eat it, but then spit it out once it is in their mouths, probably because of a combination of bad odour and taste.

Hearing
Birds generally do not have a highly developed sense of hearing. They lack any external ear flaps that would help to pinpoint sources of sound. The openings to their hearing system are located on the sides of the head, back from the eyes.

Hearing is of particular significance for nocturnal species, such as owls, which find their food in darkness. These birds are highly attuned to the calls made by rodents. The broad shape of their skull has the additional advantage of spacing the ear openings more widely, which helps them to localize the source of the sounds with greater accuracy.

Hearing is also important to birds during the breeding season. Birds show particular sensitivity to sounds falling within the vocal range of their chicks, which helps them to locate their offspring easily in the critical early days after fledging.

The Mascarene swiftlet *(Collocalia francica),* which occurs on islands in the Indian Ocean east of Madagascar, uses echo location to find its way around in the dark, rather like bats do.

Unlike bats, however, the clicking sounds of the swiftlet's calls – up to 20 a second in darkness – are clearly audible to humans. The bird interprets the echoes of its call to avoid colliding with objects in its path, although it also uses its eyesight when flying. Cave swiftlets (*Aerodramus*) from Asia and the South American oilbird (*Steatornis caripensis*) navigate in a similar way.

Touch
The sense of touch is more developed in some birds than others. Those such as snipe (*Gallinago*), which have long bills for seeking food, have sensitive nerve endings called corpuscles in their bills that pick up tiny vibrations caused by their prey. Vibrations that could suggest approaching danger can also register via other corpuscles located particularly in the legs, so that the bird has a sensory awareness even when it is resting on a branch.

Wind-borne sensing
Tubenoses such as albatrosses and petrels (Procellariiformes) have a valve in each nostril that fills with air as the bird flies. These are affected by both the bird's speed and the wind strength. The valves almost certainly act as a type of wind gauge, allowing these birds to detect changes in wind strength and patterns. This information helps to keep them airborne, as they skim over the waves with minimal effort.

Below: A combination of senses, especially touch, helps oystercatchers (Haematopus ostralegus) to detect their prey, which is normally hidden from view.

PLANT-EATERS

All over the world, many birds depend on plant matter as part of their diet, with seeds and nuts in particular providing nourishment. A close relationship between plants and birds exists in many cases. Birds fertilize flowers when feeding on nectar, and help to spread their seeds when eating fruit.

Many different types of birds are primarily plant-eaters, whether feeding on flowers, fruit, nuts and seeds, or other plant matter. Plant-eating species have to eat a large volume of food compared to meat-eating species, because of the low nutritional value of plants compared with that of prey such as invertebrates.

In the last century or so, many species have benefited from the spread of agriculture, which now provides them with large acreages of suitable crop plants to feed on. These birds' feeding habits bring them into conflict with farmers when they breed rapidly in response to a swift expansion in their food supply. Across Africa, large populations of red-billed queleas (*Quelea quelea*) descend to feed on fields of wheat, sorghum and barley, resulting in a devastating loss of grain

Below: African touracos such as this red-crested species (Tauraco erythrolophus) *are among the relatively few birds to feed on leaves. The touracos swallow these whole, and use a variable perching grip to maintain balance while feeding, even on thin branches.*

and flattening of ripening plants. They have been labelled as pests, and are increasingly being culled by pesticides. This has led to an outbreak of protest from those who argue that the arable fields have actually replaced the birds' natural food sources.

Adapting to changing seasons

Birds from temperate areas exist on a varied diet that is related to the seasons. Bullfinches (*Pyrrhula pyrrhula*), for example, eat the buds in apple orchards in spring – when they can become a pest – while later in the year they consume seeds and fruit. Their bills, like those of most other members of the finch family, are stout and relatively conical, which helps them to crack seeds effectively.

Some birds store plant food when it is plentiful, to sustain them through the winter. Nutcrackers (*Nucifraga*) collect hazel nuts, which they feed on through winter into the following year. Some woodpeckers (Picidae) drill holes in trees which they fill with acorns and other nuts and seeds, creating an easily accessible larder for the winter months, when snow may cover the ground.

Flowers

A number of birds rely on flowers rather than the whole plant as a source of food. Pollen is a valuable source of protein, while nectar provides sugars. Not surprisingly, flower-feeders tend to be confined to mainly tropical areas, where flowers are in bloom throughout the year. Hummingbirds (Trochilidae), for instance, use their narrow bills to probe into flowers to obtain nectar. Some hummingbirds have developed especially curved or elongated bills, which allow them to feed on particular flowers. These birds help to pollinate the plants on which they feed by transferring pollen from flower to flower on their bills or even on plumage.

The digestive system

Birds lack teeth, so their food must be swallowed whole. Birds have a storage organ known as the crop, which is located at the base of the neck. From here, food passes down into the proventriculus, where the digestive process starts, before entering the gizzard, which is equivalent to the mammalian stomach. Nutrients are then absorbed through the wall of the small intestine.

The digestive system of plant-eaters differs in various respects from that of predatory species. Vegetable matter is less nourishing than meat, so plant-eaters generally need longer digestive tracts to process the large quantities of food they must consume in order to obtain enough nourishment. In addition, digesting plant matter poses certain difficulties. The gizzards of seed-eating species such as many finches (Fringillidae) have especially thick muscular walls, which serve to grind up the seeds.

1 Oesophagus	6 Large intestine
2 Crop	7 Liver
3 Proventriculus	8 Spleen
4 Pancreas	9 Small intestine
5 Gizzard	

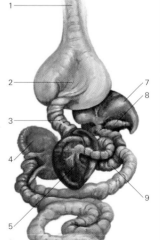

Above: Berries feature prominently in the diet of the pied barbet (Lybius leucomelas) – their stocky bill allows these birds to pluck fruits easily from their stems. However, as opportunistic feeders, they will also eat other items, including invertebrates.

The sunbirds (Nectarinidae) of Africa fill a similar evolutionary niche to America's hummingbirds, which they resemble in their small size and bright, often iridescent plumage. Unlike hummingbirds, however, they are not sufficiently agile to feed in flight, but have to perch within reach of the flower. Various members of the parrot family also feed on flowers. Their tongues are ideally equipped for this diet, with microscopic, bristle-like projections called papillae, which enable them to collect pollen easily.

Fruit

Exclusively frugivorous (fruit-eating) birds such as fruit doves (*Ptilinopus*) are found only in the tropics, where fruit is available throughout the year. These species usually dwell in tropical rainforests, where they have a valuable role to play in protecting the biodiversity of the forest. The seeds of the fruits they eat pass right through their digestive tracts unharmed, to be deposited far from the parent plant, which helps the plants to spread.

Plant matter

Relatively few birds feed almost entirely on herbage, although the bizarre hoatzin (*Opisthocomus hoazin*) from the rainforest of South America is one example. Equally unusual are the touracos (Musophagidae) of Africa, which also feed mainly on leaves, which they pluck along with fruits. Some parrots such as the eclectus (*Eclectus roratus*) are also believed to feed largely on plant matter rather than seeds or fruit.

The breakdown of vegetation presents considerable difficulty, since birds do not possess the necessary enzymes to digest the cellulose in plants. Birds such as grouse (Tetraonidae), which feed regularly on plant matter, have evolved long, blind-ending tubes known as caeca. These contain beneficial microbes that can break down cellulose.

Nuts and seeds

These dry foods are an invaluable resource to many different types of birds, ranging from parrots to finches. However, cracking the tough outer shell or husk can be a problem. Finches such as grosbeaks have evolved a particularly strong bill for this purpose. Hawfinches (*Coccothraustes coccothraustes*) are able to crack cherry stones (pits) to extract the kernel.

Above: Red-billed queleas, or weavers (Quelea quelea), are the most numerous birds in the world. Massive flocks of these birds will wipe out crops of ripening millet in parts of Africa, to the extent that they are sometimes called "feathered locusts".

The most bizarre example of bill adaptation for eating seeds is seen in the crossbills (*Loxia*) of northern coniferous forests. These birds have literally twisted upper and lower mandibles, which help them to crack open the seeds inside the larch cones, which they eat. Some cockatoos such as the Moluccan species (*Cacatua moluccensis*) have bills that are even strong enough to open coconuts.

Below: Pink-footed geese (Anser brachyrhynchus) can be a problem in agricultural areas, since they will sometimes descend in large numbers to graze on crops.

PREDATORS AND SCAVENGERS

Just as with other vertebrates, there is a food chain within the avian kingdom. Some species hunt only other birds, while others seek a more varied range of prey, including, commonly, invertebrates. Even birds that feed mainly on seeds catch protein-rich insects to feed their chicks in the nest.

Some birds are active predators, seeking and killing their own food, while others prefer to scavenge on carcasses. Many predatory birds are opportunistic feeders, hunting when food is plentiful but scavenging in times of scarcity. Both hunters and scavengers have evolved to live in a wide range of environments, and display correspondingly diverse hunting skills to obtain their food.

Birds of prey have sharp bills that enable them to tear the flesh of their prey into strips small enough to swallow. Eating whole animals can potentially cause digestive problems for these birds because of the bones, skin, feathers and other relatively indigestible body parts. Owls overcome this problem by regurgitating pellets composed of the indigestible remains of their prey. Kingfishers (Alcedinidae) produce similar pellets of fish bones and scales. These are of value to zoologists studying the feeding habits of such birds.

Below: Peregrine falcons (Falco peregrinus) *are adept aerial hunters, with pigeons – including homing pigeons – featuring prominently in their diet. These birds of prey display not just speed, but also superb manoeuvrability in flight, when pursuing their quarry.*

Birds of prey

Some avian predators feed mainly on other birds, such as the sparrowhawk (*Accipiter nisus*) – which is so called because of its preference for hunting house sparrows (*Passer domesticus*). Another avian hunter, the peregrine falcon (*Falco peregrinus*), is among the most agile of all hunting birds. Strength is a feature of some species that prey on mammals, such as the golden eagle (*Aquila chrysaetos*), which can lift young lambs in its powerful talons, but often feeds on carrion. Yet other birds of prey target different groups of vertebrates,

Above: Vision is the main sense that allows most birds of prey, such as golden eagles (Aquila chrysaetos), *to target their victims. These eagles have keen sight.*

including fish and reptiles, while a great many species hunt insects and other invertebrates.

Hunting techniques

Many predatory birds hunt during the day, but not all, with most owls preferring to seek their prey at night. Mice and other creatures that are caught by owls are killed and eaten immediately. In contrast, shrikes (Laniidae) have a grisly reputation because they kill more prey than they can eat at once. They store the surplus as a so-called larder, impaling invertebrates such as grasshoppers, and sometimes even small vertebrates, on to sharp vegetation. Having secured their prey in this manner, they will then return to feed on them later. Caching, as this behaviour is known, is especially common during the breeding period, and presumably developed as a way of ensuring that the shrikes have sufficient food to rear their young.

Some birds have evolved particular ways of overcoming prey in certain localities. In parts of Egypt, for example, eagles have learnt to prey on

Above: Like other cormorants, the white-necked cormorant (Phalacrocorax carbo) *brings fish that it catches underwater up to the surface before swallowing them.*

tortoises by seizing the unfortunate reptiles in their talons, and then dropping them on to rocky ground from the air to split open their shells.

Not all birds of prey are aerial predators. Species such as secretary birds (*Sagittarius serpentarius*), which range widely across Africa in grassland areas, prefer to seek their victims on the ground. Secretary birds have developed long, strong legs and yet have surprisingly small feet. Snakes feature prominently in the diet of these birds, which raise their wings when confronting one of the reptiles. This has the effect of breaking up the bird's outline, making it harder for the snake to strike. Meanwhile, the bird uses its feet to stun the reptile by jumping up and down on it, before killing it with a stab of its sharp bill.

Aquatic predators
The osprey (*Pandion haliaetus*) is an unusual bird of prey that literally scoops up large fish swimming close to the water's surface while in flight. Other birds actually enter the water in search of their prey. They may not have sharp talons, but many have powerful bills that enable them to grab slippery fish without difficulty.

Pelicans are equipped with a large, capacious pouch beneath the lower part of their bill, which they use like a net to trawl the water for fish.

Cormorants (Phalacrocoracidae) dive down after fish, and can remain submerged for some time. Kingfishers (*Alcedo atthis*) have sharp eyesight. Having detected the presence of a fish from the air, they dive into the water, seizing their quarry in their pointed bill and then re-emerging immediately. They then kill the fish by battering it against their perch. The speed at which the kingfisher dives provides the momentum to break through the surface, and it closes its wings once submerged to reduce resistance.

Aquatic predators always try to swallow their prey such as fish head-first. That way, gills and scales do not get stuck in their throat. On land, predatory birds that hunt victims such as rodents employ a similar technique so they do not choke on fur and tails.

Scavengers
Vultures are the best-known of all scavengers. They can home in on carcasses from a great distance away, and so have become regarded as harbingers of death. Lammergeiers (*Gypaetus barbatus*) have developed a technique that allows them to feed on bones that their relatives cannot break open. They smash the bones into pieces by dropping them from a great height. It is a skill that they learn to perfect by choosing the right terrain on which to drop the bones.

The small Egyptian vulture (*Neophron percnopterus*) survives by using its small size, which is no match

Above: Precise judgement allows a kingfisher (Alcedo atthis) *to strike with deadly accuracy from a perch. These birds frequent stretches of clear water for this reason.*

at the site of a kill, to advantage: it can become airborne soon after dawn – before the thermal air currents needed by its larger relatives have been created – and seek out overnight casualties. In some parts of Africa, these vultures smash tough ostrich eggs by repeatedly throwing stones at them.

Birds other than vultures also scavenge on occasion rather than hunting. Road kills of birds and other animals offer rich pickings for a host of such species, ranging from corvids such as crows and magpies to road-runners (*Geococcyx californianus*).

Below: Griffon vultures (Gyps fulvus) *and similar scavengers usually have bald heads, because any plumage here would quickly become matted with blood.*

DISPLAY AND PAIRING

Birds' breeding habits vary greatly. Some birds pair up only fleetingly, while others do so for the whole breeding season, and some species pair for life. For many young cock birds, the priority is to gain a territory as the first step in attracting a partner. Birds use both plumage and their songs to attract a mate.

A number of factors trigger the onset of the breeding period. In temperate areas, as the days start to lengthen in spring, the increase in daylight is detected by the pineal gland in the bird's brain, which starts a complex series of hormonal changes in the body. Most birds form a bond with a single partner during the breeding season, which is often preceded by an elaborate display by the cock bird.

Bird song

Many cock birds announce their presence by their song, which both attracts would-be mates and establishes a claim to a territory. Once pairing has occurred, the male may cease singing, but in some cases he starts to perform a duet with the hen, with each bird singing in turn.

Singing obviously serves to keep members of the pair in touch with each other. In species such as Central and

Below: An adult cock Fischer's whydah (Vidua fischeri) in breeding condition is easily distinguished from the rather plain-coloured hen by its magnificent plumage. For the remainder of the year, however, it is virtually impossible to distinguish between the sexes by sight. Whydahs occur exclusively in Africa.

South American wood quails (*Odontophorus*), the pair co-ordinate their songs so precisely that although the cock bird may sing the first few notes, and then the hen, it sounds as if the song is being sung by just one bird. Other birds may sing in unison. In African gonoleks (*Laniarius*), it may even be possible to tell the length of time that the pair have been together by the degree of harmony in their particular songs.

Studies have revealed that young males birds start warbling quite quietly, and then sing more loudly as they mature. Finally, when their song pattern becomes fixed, it remains constant throughout the bird's life.

It is obviously possible to identify different species by differences in their song patterns. However, there are sometimes marked variations between the songs of individuals of the same species that live in different places. Local dialects have been identified in various parts of a species' distribution, as in the case of grey parrots (*Psittacus erithacus*) from different parts of Africa. In addition, as far as some songbirds are concerned, recent studies

Above: A male ruff (Philomachus pugnax) at a lek, where males compete with each other in displays to attract female partners. Ruffs do not form lasting pair bonds, so the hens nest on their own after mating has occurred.

Below: Male masked weavers (Ploceus) build nests as part of their displays to attract the females. The techniques involved in nest-building are extremely complex and can be mastered only with practice. Hens are likely to choose older males as partners because they have superior nest-building skills.

Above: Mute swans (Cygnus olor) *are one of the species that pair for life. They become highly territorial when breeding, but outside the nesting period they often form flocks on large stretches of water. In spite of their common name, they can vocalize to a limited extent, by hissing and even grunting.*

have shown that over the course of several generations, the pattern of song can alter markedly.

Birds produce their sounds – even those species capable of mimicking human speech – without the benefit of a larynx and vocal cords like humans. The song is created in a voice organ called the syrinx, which is located in the bird's throat, at the bottom of the windpipe, or trachea.

The structure of the syrinx is very variable, being at its most highly developed in songbirds, which possess as many as nine pairs of separate muscles to control the vocal output. As in the human larynx, it is the flow of air through the syrinx that enables the membranes here to vibrate, creating sound. An organ called the interclavicular air sac also plays an important role, and birds cannot sing without it. The depth of song is not always proportional to size. The small Cetti's warbler (*Cettia cetti*) of Europe and north Africa will emit a sudden burst of clear, penetrating notes over a few seconds, which ceases as abruptly as it began. When breeding, males will even sing at night to attract hens.

Breeding behaviour

Many birds rely on their breeding finery to attract their mates. Some groups assemble in communal display areas known as leks, where hens witness the males' displays and select a mate. A number of different species, ranging from game birds to birds of paradise (Paradisaeidae), establish leks. Other species use a combination of factors to attract a mate. Male weaver birds (Ploceidae), for example, moult at the onset of the breeding season to display brightly-coloured plumage, which is intended to lure the female bird to their elaborate nest. These complex constructions are made from densely packed grass and twigs, and

may even boast a long and complex entrance tunnel. The successful pairing of the weavers will depend finally on the female's approval of the nest. Hens often assent to breed with older cocks, whose nest-building abilities show more sophistication than those of the younger birds.

Pair bonding

Many male and female birds form no lasting relationship, although the pair bond may be strong during the nesting period. It is usually only in potentially long-lived species, such as the larger parrots (Psittacidae) and hornbills (Bucorvidae), or waterfowl such as swans (Anatidae), that a lifelong pair bond is formed.

Pair bonding in long-lived species has certain advantages. The young of such birds are slow to mature, and are often unlikely to nest for five years or more. By remaining for a time in a family group, and sheltering the developing birds until they are strong enough to fend for themselves, adults can improve the survival prospects of their young.

Below: The dance of sandhill cranes (Grus canadensis) *is one of the most spectacular sights in the avian world, reinforcing the lifelong pair bond in this species. Dancing starts with the trumpeting calls of the birds as they stand side by side. Both sexes then start to leap into the air and display, raising their wings and tail feathers. Sometimes the birds even pick up sticks and toss them into the air.*

NESTING AND EGG-LAYING

All birds reproduce by laying eggs, which are covered with a hard, calcareous shell. The number of eggs laid at a time – known as the clutch size – varies significantly between species, as does egg coloration. Nesting habits also vary, with some birds constructing very elaborate nests.

The coloration and markings of a bird's eggs are directly linked to the nesting site. Birds that usually breed in hollow trees produce white eggs, because these are normally hidden from predators and so do not need to be camouflaged. The pale coloration may also help the adult birds to locate the eggs as they return to the nest, thus lessening the chances of damaging them. Birds that build more open, cup-shaped nests tend to lay coloured eggs, often with a mottled pattern – this acts as a useful camouflage, making them less obvious to potential nest thieves.

Nesting holes

Many birds use tree holes for nesting. Woodpeckers (Picidae) are particularly well equipped to create nesting chambers, using their powerful bills to enlarge holes in dead trees. The diameter of the entry hole thus created

Below: Ostriches lay the largest eggs in the world, which can weigh up to 1.5kg (3.3lb). In comparison, a chicken's egg, shown in front of the ostrich egg, looks tiny. The egg nearest to the viewer is a hummingbird egg. These tiny birds lay the smallest eggs in the avian world, weighing only about 0.35g (0.01oz).

Above: African bee-eaters (Merops species) nest colonially, which can make them conspicuous. They will seek to make these breeding sites inaccessible, however, typically burrowing into sandy cliffs.

is just wide enough to allow the birds to enter easily, which helps to prevent the nest being robbed. Hornbills (Bucorvidae) go one stage further – the cock bird walls the hen up inside the nest. He plasters the hole over with mud, leaving just a small gap through which he can feed the female. The barrier helps to protect the nest from attacks by snakes and lizards. The female remains entombed inside until her young are well grown. At this stage she breaks out and then helps her mate to rear the chicks, having walled them back up again.

Nest-building

Some birds return to the same nest site each year, but many birds simply abandon their old nest and build another. This may seem a waste of effort, but it actually helps to protect the birds from parasites such as blood-sucking mites, which can otherwise multiply in the confines of the nest. Most birds construct their nests from vegetation, depending on which

The reproductive systems

The cock bird has two testes located within his body. Spermatozoa pass down the vas deferens, into the cloaca and then out of the body. Insemination occurs when the vent areas of the male and female bird are in direct contact during mating. Cock birds do not have a penis for penetration, although certain groups, such as waterfowl, may have a primitive organ that is used to assist in the transference of semen in a similar way.

Normally only the left ovary and oviduct of the hen bird are functional. Eggs pass down through the reproductive tract from the ovary. Spermatozoa swim up the hen's reproductive tract, and fertilize the ova at an early stage in the process. Generally, only one mating is required to fertilize a clutch of eggs. Spermatozoa may sometimes remain viable in the hen's body for up to three weeks following mating.

1 Kidneys	7 Magnum
2 Testes	8 Isthmus
3 Vas deferens	9 Egg with shell
4 Cloaca	contained in
	the hen's
5 Ova	reproductive tract
6 Infundibulum	10 Cloaca

Male **Female**

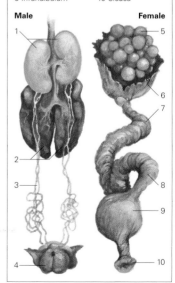

materials are locally available. In coastal areas, some seabirds use pieces of seaweed to build theirs. Artificial materials such as plastic wrappers or polystyrene may be used by some birds.

Nest styles

Different types of birds build nests of various shapes and sizes, which are characteristic of their species. Groups such as finches build nests in the form of an open cup, often concealed in vegetation. Most pigeons and doves construct a loose platform of twigs. Swallows are among the birds that use mud to construct their nests. They scoop muddy water up from the surface of a pond or puddle, mould it into shape on a suitable wall, and then allow it to dry and harden like cement.

The simplest nests are composed of little more than a pad of material, resting in the fork of a tree or on a building. The effort entailed in nest construction may reflect how often the birds are likely to nest. The platforms of pigeons and doves can disintegrate quite easily, resulting in the loss of eggs or chicks. However, if disaster does befall the nest, the pair will often breed again within a few weeks. At the other end of the scale, albatrosses expend considerable effort on nesting, because if failure occurs, the pair may not breed again for two years or so.

Cup-shaped nests are more elaborate than platform nests, being usually made by weaving grasses and twigs together. The inside is often lined with soft feathers. The raised sides of the cup nest lessen the likelihood of losing eggs and chicks, and also offer greater security to the adults during incubation. The hollow in the nest's centre is created by the birds compressing the material here before egg-laying begins.

Suspended nests enclosed by a domed roof offer even greater security. They are less accessible to predators because of their design and also their position, often hanging from slender branches. Some waxbills (*Estrilda*) build a particularly elaborate nest, comprising two chambers. There is an obvious upper opening, which is

Above: A pair of fulmars (Fulmarus glacialis) *at their nest. Choosing a location close to the sea means they can obtain food easily, and the cliffs themselves afford some shelter.*

always empty, suggesting to would-be predators that the nest is unoccupied. The birds occupy the chamber beneath, which has a separate opening.

Nest protection

Some birds rely on the safety of numbers to deter would-be predators, building vast communal nests that are occupied by successive generations and added to regularly. The so-called social weavers (*Philetairus socius*) of the African Kalahari region tend to breed in this way. A single nest, which is constructed by both sexes, may house up to 400 birds, and contain as many as 100 entrances. The nests themselves resemble an enormous thatched mass

of straw and other vegetation – often likened to a suspended haystack – and are usually built in native trees or even around manmade structures such as telegraph poles, which they tend to engulf entirely. Most incredibly of all, each entrance to the nest is reinforced with sharp grass straws, pointing down like spears, to ward off predators. The interior of the nest contains a network of cosy chambers, lined with feathers, which are used not only for breeding purposes, but also as a cool retreat from soaring daytime temperatures.

Other birds have evolved different methods not only of protecting their nests, but also of minimizing the time in which they spend incubating their eggs. Various parrots, such as the red-faced lovebirds (*Agapornis pullaria*) of Africa, lay their eggs in termite mounds. The insects tolerate this intrusion, while the heat of the mound keeps the eggs warm.

Birds that nest on the ground, such as the stone curlew (*Burhinus oedicnemus*), are especially vulnerable to predators and rely heavily on their fairly drab plumage as camouflage. Skylarks (*Alauda arvensis*) have another means of protecting their nest site – they hold one wing down and pretend to be injured to draw a predator away.

Below: Most eggs have a generally rounded shape, but seabirds such as guillemots (Uria aalge) *breeding on rocky outcrops lay eggs that are more pointed. This shape helps to prevent the eggs from rolling over the cliff.*

HATCHING AND REARING CHICKS

Birds are vulnerable to predators when breeding, especially when they have young in the nest. The chicks must be fed frequently, necessitating regular trips to and from the nest, which makes it conspicuous. The calls of the young birds represent a further danger, so the breeding period is often short.

Most birds incubate their eggs to keep them sufficiently warm for the chicks to develop inside. Larger eggs are less prone to chilling during incubation than small eggs, because of their bigger volume. In the early stages of the incubation period, when the nest may be left uncovered while the adult birds are foraging for food, eggs can withstand a lower temperature. Temperature differences also account for the fact that, at similar altitudes, incubation periods tend to be slightly longer in temperate areas than in tropical regions.

The eggshell may appear to be a solid barrier but in fact contains many pores, which are vital to the chick's well-being. These tiny holes allow water vapour and carbon dioxide to escape from the egg, and oxygen to enter it to reach the embryo.

Incubation

The incubation period often does not start until more than one egg has been laid, and sometimes not until the entire clutch has been completed. The interval between the laying of one egg and the next varies – finches lay every

Below: A fertile chicken's egg, showing the development of the embryo through to hatching. 1. The fertilized egg cell divides to form a ball of cells that gradually develops into an embryo. 2. The embryo develops, nourished by the yolk sac. 3. The air space at the rounded end of the egg enlarges as water evaporates. 4. The chick is almost fully developed and ready to hatch. 5. The chick cuts its way out, and its feathers dry off.

day, whereas gannets may lay only one egg every six days. If incubation does not start until egg-laying has finished, the chicks will all be of a similar size when they hatch, which increases their overall chances of survival.

The cock and hen may share incubation duties, as in the case of most pigeons and doves, or just one member of the pair may incubate. While this is usually the hen, there are exceptions. With ostriches (*Struthio*

Above: Breeding in one of the coldest places on Earth means that emperor penguins (Aptenodytes forsteri) can lay only a single egg, which they incubate on top of their feet, where special blood vessels help to warm it. After hatching, the chick is carried here too.

camelus) and other large flightless birds, it is the male who incubates the eggs, and cares for the resulting chicks. Anis (*Crotophaga*) breed communally, and all members of the group share the task of incubation.

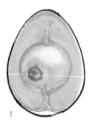
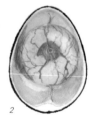

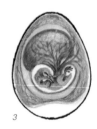

1   2   3   4   5

Below: Foster parents such as this reed warbler continue to feed the young cuckoo even when the imposter dwarfs them in size.

Hatching

Incubation periods vary among species, ranging from as few as 11 days in the case of some sparrows (*Spizella*), to over 80 days in some albatrosses (Diomedeidae). Before hatching, the chick uses the egg tooth on the tip of its upper bill to cut through the inner membrane into the air space at the blunt end of the shell, which forms as water evaporates from the egg. The chick starts to breathe atmospheric air for the first time. About 48 hours later, it breaks through the shell to emerge from the egg.

Chicks hatch out at various stages of development, and are accordingly able to leave the nest sooner or later.

Species that remain in the nest for some time after hatching, including parrots (Psittaciformes) and finches (Fringillidae), hatch in a blind and helpless state and are entirely dependent on their parents at first. Birds in this group are known as nidicolous. If not closely brooded, they are likely to become fatally chilled. In contrast, species that leave the nest soon after hatching, known as nidifugous, emerge from the egg and are able to move around on their own at this stage. They can also see, and feed themselves, almost immediately. The offspring of many game birds such as pheasants as well as waterfowl and waders are nidifugous, which gives them a better chance of survival, as they can run to escape from predators. Young waterfowl cannot take safely to the water at first, however, because they lack the oil from the preen gland above the base of the tail to water-proof their feathers.

Rearing and fledging

Many adult birds offer food to their offspring, even some nidifugous species. This can be a particularly demanding period, especially for small birds that have relatively large broods. Great tits (*Parus major*), for example, must supply their offspring with huge quantities of insects. They typically feed their chicks up to 60 times an hour, as well as keeping the nest clean.

Young birds usually leave the nest from about 12 to 30 days after hatching. However, some species develop much more slowly. Albatross chicks are particularly slow developers, spending up to eight and a half months in the nest.

When they first leave the nest, many young birds are unable to fly, simply because their flight feathers are not fully functional. If these feathers are not fully unfurled from the protective sheaths in which they emerged, they cannot function effectively. The strength of the wing muscles also needs to be built up, so it is not uncommon for young birds to rest on the sides of the nest, flapping their wings occasionally, before finally taking to the air for the first time. Chicks that

Above: Blue tits (Parus caeruleus) are typical of many birds that leave the nest before they are able to fly effectively. The young remain hidden in vegetation and are fed by their parents in these critical early days after leaving the nest.

are unable to fly immediately on fledging remain reliant on the adults, especially the cock, for food until they become fully independent.

For some young seabirds, fledging is a particularly hazardous process. From their cliff-ledge nests, they may simply flop down onto the water, where they are at risk from drowning until they master swimming skills. If they get swept out to sea, they may be caught by predators such as killer whales.

Below: The broad and often colourful gape of chicks allows parent birds such as this blackcap (Sylvia atricapilla) to feed their offspring quickly and efficiently. Weak chicks that are unable to raise their heads and gape at the approach of a parent will quickly die from starvation.

SURVIVAL

The numbers of a particular species of bird can vary significantly over time, affected by factors such as the availability of food, climate, disease and hunting. When the reproductive rate of a species falls below its annual mortality rate, it is in decline, but this does not mean it will inevitably become extinct.

For many birds, life is short and hazardous. Quite apart from the risk of predation, birds can face a whole range of other dangers, from starvation and disease through to inadvertent interference or persecution by humans. The reproductive rate is higher and age of maturity is lower in species that have particularly hazardous lifestyles, such as blue tits (*Parus caeruleus*). These species often breed twice or more each year in rapid succession.

Rising and falling numbers
Some birds will travel long distances from their native habitat when living conditions become unfavourable. Pallas's sandgrouse (*Syrrhaptes paradoxus*), for instance, a species normally found in central and eastern parts of Asia, has occasionally invaded the more temperate habitats of western Europe to breed. Large-scale irruptions of this type were recorded in 1863, 1868 and 1908, involving thousands of birds, and sightings were made from

Below: These lesser flamingos (Phoenicopterus minor) *live together in large groups, as they require a very specific habitat for dietary needs and breeding. Group living brings advantages in that it is easier to find a mate, and the presence of so many eyes will alert the birds to dangers more quickly than with pairs or lone birds.*

the Faeroe Islands in the far North Atlantic, southwards to Spain, with numerous identifications in the British Isles. Despite these often protracted relocations to ensure survival, the range of the grouse has never extended permanently into Europe.

Similar fluctuations affect other bird colonies when food runs into short supply. Snowy owls (*Nyctea scandiaca*) have a circumpolar range throughout northern Europe and North America, and the diet of the latter population depends heavily on the availability of lemmings to eat. When a combination of environmental factors causes the numbers of these small mammals to

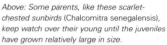

Above: Some parents, like these scarlet-chested sunbirds (Chalcomitra senegalensis), *keep watch over their young until the juveniles have grown relatively large in size.*

plummet, the predatory owls are forced to spread out over a much wider area in search of food, and their breeding success drops accordingly. As the lemming population recovers, so too will the number of snowy owls gradually rise again. This is a good example of how the interdependence of species sharing a habitat prompts cyclical change in, and subsequent control of, their numbers.

Group living
Safety in numbers is a major benefit of group living, as it can bring increased protection to birds both in the air and on the ground. For example, the way in which flocks manage to co-ordinate their flight, by weaving, dipping and rising together as a group, makes it far more difficult for an aerial predator to focus on an individual. Coloration can also disguise the number of individuals within a flock, and it serves to protect more vulnerable lone birds too. The mottled colouring on the head and upperparts of many shore and game birds, for instance, breaks up their outline so that, while on the ground,

always the case. The expansion of agriculture in various parts of West Africa, especially of crops such as millet, has resulted in the availability of more concentrated supplies of food. This, in turn, has enabled many smaller seed-eating birds such as the golden song sparrow (*Passer luteus*) to increase so rapidly in such locations that their numbers have reached plague proportions. Subsequent attempts to control the level of this increase have, in some cases, been less than humane – there are even reports of napalm gas being used against roosting sites. Other birds have, however, been boosted by direct human intervention, such as the common starling (*Sturnus vulgaris*). These birds have spread across North America, following their introduction from Europe in the late 1800s.

Similarly, the common pheasant (*Phasianus colchicus*), a native of Asia, is now found across much of Europe, thanks to human interest in these game birds, which are bred in large numbers for sport shooting. Many more survive than would otherwise be the case, thanks to the attention of gamekeepers who not only provide food, but also help to curb possible predators in areas where the birds are released.

Slow breeders
Birds that reproduce slowly, such as albatrosses (Diomedeidae) and sandhill cranes (*Grus canadensis*), are likely to be highly vulnerable to any changes in their surroundings, whether caused by

Above: Snowy owls (Nyctea scandiaca) *are often seen near coasts outside the breeding season. They are opportunistic hunters, even catching fish on occasion.*

human interference, climate change, disease, or other factors. Great concern has recently been focused on albatross numbers, which are declining worldwide. Many of these birds have been caught and drowned in fishing nets in recent years. Albatrosses are normally very long-lived and breed very slowly. Any sudden decline in their population is therefore likely to have devastating consequences that cannot easily be reversed.

Below: The black-shouldered kite (Elanus caeruleus), *seen here with its young, is an adaptable and wide-ranging bird of prey, with the ability to breed not just in Africa, but in parts of Europe and Southern Asia too.*

they merge more effectively against the land and are less conspicuous to birds of prey circling above. On sensing danger overhead, these advantageously coloured birds will often freeze into position and hold very still until the threat has passed, taking care not to betray their presence by a single movement – a far better guarantee of survival than taking flight or scurrying to find shelter.

Effects of humans
It is generally assumed that human interference in the landscape is likely to have harmful effects on avian populations. However, this is not

MIGRATION

Some birds live in a particular place all year round, but many are only temporary visitors. Typically, species fly to temperate latitudes in spring, and return to warmer climates at the end of summer. They have a wide distribution, but are seen only in specific parts of their range at certain times of the year.

Many species of birds – known as "migrants" – regularly undertake seasonal movements on specific routes. Migrations are different from so-called irruptions, when flocks suddenly move to an area where conditions are more favourable. Birds migrate to seek shelter from the elements, to find safe areas to rear their young and, in particular, to seek places where food is plentiful. Birds such as waxwings (Bombycillidae) irrupt to a new location to find food when supplies become scarce in their habitat, but such journeys are less frequent and are irregular. The instinct to migrate dates

Right: Various routes between Europe and Africa are chosen by migrants such as warblers, swallows, birds of prey and storks. Some species native to Asia also cross these pathways from the east. Crossings are not usually direct, if this would involve a potentially hazardous ocean journey. This is why birds from Iceland, for example, usually fly down across the British Isles to reach Africa, rather than veering west over the Atlantic. Even when crossing smaller bodies of water such as the Mediterranean, birds will instinctively follow routes where the land masses are close together, such as via the Iberian peninsula.

Below: Some southern European populations of Canada geese (Branta canadensis) are now losing their migratory instincts, as the winters here are less harsh and food is quite plentiful.

back millions of years, to a period when the seasons were often much more extreme, which meant that it was difficult to obtain food in a location throughout the year. This forced birds to move in search of food. Even today, the majority of migratory species live within the world's temperate zones, particularly the Northern Hemisphere, where seasonal change is pronounced.

Migratory routes

The routes that the birds follow on their journeys are often well defined. Land birds try to avoid flying over large stretches of water, preferring instead to follow coastal routes and crossing the sea at the shortest point. For instance, many birds migrating from Europe to Africa prefer to fly over the Straits of Gibraltar. Frequently

---

Banding birds

Much of what we know about migration and the lifespan of birds comes from banding studies carried out by ornithologists. Bands placed on the birds' legs allow experts to track their movements when the ringed birds are recovered again. The rings are made of lightweight aluminium, and have details of the banding organization and when banding was carried out. Unfortunately, only a very small proportion of ringed birds are ever recovered, so the data gathered is incomplete. Now other methods of tracking, such as radar, are also used to follow the routes taken by flocks of birds, which supplements the information from banding studies.

Below: A mute swan (Cygnus olor) wearing a band. Coloured bands can help to identify individual birds from some distance away.

---

birds fly at much greater altitudes when migrating. Cranes (Gruidae) have been recorded flying at 5,000m (16,400ft) when crossing the mountainous areas in France, and geese (*Anser*) have been observed crossing the Himalayas at altitudes of more than 9,000m (29,500ft). Even if the migratory routes are known, it is often difficult to spot migrating birds because they fly so high.

Speed and distance

Migrating birds also fly at greater speeds than usual, which helps to make their journey time as short as possible. The difference can be significant – migrating swallows (*Hirundo rustica*) travel at speeds between 3 and 14km/h (1.8–8.7mph) faster than usual, and are assisted by the greater altitude, where the air is thinner and resistance is less.

Some birds travel huge distances on migration. Arctic terns (*Sterna paradisaea*), for example, cover distances of more than 15,000km (9,300 miles) in total, as they shuttle between the Arctic and Antarctic. They fly an average distance of 160km (100 miles) every day. Size does not preclude birds from migrating long distances, either. The tiny ruby-throated hummingbird (*Archilochus colubris*) flies over the Gulf of Mexico from the eastern USA every year, a distance of more than 800km (500 miles).

Preparing for migration

The migratory habits of birds have long been the subject of scientific curiosity. As late as the 1800s, it was thought that swallows hibernated in the bottom of ponds because they were seen skimming over the pond surface in groups before disappearing until the following spring. Now we know that they were probably feeding on insects to build up energy supplies for their long journey ahead.

Even today, the precise mechanisms involved in migratory behaviour are not fully understood. We do know that birds feed up before setting out on migration, and that various hormonal changes enable them to store more fat

Above: Many birds, including this bluethroat (Luscinia svecica), set out on migration after moulting. Damaged plumage can make the task of flying harder.

in their bodies to sustain them on their journey. Feeding opportunities are likely to be more limited than usual when birds are migrating, while their energy requirements are, of course, higher. In addition, birds usually moult just before migrating, so that their plumage is in the best condition to withstand the inevitable buffeting that lies ahead.

Navigation

Birds use both learned and visual cues to orientate themselves when migrating. Young birds of many species, such as swans (Anatidae), learn the route by flying in the company of their elders. However, some young birds set out on their own and reach their destinations successfully without experienced companions, navigating by instinct alone. Birds such as swifts (Apopidae) fly mainly during daytime, whereas others, including ducks, migrate at night. Many birds fly direct to their destination, but some may detour and break their journey to obtain food and water before setting out again.

Experiments have shown that birds orientate themselves using the position of the sun and stars, as well as by following familiar landmarks. They also use the Earth's magnetic field to find their position, and thus do not get lost in cloudy or foggy weather, when the sky is obscured. The way in which these various factors come together, however, is not yet fully understood.

BEHAVIOUR

Bird behaviour, or avian ethology as it is known, is a very broad field. Some patterns of behaviour are common to all birds, whereas other actions are very specific, just to a single species or even to an individual population. Interpreting behaviour is easier in some cases than in others.

All bird behaviour essentially relates to various aspects of survival, such as avoiding predators, feeding, finding a mate and breeding successfully. Some behaviour patterns are instinctive, while others develop in certain populations of birds in response to particular conditions. Thus the way in which birds behave is partly influenced by their environment as well as being largely instinctual.

Age also plays a part in determining behaviour, since younger birds often behave in a very different way to the

Above: The posture a bird adopts while sunbathing can appear to indicate distress, as is the case with this Eurasian blackbird (Turdus merula), which is resting with its bill open and wings outstretched.

adults. Some forms of bird behaviour are relatively easy to interpret, while others are a great deal more difficult to explain.

Garden birds
One of the first studies documenting birds' ability to adapt their behaviour in response to changes in their environment involved blue tits (*Parus caeruleus*) in Britain. The study showed that certain individuals learned to use their bills to tap through the shiny metallic foil covers on milk bottles to reach the milk. Other blue tits followed their example, and in certain areas householders with milk deliveries had to protect their bottle tops from the birds.

The way in which birds have learned to use various types of garden feeders also demonstrates their ability to modify their existing behaviour in response to new conditions when it benefits them. A number of new feeders on the market designed to thwart squirrels from stealing the food

exploit birds' ability to adapt in this way. The birds have to squeeze through a small gap to reach the food, just as they might enter the nest. Once one bird has been bold enough to enter in this fashion, others observe and soon follow suit.

Preening
Although preening serves a variety of functions, the most important aspect is keeping the feathers in good condition. It helps to dislodge parasites and removes loose feathers, particularly during moulting. It also ensures that the plumage is kept waterproof by spreading oil from the preen gland at the base of the tail.

Preening can be a social activity too. It may be carried out by pairs of males and females during the breeding season, or among a family group.

Aggression
Birds can be surprisingly aggressive towards each other, even to the point of sometimes inflicting fatal injuries. Usually, however, only a few feathers are shed before the weaker individual backs away, without sustaining serious injury. Conflicts of this type can break out over feeding sites or territorial disputes. The risk of aggressive outbreaks is greatest at the start of the breeding season, when the territorial instincts of cock birds are most aroused. Size is no indicator of the potential level of aggression, since some of the smallest birds, such as sunbirds (Nectariniidae), can be ferociously aggressive towards each other.

Below: A dispute breaks out between a pair of European nutcrackers (Nucifraga caryocatactes). Birds often fight with their wings outstretched, as they seek to batter their opponent into submission.

This behaviour is seen in a variety of birds, ranging from parrots to finches. Some parrots perform mutual preening throughout the year, which reinforces the pair bond. In some species of psittaculid parakeets, however, such as the African ring-necked (*Psittacula krameri*), the dominant hen allows her mate to preen her only when she is in breeding condition, and therefore preening in this instance may be seen as a prelude to mating.

Bathing

Preening is not the only way in which birds keep their plumage in good condition. Birds often bathe to remove dirt and debris from their plumage. Small birds wet their feathers by lying on a damp leaf during a shower of rain, in an activity known as leaf-bathing. Other birds immerse themselves in a pool of water, splashing around and ruffling their feathers.

Some birds, especially those found in drier areas of the world, prefer to dust-bathe, lying down in a dusty hollow known as a scrape and using fine earth thrown up by their wings to absorb excess oil from their plumage. Then, by shaking themselves thoroughly, followed by a period of preening, the excess oil is removed.

Sunbathing

Sunbathing may be important in allowing birds to synthesize Vitamin D3 from the ultraviolet rays in sunlight, which is vital for a healthy skeleton. This process can be achieved only if light falling on the bird's skin, which explains why birds ruffle their plumage at this time. Some birds stretch out while sunbathing, although others, such as many pigeons (Columbidae), prefer to rest with one

wing raised, leaning over at a strange angle on the perch. Vasa parrots (*Coracopsis*), found on the island of Madagascar, often behave in this fashion – however, sunbathing is generally not common among parrots.

Maintaining health

Some people believe that when birds are ill, they eat particular plants that have medicinal properties, but this theory is very difficult to prove. One form of behaviour that does confer health benefits has been documented, however: it involves the use of ants. Instead of eating these insects, some birds occasionally rub them in among their feathers. This causes the ants to release formic acid, which acts as a potent insecticide, killing off lurking parasites such as mites and lice. Jays (*Garrulus glandarius*) and also starlings (Sturnidae) and Eurasian blackbirds (*Turdus merula*) are among the species that have been observed using insects in this way. Members of the crow family have also been seen perching on smoking chimney pots or above bonfires, ruffling their feathers and allowing the smoke to penetrate their plumage. The smoke is thought to kill off parasites in a process that confers the same benefits as anting.

Above: Birds such as the African yellow-billed oxpecker (Buphagus africanus) form unusual associations with large mammals. These starlings frequently hitch a ride on the backs of animals such as rhinoceroses, as seen here, and buffaloes, where they are relatively safe from predators, and can feed on the animal's resident colony of ticks.

Below: The Eurasian green woodpecker (Picus viridis) uses its strong, pointed bill to pluck invertebrates from the ground.

Right: The natural waterproofing present on the plumage ensures that birds do not become saturated when swimming or caught in a shower of rain. This would destroy the warm layer of air surrounding the body created by the down feathering, and leave them vulnerable to hypothermia. Nevertheless birds do need to dry their plumage, which is what this Galapagos cormorant (Nannopterum harrisi) is doing, with its wings outstretched.

BIRDWATCHING

Thanks to their widespread distribution, birds can be seen in virtually any locality, even in the centre of cities. You don't need any special equipment to watch birds, but a pair of binoculars will help you to gain a better insight into avian behaviour, by allowing you to study birds at close range.

Birdwatching can be carried out almost anywhere around the world. Many people enjoy simply watching the birds that visit their garden. A greater variety of species can be seen if the birdwatcher ventures further afield, to local parks, woods or wetlands for example. Birdwatching holidays and sponsored birdwatching competitions offer opportunities to see an even greater variety of birds in different locations. Seasonal changes in bird populations mean that even if you visit the same area through the year, you will see new species at different times.

Above: At many major reserves where birds congregate, special permanent birdwatching hides have been set up to give visitors a good view without disturbing the birds themselves.

Getting a good view

Binoculars can be purchased from camera stores and similar outlets, but it is important to test them before deciding which model to buy, particularly as they vary quite significantly in price. When purchasing binoculars, you will need to consider not only the power of magnification, but also how closely the binoculars can be focused, particularly if you going to use them at home, where the bird table is likely to be relatively close.

Binoculars vary according to their power of magnification and the diameter of the objective lens in millimetres. The lens' diameter and magnification are given in the specifications: binoculars described as 8x45 multiply the image by 8 in comparison with how it would appear to the naked eye and have an objective lens of 45mm, which determines how much light is gathered.

Two important considerations stem from the power of magnification. First, the depth of field is important, since it affects the area of the image that is in

---

Drawing birds for reference

1. Sketching birds is relatively straightforward if you follow this procedure. Start by drawing an egg shape for the body, with a smaller egg above, which will become the head, and another to form the rump. A centre line through the head circle will form the basis for the bill. Now add circles and lines to indicate the position of the wings and tail. Add lines for the legs and then sketch in the feet and claws.

2. Use an indelible fine-line felt-tip pen to ink in the shape of the bird that you have drawn previously in pencil, avoiding the unwanted construction lines.

3. Coloured pencils will allow you to add more detail after you have rubbed out any unwanted pencil markings.

4. If you take a number of prepared head shapes with you into the field, you can fill in the detail quickly and easily, enabling you to identify birds later.

focus. The greater the magnification, the shallower the depth of field. A greater depth of field can be helpful, chiefly because it ensures that a larger proportion of the birds on view are in focus, which avoids the need to refocus constantly. If the depth of field is shallow, only the birds in the centre will be in focus. Second, the degree of magnification also affects the field of vision – the area that you can see through the binoculars. A wide field of vision will help you to locate birds more easily.

Buying binoculars

A number of other factors may be considered when buying binoculars.
• Weight is important. Consider buying a lightweight pair if you intend using binoculars for long periods. They should also feel balanced in the hands.
• For people with large hands, small binoculars may be hard to adjust and not very comfortable to hold. Pay attention to the focusing mechanism – it should be easy to operate.
• Try the eyecups of the binoculars to see how comfortable they feel. If you wear spectacles, it is important that the cups give you a full field of vision. Binoculars with adjustable eyecups are more suitable for spectacle-wearers.
• Is the design of good quality? It could be worthwhile paying extra for waterproofing. The better-quality

Above: A garden bird table will attract many species to feed, and if it is carefully sited, you should be able to see the birds easily, even from inside your home.

Right: Hanging cages are a compact type of food dispenser. They should be filled with special peanuts that are safe for birds. They may attract a wide variety of birds, including various tits, finches and even more unusual species, such as this great spotted woodpecker (Dendrocopos major).

Below: A view of a hide. External camouflage, easy access and good viewing positions are essential features in the design of such units. Even so, it may take birds some time to accept the presence of a hide.

models have their chambers filled with nitrogen gas to prevent any condensation developing.
• The design should be robust, with a solid protective casing.

Fieldscopes

Apart from binoculars, dedicated bird-watchers often use birding telescopes, called fieldscopes. These are ideal for use in hides as they can be mounted in various ways, using either a bench clamp fitting or a tripod. Fieldscopes are equipped with lenses similar to those in binoculars, but are more suited to long-term use, when you are watching a nest for example, as you do not have to keep holding the scope while waiting for a bird to return. Instead, attach the scope to a branch or bench and train it on the nest, then simply be patient until you see the bird return.

Making notes

When observing birds either in the garden or further afield, it is always useful to have a notebook handy to write down details and make sketches.

When sketching, proceed from a few quick pencil lines to a more finished portrait as time allows. Water-soluble pencils are helpful for colouring sketches, as the colours can be spread using water and a small paintbrush. If you spot a bird you cannot identify, jot down the details quickly in your notebook. Note the bird's colours and markings. Write down the length of the neck and legs, and note the bill shape. Assess the bird's size in relation to familiar species, and try to decide which family you think it belongs to. Your notes can then be compared with a field guide or other sources of information to identify the bird.

FIELDCRAFT

If you are seriously interested in birdwatching, you will need to develop fieldcraft skills. There is a significant difference between watching birds casually in a garden and tracking down particular species in remote areas, where preparation is important. Don't neglect your own safety in the wild.

Left: Hand-held binoculars or a viewing scope attached to a tripod can help you to study both common and rare species. Taking notes is useful, especially if you intend to write up details of your observations.

Photography
In the past, birdwatchers relied on 35mm SLR cameras and telephoto lenses to record their sightings. Today, however, birders are increasingly using digital cameras. These work very well when combined via a connector to a viewing scope that magnifies the image, like a telephoto lens. Digital cameras have the further advantage that they do not require film, but store images in their memory. Unwanted pictures can simply be deleted, while the best images can be transferred to a computer and printed out. Although you will not run out of film, digital cameras do use a surprising amount of power, so remember to take spare

Research and careful preparation are vital to the success of any field trip. You should also select clothing and equipment suited to the particular place where you intend to study birds.

Clothing and equipment
Suitable clothing is vital to keep you warm and dry when birdwatching. Waterproof footwear will be needed when visiting wetlands, or after rain. Dull-coloured clothing will allow you to blend in with the landscape so you can approach the birds more closely. A camping mat can be useful if you intend spending time on the ground.

In addition to packing your binoculars, camera equipment and perhaps a viewing scope, you may also want to take a notebook or sketchpad. A field guide will help to identify birds, while a waterproof rucksack will protect all your belongings.

Preparation
It always helps to do your homework before setting out. Investigating the habits of the birds you hope to see will help you to decide on the best place to go, and the time of day when they are

most likely to be seen. It may be useful to draw up a checklist highlighting key features of the species concerned in advance. You can then refer to these in the field. Studying a local map prior to your visit will help you to orientate yourself in new surroundings. Good preparation is especially important in areas where you are likely to be unfamiliar with the birds concerned.

Below: Plumage details, such as the handsome markings of this nutcracker (Nucifraga caryocatactes), may be captured using a conventional camera with a telephoto lens, or using a digital camera or camcorder linked to a viewing scope.

batteries with you on field trips. Digital camcorders can also be linked with viewing scopes, and are more flexible than cameras. Not only does a camcorder enable you to record the bird's song – which can be significant, especially if there is any doubt about identification – but you can also obtain a sequence of still images, especially if you can see the bird from different angles. Flight patterns can be recorded in this way, which again can help with identification. Even in relatively dark surroundings, some camcorders will function well.

Using hides and cover

On recognized reserves, there are likely to be hides in the best localities for birdwatching. Hides allow you to observe birds at relatively close quarters, and also offer excellent opportunities to photograph or film birds in their natural habitat. Even so, patience is likely to be needed for successful birding, as there will be no guarantees that you will see the species you hope to spot.

In areas where no hide is available, take cover behind shrubs, tree trunks or raised banks, or even in a parked car. Birds are highly attuned to the

Below: There are now many organized trips taking keen birders to far-flung parts of the world, offering unique opportunities to see new birds in exotic localities.

slightest hint of danger, such as humans approaching. In areas where no cover is available, stand, kneel or lie in a comfortable position and try to move as little as possible. When approaching birds, make sure your position is downwind, so the sounds of your approach don't frighten them away.

Seeking rarities

Birdwatching magazines can be useful in identifying sites where rarities have been spotted. For up-to-the-minute news, you will need to seek out either a regularly updated website or an information phone line giving details of the latest sightings. Birders with access to email can also receive

Above: In some areas, there may not be any natural cover or hides available. To get very close, it is vital to dress inconspicuously so that you blend into the background, and try to keep as still as you possibly can. Birdwatching requires plenty of patience.

bulletins listing where particular rarities have cropped up. These are most likely to be recorded after bad weather such as fierce storms which can blow migrant birds off-course.

Bear in mind that many people will be drawn to a place where an unusual species has been sighted, and it is important not to create a disturbance or to trespass on private land. Similarly, it is a criminal offence in some areas to disturb breeding birds. Always act in a responsible manner when birdwatching.

Getting the best results

• Plan well beforehand, including checking tide times if relevant. Tidal areas can be particularly hazardous where there is quicksand.
• Remember that bird populations may vary according to the time of year.
• Never neglect your own safety. Let someone else know where you are going, and when you intend to return.
• Check the weather forecast first, and take a mobile phone in case you get into difficulties.
• Take a local map and also a compass to guide you if you get lost. Allow enough time to locate and then observe the birds.

ZONES AND HABITATS

Birds have been exceedingly successful in colonizing the planet. Their warm-blooded nature and ability to fly have helped them to reach and then adapt to life in some of the world's most inaccessible places. They are found naturally on all continents, even successfully inhabiting Antarctica.

Zoologists divide the world into broad geographical zones, within which there are many different habitats. This approach reflects the movements of the Earth's landmasses through geological time, and so helps to show relationships between species occurring in various parts of the world today.

The Americas

In the distant past, North America was separated from its southern neighbour, and they had different origins. North America was originally attached to what is now Europe and later drifted westwards, while South America was once joined to a huge southern landmass that geologists call Gondwana, which included what is now the Indian subcontinent, Australia, Africa and Antarctica. South America split off at an earlier stage in

geological history than did North America – more than 100 million years ago – at a time when dinosaurs were in the ascendancy and the skies were occupied by flying reptiles called pterosaurs, rather than birds.

When birds began to evolve on this southern continent, they did so in isolation from the rest of the world. For this reason, the bird life that occurs today in this southern zone is known as neotropical, to distinguish it from that found in North America, which is known as nearctic. Later the avian populations of the Nearctic and Neotropical zones mingled somewhat by way of the Central American land bridge that was created when these two vast landmasses joined. However, unique forms still exist that are found only in South America, reflecting their isolated development in prehistory.

Above: This map shows how the different continents are believed to have formed and divided, giving rise to the familiar continents that we know today (see map below). These continental movements have had a direct effect on the distribution of avian life.

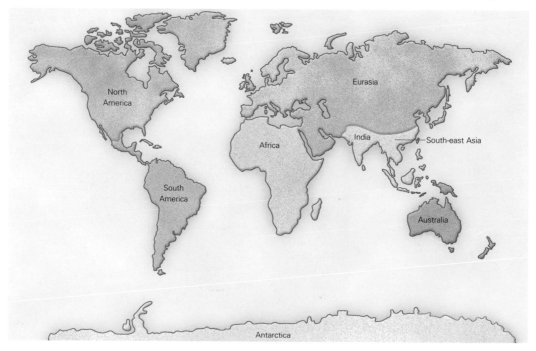

Above: The Indian subspecies of ring-necked parakeet (Psittacula krameri) *has succeeded in adapting to an urban existence in the suburbs of various European cities, including London and Amsterdam. Here the birds survive the winter mainly on bird-table offerings of seed put out for native birds.*

The Palaearctic

Europe has been separated from North America by the Atlantic Ocean for more than 50 million years, but the bird species of these now separate areas still show some evidence of their common past. In prehistory, Europe formed, and still forms, part of a much broader area known as the Palaearctic realm, which extends right across the northern continent from Iceland eastwards to Japan. Fossilized remains suggest that this region was the cradle of avian evolution, where the first members of the group probably originated more than 80 million years ago. Most zoologists believe that the oldest known bird, *Archaeopteryx,* was not in fact the first of the avian line, but as yet its immediate ancestors have not been discovered.

The distribution of avian species in the Northern Hemisphere has been affected in the more recent geological past by the spread and subsequent retreat of the ice sheets from the far north. Today, Europe and Asia experience a climate similar to that of the corresponding area of North America, ranging from arctic to subtropical according to latitude. The two regions even have some birds in common, especially in the far north, where certain species have a circumpolar distribution – they are found right around the polar region.

Africa, southern Asia and Australasia

As part of the great southern continent of Gondwana, Africa used to be attached to South America, but subsequently remained in contact with what is now the Indian subcontinent during the critical early phase in avian evolution approximately 60 million years ago. This distant history is reflected even today by the large number of avian species found south of what has become the Sahara Desert. This zone is now described as the Ethiopian realm, although it covers virtually all of Africa.

The Indian subcontinent became a separate landmass when Gondwana broke up. It ultimately drifted north, colliding and eventually joining with what is now the Asian landmass, and creating the Himalayan Mountains in the process. As in Africa, the broadly tropical climate and the landscape have altered little since then, which has meant that a number of the species that evolved here are found nowhere else in the world.

East and south of India lie the islands that comprise the Australasian realm, which includes Australia, New Guinea and New Zealand. These islands once formed part of the vast landmass of Gondwana, but later broke away and have been isolated from the rest of the world for millions of years. A diversity of bird species found nowhere else in the world can be seen here as a result.

Present distribution

Birds' current distribution throughout the world is affected by a number of different factors, as well as the history of their evolution. The ability to fly has allowed birds to become very widely distributed, as has their warm-blooded nature, which has meant that they are far less vulnerable to climatic factors than cold-blooded creatures. Lifestyle, and particularly the range of foods that are available, also play a part. When birdwatching, there are certain groups of birds that you are most likely to encounter in specific types of habitat as a result of all these factors. The major avian habitats of the world are as listed on the pages that follow.

Below: Common, or European, starlings (Sturnus vulgaris) *are now well established outside their natural range. They are now resident in the USA, having been introduced there in the 1800s. They have since spread out across North America, and can also be seen in other locations, including Australia.*

THE SEA

The world's oceans provide a very rich source of food for all birds able to exploit it. Fish and invertebrates such as squid and krill form the basis of the diet of seabirds, some of which range extensively across the world's oceans and are frequently sighted long distances from land.

The huge expanse of the oceans, and the difficulty of observing seabirds, means that relatively little is known about many species. This lack of knowledge was confirmed by the case of the Bermuda petrel (*Pterodroma cahow*). This species was believed to have become extinct during the 1600s, but, remarkably, a surviving population was rediscovered in 1951 after more than three hundred years. Seabirds survive out at sea with the help of special salt-excreting glands in

the nasal area (just above their bills) that allow them to drink seawater without getting dehydrated.

Breeding habits

Many seabirds are social by nature, forming huge breeding colonies on rocky outcrops by the sea. Indeed, one of the main factors restricting seabird populations can be the lack of nesting sites. By congregating in this way, the birds can maximize their reproductive success while reducing the attacks of predators on their numbers. Nest-raiders such as great black-backed gulls (*Larus marinus*) may be unable to inflict major damage on a breeding colony if the birds are so densely packed that the raiders cannot land.

Feeding

The feeding habits of seabirds have a significant impact on their lifestyle. Albatrosses (Diomedeidae), for example, spend most of their lives flying above the oceans. Their large wingspan allows them to glide almost effortlessly for long periods, swooping down to take food from the surface or even catching flying fish above the waves, rather than entering the water. Other species, such as gannets (Sulidae), dive beneath the surface to feed.

Above: Birds have come to recognize trawlers as sources of fish, swooping down to feed on whatever is thrown overboard, and haunting shipping lanes. Fulmars (Fulmarus glacialis) and gannets (Sula bassana) can be seen here in the wake of a trawler off the Shetland Islands of Scotland.

Below: Not all seabirds feed on fish. This white-vented storm petrel (Oceanites gracilis) is feeding on planktonic debris, while paddling with its feet on the surface of the sea.

Right: All seabirds are forced back to land to breed, and some long-distance travellers seek out remote oceanic islands for this purpose. Cliff faces and nearby offshore stacks are the next best thing for other seabird colonies, offering shelter from the elements, although there is also less protection from opportunistic nest raiders, such as the larger gulls. Seabirds usually return year after year to the same nesting grounds, but will abandon them if their fish stocks plummet.

Birdwatching tips

• Seabirds such as albatrosses are attracted to passing ships because of the food that is thrown overboard. This means they are relatively easy to locate in certain areas – for example near shipping lanes.

• Ornithologists can often take trips on local boats to view seabird colonies. These and other sea crossings may present a good opportunity to watch birds feeding out at sea.

• If you are prone to seasickness, don't forget to take medication beforehand if you think you may feel ill on a trip.

• Binoculars can easily be lost overboard from a small boat in choppy seas. Always sling them (and any camera equipment) around your neck, rather than simply holding them in your hands.

Typical sightings in seas and oceans, depending to some extent on location:

• Auks
• Gannets
• Albatrosses
• Petrels

Below: For most ornithologists, organized charter boat trips present the only way to reach seabird colonies.

1 Peregrine falcon
2 Kestrel
3 Rock dove
4 Stonechat
5 Fulmar
6 Great black-backed gull
7 Herring gull
8 Rock pipit
9 Oystercatcher

SEASHORE AND ESTUARY

Tidal rhythms have a significant impact on the habits of birds found on seashores and estuaries. These birds usually group together to feed on mudflats and sandbars that are uncovered at low tide. As the incoming tide encroaches, the birds are forced to retreat to the shoreline.

Gulls typify the image of the seashore more than any other group of birds, being a familiar sight on coasts the world over. These adaptable birds also venture well inland, especially to locations where food is available, such

Above: Sanderlings (Calidris alba) *demonstrate the features of a typical wader. The daily lives of such birds are directly influenced by the movements of the tide.*

Below: *The appearance of black-headed gulls* (Larus ridibundus) *differs subtly between the seasons. In winter, the marked black plumage on the crown is reduced to a thin crescent of black which sits on either side of the head.*

as public parks with ponds and even the less salubrious surroundings of refuse dumps.

Lifestyle and feeding

Wading birds that frequent seashores typically have relatively long legs compared with perching birds, which enable them to walk through shallow water. Their narrow bills allow them to probe for invertebrates concealed in the mud. Some waders have evolved more specialized feeding habits, which are reflected in the shape of their bills. The oystercatcher (*Haematopus ostralegus*), for example, has a chisel-like tip to its bill that allows it to split open mollusc shells.

Shorebirds feed on a range of creatures, and can therefore be sighted further inland, even if only seeking sanctuary from storms. Some shorebirds are migratory, spending summer as far north as the Arctic Circle before heading south for winter again.

Breeding habits

Many birds that live close to the shoreline have to breed in the open. The eggs and chicks of such species,

which include curlews (*Numenius arquata*) have markings that conceal them well among the sand or pebbles. Even the colouring of the adult birds often helps to conceal their presence, with typical shades of grey, brown and white plumage merging into the background of the shoreline.

Within the tropics, a number of waterbirds have adapted to living in coastal mangrove forests, the roots of which are submerged by the incoming tide. They include some of the most spectacular members of the group, such as the pink-backed pelican (*Pelecanus rufescens*), which capitalizes on the abundance of cover, food and water in the mangroves to breed.

Right: *The day-to-day distribution of seashore and estuarine birds is likely to be influenced by the weather. If conditions are stormy, birds often retreat to estuaries and coastal lagoons; in icy winter weather, a variety of unexpected species may be seen at estuaries, since these stretches of water do not freeze over, unlike surrounding areas of freshwater such as lakes.*

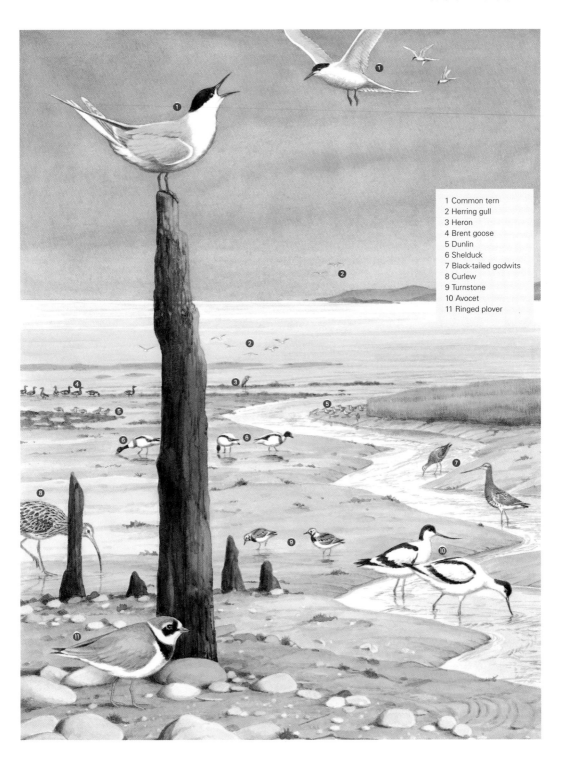

1 Common tern
2 Herring gull
3 Heron
4 Brent goose
5 Dunlin
6 Shelduck
7 Black-tailed godwits
8 Curlew
9 Turnstone
10 Avocet
11 Ringed plover

FRESHWATER LAKES, PONDS AND RIVERS

The speed of the water flow in freshwater habitats has a direct impact on the vegetation that grows there, which in turn influences the types of birds that may be seen. Some birds are drawn to lakes, ponds and rivers mainly for food, whereas others seek sanctuary from would-be predators there.

A wide variety of birds can be encountered by lakes, ponds and rivers, but not all are easy to observe. In areas of slow-flowing or still, shallow water where reed beds are well established, rails of various types (Rallidae) are often present, but these birds are shy by nature. Their mottled plumage provides camouflage, while their slim, tall body shape coupled with long, narrow toes allows them to move quietly through the vegetation.

Above: A sharp bill, narrow head and powerful neck mean that birds such as the red-necked grebe (Podiceps grisegena) are well equipped to seize aquatic prey.

Finding food

Many birds of prey hunt in freshwater habitats, swooping low over the water to seize fish by day and even at night. Fishing owls (*Scotopelia*) have sharp spines on the undersides of their feet that allow them to tighten their grip on fish hooked by their sharp talons. Other hunters rely on different strategies to catch food. Herons (Ardeidae) wait in the shallows and seize fish that swim in range of their sharp, powerful bills. Some fish-eating birds, notably some kingfishers (Alcedinidae), dive to seize their prey, which they may feed to their young in river bank nests.

Nesting

Some birds are drawn to lakes and rivers not so much by food but by nesting opportunities. Swallows (*Hirundo rustica*) collect damp mud from the

water's edge to make their nests, and may also catch midges flying above the water. Most birds that actually nest by ponds and rivers seek seclusion when breeding. They hide their nest away, or make it hard to reach by choosing a spot surrounded by water, while taking care to avoid sites that may flood. Mute swans (*Cygnus olor*) construct large nests, which restricts their choice of sites. Both sexes, but especially the cob (male), defend the nest ferociously. These largish birds are capable of inflicting painful, damaging blows with

their wings on would-be wild predators, dogs or even people who venture too close.

Birdwatching tips
• Patience is essential when watching freshwater birds, as many species are shy and easily frightened away.
• Certain localities, such as large lakes and gravel pits, are particularly good for spotting waterfowl in winter. Check local details in field guides or websites.
• Quietly paddling a canoe up a river can be a good way to spot birds, but plan carefully and be alert to possible dangers, such as strong currents, weirs or waterfalls on the route.
• Take great care near rivers when there is a risk of flooding, such as after heavy rain.

Typical sightings by lakes, ponds and rivers, depending on location:
• Ducks, geese and swans
• Rails
• Herons
• Birds of prey

Below: The keen eyesight, long legs and prominent bill of birds such as this yellow-billed stork (Mycteria ibis) help them to hunt and feed in freshwater habitats.

Below: An African jacana (Actophilornis africanus) on a hippopotamus. This bird's long toes support its weight when walking over lily pads, so it does not sink down.

Right: Lakes provide a range of different benefits for birds, ranging from calm, open water in which to swim, to the dense cover provided by reedbeds at the perimeter. The narrow body shape of birds such as crakes (Rallidae) allows them to move easily through the dense vegetation, while taller reeds further inland make excellent vantage points for kingfishers (Alcedinidae) spotting prey.

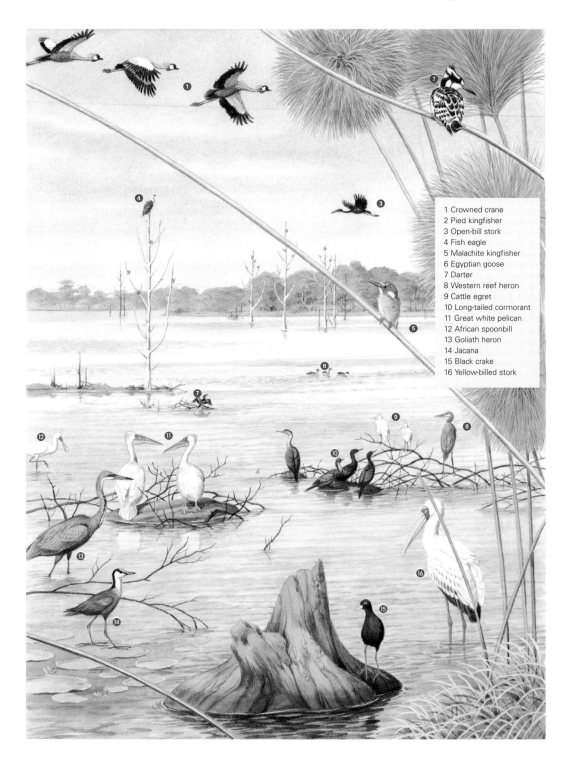

1 Crowned crane
2 Pied kingfisher
3 Open-bill stork
4 Fish eagle
5 Malachite kingfisher
6 Egyptian goose
7 Darter
8 Western reef heron
9 Cattle egret
10 Long-tailed cormorant
11 Great white pelican
12 African spoonbill
13 Goliath heron
14 Jacana
15 Black crake
16 Yellow-billed stork

TEMPERATE WOODLAND

The temperate woodlands of the Northern Hemisphere have altered significantly over time owing to climate change, receding in cold periods and expanding in warmer eras. Coniferous forests extend north to the treeless area known as the tundra, where it is too cold for even hardy trees to grow.

Bird life in coniferous forests is less varied than in deciduous, broad-leaved woodlands, largely because there are fewer feeding opportunities. A variety of species opt to live in this cooler habitat, however.

Coniferous woodlands

One resident is the spotted nutcracker (*Nucifraga caryocatactes*) of European and Asian forests. Their pointed bills allow these specialized members of the crow family to extract the seeds from pine cones very effectively.

The food supply in this habitat is not guaranteed, however. There are barren years when the trees do not produce as many cones as usual, forcing the birds to abandon their regular haunts and fly elsewhere. These unpredictable movements, known as irruptions, occur when birds suddenly appear in large numbers outside their normal range, searching for alternative sources of food. They later disappear

Below: Some predatory birds have adapted to life in temperate forests, especially owls such as this Tengmalm's owl (Aegolius funereus). These hunters mainly feed on rodents.

Above: Ground birds such as the capercaillie (Tetrao urogallus) breed on the ground, concealing their presence as far as possible. Their chicks are able to move immediately after they hatch out.

just as suddenly as they arrived, and may not return again for years. In northerly areas the landscape is covered in snow for much of the winter. Some species, including various corvids (Corvidae) and woodpeckers (Picidae), prepare for the cold weather by burying stores of nuts.

Owls are frequently found in coniferous forests, preying on the rodents that can be quite plentiful there. However, owls may also be forced to hunt elsewhere if the numbers of their prey plummet, as occasionally happens when there is a shortage of pine cones.

Deciduous woodlands

A greater variety of feeding opportunities exists for birds in deciduous forests. Such woodland is more open, which means that there is a significant understorey of vegetation, and insects are more plentiful. Migratory birds also take advantage of the feeding opportunities in these forests in summer. These birds eat a variety of foods, ranging from seeds to berries and invertebrates, depending on the time of year. Ground birds of various types, including Eurasian woodcocks (*Scolopax rusticola*), are

Above: A great spotted woodpecker (Dendrocopos major) returns to the nest site. Trees provide relatively safe nesting havens, especially for birds such as woodpeckers that can create their own nesting holes.

also found here. During the breeding season, the males become territorial and are often highly active at dusk.

Birdwatching tips
• Spring is a good time to spot birds in deciduous woodlands, before the trees are covered in leaves.
• Woodlands and particularly coniferous forests can be disorientating, so take a map and compass if you're going any distance in case you lose your bearings.
• In summer, woodland glades attract invertebrates, which in turn attract insectivorous birds in search of prey.
• Stand quietly in woodlands and listen – the song of woodland birds helps to reveal their presence.

Typical sightings in temperate woodlands, depending to some extent on location:
• Woodpeckers
• Finches
• Owls
• Warblers

Right: In many ways, temperate woodland is an ideal avian habitat during the warm months of the year, providing a wide range of food, excellent cover and a variety of nesting sites. During the winter months, however, life here can become much harsher. Once the leaves have fallen, the birds will be much more conspicuous, and food is likely to be scarcer. Survival will become even harder if snow blankets the ground.

1 Redstart
2 Hobby
3 Wood warbler
4 Treecreeper
5 Tawny owl
6 Blackcap
7 Jay
8 Great spotted
  woodpecker
9 Pheasant
10 Song thrush

TROPICAL RAINFOREST

Over long periods, tropical rainforests have provided relatively stable environments compared with temperate woodland, and are home to some spectacular species. Unfortunately, many tracts of forest are not easily accessible. Choose locations carefully to maximize your chance of seeing a wide range of birds.

Many of the birds inhabiting tropical rainforest are brightly coloured, but their vibrant plumage is very effectively concealed in this dark, shadowy environment. Only flashes of colour may be seen as the plumage is lit by shafts of sunlight penetrating through the dense canopy of the forest.

Rainforest diversity

The stable environment of this dense forest has undoubtedly contributed to the diversity of bird life found there. Fruit is especially plentiful, and specialist fruit-eating birds, known as frugivores, are therefore numerous. Their presence is essential to the long-term well-being of the rainforest, as they help to distribute the seeds of fruits on which they feed. The seeds are excreted in their droppings, often some distance away from where the fruit was originally eaten. This method of seed dispersal helps to ensure the continued regeneration of the forest.

Birds of prey can also be observed in tropical rainforests, having adapted well to forest life, and there are even a

Below: Cape parrots (Poicephalus robustus) can be encountered in rainforest areas. The unchanging climatic conditions there means that food is available throughout the year.

number of species that specialize in hunting other birds. These predators are relatively few in number, however, compared with the overall numbers of birds found in this habitat.

Many rainforest species have highly specialized distributions. Touracos (Musophagidae) are found only in Africa, and the range of the distinctive black parrot (*Coracopsis*) is smaller still, confined to Madagascar and neighbouring islands. Vast tracts of the world's tropical forests are still so inaccessible and remote, particularly in South America, that even today new species of birds are being discovered by explorers on a regular basis.

Threatened habitat

It is well documented that the world's rainforests are being felled at an alarming rate. The sheer speed of destruction means that some species may become extinct before a genetic profile can be made. This was feared to be the fate of the rare Congo bay owl (*Phodilus prigoginei*), once documented solely from the remains of a single bird skin obtained from eastern Zaire in 1951. The species was rediscovered in the region in 1986, but remains extremely vulnerable.

Above: Touracos are uniquely African birds, and are among some of the most colourful species living in the western rainforests. This vivid example is a violet-crested touraco (Muporphyreolopha porphyreolopha).

Birdwatching tips
• Rainforests are potentially dangerous places, so go with an experienced guide or group, and don't be tempted to wander off into the forest on your own.
• You are often more likely to hear rather than see birds in this leafy environment.
• Pausing quietly for a time should allow you to spot bird life more easily.
• Photography is often difficult in the forest because of the low light.
• The high humidity, almost daily rainfall and biting insects in rainforests can create additional problems.

Typical sightings in tropical rainforests, depending to some extent on location:
• Parrots
• Barbets
• Hornbills
• Trogons

Right: The dense upper canopy of the rainforest provides both a screen and a vantage point for birds, depending on their lifestyle. Hunters may perch among the tallest trees or fly over the canopy, seeking signs of possible prey beneath, while nearer to the ground, nectar-eating birds seek flowers to feed from. Fruit is also abundant in these lush forests, so frugivorous species are commonly encountered here too.

1 Crowned hawk-eagle
2 Narina trogon
3 Black-casqued hornbill
4 Green-crested touraco
5 Grey parrots
6 Fire-bellied woodpecker
7 Crested guinea fowl
8 Emerald cuckoo
9 White-tailed ant thrush
10 Lemon-rumped tinkerbird
11 Collared sunbird

TUNDRA AND POLAR REGIONS

Birds have successfully colonized many harsh environments, including the treeless tundra and freezing Antarctic. A surprisingly wide range of birds may be sighted on the tundra, especially in summer, when many migratory birds arrive to breed.

The treeless lands of the far north are inhospitable in winter, so many birds visit only for the summer. Icy Antarctica is even harsher, yet birds such as penguins are year-round residents on coastlines.

Antarctic survivors

As the huge landmass of Antarctica drifted gradually southwards millions of years ago, so the seabirds there adapted their lifestyle to survive the harshest conditions on Earth. The freezing cold and biting winds combine to create a numbing wind-chill factor that few creatures could survive, but penguins have adapted to thrive in this habitat, as have other seabirds such as petrels (Procellariidae), which return there every year to nest.

Penguins have reversed the general evolutionary path of birds to survive in this harsh environment. In the course of millions of years, most birds evolved increasingly lightweight bodies to

Above: A rock ptarmigan (Lagopus mutus) hidden in the snow. This bird's white winter plumage provides excellent camouflage, and it becomes immobile at the hint of danger to complete its disguise.

facilitate flight, but the body weight of penguins increased because of a build-up of the subcutaneous fat that helps to insulate them against the bitter cold. The evolution of their wings into flippers and their streamlined shape combine to make them highly effective marine predators.

The northern tundra

In the far north, the treeless tundra landscape is transformed during the brief summer months when the snow melts. The topsoil thaws and the

ground becomes boggy because the melt water cannot drain away through the permanently frozen layer beneath. Instead, water forms shallow pools at the surface, where mosquitoes and other insects breed in large numbers. These invertebrates and other food attract a variety of birds as temporary visitors. The migrants nest and quickly rear their young before the weather turns cold and the time comes to head south again. In some cases, adult birds may leave in advance of their young, leaving these newly independent birds to continue feeding for some weeks on the rich source of protein provided by invertebrates. This helps to build up their body strength for the journey to the wintering grounds, which may extend as far south as parts of Africa.

Right: The tundra landscape alters dramatically in appearance during the year, with the snow being replaced by a carpet of vegetation in the spring. This change heralds a rapid influx of birds which breed here over the brief summer before departing again. The species which remain during the harsh winter often develop a snow-white plumage for camouflage.

Birdwatching tips

• Wear pale or dull-coloured clothing to conceal your presence in these cold, treeless areas where there is little natural cover. Of course, all clothing must be warm as well.

• Take mosquito repellent when visiting the tundra during the summer.

• Allow for the bright light when photographing in snowy landscapes. Glare reflecting off the snow may distort your camera's light readings, so you may need to compensate.

• An increasing number of ornithological trips to the Antarctic allow you to visit this part of the world accompanied by experienced guides.

Typical sightings in tundra or polar landscapes, depending on your location in the Northern or Southern Hemisphere:

• Waterfowl
• Snowy owls
• Waders
• Penguins

Below: Wide-ranging seabirds such as the cape petrel (Daption capense) benefit from the rich food supply in the southern oceans. These birds fly north to escape the worst winter weather, and only return to the shores of Antarctica during the brief summer to nest.

1 Pink-footed geese
2 Snowy owl
3 Hooded crow
4 Barnacle goose
5 Bewick's swan
6 Red-necked
  phalarope
7 Gyr falcon
8 Wheatear
9 Knot
10 Grey-headed
   wagtail
11 Lapland longspur

GRASSLAND, STEPPE AND MOORLAND

Open grasslands offer relatively little cover to birds, and some are harsh, treeless places where both water and food may be scarce. A number of birds found in these areas are ground-dwellers, and they are often well camouflaged, which makes them hard to spot unless flushed from their hiding places.

Moors and grasslands are among the best habitats in which to spot predatory birds as they fly overhead seeking live quarry or carcasses to scavenge. Prey species are also present in numbers, but they are more difficult to spot because of their camouflage.

Spotting predatory birds
Large predators and scavengers such as condors (Cathartidae) fly high over grasslands, utilizing the warm air

Above: Open country predators such as this golden eagle (Aquila chrysaetos) *benefit from keen eyesight, which enables them to spot quarry on the ground while in flight.*

currents known as thermals, which allow them to remain airborne with minimal effort. Smaller hunters such as hawks swoop down much lower over the open countryside as they search for the small mammals or birds that form the basis of their diet.

Survival of terrestrial birds
Many birds occupying grassland areas have evolved either to become very large, as in the case of the ostrich (*Struthio camellus*), or are small and inconspicuous as increased protection against predators. Many terrestrial birds rely on their ability to remain undetected if danger threatens, only taking flight as a last resort. Skylarks (*Alauda arvensis*) have developed an unusual way of drawing a would-be predator away from their nest site by feigning an injury, often to the wing.

These birds have also been disrupted by human intervention, however, such as the cultivation of open fields which

Left: The northern wheatear (Oenanthe oenanthe) *migrates to Africa after breeding in Europe. This is a hen in autumn plumage.*

has disturbed the nesting patterns of both skylarks and corncrakes (*Crex crex*). Furthermore, insecticides have reduced their natural food resources, which are vital to the successful rearing of their young.

Moorland camouflage
On moorlands and steppes the weather can become cold and snowy in winter. Some of the birds found in this terrain undergo a seasonal moult at the onset of winter, from which they emerge transformed by lighter-coloured plumage to help conceal their presence.

Birdwatching tips
• Seek a good vantage point to increase your chances of spotting and following birds of prey.
• You will need a pair of powerful binoculars in grassland environments, as you will be combing relatively large and distant expanses of sky and land in search of birds.
• Use whatever natural cover is available to conceal your presence, such as tall vegetation and outcropping rocks.
• Horse riding can be a good way to cover long distances in grasslands and yet have a reasonable chance of spotting bird life, because birds are often less fearful of people on horseback.

Typical sightings in grassland habitats, depending to some extent on location:
• Eagles
• Vultures
• Grouse
• Hawks

Right: Open countryside can range from bleak moorland or arid steppeland to agricultural areas where trees have been cleared to create fields. These may then be ploughed to grow cereal crops, or left as meadows which can support a rich diversity of plant and animal life, including birds, although any resulting avian life may not be especially conspicuous to the observer. Grasslands offer better prospects of spotting birds of prey, however, since they are forced to spend relatively long periods on the wing scanning the ground for food.

1 Buzzard
2 Long-tailed tit
3 Skylark
4 Yellowhammer
5 Swallow
6 Goldfinch
7 Grey partridge
8 Lapwing
9 Snipe

URBAN LIFE

Some birds display a remarkable ability to adapt to modern life, occurring right in the centre of cities.
They use buildings for nesting and, in the case of birds of prey, as vantage points for hunting, just as they
would use trees or rocky crags in the wild. City parks, in particular, have become major refuges for birds.

Cities tend to be slightly warmer than the surrounding countryside, and this warm microclimate offers a number of advantages for birds. Drinking water is less likely to freeze in cold weather, and in spring, insects are more abundant at an earlier time, as plants bud and grow more quickly because of the warmth.

Residents and visitors
Some birds live permanently in cities, taking advantage of parks, whereas

Above: Out of all birds, the feral pigeon (Columba livia) has adapted best to urban life, to the extent that it is now a common sight in cities around the world.

Below: Cattle egrets (Bubulcus ibis) have proved remarkably adaptable in their invasion of cities, and are often found scavenging around markets or refuse dumps. They can prove surprisingly bold in such surroundings, unfazed even by the presence of vehicles.

Above: Buildings can represent safe localities for nest-building. White storks (Ciconia ciconia) such as these have nested on town roofs for centuries in some parts of their range.

others are more casual visitors, flying in to roost at night from outlying areas, or pausing here on migration. Deserted buildings offer a snug and relatively safe retreat for birds that roost in flocks, whereas birds of prey seek the inaccessible ledges of high-rise buildings. The abundance of feral pigeons (*Columba livia*) in built-up areas attracts peregrine falcons (*Falco peregrinus*), proving that they are just as adaptable as their prey. The falcons may keep pigeon populations in check, but if not, their numbers can be also curbed by feeding them with corn, which acts as a contraceptive.

A life above the bustle of city streets generally offers predatory species a fairly safe existence, compared with more rural areas where they risk being shot illegally. There are still dangers lurking on the city streets, however. High-rise office blocks with large expanses of glass can lure birds to a fatal collision.

Migrating birds still pass through cities on occasions, notably huge flocks of common starlings (*Sturnus vulgaris*). These congregate not just in city parks, but also roost on buildings and tree-lined streets when breaking their journey, creating a noisy chatter and plenty of mess.

Birdwatching tips
• City parks offer the best chances of spotting the largest number of species in urban environments, particularly if there is a sizeable pond or lake.
• Early morning is a good time to spot birds at close quarters in cities, before many people are on the streets.
• Don't forget about the dangers of traffic in your enthusiasm to spot particular birds.
• Join the local ornithological society to gain insight into the more unusual species found in local towns and cities.

Typical sightings in urban environments, depending to some extent on location:
• Falcons
• Owls
• Pigeons and doves
• Gulls

Right: Urbanization has inevitably influenced resident avian populations by altering the surrounding habitat. Only opportunists such as pigeons – with their extremely adaptable dietary habits – will actually thrive in crowded city centres, but a much wider variety of bird life can be seen in city parks. Various species of waterfowl, for example, have been introduced to man-made ponds and lakes, while coastal birds such as gulls will also scavenge in this habitat.

1 Jackdaw
2 Starling
3 Pigeon
4 Magpie
5 Black-headed gull
6 Coot
7 Mute swan
8 Tufted duck
9 Mallard
10 Pintail
11 Wigeon
12 Goldeneye
13 House sparrow
14 Wood duck

GARDENS

An amazingly wide variety of birds have been recorded as regular garden visitors. It is possible to observe as many as 40 species regularly visiting bird tables in urban areas of north-western Europe. Feeding stations undoubtedly help to draw birds to gardens, but birds also visit as part of their natural behaviour.

Tidy, immaculately manicured gardens generally support less bird life than well-established gardens with plenty of mature shrubs that can be used for roosting and nesting. If there are stands of trees nearby, or even just lining the road outside, the range of birds visiting the garden will increase, and larger species will become more common. Artificial nesting sites, such as nest boxes of various types and sizes, can also help to increase the variety and numbers of birds that visit gardens regularly.

Birds face a major danger in gardens in the guise of the domestic cat. Huge numbers of individuals fall victim to these pets annually. The majority of the casualties are young fledglings, which lack the awareness and caution of adult birds. In areas where the cat population is especially high, there

Above: Bird tables and feeders help to attract birds into gardens by providing them with additional food sources. These are especially valuable during cold winter weather.

may be local declines in bird numbers. However, studies suggest that bird populations do not seem to be adversely affected by cats overall.

Helpers and pests
Birds are often regarded as gardeners' friends because they help to control the number of invertebrate pests in gardens. For example, tits (*Parus*) eat aphids on rose bushes, and thrushes (*Turdus*) hunt snails. At certain times of year, however, some birds can themselves become pests. Pigeons (*Columba*), in particular, often dig up newly planted seeds and eat them before they can germinate, unless the seeds are protected in some way. Later in the year, some species eat ripening berries.

Residents and migrants
Some birds are resident in garden settings throughout the year. Others are temporary visitors, migrating to warmer climates for the winter period. Many warblers (Sylviidae) can be seen in northern Europe for only part of the year, before heading south to winter in Africa. At this time, migrants from further north may descend on gardens to replace the species that have left, as

occurs with the fieldfare (*Turdus pilaris*). Studies provide clear evidence that actual shifts in the behaviour and distribution of birds are currently occurring because of the availability of garden habitat and the provision of food there. The Eurasian blackbird (*Turdus merula*), a native of field and woodland, has become a common sight in gardens, while the Eurasian collared dove (*Streptopelia decaocto*), native to India, has undoubtedly benefited from bird table fare as it has spread from Asia into parts of Europe.

Above: Fieldfares (Turdus pilaris) *arrive from their northerly breeding grounds to winter in European gardens and farmland, where they like to feed on fallen fruit. These thrushes can be identified by their harsh, chuckling calls.*

*Right: In many respects, gardens offer an ideal habitat for birds. Food is readily available in these surroundings, as well as trees and shrubs, which provide good opportunities for roosting and nesting. Unfortunately, gardens can often be dangerous places for birds to visit, thanks to the popularity of cats as pets. Nor are cats the only danger in this type of habitat. Predatory birds, notably magpies (*Pica pica*), will raid the nests of smaller birds, taking both eggs and chicks.*

Birdwatching tips
• You can encourage invertebrate-eating birds to visit your garden by creating a wild area or by establishing a compost heap where invertebrates can multiply.
• Positioning a bird table near a window will allow you to watch birds from inside the house, but take care to site it well away from cover where cats could lurk and ambush the birds.
• Keep a pair of binoculars handy indoors so you can get a better view of the bird table and any unexpected visitors to it, plus a notepad to record descriptions of any unusual birds you see.
• Try to avoid using insecticides on your garden, as these reduce the food that will be available for birds.
• Ordinary slug pellets will poison slug-eaters such as thrushes feeding in your garden. Use pellets that are described as safe for birds instead.

Typical sightings in gardens, depending to some extent on location:
• Tits
• Thrushes
• Starlings
• Finches

1 Rooks
2 Spotted flycatcher
3 Collared dove
4 Chaffinch
5 Robin
6 Mistle thrush
7 Blackbird
8 Blue tit
9 Wren
10 Dunnock

ENDANGERED SPECIES AND CONSERVATION

It has been estimated that three-quarters of the world's birds may come under threat in the 21st century. Habitat destruction poses the most serious danger, so conservationists are striving to preserve bird habitats worldwide. Direct intervention of various kinds is also used to ensure the survival of particular species.

Around the world, threats to birds are varied and complex, but most are linked to human interference in the ecosystem, and will thus continue to grow as human populations increase.

Habitat destruction

Habitat destruction includes the deforestation of the world's tropical rainforests, which host a wide variety of birds, and also the conversion of many grassland areas into crop fields or livestock pasture. The first casualties of habitat destruction are often species with specialized feeding or nesting requirements, which cannot easily adapt to change.

In recent years, there have been a number of instances of opportunistic species adapting and thriving in altered habitats. One example is the common mynah (*Acridotheres tristis*), whose natural distribution is centred on India but has been introduced to many other localities worldwide, often to control locust numbers. Its range now includes southern Africa and the Seychelles.

Below: The waldrapp, or bald ibis (Geronticus eremita), is now the subject of intense conservation efforts, with captive-breeding programmes in force to build on its numbers.

Above: Aquatic birds, such as these wattled cranes (Grus carunculatus) may be vulnerable to marshland drainage schemes or other commercial initiatives.

Generally, the diversity of bird life in an area declines drastically when the land is modified or cleared.

Hunting and pollution

Unregulated hunting of adult birds, eggs or young threatens a variety of species worldwide. The birds may be killed for their meat or feathers, or captured live and sold through the pet trade. In many countries, laws are now in place to protect rare species, but hunting and trading still go on illegally.

Overfishing is a related hazard facing seabirds, especially now that trawling methods have become so efficient. Global shortages of fish stocks are forcing fishermen to target fish that had previously been of little commercial value, but that are an important part of seabirds' diets.

In agricultural areas, pesticides and herbicides sprayed on farmers' fields decimate bird populations by eliminating their plant or animal food supplies. Deliberate or accidental contamination of the soil, air or water by industrial chemicals is another hazard, while in the oceans, seabirds are killed by dumped toxins and oil spills. Disease is another major threat that may increase.

Climate change

In the near future, global warming caused by increased emissions of carbon dioxide and other gases is likely to impact on many bird habitats, and will almost certainly adversely affect birds' food supplies. If plants or other foods become unavailable in an area, birds must adapt their feeding habits or face extinction. As temperatures rise, the melting of the polar ice caps will threaten seabird populations by destroying their traditional nesting areas. Rising sea levels will also threaten low-lying wetlands favoured by wading birds.

Threats to island birds

Some of the world's most distinctive birds have evolved in relative isolation on islands. Unfortunately, these species are also extremely vulnerable to changes in their environment, partly because their populations are small. One of the greatest threats comes from

Above: This guillemot (Uria aalge) *killed in Scottish waters is just one of the countless avian victims claimed by oil spillages each year. Large spills of oil can have devastating effects on whole populations.*

introduced predators, particularly domestic cats. Most famously, off the coast of New Zealand in 1894, the resident lighthouse keeper's cat killed the last Stephen Island wren *(Xenicus lyalli)*, which was unique to this habitat, before any official record of the species had been made.

Cats are not the only introduced predators that can cause serious harm to avian populations. Grazing animals such as goats, introduced to islands by passing ships to provide future crews with fresh meat, have frequently destroyed the native vegetation, so reducing the birds' food supply. Rats and pigs threaten ground-nesting birds as they will prey on both their eggs and even young chicks.

Today, control of harmful introduced species is helping to protect surviving populations of endangered island birds, but sadly for some species this action has come too late to save them from total extinction.

Conservation and captive-breeding

Preserving habitat is the best and most cost-effective way to ensure the survival of all the birds that frequent a particular ecosystem. A worldwide network of national parks and reserves

now helps to protect at least part of many birds' habitats. In addition, conservationists may take a variety of direct measures to safeguard the future of particular species, such as breeding in captivity, or translocation. The latter method sees conservation officials remove the youngest chicks from wild nests, which are subsequently reared to independence and released into a new location, where it is hoped they will thrive. Using this approach, golden eagles *(Aquila chrysaetos)* have been translocated to Ireland from their native home in the Scottish highlands.

Artificially or naturally fertilized eggs can be transferred to incubators to be hatched, effectively doubling the number of chicks that can be reared. This is because removing the eggs often stimulates the hen to lay again more quickly than usual. Hand-rearing chicks on formulated diets helps to ensure the survival of the young once hatched. When hand-reared chicks are later released into the wild, it is vital that they bond with their own species and retain their natural fear of people, so glove puppets shaped like the parent birds are often used to feed the chicks.

Reintroduction programmes

Breeding endangered species is relatively easy compared with the difficulties of reintroducing a species to

Above: Glove puppets resembling the parent bird's head are often used when hand-rearing chicks such as this peregrine falcon (Falco peregrinus), *to encourage the birds to bond with their own kind when eventually released.*

an area of its former habitat. The cost of such reintroduction programmes is often very high. Staff are needed not only to look after the aviary stock and rear the chicks, but also to carry out habitat studies. These assess the dangers that the birds will face after release and pinpoint release sites. The released birds must then be monitored, which may include fitting them with radio transmitters.

Ecotourism

Working with local people and gaining their support is often essential to the long-term successes of conservation initiatives. On Mauritius, an island home to unique indigenous species such as the echo parakeet *(Psittacula echo)* and the pink pigeon *(Columba mayeri)*, international assistance from organisations such as the Jersey Wildlife Preservation Trust has helped both to increase the numbers of these critically endangered birds, and also to make local people more aware of the significance of their native wildlife as part of the island's heritage. It has also raised the profile of these particular species on a global scale, increasing the flux of tourists to this island and bringing in some much needed foreign currency to boost the local economy.

Left: Around 20% of the world's surviving rainforest is located in Africa, such as the Uluguru montane forests in Tanzania. Yet ongoing clearance of land continues to threaten the many birds living there.

DIRECTORY OF BIRDS

Identifying birds in many cases is not easy, particularly if you have only a relatively brief sighting. This part of the book has therefore been divided into the key habitat groups – including sea, estuarine, freshwater, woodland, open country and urban locations – designed to simplify the task of identification as much as possible by allowing you to link your sightings with the place in which you spotted the bird. It should be pointed out that this system is not infallible, as some birds are highly adaptable and range widely through different environments, but it is a useful starting point. Distribution maps accompanying all the illustrated entries provide a visual guide as to where exactly bird species are likely to be found within these regions, while the text indicates the various locations in which migratory species can be seen at differing times of the year.

The associated descriptions will help to clarify whether you have seen a cock bird or a hen, since there are often plumage differences between the sexes. Other information in these fact boxes about habitat, feeding and breeding behaviour should provide further help when it comes to identifying a particular bird. A bird's general shape, its habits, and the characteristic way in which it moves, all add up to what birdwatchers call its "jizz", which can help to pinpoint birds even from a tiny speck in the sky or a dark shape scuttling behind a hedge. Where this is a notable discrepancy between the size of the male and females birds, both measurements are given.

Not every species within the terrain of Great Britain, Europe and Africa is covered, but the representative sample featured in the following pages – which are grouped with similar "types" or family members – should at least allow you to narrow down the search. Browsing through these pages also affords an opportunity to learn more about the diverse avian life of these continents, ranging from the hornbills of the west African rainforests, to the eider ducks breeding within the Arctic Circle, not overlooking the many predatory birds and Columbiforms that have made a home in our city centres.

Left: Bee-eaters (Meropidae) are colourful and social birds, and species can be found in both Europe and Africa. They live in colonies, carving out nesting holes in sandy river banks with their long, pointed bills. Bee-eaters feed mainly on bees and wasps, and rub their insect prey on the ground before consuming it, either to remove the sting or kill them outright.

THE AVIFAUNA OF GREAT BRITAIN, EUROPE & AFRICA

The distribution of birds occurring on these continents, especially those found in Europe, often extends eastwards into Asia as well. Many northerly species also undergo regular seasonal movements in response to the climate, overwintering in more southerly latitudes, with some even flying as far as southern Africa. Those groups of birds most commonly associated with tropical areas – such as parrots, for example – are poorly represented in this region of the world, partly because of the absence of suitable feeding opportunities in Europe. Urban development has also had a marked impact on the distribution of a number of species, and some have adapted to urban environments better than others. Human involvement has also seen the introduction of avian species into Europe from outside their natural range, often for sporting purposes, as in the case of various species of pheasants and partridges.

Above from left: kestrel (Falco tinnunculus), *eagle owl* (Bubo bubo), *malachite kingfisher* (Alcedo cristata).

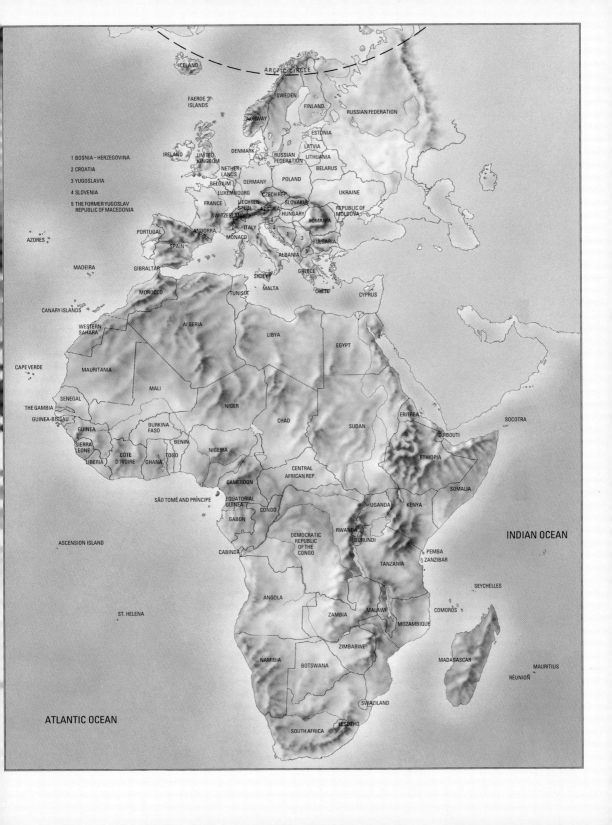

OCEAN WANDERERS

These seabirds typically have a very wide distribution, effortlessly roaming over the oceans far away from the shore. They return to land only in order to nest, though are unlikely to be seen by the casual observer, as they frequently choose remote islands on which to breed. However, they may be attracted to passing ships in search of offerings of food.

Black-browed albatross

Diomedea melanophris

Distribution: Throughout the entire southern oceanic region, in a broad band extending from just off Antarctica as far north as southern Africa.
Size: 93cm (37in).
Habitat: Over the ocean.
Nest: Earth mound incorporating plant matter.
Eggs: 1, white.
Food: Mainly crustaceans, fish and squid.

This is the most common of the black-backed albatross species seen off the coast of Africa. Despite roaming widely over the ocean, they are also likely to be sighted close to the shore, where they seek out bays and similar stretches of tranquil water when the weather becomes stormy. Here they are easily distinguished in flight from gulls by their much longer wings. These albatrosses will often follow trawlers, seeking offal thrown overboard, and as many as 3000 individuals have been sighted around a single boat. In these circumstances they will descend to the sea to feed, although more commonly they will pick up their prey in flight from the surface of the water, only occasionally venturing beneath the waves. Black-browed albatrosses choose remote islands for their breeding grounds, and ringing studies reveal that many of the birds seen off the coasts of South Africa originate from the population breeding on the island of South Georgia, off the east coast of South America.

Identification:
Black upper surface to the body, with relatively dark underwing coloration, especially around the edges. Underside of the body is white, as is the rump. Bill is orangish with a pinkish tip. Sexes are alike.

Shy albatross

Diomedea cauta

Despite its name the shy albatross is a bold scavenger, swooping down to feed on offal thrown overboard from trawlers and driving away other seabirds. It also feeds by scooping at the surface, sometimes even diving under the water. These albatrosses frequent African waters during the southern winter, although they can be seen off the western Cape throughout the year. Unlike most other albatrosses this species often ventures near to the shoreline. Younger, non-breeding birds may fly further afield than adults, but little is known about their migratory habits. They breed on the smaller islands around Australia and New Zealand, with pairs returning to their breeding grounds in September. Incubation lasts nearly 11 weeks, after which the chick remains in the nest for a further four months.

Identification: Black back and wings, with black edging on the undersides. Underparts white. Pale head with a prominent white cap and a blackish band beneath running through the eyes. Grey area below on the sides of the face. Young birds have dark bills, whereas adults are greyish, with a lighter yellowish tip. Sexes are alike.

Distribution: Occurs widely from the western coast of southern South America via New Zealand and Australia to the southern tip of Africa.
Size: 98cm (38½in).
Habitat: Over the ocean.
Nest: Earth mound incorporating plant matter.
Eggs: 1, white.
Food: Mainly fish and squid.

Wandering albatross

Snowy albatross *Diomedea exulans*

Distribution: Occurs throughout the southern oceans, extending slightly further north up the Atlantic coastline of Africa than on the eastern side of the continent, and breeding on islands to the south.
Size: 135cm (53in).
Habitat: Over the ocean.
Nest: Pile of mud and grass.
Eggs: 1, white with reddish-brown speckling.
Food: Mainly squid, but will also take fish, crustaceans and carrion.

As their name suggests, these albatrosses range widely over the southern oceans, often following ships and scavenging on galley scraps thrown overboard. They are also active hunters, scooping up squid from the sea after dark, when these cephalopods come closer to the surface. Pairs separate at the end of the breeding period, though some will reunite later on the breeding grounds. They breed only every second year since it takes nearly 40 weeks for a newly hatched chick to grow large enough to leave the nest.

Identification: Predominantly white. Black patches over much of the wings, although those closest to the body have only a black edging. There is often a pinkish area near the ear coverts, and there may be a greyish area on the crown. The bill is pink with a yellowish, hooked tip. Hens are slightly smaller, and may display a light greyish band around the chest and black on the edges of the tail feathers.

Grey-headed albatross (*Diomedea chrysostoma*): 80cm (31¹/₂in) Circumpolar, occurring northwards to the Cape of Good Hope. Characteristic grey head, with blackish back and wings. Wings have black M-shaped pattern when seen from below. Bill is yellow on its upper and lower edges, black on the sides and reddish at the tip, but blackish overall in young birds. Sexes are alike.

Light-mantled albatross (*Phoebetria palpebrata*): 80cm (31¹/₂in) Circumpolar, reaching the extreme southern coast of Africa. Moves further north in the southern winter as the pack ice around Antarctica extends. Predominantly blackish overall, apart from a distinctive pale grey area on the mantle. Fairly indistinct yellow eye ring. Sexes are alike.

Sooty albatross (*Phoebetria fusca*): 89cm (35in) Southern oceans south of Australia across to southern Africa and extending westwards close to the Falkland Islands. Lives over on the open ocean, breeding on isolated islands through its range, such as Tristan da Cunha. Even smoky-black coloration, with a dark bill. Long, rather angular wings when seen in flight. Sexes are alike.

Yellow-nosed albatross

Diomedea chlororhynchos

Two races of this albatross frequent South African waters: the grey-headed (*D. c. chlororhynchos*) and white-headed (*D. c. bassi*) subspecies, with the former most often sighted off the western Cape. The white-headed population, which breeds in the Indian Ocean, is most common on the east coast, especially off Natal during the winter months. Their appearance here is linked not just to the end of the nesting period but also the seasonal availability of sardines, which feature prominently in their diet. Breeding grounds of the yellow-nosed albatross include Gough and Prince Edward Islands, with pairs nesting in much looser associations in the former locality. Pairs return to breed annually, constructing large, platform-style nests. Young birds may not nest for the first time until they are about 10 years old, but like others of their kind, these albatrosses have a life expectancy extending over four decades.

Identification: Black wings with prominent black wing tips on the undersides and along the leading edges. Underparts white. Bill is blackish on the sides, with a central yellow stripe and a red tip. Crown white, rest of the head pale grey with a black stripe through the eyes. Young birds have white heads and black bills. Sexes are alike.

Distribution: Extends through the southern oceans, from New Zealand westwards via southern Africa across the southern Atlantic to South America.
Size: 80cm (31in).
Habitat: Over the ocean.
Nest: Earth mound incorporating plant matter.
Eggs: 1, white.
Food: Mainly fish and squid.

STORM PETRELS

Keen eyesight, possibly assisted by a sense of smell, helps these seabirds find food in the oceans. Marine invertebrates feature prominently in their diet, and they will often congregate in areas where krill are to be found, along with other predatory creatures such as whales. They seek out inconspicuous places to nest, such as underground burrows or the crevices in a rocky cliff face.

White-faced storm petrel

Pelagodroma marina

Distribution: Two separate breeding populations present in the Atlantic, either side of the equator. A third area of distribution extends through the Pacific region from the Red Sea to the north-west coast of South America.
Size: 20cm (8in).
Habitat: Over the ocean.
Nest: Underground burrow.
Eggs: 1, white.
Food: Mainly plankton and small fish.

Unlike many storm petrels, these seabirds are rarely attracted to ships seeking offal. They will, however, congregate in the vicinity of whales, since the presence of these creatures often indicates a plentiful source of krill and similar planktonic crustaceans, which feature prominently in their diet. Pairs nest both north and south of the equator, with the breeding period depending on the locality of each individual population, but invariably taking place during the warmer months of the year. Due to their subterrestrial breeding habits in certain locations, these storm petrels are vulnerable to introduced predators that favour similar surroundings, for example mice and rats. These predators not only disturb the sitting bird but may also prey on the egg or chick. There has been a tendency for colonies to adapt though, by moving from the cliffs to offshore rocky stacks away from such danger. Outside the breeding season, white-faced storm petrels are rarely observed near land.

Identification: Characterized by white plumage on the sides of the head, broken by a dark stripe running back through each eye to the neck. Remainder of the upper body is dark brownish-grey, becoming greyer on the rump. The underparts are white. Sexes are alike.

Black-bellied storm petrel

Fregetta tropica

Distribution: Occurs virtually throughout the oceans of the southern hemisphere up to the equator on the western side of Africa and right up to the Red Sea region on the eastern side.
Size: 20cm (8in).
Habitat: Over the ocean.
Nest: Underground burrow or crevice.
Eggs: 1, white.
Food: Small fish and squid.

Widely distributed throughout the southern oceans, these storm petrels are most likely to be sighted off the western Cape when migrating during October and November, and then again during February. At a distance they can be confused with the white-bellied storm petrel (*F. grallaria*), but their behaviour will usually set them apart. Although they will often congregate close to ships in small groups of up to five individuals, they prefer to dart in front of the vessels or fly alongside them, rather than swoop down over the stern as in the case of most other species. They tend not to dive into the water but patter along on the surface, with the movements of their wings keeping them above the waves. When nesting, black-bellied storm petrels do not spend any time brooding their chick once it has hatched. Instead, it relies on the warmth of the burrow and the insulating effect of its thick grey down feathering to maintain its body temperature.

Identification: Seen from beneath, a well-defined and characteristic central black stripe bisects the white plumage on the breast, extending down to the black lower belly and undertail coverts. Whitish areas also present on the undersides of the wings. Sexes are alike.

European storm petrel

Hydrobates pelagicus

Like others of its kind, the European storm petrel prefers to nest on islands, its traditional nesting grounds including the Balearics and similar localities in the Mediterranean region. Unfortunately however, coastal development is having an adverse effect on breeding populations in some areas. The storm petrels may be resident here throughout the year, but the majority of the North Atlantic population moves south for the winter, where they can be seen off Namibia and South Africa. As with other storm petrels, this species is only able to feed on smaller items of food due to its restricted gape. It is thought that they are able to locate food not only by sight but also by smell, which is rare in birds. Their usual diet is comprised of planktonic creatures such as krill, but they have learned to scavenge for edible items thrown overboard from ships, especially trawlers. If threatened at close quarters, they regurgitate their foul-smelling stomach contents as a deterrent.

Identification: Dark brownish-grey in colour overall, with a pale whitish area on the undersides of the wings, and on the sides of the rump. Square-shaped tail, with the legs not extending beyond the tip when in flight.

Distribution: Ranges from Norway and southern Iceland via the western side of Great Britain right down to the Cape of Good Hope. Also present through much of the Mediterranean Sea.
Size: 18cm (7in).
Habitat: Over the ocean.
Nest: Rocky crevice.
Eggs: 1, white.
Food: Small fish, crustaceans and squid.

Grey-backed storm petrel (*Garrodia nereis*): 20cm (8in)
Three isolated breeding populations occur in the southern oceans: one extends from south-eastern South America across towards south-western Africa; the second lies to the east of this; the third population is restricted to the region of Australia and New Zealand. Head and leading edges of the wings are dark, while the remainder of the underparts and wings are white. Grey rump and uppertail coverts, with a black bar edging the tail feathers. Legs are long, extending beyond the tail feathers when in flight. Sexes are alike.

Matsudaira's storm petrel (*Oceanodroma matsudairae*): 25cm (10in)
Ranges from south-east of Japan down through the Indonesian region and across the Indo-Pacific to the eastern side of Africa. Brownish-grey overall, with paler wing bars extending to the leading edges of the wings. This storm petrel is also distinguishable by its more prominent forked tail. White shafts to the outermost primary feathers may also be evident. Sexes are alike.

Madeiran storm petrel (*Oceanodroma castro*): 20cm (8in)
Present in the eastern Atlantic, from the Iberian coast southwards across the equator to the Tropic of Capricorn. Prefers to breed on islands. Brownish-grey overall, with lighter plumage across the wings. Rump is white, as are the underparts, and the tail is slightly forked. Sexes are alike.

Leach's storm petrel

Oceanodroma leucorhoa

With an extensive distribution and a population comprised of more than 10 million individuals worldwide, Leach's storm petrel is regarded as a very common species. However, these birds are vulnerable to predators when breeding, even in the isolated locations that they frequent. Their relatively small size means they can suffer attacks by larger seabirds such as gulls, which prey especially on newly fledged chicks. Should they survive this critical early period of their development, the young Leach's storm petrels have a life expectancy of nearly a quarter of a century. Soon after the breeding period has ended, the North Atlantic population moves southwards for the duration of the winter, extending to the coast of South Africa with occasional reports also from the Indian Ocean. As with other storm petrels, they may follow pods of whales, feeding on the food churned up by these cetaceans, and also scavenging on their faeces.

Distribution: Atlantic population extends from Norway southwards around both coasts of Great Britain, being present in the North Sea and the Baltic Sea. Does not range through the Mediterranean. Extends right down to the tip of Africa. There is also a separate, widespread population in the Pacific.
Size: 22cm (9in).
Habitat: Over the ocean.
Nest: Underground burrow or rocky crevice.
Eggs: 1, white.
Food: Mostly small fish, crustaceans and squid.

Identification: Relatively brown head and back. Rump is predominantly white, with a brown stripe running down its centre. Broad, forked tail feathers. Sexes are alike.

SOUTHERN OCEAN PETRELS

Many of the seabirds found in southern African waters have a wide distribution, which can be pan-global, often extending around the southern oceans and sometimes even further afield. Petrels are well adapted to spending virtually their entire lives over these waters, being able to scoop up their food directly from the surface of the ocean and even sleeping on the wing as they glide.

Common diving petrel

Pelecanoides urinatrix

The common diving petrel ranks as one of the most numerous of all seabirds, certainly in the southern hemisphere, although the breeding population on Tristan da Cunha and neighbouring islands off the south-west coast of Africa is smaller than the populations occurring elsewhere in its range. Overall numbers are estimated as being close to 10 million individuals. Pairs nest on remote islands in burrows of up to 1.5m (5ft) in length, the ground underfoot sometimes being a mass of such tunnels. Although the vast majority of young birds will survive through to fledging, which occurs approximately eight weeks after hatching, their mortality rate soars once they take to the water, where few individuals can expect to live for more than 4 years. They do not stray very far from the islands that form their breeding grounds, feeding in these waters too. As their name suggests, common diving petrels will often pursue their quarry underwater, although they may occasionally feed at the surface as well.

Identification: Blackish head and upperparts, with a more whitish area behind the eyes. Underparts, including the undersides of the wings, are also white. Sexes are alike.

Distribution: One population occurs off the south-west African coast, and another can be found further south-east of the Cape. Two other populations exist: one off the eastern coast of southern South America, the second around New Zealand and the south-east Australian coast.
Size: 25cm (10in).
Habitat: Over the ocean.
Nest: Underground burrow.
Eggs: 1, white.
Food: Planktonic crustaceans, including krill.

Kerguelen petrel

Aphrodrama brevirostris

Kerguelen petrels begin nesting in August, when groups form colonies on islands to the south of Africa where conditions are favourable. They seek relatively soft soil in which they can excavate their burrows without great difficulty. Incubation is a fairly lengthy process, taking seven weeks, and it will be a further nine weeks before the young birds are ready to emerge from their burrows. Breeding pairs, especially on Gough Island and Tristan da Cunha, face predation of their young from skuas, which also live in the vicinity, but by nesting together a higher percentage of the young manage to escape these larger, aggressive seabirds. They then have to master the feeding skills that enable them to survive life over the ocean, which is liable to be a harsh environment. Kerguelen petrels generally feed at night, when the squid that feature prominently in their diet move up from deeper water, allowing them to be seized directly from the surface.

Identification: Dark overall, but with a slight iridescence over some areas that can make the plumage appear a little paler, especially over the wings. Sexes are alike, but hens are slightly smaller in size.

Distribution: Circumglobal through the southern oceans, via Cape Horn in southern South America, New Zealand, south Australia and the Cape of Good Hope at Africa's southern tip.
Size: 36cm (14in).
Habitat: Over the ocean.
Nest: Underground tunnel.
Eggs: 1, white.
Food: Squid, plus some krill and small fish.

Cape petrel

Pintado petrel *Daption capense*

Distribution: Circumglobal range throughout the southern oceans, extending from the shore of Antarctica northwards to a line roughly corresponding to the Tropic of Capricorn, including the southern tip of Africa.
Size: 40cm (16in).
Habitat: Over the ocean.
Nest: Often in a crevice on the ground.
Eggs: 1, white.
Food: Krill, squid and fish.

Cape petrels are very common in South African waters over the winter period, when harsher conditions in the Antarctic drive them further north. They are also very bold, with contemporary records describing how they followed whaling ships from the open ocean right into Durban harbour, in the hope of being able to scavenge on offal. Today, they are often seen in large numbers around fishing boats for the same reason, and it is this social side to their nature that has led to them being known rather confusingly as 'Cape pigeons'. They are adept at catching their own food on the wing, however, by flying with heads submerged beneath the waves, sieving water through their partially closed bills. The bill has a series of serrations running down each side, which serve as a filter to trap edible items in the mouth. Cape petrels often settle on the surface of the water when seeking food, which aids identification. Individual birds can also be distinguished by their mottled patterning.

Identification: A combination of brown and white plumage, with the back being speckled brown in the case of subspecies *D.c. capense*, rather than solid brown as in *D.c. australe*, which nests in the vicinity of New Zealand. Rump in both cases is white with brown markings, while the head and neck are also brown. Sexes are alike.

Northern giant petrel (Hall's giant petrel, *Macronectes halli*): 94cm (37in)
Circumglobal in the southern hemisphere, ranging some distance off the coast of Antarctica northwards, reaching the Cape of Good Hope at Africa's southern tip. Variable amount of dark plumage on the head, and relatively dark, more even coloration on the underparts help to distinguish this species from its Southern relative (see right). The pinkish bill tip is another distinguishing feature.

Great-winged petrel (grey-faced petrel, *Pterodroma macroptera*): 40cm (16in)
Distribution extends from east of New Zealand around the Cape of Good Hope and some distance up the western coast of Africa, continuing across the southern Atlantic to an area to the east of the Falkland Islands off the coast of South America. Breeding grounds include islands to the south-west and south-east of Africa. Characterized by its its consistent dark brown coloration. Sexes are similar, but hens are smaller in size.

Soft-plumaged petrel (*Pterodroma mollis*): 37cm (14½in)
Distribution extends from the seas around New Zealand westwards round the southern tip of Africa and a short distance up the west side, and across the southern Atlantic to southern South America. Generally only exists in a light colour phase, although the breadth of the dark throat collar varies in width and definition. Basic coloration similar to related petrels, with dark upperparts and largely white underparts.

Southern giant petrel

Macronectes giganteus

With a wingspan of more than 2m (78in) and weighing as much as 5kg (11lb), these aerial giants are capable of covering huge distances over the oceans around the southern hemisphere. Southern giant petrels feed on the carcasses of marine mammals such as seals left on the shoreline, as well as scavenging on dead seabirds. They may also be sighted close to trawlers, seeking offal and fish thrown overboard, which they scoop up from the surface of the water. These petrels nest on grassy islands in colonies of up to 300 pairs. The single chick develops quite slowly and may not fledge until it is nearly 20 weeks old. It is unlikely to breed for the first time until it is seven years old.

Identification: Brownish overall, although darker on the lower underparts towards the vent. Head and neck are paler greyish-brown. Bill is yellow. The white morph of this species displays odd speckled brownish feathering on a white background. Hens are smaller.

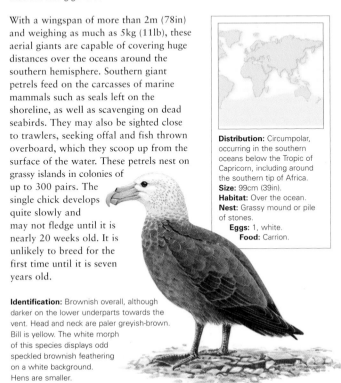

Distribution: Circumpolar, occurring in the southern oceans below the Tropic of Capricorn, including around the southern tip of Africa.
Size: 99cm (39in).
Habitat: Over the ocean.
Nest: Grassy mound or pile of stones.
Eggs: 1, white.
Food: Carrion.

ISLAND SEABIRDS

Whereas some seabirds have evolved to live largely on the wing, roaming large areas of the ocean, others like the little auk, misleadingly dubbed the "penguin of the north" in spite of its small size, have adapted to a more aquatic lifestyle. A number of seabirds have a very limited distribution, breeding on just a few islands, where their populations are potentially under threat from human interference in the landscape.

Puffin

Fratercula arctica

These auks have unmistakable bills, rather akin to those of parrots. Young puffins have much narrower and less brightly coloured bills than the adults. Puffins come ashore to nest in colonies on cliffs and coastal areas where they can breed largely hidden from predators. Sand eels figure prominently in their diet at this time, and adult birds often fly quite long distances to obtain food. When underwater, puffins use their wings like flippers, enabling them to swim faster. Adult birds fly back to their young with the sand eels arranged in a row, hanging down each side of their bills. They are able to carry as many as ten eels at a time in this way.

Identification: Whitish sides to the face. Black plumage extends back from the top of the bill over the crown and around to the neck. The back and wings are also black. Underparts are white, with a grey area on the flanks. Distinctive broad, flattened bill with a red area running down its length and across the tip. Greyish base with yellow area intervening. Bill is less brightly coloured and the sides of the face are greyish during the winter. Sexes are alike.

Left: The appearance of the puffin's bill varies depending on the bird's age and the time of year.

Distribution: Throughout the northern Atlantic, including Spitzbergen, as far as the west coast of Africa.
Size: 32cm (13in).
Habitat: Sea, coastal areas.
Nest: Underground burrow.
Eggs: 1, white.
Food: Fish.

Right: Puffins excavate nesting tunnels underground or use existing holes.

Little auk

Alle alle

Despite its relatively restricted distribution, the little auk is considered to be one of the most numerous seabird species in the world. These birds form huge nesting colonies in the Arctic region during the brief summer, before heading south at the approach of winter as the sea begins to freeze. Little auks are often more likely to be spotted at this time of year, frequently flying very low over the waves or even through them on occasion. Sometimes, however, fierce storms make feeding virtually impossible, and in a weakened state little auks are driven into coastal areas, a phenomenon often described as a "wreck".

Identification: In summer plumage, the head and upper part of the chest are black. The back, wings and upper surface of the tail feathers are also black, aside from white streaks apparent over the wings. During the winter, the black on the face is broken by white, leaving a black band across the throat. The bill is small and black. Sexes are alike.

Distribution: Entire coastline of Greenland and Iceland to northern Scandinavia, across the North Sea to the coast of eastern England.
Size: 20cm (8in).
Habitat: Sea, coastal areas.
Nest: Cliff or crevice.
Eggs: 1, pale blue.
Food: Microscopic plankton.

Gannet

Northern gannet *Morus bassana*

Distribution: Along the eastern seaboard of North America, extending across the Atlantic via southern Greenland and Iceland to eastern Scandinavia, and southwards through the Mediterranean and down the western coast of Africa.
Size: 88–100cm (35–39in).
Habitat: Sea.
Nest: Usually on a cliff, built from seaweed and other marine debris held together by droppings.
Eggs: 1, whitish.
Food: Fish.

The largest of all gannets, this species can weigh up to 3.6kg (8lb). It is the only member of this group found around the North Atlantic. These gannets are powerful in the air, and their keen eyesight allows them to detect shoals of fish such as herring and mackerel in the sea below. When feeding, gannets dive down into a shoal, often from a considerable height, seizing fish from under the water. Their streamlined shape also enables them to swim. Breeding occurs in the spring, when the birds form large colonies in which there is often a lot of squabbling. The young mature quite slowly, and are unlikely to breed until they are at least four years old.

Identification: Mainly white, aside from pale creamy yellow plumage on the head extending down the neck. Black flight feathers. Tail feathers are white, and the feet are dark grey. Sexes are alike. Young birds are dark brown in colour.

Fea's petrel (Cape Verde petrel, *Pterodroma feae*): 36cm (14in)
Restricted to Muddier and Cape Verde Islands in the Atlantic, off north-west Africa. Head is white around the bill, grey extending back and down on to the sides of the neck and over the central areas of the wings. Remainder of wings is black, creating a two-tone effect evident in flight. Black semi-circular areas around the eyes, and a stocky black bill. Sexes are alike.

Zino's petrel (*Pterodroma madeira*): 34cm (13in) (E)
Occurs alongside Fea's petrel on Madeira. Very rare, the population reduced to approximately 20 pairs, making it one of the region's most endangered seabirds. Distinguishable from its relative by paler grey feathering on the head and reduced areas of black on the sides of the face, which are more like streaks running through the eyes than circles. Sexes are alike.

Bulwer's Petrel (*Bulweria bulwerii*): 29cm (11in)
Another Madeiran species, which also occurs on some Canary Islands, but range also extends across the Atlantic to South America. Also represented widely through the Pacific, from off the east coast of Madagascar to near the western seaboard of South America. Dark in colour, with grey underparts and dark leading edges to the wings when seen from below. Paler grey band along the upper surface of the wings. Tail appears narrow in flight. Sexes are alike.

Cape gannet

South African gannet *Morus capensis*

Cape gannets nest between September and April, with five of their six major colonies lying off south-west Africa, where pilchards and anchovies are plentiful. Their young hatch after six weeks, leaving the nest at 14 weeks old, and are occasionally sighted in southern Europe. Adult birds tend to remain closer to their breeding grounds. The young return to breed at three years old. Several thousand tons of their droppings (guano) are still collected annually and sold as a fertilizer.

Distribution: Ranges widely around the African coast, from the Gulf of Guinea on the western side via the Cape of Good Hope to Mozambique on the eastern side. Breeding range is restricted to Namibia and South Africa.
Size: 90cm (35in).
Habitat: Over the sea.
Nest: Flotsam, on the ground.
Eggs: 1, white.
Food: Mainly fish.

Identification: Straw-yellow head, extending down the back of the neck. Body is white, flight feathers black. Black edging to the tail and a more extensive black throat stripe than Gannet. Bill pale yellowish-blue. Legs and feet black. Young birds are dark brown. Sexes are alike.

SKUAS AND FRIGATE BIRDS

It is remarkable how far some seabirds will fly to and from their nesting grounds each year. They may effectively traverse the globe, nesting in the far north and then returning to the Antarctic region by the start of the northern winter, or vice versa. These extensive journeys are made all the more remarkable since they entail little or no rest on land.

Long-tailed skua

Long-tailed jaeger *Stercorarius longicaudus*

This species is the smallest member of the jaeger family, even though as much as 23cm (9in) of its overall length is accounted for by its distinctive tail feathers. Long-tailed jaegers breed in the Arctic region of Europe, spending the winter at sea. Only on rare occasions are they observed on freshwater lakes. Jaegers can be considered the pirates of the skies, menacing gulls and terns and harrying them into dropping fish or other quarry, which they quickly swoop down on and seize before the prey disappears into the water. Long-tailed jaegers are especially agile in flight, thanks to their long and pointed wings, while their hooked bills are quite formidable weapons. On occasions, these jaegers have also been known to attack other nesting seabirds, taking both their eggs and their chicks.

Identification: Characteristic long, narrow tail feathers. Underparts are whitish, with a greyer tone on the flanks and around the vent. Head is blackish and the wings are dark. Sexes are alike.

Distribution: During the summer breeding period occurs right across the far north of Scandinavia and Russia, and into the Arctic. Flies south to overwinter around the western coast of South Africa and throughout the southern oceans, extending almost as far as Antarctica.
Size: 58cm (23in).
Habitat: Mainly open ocean.
Nest: Depression or scrape on the ground.
Eggs: 1–2, olive with dark spots.
Food: Fish and other small

Arctic skua

Parasitic jaeger *Stercorarius parasiticus*

Arctic skuas are very adept at stealing fish from other seabirds, preferring this method of feeding more than any related species. Yet they are also effective hunters, easily catching lemmings and other small rodents in their northern breeding grounds. Their diet alters dramatically though the year, and they will feed on insects and even berries during the brief Arctic summer. Their nests, in turn, are frequently raided by Arctic foxes (*Alopex lagopus*). Once all the surviving chicks have migrated southwards, beginning their journey in August, they may remain in the southern hemisphere for their first year rather than returning back north. Unlike many seabirds, these skuas often migrate over land, possibly because they will stay close to the coasts on arrival, rather than ranging over the ocean.

Identification: Sleek, gull-like appearance with long, narrow tail extensions averaging nearly 9cm (3.5in) in the summer. Dark crown, with brownish-grey wings and tail, and white underparts at this stage too. The dark colour morph displays no white plumage, while youngsters have a barred appearance. Sexes are alike. Young birds have blue legs.

Distribution: Overwinters south of the equator, mainly on Africa's southern Atlantic seaboard but also on the south-eastern coast. Breeds in the far north of Europe, including parts of Scotland and Scandinavia.
Size: 44cm (17in).
Habitat: Open ocean.
Nest: Scrape on the ground.
Eggs: 1–2, olive with dark spots.
Food: Fish and rodents.

Great skua (northern skua, *Catharacta skua*): 58cm (23in)
Breeds in Iceland, the Faroes and northern Scotland, and to a lesser extent in Norway and north-western Russia. Winters south around the Iberian peninsula, including the western Mediterranean. Some birds migrate further afield to Newfoundland, the Caribbean and northern Brazil. Predominantly brown, with a powerful black bill. Sides and top of the head are entirely dark in colour, with lighter streaking down the neck and on to the chest, broadening out over the wings. Short tail and dark webbed feet. Sexes are alike.

Brown skua (*Catharacta antarctica*): 64cm (25in)
Widely distributed through southern latitudes, including off the southern tip of Africa. Breeds further south on islands including Tristan da Cunha and Gough Island. Large size, stocky appearance. Predominantly brown in colour, with paler streaking extending down from the neck around the wings, which tend to be of a darker shade, although there can be considerable variation between individuals. Sexes are alike.

South Polar skua (*Catharacta maccormicki*): 55cm (22in)
Winters from the Atlantic seaboard off the coast of North America across to the mid-Atlantic, south of Iceland and west of Ireland. Breeds in the Antarctic, notably in the vicinity of the Ross Sea. Two distinctive colour morphs: dark morph (Antarctic Peninsula) is brown, with wings slightly darker than the body; pale morph has brown wings with significantly paler head and underparts. Males are darker overall and smaller.

Pomarine skua

Pomarine jaeger *Stercorarius pomarinus*

Pomarine skuas are exceedingly effective predators of lemmings, and are even able to dig these small rodents out of their underground burrows using their strong bills. There is a direct link between the number of lemmings and the breeding success of the skuas: when lemmings are plentiful, it is not uncommon for young pomarine skuas to breed before they have acquired full adult plumage. However, food becomes scarce during the period following a collapse in the lemming population, forcing the skuas to turn their attention to other prey, which can include anything from carrion to the eggs of other birds. They will also kill and eat smaller seabirds. Pairs lay in the far north, directly on the ground, without attempting to construct a nest of any kind. After leaving the tundra region in September, pomarine skuas will feed mainly on fish, which they prefer to steal from other seabirds rather than catch themselves.

Distribution: Breeds in the Arctic region of Russia, but overwinters on both the Atlantic coast of Africa, from the Tropic of Cancer southwards, and in the vicinity of the Red Sea, extending to the Horn of Africa. The more easterly Russian populations generally migrate to an area extending from South-east Asia to Australia.
Size: 50cm (20in).
Habitat: Open ocean.
Nest: Scrape on the ground.
Eggs: 2, olive with dark spots.
Food: Fish and lemmings.

Identification: Mainly black head; back of neck is pale yellowish. Back, wings and vent area dark grey. White underparts, with grey barring on chest and flanks. Bill pinkish with dark tip. Juvenile has white wing bars.

Greater frigate bird

Fregata minor

The greater frigate bird is an impressive aerial hunter, attracted to shoals of flying fish as well as squid, scooping up their prey from the surface of the water. These large birds are very opportunistic feeders, and will swoop over beaches where turtles nest in order to catch and eat the hatchling reptiles as they head across the sand for the relative safety of the sea. They will also harry other seabirds in skua fashion, forcing them into dropping their catches, which they then take for themselves. Greater frigate birds breed in colonies on remote islands. Their chicks develop very slowly and are cared for by both parents for up to a year and a half after hatching.

Identification: Dark overall with a bright red throat sac. Abdomen is black. Has a long, hooked bill and a streaming tail. Brownish wing bars on the upper side of the wings. Angular wing posture is evident in flight. Black areas of plumage can have a glossy green suffusion. Sexes are similar, but hens are larger with a greyish white throat and white chest.

Left: Greater frigate bird with throat sac inflated for displaying.

Distribution: Mainly in the Pacific, from the west coast of South America to the northern coast of Australia and South-east Asia to eastern Africa. A smaller population also occurs in the South Atlantic.
Size: 105cm (41in).
Habitat: Islands and mangroves.
Nest: Platform of sticks.
Eggs: 1, chalky white.
Food: Mainly fish, sometimes squid and carrion.

AGILE AND ADAPTABLE FEEDERS

Seabirds are highly adaptable by nature, as shown by their readiness to scavenge, often following trawlers for miles over the ocean seeking unwanted parts of a catch thrown back overboard. The more agile hunters, such as tropic birds, are often harried into dropping their catches by other equally resourceful but more aggressive seabirds such as skuas.

Manx shearwater

Puffinus puffinus

In March, large numbers of Manx shearwaters gather to breed in remote coastal areas, typically on islands through their range. Incubation is shared, with both members of a pair sitting individually for up to six days. The eggs hatch after a period of about eight weeks, and the young birds will finally emerge from the nesting chamber at the age of 11 weeks. They mature slowly, and may not start breeding themselves until they are about six years old. Despite their arduous migration they are potentially long-lived birds, surviving for at least 30 years in the wild. While the majority of Manx shearwaters cross the Atlantic to overwinter off South America, a small number head directly south, being recorded along the coasts of Namibia and the Cape, where they can be observed hunting shoals of both anchovies and sardines.

Identification: Sooty-black upperparts, with white plumage beneath, including the undertail coverts. Sexes are alike.

Distribution: Widely distributed from north of Norway and Iceland to the coast of northern Africa during the summer breeding period. Migrates south along the eastern seaboard of South America and across the Atlantic to South Africa.
Size: 35cm (14in).
Habitat: Over the ocean.
Nest: Underground burrow.
Eggs: 1, white.
Food: Small fish, also squid.

Audubon's shearwater

Puffinus lherminieri

Distribution: The African population extends from along the western coast of India through the Red Sea region and down the adjacent coast of Africa, to the eastern side of Madagascar and further south.
Size: 33cm (13in).
Habitat: Over the ocean.
Nest: Rocky hollow or sometimes underground.
Eggs: 1, white.
Food: Fish, krill, and squid.

Audubon's shearwater has a discontinuous distribution through the world's oceans. There is a distinct and separate Pacific population off the coasts of Asia and Australia, and another in the Indian Ocean. Breeding periods vary accordingly in different parts of its range. Small, remote islands, many of which are uninhabited, are favoured for breeding. These shearwaters usually stay close to the shore when nesting, breeding colonially yet preferring an inconspicuous site, which may sometimes be underground rather than on the bare cliff face. The young disperse to the sea after fledging, which may not be until they are nearly 11 weeks old. They are slow to mature, and unlikely to breed until they have reached approximately eight years old. Individuals from the Caribbean population have occasionally been recorded as far north as north-eastern Canada.

Identification: Brownish back and wings, with brown coloration extending to the sides of the head. Throat area and underparts are white, with brown edging visible on the extended undersides of the wings. This species has a dark bill, pinkish legs and brown undertail coverts. Sexes are alike, and younger birds often closely resemble adults.

Red-billed tropic bird

Phaethon aethereus

These sleek, elegant birds swoop down from their cliff-top roosts and fly out over the sea, catching prey by diving into the water. The red-billed species is the largest of the tropic birds, its long, streaming white tail distinguishing it from the red-tailed tropic bird (*P. rubricauda*), which has paler wings and ranges further across the Indo-Pacific Ocean to the south. The bill of the Indian Ocean population is less brightly coloured, serving to distinguish these birds from others of the species occurring elsewhere in the world. Islands, rather than mainland areas, are favoured breeding sites, since their isolation means that the birds will be in less danger from predators.

Above: Red-billed tropic birds nest in crevices in the ground.

Identification: Predominantly white with a black streak surrounding both eyes. Black is clearly visible on the primary flight feathers at the ends of the wings. Black streaking runs over the back and rump down to the base of the tail. Tail streamers are longer in the cock than the hen. Bill is reddish-orange with black edging.

Distribution: The main Atlantic population extends from Brazil to the west coast of Africa between the equator and the Tropic of Capricorn, while a second is centred on the Canary Islands. Another occurs off the north-east coast of Africa in the Red Sea.
Size: 104cm (41in) including streamers of 56cm (22in).
Habitat: Tropical and subtropical seas.
Nest: Rocky crevice or hollow on the ground.
Eggs: 1, pinkish with darker markings.
Food: Fish and squid. Agile enough to catch flying fish.

Yelkouan shearwater (Mediterranean shearwater, *Puffinus yelkouan*):
40cm (16in)
Southern Scandinavia around Great Britain down to the coast of northern Africa. Also through the Mediterranean and the Black Sea. Resembles Manx shearwater but has paler upperparts, resulting in more even coloration, although subspecies *P. y. mauretanicus* (Balearic shearwater) tends to have dark underparts. Relatively short tail, with brown suffusion on the undertail coverts and flanks. Sexes are alike.

Salvin's shearwater (*Pachyptila salvini*):
28cm (11in)
Southern oceanic range, from New Zealand to south-east Africa. Bluish-grey coloration on the head and back, with a black M-shape running across the wings. White stripe beneath each eye; underparts are also white. Sexes are alike.

Great shearwater (*Puffinus gravis*): 50cm (20in)
From Scandinavia and southern Iceland southwards, but absent from the Atlantic off west-central Africa. Dark upperparts and a white band on the uppertail coverts. Underparts below the eyes are whitish, with variable darker mottling on the belly and dark edges to the undersides of the wings. Sexes are alike.

Northern fulmar

Fulmarus glacialis

Northern fulmars are versatile feeders, tracking trawlers or congregating in large groups in the wake of boats. These seabirds will scoop up fish during the day and hunt squid at night, as these invertebrates rise up from the ocean depths. If necessary, they will dive into the water to catch food. They are also adept scavengers, feeding on the remains of whales and other marine mammals washed up on to beaches. They nest communally, usually on sheer cliff faces, where they can colonize inaccessible ledges. In some parts of their range they may even build nests inland on buildings, but they generally favour islands and other remote sites rather than the mainland. Northern fulmars are thought to have a life expectancy of around 34 years, but it may be more than a decade after fledging before the chicks are ready to breed.

Distribution: Present in much of the Northern Hemisphere, in the Arctic region and much of the north Atlantic. Reaches the Iberian peninsula at the most southerly tip of its range.
Size: 50cm (20in).
Habitat: Open ocean.
Nest: Bare cliff ledge.
Eggs: 1, white.
Food: Fish, squid and sometimes carrion.

Identification: Varies in colour throughout its range, with both light and dark morphs: light form has a whitish head and underparts with grey above; dark morphs are greyish-brown overall. Sexes are alike, but males are larger.

COASTAL SEABIRDS

Most seabirds are not brightly coloured, with white and black as well as hues of grey predominating in their plumage. They are often highly social, especially when breeding, nesting in large colonies on rocky stacks or inaccessible cliffs, which afford them some protection from predators. Food for their offspring is gathered often some distance from the nest site.

Guillemot

Common murre *Uria aalge*

Distribution: From north of Iceland and Scandinavia southwards to the Atlantic coast of the Iberian Peninsula, and west across the Atlantic to North America. Also present throughout the northern Pacific.
Size: 43cm (17in).
Habitat: Ocean and shore.
Nest: Cliff ledges.
Eggs: 1, bluish-green with dark spots.
Food: Fish and invertebrates.

The upright resting stance of the guillemot and its ability to hop, together with its black and white coloration and fish-eating habits, have led to these birds being described as the penguins of the north. However, unlike penguins they can fly. This enables them to reach their rocky and inhospitable nesting sites, where large numbers pack on to the cliff ledges to breed; as many as twenty breeding pairs can crowd every square metre (11 sq ft). The sheer density of numbers here offers protection against raiding gulls since there is little space for the predators to land, and they will be met with a fearsome barrier of sharp, pointed bills if they try to swoop down. Fall-offs in fish stocks can have an adverse effect on guillemot numbers, as will oil pollution.

Identification: Black head, neck and upperparts, with white edges to the wing coverts. Slight mottling on the flanks, otherwise underparts white. Throat and sides of the neck are white in non-breeding plumage. Sexes are alike. Dark sides to the neck in young birds.

Black guillemot

Cepphus grylle

These guillemots occur inshore throughout the Arctic Circle. Populations are sedentary, not moving significantly unless forced to do so by expanding ice sheets. They seek food on the sea floor, typically diving to depths of 20m (66ft), remaining submerged for a maximum of around 40 seconds. Pairs generally stay together, breeding each year in the same location. In the far north, colonies may consist of as many as 1,000 pairs, but elsewhere individual pairs may nest on their own. Both sexes share the incubation, which takes about 30 days. Fish is the preferred rearing food for the chicks, who may be fed up to 15 times a day, though during the winter crustaceans feature more prominently in their diet. Black guillemots are common in many parts of their range: the Icelandic population alone is estimated at 50,000 pairs.

Identification: Characteristic jet black coloration, with prominent white patches on the wings. Long, pointed black bill and red feet. In winter, has white underparts and white barring on the back, while retaining its black-and-white wing pattern. Young birds have darker upperparts at first, with spotting rather than barring on their wings in winter. Sexes are alike.

Distribution: Occurs from Iceland around much of the coast of Great Britain, although not typically encountered in the English Channel, via Scandinavia and the Baltic Sea up to the coast of Russia. Circumpolar range continues via Asia to North America.
Size: 32cm (12½in).
Habitat: Sea and rocky cliffs.
Nest: Scrape on cliff.
Eggs: 1–2, whitish-coloured with dark markings.
Food: Fish and invertebrates.

Razorbill

Alca torda

The distinctive broad, flattened shape of the bill, resembling a cut-throat razor, explains the common name of these auks. They can often be observed swimming with their tails held vertically, rather than flat, enabling them to be distinguished from seabirds of similar size and coloration. Razorbills are adaptable feeders, and their diet varys according to location. Pairs display a strong bond and return to their traditional breeding sites, which may sometimes be no more than steep, inaccessible rocky stacks off the coast. They show no tendency to construct a nest of any kind, and the hen will lay her single egg on a narrow ledge directly above the ocean. The pear-like shape of the razorbill's egg helps to prevent it from rolling over the edge if accidentally dislodged. Even so, losses of eggs are fairly high, with predators such as gulls swooping down on unguarded sites.

Identification: Black upperparts, with white edging along the back of the wings and a vertical white stripe across the bill. Black coloration more strongly defined in breeding birds, with a white horizontal stripe reaching from the eyes to the bill. Sexes are alike. Young birds have smaller bills with no white markings.

Distribution: From north of Iceland and Scandinavia south to the Iberian Peninsula and northern Africa, extending into the eastern Mediterranean. Also present throughout the North Atlantic to the American coast.
Size: 39cm (15in).
Habitat: Ocean and shore.
Nest: Cliff-face crevices.
Eggs: 1, whitish-coloured with brown spots.
Food: Fish and crustaceans.

Thick-billed murre (*Uria lomvia*): 43cm (17in)
Right around the northern hemisphere, in the vicinity of the Arctic region. Ranges southwards around Iceland and along the north-western coast of Scandinavia. Resembles the guillemot, but distinguishable by its broader, shorter bill and whitish line extending along the top of the lower mandible. In winter, black head, back and wings with white underparts. In summer, black plumage extends on to the throat and lower part of the face. Young birds resemble adults in winter plumage, but are smaller. Sexes are alike.

Gentoo penguin (*Pygoscelis papua*): 81cm (32in)
Circumpolar throughout the southern oceans, found south of southern Africa. Black upperparts extending down across the throat, with white underparts. White plumage above the eyes, which are also encircled with white. White edging to the flippers, especially evident along the rear edge. The rump also has whitish feathering. Reddish, relatively narrow bill which is dark on its upper surface. White on the head less evident in young birds. Sexes are alike.

Macaroni penguin (*Eudyptes chrysolophus*): 70cm (27¹/₂in)
Confined to southern waters, from the southern tip of South America to below south-eastern Africa, breeding on remote islands in this area. Black on the head, extending to the upper chest and down over the back and wings. Remaining underparts are white. Prominent golden-yellow plumes extend back over the eyes. Iris is red, as are stout bill, legs and feet. Young birds are greyish below the bill, with a less prominent crest. Males are larger than females.

Jackass penguin

Spheniscus demersus

The unusual name of these penguins derives from their calls, which resemble a braying donkey. They remain close to the coast and are the only penguin species occurring on the African mainland, although their breeding colonies (rookeries) are more often located on small offshore islands. Breeding can occur throughout the year, with both adults sharing the six-week incubation. Young penguins leave the nest from 10 weeks onwards. Numbers of jackass penguins have declined significantly over the past century, and especially over recent years, because overfishing has reduced their food supply. Some populations have also suffered badly from oil spillages and coastal development. These penguins spend much of the day searching for shoals of fish. They may dive to depths as great as 90m (295ft) and can remain submerged for several minutes at a time.

Distribution: From Namibia right around the coast of southern Africa extending up to Mozambique on the eastern seaboard.
Size: 70cm (27¹/₂in).
Habitat: Coastal areas.
Nest: Under rocks; burrows.
Eggs: 2, greenish.
Food: Anchovies and other schooling fish.

Identification: Head, back and wings black. Underparts white, extending up the sides of the face. Black band encircles lower body. Pink area above each eye. Bill is black, lighter at the tip. Young have grey heads. Sexes are alike.

FISH-EATERS

Not surprisingly, birds living close to the coast often catch fish and other forms of aquatic life, though there are differences in their feeding methods. Pelicans, for example, use their large bills to trawl for fish near the surface, whereas snakebirds dive underwater to pursue their quarry. Many of these birds are at risk from overfishing in coastal waters, which deprives them of their food supply.

Pink-backed pelican

Pelecanus rufescens

Identification: Pale greyish coloration overall, with pinkish suffusion on the underparts and wings. Bill is yellowish, as is the bare skin forming the pouch. Skin around the eyes also yellowish with black surround. Young birds resemble adults but with a browner shade to the upperparts, and less pink suffusion. Sexes alike but hens smaller.

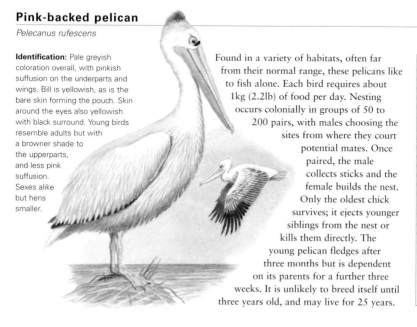

Found in a variety of habitats, often far from their normal range, these pelicans like to fish alone. Each bird requires about 1kg (2.2lb) of food per day. Nesting occurs colonially in groups of 50 to 200 pairs, with males choosing the sites from where they court potential mates. Once paired, the male collects sticks and the female builds the nest. Only the oldest chick survives; it ejects younger siblings from the nest or kills them directly. The young pelican fledges after three months but is dependent on its parents for a further three weeks. It is unlikely to breed itself until three years old, and may live for 25 years.

Distribution: Ranges across Africa between the tropics, from Senegal to Sudan and south to Botswana and Natal in South Africa.
Size: 132cm (52in).
Habitat: Coastal regions and inland waters.
Nest: Made of sticks in trees.
Eggs: 1–3, whitish.
Food: Almost entirely fish.

African darter

Snakebird *Anhinga melanogaster*

Distribution: Found right across Africa south of the Sahara, and in Madagascar. Also present in South-east Asia and Australia.
Size: 97cm (38in).
Habitat: Coastal mangroves, inland areas.
Nest: Made of reeds and other aquatic vegetation.
Eggs: 2–6, chalky-white.
Food: Fish and amphibians.

Darters are so called because of their fishing style. Diving in search of prey, their powerful neck muscles enable them to lunge forward and seize quarry with their sharp, pointed bill. African darters swim low in the water, propelled by strong webbed feet, with just their narrow neck visible, hence the characteristic snake-like appearance. Out of water they adopt a cormorant posture, resting with wings held open, which dries their plumage and may also help to maintain body temperature. Darters typically nest off the ground alongside cormorants and other birds. The largest recorded breeding colony was documented in 1962 at Chagana in Tanzania, eastern Africa, and consisted of an estimated 10,000 nests.

Identification: Brownish-black body with a white stripe down each side of the neck. Pale throat with dark-edged whitish plumage over the wings. Hens have pale underparts. Young birds resemble hens, but have buff rather than white markings.

Blue-faced booby

Masked booby *Sula dactylatra*

The blue-faced is the largest of the booby family. It catches correspondingly larger prey, swallowing without difficulty fish of up to 41cm (16in). Although these birds often dive quite deep in search of fish, they will also catch flying fish at the surface. They sometimes lose their catch to frigatebirds that harry them as they fly back to land. Blue-faced boobies live in colonies, preferring to nest on cliff faces, but on remote islands in the absence of major predators pairs may breed on the ground. While the hen lays two eggs only one chick is normally reared, since the weaker chick eventually loses out to its stronger sibling in the competition for food. The young may not breed until their third year. Blue-faced boobies frequent tropical oceans on both sides of America. Although long-lived birds, sadly their numbers are declining in some areas due to increased development disturbing their habitat. A large colony can still be found around the Galapagos Islands, off the western coast of South America.

Identification: Predominantly white but with black on the wings and a distinctive black tail. Has dark feathering on the face around the eyes, with a bluish tinge extending on to the yellowish bill. In hens, the bill is significantly duller.

Distribution: Extensive distribution in the western Indian Ocean off the east coast of Africa and around Madagascar, north to the Red Sea. Also present off the coast of South-east Asia right through the Pacific and into the Atlantic, approaching the western coast of Africa.
Size: 91cm (36in).
Habitat: Tropical oceans.
Nest: Constructed from accumulated droppings.
Eggs: 2, pale blue.
Food: Mainly fish.

Half-collared kingfisher (*Alcedo semitorquata*): 20cm (8in)
A northerly population of this colourful African species is present in Ethiopia, with its more southerly representatives centred on south-eastern Africa. Distinctive, deep blue coloration on the head and cheeks, with a prominent white collar across the nape of the neck. The throat area is also white, although the remainder of the underparts are orangish in colour. The sides of the chest, back and wings are greenish-blue, although plumage is not particularly bright. Adult birds have pinkish feet; in young birds these are black. Bill is black with a small patch of orange either side. Sexes are alike.

Green-backed heron (*Butorides striatus*): 40cm (16in)
Widely distributed across all continents, with more than 30 distinctive subspecies recognized. Present across much of Africa south of the Sahara, as well as the Red Sea, apart from the southern tip. Also present on Madagascar and nearby islands. Very variable in appearance. The most widely distributed African race (*B. s. atricapillus*) is predominantly greyish, with white stripes on the face and on the mid-line of the body. White edging to the wing coverts, with green plumage on the back. Bill is blackish above, more yellowish beneath. Legs and feet are yellow. Young birds tend to be of a browner shade overall. Sexes are alike.

Brown booby

Sula leucogaster

The noise of these boobies in a colony is deafening, but out over the ocean they hunt quietly, often not far from the coast. They are very agile both above and below the water, able to catch flying fish as they break above the waves as well as pursuing prey underwater using their wings like paddles. However, brown boobies are rarely seen on the surface of the ocean. Females especially will also rob other seabirds of their catches as they head back to shore. Pairs usually nest on the ground, favouring offshore islands, nesting almost throughout the year in some parts of their range. Normally only one chick survives through to fledging. Once they have flown the nest the young boobies spend several months with their parents before leaving the colony, learning the basic fishing techniques that will be essential to their survival.

Distribution: Brazillian coast across the Atlantic to Africa's west coast, and from the eastern coast extending to the central-eastern Pacific. A third population exists around Central America.
Size: 81cm (32in).
Habitat: Ocean and shore.
Nest: Loose pile of twigs.
Eggs: 2, pale chalky-blue.
Food: Flying fish and squid.

Identification: Adults generally have dark brownish head, upperparts and wings. The remainder of the body is white, including much of the underwing area. Bill and feet are pale yellowish. Sexes are alike. Young birds are entirely brown at first, and have duller coloration around the face.

SEA DUCKS AND COASTAL WATERFOWL

Although more commonly encountered on inland waters, a number of waterfowl species have adapted to life in coastal waters, and some will even venture far out to sea. These include the eider ducks, whose plumage was once highly sought-after to make eiderdown, before artificial substitutes for stuffing pillows became available. These ducks will insulate their nests with their own feathers once eggs are laid.

King eider

Somateria spectabilis

Like most birds from the far north, the king eider has a circumpolar distribution that reaches right around the top of the globe. Seasonal movements of these sea ducks tend to be more widespread than in other eiders. They are remarkably common, with the North American population estimated at two million individuals. Huge groups of up to 100,000 birds congregate when moulting, although for the breeding season they split up and pairs nest individually across the Arctic tundra. King eiders are very powerful swimmers and generally dive to obtain their food.

Identification: Drakes in breeding condition have an orange area edged with black above a reddish bill. Light grey head plumage extends down the neck. Chest is pale pinkish-white, with black wings and underparts. Ducks are mainly a speckled shade of brown, with the pale underside of their wings visible in flight. In eclipse plumage, drakes are a darker shade of brown, with an orangish-yellow bill and white plumage on the back.

Distribution: From the coast of Iceland westwards around the British Isles and along northern Scandinavia. Also present in northern latitudes of eastern Asia and on both coasts of North America, as well as Greenland.
Size: 63cm (25in).
Habitat: Tundra and ocean.
Nest: Hollow on the ground lined with down.
Eggs: 4–7, olive-buff.
Food: Mainly crustaceans and marine invertebrates.

Common eider

Somateria mollissima

This is the most common European sea duck. Along the Norwegian coast the population is estimated at some two million individuals, and may even be increasing. Common eiders occur in large flocks and nest in colonies on islands, where they are safe from predators such as Arctic foxes (*Alopex lagopus*). The start of the breeding period depends on latitude, often not commencing until June in the far north. The nest is lined with their dense down, which safeguards the eggs from being chilled. While the ducks are incubating, drakes congregate to moult out of their breeding plumage. Outside the nesting period, common eiders are most likely to be observed close to shore. They do not generally migrate far, although ducks and young birds disperse further than drakes. They usually forage for food underwater.

Identification: Drake in colour has a black cap to the head, with black underparts and flight feathers. Rest of the body is white, and the bill is greyish. Out of colour, drakes are blackish-brown, lacking the barring seen in ducks, and have white upperwing coverts. Ducks are predominantly a combination of black and brown in colour, with a dark bill and legs.

Distribution: Northern and north-western parts of Europe extending to Siberia. Also from eastern Asia to both Pacific and Atlantic coasts of North America.
Size: 70cm (27¹/₂in).
Habitat: Coastal areas.
Nest: Hollow on the ground lined with down.
Eggs: 1–8, yellowish-olive.
Food: Mainly invertebrates.

Long-tailed duck

Oldsquaw *Clangula hyemalis*

These sea ducks often congregate in large numbers, although in winter females and young birds tend to migrate further south in flocks than do adult drakes. They spend most of their time on the water, obtaining food by diving under the waves. They come ashore to nest on the tundra, where the ducks lay their eggs directly on to the ground under cover. The drakes soon return to the ocean to moult. When migrating, oldsquaws fly low in lines, rather than in any more organized formation.

Identification: Black head, neck and chest, with white around the eyes and white underparts. Head becomes white across the top outside the breeding season, with patches of black evident on the sides. Grey rather than brown predominates on the wings. Long tail plumes present throughout the year. The smaller ducks undergo a similar change in appearance, with the sides of the face becoming white rather than blackish.

Distribution: Circumpolar, breeding in Northern Europe and the Arctic. Winters further south.
Size: 47cm (18¹/₂in).
Habitat: Coasts and bays.
Nest: Hidden in vegetation or under a rock.
Eggs: 5–7, olive-buff.
Food: Mainly crustaceans and marine invertebrates.

South African shelduck (*Tadorna cana*): 64cm (25in)
Southern Africa north into Namibia, occurring in freshwater and coastal areas. Drake is golden-brown overall, lighter on the upper chest, with a grey neck and head. Tail and flight feathers are dark brown. Mature ducks have prominent white plumage over much of the head and face, except for a dark crown. Young females display less white here, the white largely confined to around the eyes. Young drakes are similar but duller in coloration than adult drakes.

Cape teal (*Anas capensis*): 46cm (18in)
Namibia southwards, though more restricted in south-eastern southern Africa. Also found inland on salt marshes. Able to excrete salt through specially-adapted tear glands. Brown overall, with the feathers typically having dark centres, which are especially apparent on the flanks. Prominent white and dark green wing speculum, most evident in flight. Bill is pinkish, dark at its base. Legs and feet blackish. Sexes are alike.

Barnacle goose (*Branta leucopsis*): 71cm (28in)
Breeds in the far north, overwintering in the British Isles and north-western Europe. Broad white area on the forehead, extending across the face to the throat. Rest of the head, neck, upper back and chest are black. Black stripe runs back from the bill to the eyes. Underparts are whitish, becoming greyer with more distinct barring on the flanks. Wings have alternating broad grey bars and narrow black bars edged with white. Bill, legs and feet are black. Young birds have brownish suffusion to the upperparts. Sexes are alike but males generally larger.

Brent goose

Brant goose *Branta bernicla*

Brent geese start breeding in June. A site close to the tundra shoreline is favoured, with pairs lining the scrape with plant matter and down. It takes nine weeks from egg-laying to the young geese leaving the nest, after which they head south with their parents. Goslings may not breed until they are three years old. On the tundra, brent geese graze on lichens, moss and other terrestrial vegetation, while in winter they feed mainly on aquatic plants like seaweed, which is plucked from under the water as the geese up-end their bodies. On land, they graze by nibbling the shoots of plants.

Identification: Black head and neck, with trace of white on lower neck. Wings grey-black. White flanks with barring. Abdomen is white in the American brant (*B. b. hrota*) from the east, but often dark in its western relative, the black brant (*B. b. nigricans*). Sexes are alike. Young geese may lack white neck patches.

Distribution: Breeds in the Arctic, overwintering in Ireland and parts of north-western Europe. Other populations overwinter in eastern Asia and along both coasts of North America.
Size: 66cm (26in).
Habitat: Bays and estuaries.
Nest: Scrape on the ground.
Eggs: 1–10, whitish.
Food: Plant matter.

COMMON GULLS

Gulls are linked in many people's minds with the seaside, but some species have proved very adept at adjusting to living alongside people, and generally profiting from the association. A number of gulls have now spread to various locations inland. Shades of white and grey generally predominate in the plumage of these birds, making them quite easy to recognize.

Herring gull

Larus argentatus

These large gulls are often seen on fishing jetties and around harbours, searching for scraps. They have also moved inland and can be seen in areas such as rubbish dumps, where they scavenge for food, often in quite large groups. Herring gulls are noisy by nature, especially when breeding. They frequently nest on rooftops in coastal towns and cities, a trend that began in Britain as recently as the 1940s. Pairs can become very aggressive at breeding time, swooping menacingly on people who venture too close to the nest site (and even including the chicks once they have fledged).

Left: The herring gull's pink legs are a distinctive feature.

Identification: White head and underparts, with grey on the back and wings. Prominent large, white spots on the black flight feathers. Distinctive pink feet. Reddish spot towards the tip of the lower bill. Some dark streaking on the head and neck in winter. Sexes are alike. Young birds are mainly brown, with dark bills and prominent barring on their wings.

Distribution: The northern Atlantic north of Iceland and south to northern Africa and the Mediterranean. Also the North Sea and Baltic areas to northern Scandinavia and Arctic Russia.
Size: 60cm (24in)
Habitat: Coasts and inland.
Nest: Small pile of vegetation.
Eggs: 2–3, pale blue to brown with darker markings.
Food: Fish and carrion.

Black-headed gull

Larus ridibundus

These gulls are a common sight not only in coastal areas but also in town parks with lakes. They move inland during the winter, where they can often be seen following ploughing tractors searching for worms and grubs disturbed in the soil. Black-headed gulls nest close to water in what can be quite large colonies. Like many gulls, they are noisy birds, even calling at night. On warm, summer evenings they can sometimes be seen hawking flying ants and similar insects in flight, demonstrating their airborne agility.

Identification: Throughout the summer, distinctive black head with a white collar beneath and white under-parts. The wings are grey and the flight feathers mainly black. In the winter, the head is mainly white except for black ear coverts and a black smudge above each eye, while the bill is red at its base and dark at the tip.

Distribution: Greenland and throughout Europe, south along the coast of north-western Africa and into Asia.
Size: 39cm (15in).
Habitat: Coastal areas.
Nest: Scrape on the ground lined with plant matter.
Eggs: 2–3, pale blue to brown with darker markings.
Food: Typically molluscs, crustaceans and small fish.

Above: The black feathering on the head is a transient characteristic, appearing only in the summer (above right).

Great black-backed gull

Larus marinus

These large gulls can be extremely disruptive when close to other nesting seabird colonies. Not only will they harry returning birds for their catches, but they will also take eggs and chicks on occasion. In winter, great black-backed gulls move inland to scavenge on rubbish tips, although they are generally wary of people and are unlikely to be seen in urban areas. Banding studies have revealed that many of those that overwinter in Britain are actually birds of Norwegian origin, which return to Scandinavia to breed the following spring. Pairs are often quite solitary at this time, especially when nesting near people, though they are more likely to nest in colonies on uninhabited islands.

Identification: Very large gull. White head and underparts with black on the back and wings. White-spotted black tail. Large area of white is apparent at the wing tips in flight. Bill is yellow with a red tip to the lower side. Pale pinkish legs. Sexes are alike.

Distribution: From northern Spain north to Iceland and eastwards through the North Sea and Baltic to Scandinavia. Also present on the eastern side of North America.
Size: 74cm (29in).
Habitat: Coastal areas.
Nest: Pile of vegetation.
Eggs: 2–3, brownish with dark markings.
Food: Fish and carrion.

Lesser black-backed gull (*Larus fuscus*): 56cm (22in)
Breeds around the shores of the extreme north of Europe, moving as far south as parts of northern Africa in the winter. Similar to the great black-backed but smaller and lacks the prominent white seen on the flight feathers when the wings are closed. Legs are yellow rather than dull pink. Much smaller area of white on the outstretched upper surface of the wings in flight. Sexes are alike.

Glaucous gull (*Larus hyperboreus*): 68cm (27in)
Coastal areas of northern Europe, including Iceland. Very pale bluish-grey wings with white edges. Head and underparts white in summer, developing grey streaks in winter. Sexes are alike. As with other species, young birds are more mottled overall.

Yellow-legged gull (*Larus cachinnans*): 58cm (23in)
Found in coastal areas of southern England and mainland Europe to northern Africa, and also around the Black and Caspian seas. It has a white head and underparts, grey back and wings, and small white spots on the black flight feathers. The wings have large black areas towards the tips. The bill and legs are yellow, and there is a red spot on the lower bill. Grey suffusion on the head in winter. Sexes are alike. Was recognized as a form of the herring gull (*L. argentatus*) but now considered a separate species.

Hartlaub's gull (*Larus hartlaubii*): 38cm (15in)
Restricted to the western seaboard of southern Africa, from Walvis Bay in Namibia south to Cape Agulhas. White head, chest and underparts, with grey on the back of the neck becoming darker on the wings. White tips to the black flight feathers. Bill blackish with a slight reddish hue. Young birds have brown areas on the wings, and a similar band across the tail. Sexes are alike.

Common gull

Mew gull *Larus canus*

Common gulls often range inland over considerable distances, searching for earthworms and other invertebrates to feed on. In sandy coastal areas they will seek out shellfish as well. There is a distinct seasonal variation in the range of these gulls. At the end of the summer they leave their Scandinavian and Russian breeding grounds and head further south in Europe, to France and various other locations in the Mediterranean. Here they overwinter before migrating north again in the spring. In spite of its rather meek appearance, this species will bully smaller gulls such as the black-headed gull and take food from them. Common and black-headed gulls are often found in the same kind of inland environment, both showing a preference for agricultural areas and grassland.

Distribution: Iceland and throughout Europe, with the main breeding grounds in Scandinavia and Russia. Extends across Asia to western North America.
Size: 46cm (18in).
Habitat: Coasts and inland areas close to water.
Nest: Raised nest of twigs and other debris.
Eggs: 2–3, pale blue to brownish-olive in colour, with dark markings.
Food: Shellfish, small fish and invertebrates.

Identification: White head and underparts with yellow bill and yellowish-green legs. Wings are greyish with white markings at the tips, which are most visible in flight. Flight feathers are black with white spots. Tail is white. Dark eyes. Greyish streaking on the head in winter plumage. Sexes are alike. Young birds have brown mottled plumage, and it takes them more than two years to obtain adult coloration.

WIDE-RANGING GULLS

The adaptability of gulls ensures that the group has a worldwide representation, and there is evidence that some species are starting to colonize new areas, even moving across the Atlantic in the case of the ring-billed gull. While a number of species are sedentary through the year, others undertake regular seasonal movements, depending partly on the individual population concerned.

Kelp gull

Larus dominicanus

These gulls have a wide global distribution, present in the southern hemisphere along the shores of southern Africa, Australia and New Zealand, and South America. Birds from the latter population may venture inland, sometimes being found on lakes in the Andean region. The kelp gulls' extensive range is matched by their opportunistic feeding habits. In addition to taking fish and crustaceans they may attack other creatures ranging from geese and lambs to whales. Those gulls found in the Antarctic, below Tierra del Fuego, remain there all year, frequenting open water away from the pack ice. They breed between October and December. Pairs construct a relatively bulky nest from seaweed and similar material gathered on the shore, often concealed by rocks or trees, which offer some security. The young fledge when they are seven weeks old.

Identification: A large, black-winged species with a white area at the rear of the flight feathers (most evident in flight). A red spot is present near the tip of the lower mandible. Sexes are alike. Dark area mottled brown in maturing young birds.

Distribution: Southern Africa, from Cape Cross in Namibia to Cape Province in South Africa, and also on southern Madagascar. Represented on the other southern continents.
Size: 65cm (26in).
Habitat: Ocean and shore.
Nest: Pile of vegetation.
Eggs: 3, olive-brown in colour and speckled.
Food: Animal matter.

Black-legged kittiwake

Rissa tridactyla

Identification: Head whitish with a black marking on the back. Back and wings greyish. Flight feathers black, with white spots on the tips. Bill yellow, legs are black. Sexes alike. Young birds have a black bill, plus a black band across the neck, wings and tail tip.

The largest black-legged kittiwake breeding colonies in the Arctic comprise literally hundreds of thousands of birds. They seek out high, steep-sided cliffs, with so many birds packing on to these ledges that both adults may encounter difficulty in landing at the same time. These sites are defended from takeover for most of the year, not just during the nesting period. The nest is made from scraps of vegetation, especially seaweed, combined with feathers and bound together with mud. The narrow, shelf-like nature of the site makes it difficult for aerial predators to attack the kittiwakes, although in some parts of their range, such as Newfoundland, it also reduces breeding success. Away from the nest, these birds remain largely on the wing, swooping down to gather food from the surface of the ocean.

Distribution: Circumpolar range. Present beyond Iceland and northern Scandinavia in the summer, and around the British Isles and western Europe throughout the year. Winters up to southern Scandinavia. The commonest gull in the Arctic region.
Size: 40cm (16in).
Habitat: Ocean and shore.
Nest: Cliff ledge.
Eggs: 2, buff-olive, blotched.
Food: Fish and invertebrates.

Little gull (*Larus minutus*): 28cm (11in)
Distribution extends through north-eastern parts of Europe and into Asia during the summer. Overwinters around the shores of western Europe, including the British Isles, down to the Mediterranean region. Pale grey back and wings. Black head, with the black extending right down on to the neck. Red legs and feet. In winter, has a dark spot towards the rear of the head, which is otherwise whitish apart from a mottled area on the crown. Sexes are alike.

Audouin's gull (*Larus audouinii*): 52cm (20¹/₂in)
Restricted to parts of the Mediterranean, and the western coast of northern Africa. Adults are predominantly whitish. Wings are grey, with a white edge along the back, and black flight feathers tipped with white markings. Bill is relatively short and reddish, with a black band towards its tip. Eyes are dark, as are the legs. Young birds are mottled brown, gaining grey on the wings first. Sexes are alike.

Bonaparte's gull (*Larus philadelphia*): 34cm (13in)
Essentially a North American species; European sightings are birds from the Atlantic population, which normally overwinter from New England down to the Gulf Coast. Identified by its black head, with a white collar on the neck. Pale grey wings and white underparts. The bill is black throughout the year, but the black plumage on the head can be reduced to a spot beneath each eye. Legs and feet are red. Sexes are alike.

Iceland gull

Larus glaucoides

The name of this gull is misleading, since it is only present on Iceland (and in Europe) outside the breeding season. The gulls found here are those that breed in north-eastern Greenland; birds further south on Greenland are resident throughout the year. Young birds travel further afield, and are often seen with other gulls, frequently scavenging for food in coastal waters and inland at rubbish dumps. Iceland gulls will consume almost anything edible. At sea they prefer to feed on the surface, although they may dive to catch fish or invertebrates. Breeding typically starts on Greenland around the middle of May, with pairs nesting on steep, inaccessible cliffs, often in the company of other seabirds, whose eggs and chicks may be preyed upon by the Iceland gulls.

Identification: Predominantly white, with pale grey coloration on the wings. Bill is yellowish, with a red spot near the tip of the lower bill. Legs and feet pink. Sexes are alike. Out of breeding condition, adult birds display brownish markings on the head, extending on to the breast. Young birds are very pale in colour, with a brownish bill.

Distribution: The Greenland population overwinters on Iceland, around the British Isles and in parts of Scandinavia. North-eastern Canadian population overwinters south to Virginia in the US and inland to the Great Lakes.
Size: 64cm (25in).
Habitat: Typically near cliffs adjoining sea coasts.
Nest: Made from seaweed and other vegetation.
Eggs: 2–3, olive-brownish in colour.
Food: Fish and other edible items.

Ring-billed gull

Larus delawarensis

Identification: A black ring encircles the yellow bill, close to its tip. Typical gull patterning, with white head showing mottling in winter. Wings are greyish, with white markings on the black wing tips. Legs are yellow. Sexes are alike. Young birds are lightly mottled.

Winter sees a return to the coastline for these gulls. Most move to the more southerly parts of their range, although some wander north as far as Alaska. Over recent years they have become relatively common in Florida, where they were first recorded in 1930. On the west coast their distribution extended from California in 1940 up to British Columbia by 1974. Even more remarkably, since the 1970s they have been crossing the Atlantic in large numbers, and are no longer considered rare vagrants in the UK. Ring-billed gulls are adaptable feeders, and on the prairies will congregate in flocks to pick up grubs from the soil as the land is ploughed. They also catch fish by diving underwater when hunting at sea.

Distribution: Originates from North America, down the Atlantic seaboard and elsewhere, but observed annually in western Europe, especially in the British Isles, where it appears to be taking up residence.
Size: 53cm (21in).
Habitat: Coasts and inland, including agricultural areas.
Nest: Made of vegetation.
Eggs: 3, usually buff-coloured with blotches.
Food: Omnivorous.

TERNS

Terns are easily distinguished, even from gulls, by their relatively elongated shape. Their long, pointed wings are an indication of their aerial ability. Some terns regularly fly great distances on migration, further than most other birds. Not surprisingly, their flight appears to be almost effortless. When breeding, terns prefer to nest in colonies.

Common tern

Sterna hirundo

These graceful birds are only likely to be encountered in northern parts of their range between April and October, after which time they head south to warmer climes for the duration of the winter period. Travelling such long distances means that they are powerful in flight, and yet are also very agile. Their strongly-forked tail helps them to hover effectively, allowing them to adjust their position before diving into the water in search of quarry. They are very versatile feeders and may also hawk food on the wing. Common terns are represented on all the continents, their long bills providing a simple way of distinguishing them from gulls.

Identification: Long body shape, with black on the top of the head extending down the back of the neck. Rest of the face and underparts whitish-grey. Back and wings greyish, with long flight feathers. Narrow white streamers on the tail. Bill is red with a dark tip, which becomes completely black in the winter. The plumage in front of the eyes becomes white during winter. Legs and feet are red. Sexes are alike.

Distribution: Great Britain, Scandinavia and much of Central Europe during the summer. Migrates south to parts of eastern and southern Africa for the winter.
Size: 36cm (14in).
Habitat: Near water.
Nest: Scrape on the ground.
Eggs: 3, pale brown with dark spots.
Food: Mainly fish, but also eats crustaceans.

Sandwich tern

Cabot's tern *Sterna sandvicensis*

A summer visitor to northern Europe, this species is often sighted slightly earlier than the common tern, and also leaves just before its relative. The sandwich tern is significantly larger and is surprisingly noisy, with the sounds of its calls having been likened to a grating cartwheel. Although these terns will skim over the water surface seeking food, they can also dive spectacularly from heights of up to 10m (33ft). Sandwich terns usually breed in high-density colonies in the open on sand bars and similarly exposed coastal sites, although they may sometimes nest on islands in lakes.

Identification: Shaggy black crest evident at the back of the head. The entire top of the head is black during the summer, while a white forehead is characteristic of the winter plumage. The bill is long and black with a yellow tip. Rest of the head and underparts are white, and the wings are grey. Sexes are alike.

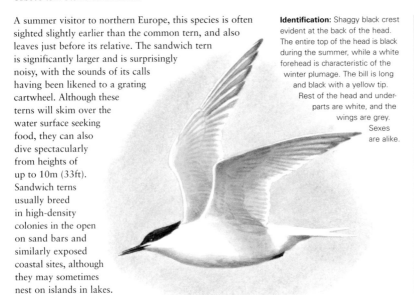

Distribution: Around the shores of Great Britain and northern Europe, as well as the Caspian and Black seas. Winters further south in the Mediterranean region and northern Africa. Also found in South-east Asia, the Caribbean and South America.
Size: 43cm (17in).
Habitat: Coastal areas.
Nest: Scrape on the ground.
Eggs: 1–2, brownish-white with darker markings.
Food: Fish and especially sand eels.

Roseate tern

Sterna dougallii

In northern parts of their range these terns are brief summer visitors, only likely to be present from about the middle of May until the end of August. Their distribution is quite localized. They are most likely to be seen where the shore is shallow and sandy, providing them with better fishing opportunities. They dive into the water to catch their prey from heights of no more than 2m (7ft), and may also take fish from other terns. Their shorter wings and quicker wing beats make them incredibly agile in flight. Roseate terns avoid open areas when nesting, preferring sites that are concealed among rocks or vegetation.

Identification: This tern gets its name from the slight pinkish suffusion on its whitish underparts. Compared to other terns, it has relatively long tail streamers and quite short wings. The bill is primarily blackish with a red base in the summer. Entire top of the head is black in summer, and the forehead turns white in winter. Sexes are alike. Subspecies differ in both wing and bill length.

Distribution: From the British Isles south to Spain and north-western Africa. Winters along the west African coast.
Size: 36cm (14in).
Habitat: Coastal areas.
Nest: Scrape on the ground.
Eggs: 1–2, cream or buff with reddish-brown markings.
Food: Mainly fish.

Caspian tern (*Sterna caspia*): 55cm (22in)
Baltic region, overwintering in western Africa. Sometimes seen in the Mediterranean. Black top to the head becoming streaked in winter. Grey wings, with a white chest and underparts. Large red bill with a black tip. Sexes are alike.

Black-naped tern (*Sterna sumatrana*): 35cm (14in)
Western Indian Ocean, from the horn of Africa to Mozambique, and across the Indo-Pacific to western India. Separate population occurs off South-east Asia, on islands to the north and east of Australia. Mostly white, with a silvery back and strongly-forked tail. Distinctive black area extending back from the eyes around the nape. Bill also black. Sexes are alike.

Saunders' Tern (*Sterna saundersi*): 28cm (11in)
Red Sea to Tanzania, and southern Madagascar. Also in the Indo-Pacific, including Sri Lanka, to South-east Asia. Black streaks from the sides of the bill to the eyes, with a white crown. Black above the eyes to the nape of the neck. Back, rump and wings are grey, with darker flight feathers. Underparts are white. Non-breeding plumage is darker. Bill is yellow with a blackish tip. Legs and feet greyish-yellow. Young have blackish areas over the wings. Sexes are alike.

White-cheeked tern (*Sterna repressa*): 35cm (14in)
Red Sea to Kenya. Also further east, along the Asian coast to south-western India. Black from the upper bill back over the head to the neck, encompassing the eyes, with white cheeks. Throat, underparts, back and wings all grey. Bill is reddish with a dark tip. Legs and feet also reddish. Non-breeding: white on the head more extensive, and dark areas confined to around the eyes. Young have brownish upperparts.

Arctic tern

Sterna paradisaea

It can be very difficult to distinguish this species from the common tern, but the Arctic tern's bill is shorter and does not have a black tip in the summer. The tail too is longer, and the tail streamers are very evident in flight. Arctic terns undertake the most extensive migration of all birds, flying virtually from one end of the globe to the other. After breeding in the vicinity of the Arctic Circle the birds head south, often beyond Africa to Antarctica, before repeating the journey the following year, though it appears that at least some of the young birds stay in the Antarctic for their first full year. Arctic terns nest communally, often choosing islands on which to breed. They will react aggressively to any potential predators in their midst, with a number of individuals turning on and mobbing an intruder. Arctic terns may steal food from other birds, for example from puffins in the Faroe Islands.

Identification: Black area covering the entire top of the head, with white chest and underparts. Wings grey. Bill is dark red, becoming black in the winter, when the forehead is white. Sexes are alike.

Distribution: Breeds in the Arctic and northern Europe. Migrates south to overwinter in southern Africa.
Size: 38cm (15in).
Habitat: Sea and fresh water.
Nest: Hollow on the ground, lined with vegetation.
Eggs: 2, can be brownish, bluish or greenish in colour, with dark markings.
Food: Fish and invertebrates.

LONG DISTANCE TRAVELLERS

Many terns have a very wide distribution through the world's oceans, with individual populations ranging across large areas. By nature they are quite adaptable, and may sometimes modify their feeding habits depending on the type of food available. Their breeding grounds are often small, remote islands, where the terns can nest in relative safety on the ground.

Bridled tern

Sterna anaethetus

This tern has a pantropical distribution, but rarely ventures further than 50 km (30 miles) from the shore. It feeds mainly on small fish that school near the surface, swooping down to seize them in its bill. Breeding birds typically return to the same beach each year, and will attempt to conceal the nest site among rocks or vegetation. Bridled terns often associate with related species, such as sooty terns, when nesting. Incubation lasts about a month. The young stay in the nest for seven weeks, and remain with the colony a further month or so after fledging. They are unlikely to nest themselves until four years old. Bridled terns live for about 18 years.

Identification: Long, narrow wings are brownish-black with a white collar. A black patch towards the back of the head narrows to a stripe connecting the eyes and bill. White patch above the eye. White underparts and underwing coverts with black flight feathers. Deeply-forked tail. Young have white edging to dark plumage on back and wings, and black area on head is mottled.

Distribution: Separate African populations, on the west and east coasts. Also in Australasia and on both sides of Central America.
Size: 38cm (15in).
Habitat: Ocean and shore.
Nest: Scrape on the ground.
Eggs: 1, brownish with darker markings.
Food: Mostly fish, also squid and crustaceans.

Gull-billed tern

Sterna nilotica

Although more commonly sighted around coastal areas, these terns can also be found some considerable distance inland, for example when overwintering in the vicinity of the River Niger in West Africa, as well as through the Rift Valley lakes of eastern Africa. Gull-billed terns are adaptable and highly opportunistic feeders, with terrestrial invertebrates ranging from grasshoppers to spiders frequently making up a significant part of their diet. The terns may congregate in large numbers in areas where food is plentiful. When hunting over grassland, the terns will fly low and swoop down quickly to seize their quarry, a technique similar to the one used when hunting for fish over the water. Small mammals such as voles may also fall prey to them in this fashion, as may reptiles including lizards, which are killed by blows from the terns' short but strong bill. Gull-billed terns prefer to nest in colonies, and their overall success rate is significantly higher when they associate in large groups. This is because collectively the terns are more able to drive off gulls and other predatory species seeking to seize their eggs and chicks.

Identification: Black cap on the head extends down to the nape of the neck. Frosty grey wings, back and tail feathers, the latter having white edges. Remainder of the plumage is white. In winter plumage the black cap is replaced by blackish ear coverts. Bill is relatively short and black. Sexes are alike.

Distribution: Ranges along the southern coasts of mainland Europe to the Mediterranean, extending east into Asia. Overwinters in Africa. Other populations present through southern Asia to Australia, and from the USA down to Argentina in South America.
Size: 42cm (16¹/₂in).
Habitat: Coastal areas and inland lakes.
Nest: Scrape on the shore.
Eggs: 1–5, pale-coloured with darker blotches.
Food: Invertebrates and small vertebrates.

Lesser crested tern

Sterna bengalensis

The lesser crested tern's northern range extends as far as the Mediterranean, though its main centre of distribution is located within the tropics. It is less migratory than many tern species, with northern populations overwintering along the northern and north-western coast of Africa. Those terns encountered on the eastern coast of Africa, occurring as far south as Natal, migrate to this region from the Middle East. Outside the Mediterranean, breeding often occurs on coral islands, where the birds will be relatively safe from predators. Here, their large nesting colonies may comprise as many as 20,000 individuals. During breeding, lesser crested terns sometimes associate with other related species, and have even been recorded as hybridizing with sandwich terns (*Sterna sandvicensis*) on their European breeding grounds. They prefer to seek their food in sheltered bays rather than over the open sea, and will sometimes venture into estuarine waters.

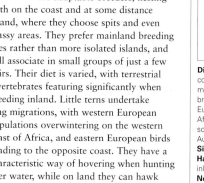

Identification: Black top to the head, with a crest. Wings, rump and upper tail are grey, and the remainder of the plumage is white. Bill is slender and yellow in colour, while the legs are black. In winter plumage, the area of black on the head is reduced. Sexes are alike.

Distribution: Found along the north African coast and less commonly in the Gulf of Suez and the Red Sea, extending through the Indo-Pacific region to Australia. Occasionally seen in Europe.
Size: 40cm (16in).
Habitat: Mainly tropical areas of coast.
Nest: Scrape on the shore.
Eggs: 1–2, brownish with dark markings.
Food: Fish and crustaceans.

Black noddy (white-capped noddy, *Anous minutus*): 39cm (15in)
From the Gulf of Guinea, off Africa's west coast, across the Atlantic to the northern coast of South America and the eastern Caribbean. Also in the Pacific, north and east of Australia. All *Anous* noddies, which are members of the tern family, are similar in appearance. Whitish plumage extends from the bill across the crown. Remainder of the body is dark greyish, and the flight feathers are blackish. Sexes are alike.

Brown noddy (noddy tern, common noddy, *Anous stolidus*): 45cm (18in)
From the Gulf of Guinea across the Atlantic to the Caribbean. Also throughout the Indian Ocean and the Pacific, from the east coast of Africa to Hawaii and East Island. Dark chocolate-brown, with greyish-white on the crown and a narrow broken area of white plumage encircling the eyes. Long, pointed black bill, with black legs and feet. Young birds have a brown crown. Sexes are alike.

Lesser noddy (*Anous tenuirostris*): 34cm (13in)
Restricted to the Indian Ocean and Pacific, but mainly around Madagascar. Breeds on the Seychelles and Mascarene Islands, the Maldives, and the Houtman Abrolhos Islands, off the western coast of Australia. Relatively small, with a more extensive whitish area on the head, which extends down beneath the eyes. Greyish hindcrown and nape. Blackish-brown elsewhere. Young birds have more prominent white area on the head, and brownish bodies. Sexes are alike.

Little tern

Sterna albifrons

Little terns are adaptable breeders, nesting both on the coast and at some distance inland, where they choose spits and even grassy areas. They prefer mainland breeding sites rather than more isolated islands, and will associate in small groups of just a few pairs. Their diet is varied, with terrestrial invertebrates featuring significantly when breeding inland. Little terns undertake long migrations, with western European populations overwintering on the western coast of Africa, and eastern European birds heading to the opposite coast. They have a characteristic way of hovering when hunting over water, while on land they can hawk invertebrates directly off branches. They will also pick up worms from sandbanks or soil.

Identification: Prominent white forehead with black edges, which form a black cap that extends down the nape of the neck. The chest and underparts are white and the wings are grey, except for the black edges to the primary feathers. The bill is yellow with a black tip, and the legs are orangish-yellow. Sexes are alike.

Distribution: Occurs in coastal waters throughout most of Europe, also breeding inland in central Europe. Overwinters in Africa. Present too in parts of southern Asia, ranging to Australia and New Zealand.
Size: 25cm (10in).
Habitat: Coastal areas and inland rivers.
Nest: Usually a bare scrape.
Eggs: 2–3, often brownish with darker markings.
Food: Fish and invertebrates.

SOUTHERN TERNS

Although terns are generally widespread around the globe, and often particularly well-travelled on migration, some are confined mainly to the southern hemisphere, rarely crossing the equator. Occasionally, breeding colonies of southern terns may include odd pairs of related species, which have joined up with them for the nesting period.

White tern

Fairy tern *Gygis alba*

These unmistakable terns have long flight feathers that reach to the tip of the tail when the wings are folded. They rarely venture to mainland areas, preferring to nest on remote tropical islands. Unlike most terns they do not choose a site on the ground, selecting instead a large leaf, such as that of a banana plant, often close to the trunk, where the egg will be relatively secure. This unusual behaviour in island-nesting birds, which instinctively lay on the ground, helps to protect their nests from introduced predators such as rats. In some parts of their range, notably on Ascension Island, where vegetation is scarce, pairs will breed on cliffs. Hatching takes about five weeks, and the single chick is equipped with strong claws that anchor it to its insecure nest site. It is reared mainly on small fish.

Identification: Predominantly pure white, but the African subspecies *G. a. candida* has a bluish-grey base to its otherwise black bill. Legs and feet are greyish. Sexes are alike.

Distribution: A population occurs in the vicinity of the Seychelles and Mascarenes, extending to the Indo-Pacific region. Also present off the coast of South-east Asia out across the Pacific, past Hawaii reaching western Mexico, and possibly extending down as far as western Colombia.
Size: 30cm (12in).
Habitat: Coral islands.
Nest: Lays on branches.
Eggs: 1, greyish-white with dark markings.
Food: Mainly eats fish and marine invertebrates.

Antarctic tern

Sterna vittata

Confined to the far south as their name suggests, Antarctic terns nest on remote islands during the brief summer, flying north to the southern coastal tip of Africa, where they will overwinter. Here they are most likely to be observed along craggy stretches of coastline. Ringing studies have helped to unravel the movements of the different populations of Antarctic tern, and have also revealed them to be relatively long-lived birds. One individual rung on the south-western Cape was eventually recaptured by ornithologists on Gough Island, close to the Antarctic, around 18 years later. Their survival may be due in part to their adaptability, since their feeding habits alter depending on the prevailing weather conditions. Antarctic terns avoid diving when the sea is rough, preferring instead to scoop up food from the surface.

Identification: Black cap, from the base of the upper bill over the head to the nape of the neck, including the eyes. White forehead (white streaking on the crown in non-breeding). Rest of the face is white. Lower back and forked tail are white, as are the lower underparts. Throat, chest and wings pale grey. Bill bright red, with darker legs and feet. Young birds have a black bill and legs, with barring when seen from below. Sexes are alike.

Distribution: Extends from the Antarctic north to the southern tip of South Africa. Other populations extend from Antarctica north to the Falklands and south-eastern South America, and also to New Zealand.
Size: 40cm (16in).
Habitat: Mostly rocky areas, including cliffs.
Nest: Scrape on the ground.
Eggs: 1–2, whitish-coloured with dark markings.
Food: Fish and crustaceans.

Sooty tern

Sterna fuscata

Throughout their range, sooty terns seek out inaccessible islands on which to breed, where they can nest in relative safety. They congregate in large colonies, with nesting pairs often less than 50cm (20in) apart. The breeding period varies according to location, typically beginning in June in the Seychelles but not until November further north. Pairs and offspring subsequently leave their island breeding grounds and spend up to three months over the oceans, before the adult terns head back to the colonies. It will be at least six years before the young return to breed. Remarkably, these terns cannot swim, and so are confined to an aerial existence, even to the extent of sleeping in flight. They often feed at night, scooping prey out of the water, but will also catch flying fish as they leap over the waves. Sooty terns have been known to live for over 30 years.

Identification: Black plumage extends from the base of the bill through the eyes, joining the black cap on the head which extends over the back and wings. The tail is black too, and deeply forked. The underparts are white, and the bill and legs are black. Young birds have blackish-brown upperparts, and are greyish-brown below. Sexes are alike.

Distribution: Two separate populations exist. One extends from the Caribbean right across the Atlantic Ocean to the west coast of Africa, while the other is present along the eastern side of the continent from the Horn of Africa to below Madagascar. Also ranges from South-east Asia into the Pacific Ocean.
Size: 45cm (18in).
Habitat: Oceanic islands.
Nest: Lays on the ground.
Eggs: 1, whitish-coloured with dark markings.
Food: Fish and squid.

Whiskered tern (*Chlidonias hybridus*): 27cm (11in)
Southern Africa to Asia, south to Australia. Cock has a black cap and grey body, except for white on the sides of the face. In non-breeding, this area is speckled, and the underparts are white. Young are buff on the sides of the face, grey on the hindneck. Sexes are alike, but hens smaller.

Kerguelen tern (*Sterna virgata*): 33cm (13in)
Restricted to Kerguelen, Marion, Prince Edward and Crozet Islands in the southern Indian Ocean. Similar to Antarctic tern, but has pale grey rather than white tail, and white on the upperparts is confined to the lower back. Grey on the body, the chest especially being darker.

Damara tern (*Sterna balaenarum*): 23cm (9in)
Endemic to south-western Africa, from Namibia to the eastern Cape. Similar to little tern, with a black cap on the head in breeding plumage. Wings are pale grey and the underparts white. Black bill, legs and feet. Sexes are alike.

Royal tern (*Thalasseus maxima*): 51cm (20in)
East African coast, winters in Namibia, breeds in the Gulf of Guinea. Separate population in the Americas, centred on Central America and the Caribbean. Large, with black on the head encompassing the eyes, and plumes on the nape of the neck. Underparts white, back and wings light grey. Bill orange-red. Black legs and feet. Young have a grey hindcrown, yellow legs and feet. Sexes are alike.

Black tern

Chlidonias niger

The change in coloration between this species' breeding and non-breeding plumage is unique among terns. In Europe they breed in wetland areas far from the coast, with nesting colonies often comprising fewer than 20 pairs. The nest is made of vegetation, built on a bed of reeds, directly above the water. If a sitting bird is disturbed by a predator, other members of the colony will make no attempt to swoop down and harry the intruder. Black terns feed largely on insects while nesting, though will also catch fish and other vertebrates, usually without diving into the water. In August the terns migrate south, the majority heading to the west coast of Africa. Young birds remain behind another month, building up their strength before under-taking the journey.

Distribution: From southern Scandinavia to Spain, with the mainland European population extending into Asia. Mostly winters along the west coast of Africa. Also found inland in the Nile valley. Distinct American population.
Size: 28cm (11in).
Habitat: Coastal areas, marshland and lakes.
Nest: Made of vegetation.
Eggs: 2–3, olive-brown with dark markings.
Food: Both vertebrates and invertebrates.

Identification: Black head and chest, greyer back and wings, with a white vent. Hens may be greyer overall. Bill black, legs and feet reddish-black. Non-breeding: much of the head is white, as are the underparts, with black on the sides of the breast. Young have a brownish forehead suffusion.

CORMORANTS AND SHAGS

Widely distributed around the world, and particularly in the southern hemisphere, these coastal seabirds are not only restricted to the marine environment. A few species inhabit freshwater, and some will move inland if fishing opportunities are better, which has brought them into conflict with anglers. Others are found only on tiny islands lying to the south of Africa.

Cormorant

Great cormorant *Phalacrocorax carbo*

This is the most common species, although there are disagreements about certain races. The isolated South African form *P. c. lucidus* ('white-breasted cormorant') is often regarded as a distinct species since it differs markedly in appearance, with a more extensive white throat extending on to the upper chest, and dark, greenish-black wing plumage. Cormorants can be seen in habitats ranging from the open sea to inland freshwater lakes, where they are despised by fishermen, as they prey on their quarry, diving and chasing the fish underwater. Although they nest colonially in a wide variety of sites, it is not uncommon to see odd individuals perched on groynes and similar places. While human persecution and oil spillages represent dangers, these cormorants can have a life-expectancy approaching 20 years.

Identification: Predominantly black once adult, with a white throat area. A white patch is present at the top of each leg in birds in breeding condition. Some regional variations. Bluish skin around the eyes. Bill is horn-coloured at its base and dark at the tip. Young birds are brownish with paler underparts. Sexes are alike.

Distribution: Scandinavia and the British Isles southwards via the Iberian peninsula, through the Mediterranean, and on to north-western Africa. May occur in southern Africa. Range also extends to North America, southern Asia and Australia.
Size: 94cm (37in).
Habitat: Mainly coastal, sometimes inland.
Nest: Made of seaweed and other flotsam.
Eggs: 3-4, chalky white.
Food: Largely fish.

Common shag

Green cormorant *Phalacrocorax aristotelis*

These shorebirds range over a wide area, but in contrast to the more common cormorant they very rarely venture into reservoirs or other freshwater areas. They also shy away from artificial structures such as harbour piers, roosting instead on cliffs and rocky stacks. Young birds may disperse far from where they hatched, especially those of the more northerly populations, but are likely to return in due course to breed in the same area. However, younger birds command only the less favourable sites, often around the perimeter of the nesting colony. The common shag's breeding season varies according to latitude, typically not commencing until March in the far north of its range, by which time the northern African population will have almost ceased nesting. The number and size of colonies fluctuates quite significantly, depending on the availability of food. Common shags catch fish underwater, diving to pursue their quarry, but unlike some cormorants never appear to hunt co-operatively.

Identification: Black with a slight greenish suffusion to the plumage, and an upturned crest on the head. Iris is blue. The bill is dark grey with a bare yellowish area of skin at its base. Legs dark grey. Non-breeding adults lose their crest and display mottled brown coloration on the throat. Young birds are entirely brown. Sexes are alike.

Distribution: Ranges around much of coastal Iceland and eastwards along the northern Scandinavian coast, south around the British Isles and the North Sea, around coastal Europe and through the Mediterranean to the Black Sea and northern Africa.
Size: 80cm (32in).
Habitat: Coastal areas.
Nest: Made of seaweed with a grass lining.
Eggs: 3-5, a chalky, bluish-white colour.
Food: Mainly fish.

Crowned cormorant

Phalacrocorax coronatus

The crowned cormorant's distribution falls within that of its relative the Cape cormorant (*P. capensis*), and both populations are sustained by the food-rich Benguela current which nourishes fish stocks in this region, some 10km (6.25 miles) offshore. There are very distinct differences in their feeding preferences however, since the crowned cormorants prefer to catch slower-swimming fish and a higher percentage of marine invertebrates, often quite close to the shoreline in the tidal zone, making them much easier to observe. They also breed in far smaller groups than Cape cormorants, with colonies usually comprising fewer than 150 pairs. This means they can occupy smaller sites, and will even take the opportunity to nest on wrecked ships close to this treacherous stretch of the African coastline. Crowned cormorants are relatively scarce birds, and their population probably consists of no more than 6,000 individuals, although there is no evidence that they have declined in numbers over recent years.

Identification: Relatively conspicuous crest above the bill. Overall body plumage is blackish, with no lighter areas over the wings. Reddish eyes and facial skin. Young birds are a browner shade. Sexes are alike in colour, but hens are smaller.

Distribution: Restricted to the south-western coast of Africa, extending from Namibia down to Cape Agulhas in South Africa.
Size: 55cm (22in).
Habitat: Coasts, especially rocky areas.
Nest: Made from seaweed and flotsam.
Eggs: 2-4, chalky-white.
Food: Fish and invertebrates.

Pygmy cormorant (*Phalacrocorax pygmaeus*): 55cm (22in)
Restricted to parts of south-eastern Europe and adjacent areas of Asia, including parts of Italy and Turkey, extending to the Aral Sea. Still recorded occasionally in Israel but extinct in Algeria. Relatively small. Predominantly black with a fairly indistinct crest and a long neck. Browner overall out of breeding condition, with paler, silvery coloration across the wings. Yellow bill. Young birds have whitish underparts. Sexes are alike but hens smaller.

Crozet shag (*Phalacrocorax melanogenis*): 70cm (27¹⁄₂in)
Confined to Crozet and nearby Prince Edward Island, lying to the south-east of Africa in the southern Indian Ocean. Black and white, with a black crest in breeding condition. White extends from the throat down the sides of the neck to the underparts and vent. Narrow white band evident across each wing, with black on the sides of the flanks, extending to the legs. Legs are pink, as are the feet. Blue skin encircles the eyes, with white plumes on the sides of head. Young birds are brownish rather than black, with no white on the wings. Sexes are alike.

Heard shag (*Phalacrocorax nivalis*): 77cm (30in)
Present only on Heard Island, which lies south-east of mainland Africa. Piebald, with similar patterning to the Crozet shag (above), but is much larger and has broad white wing patches. Also has more extensive white plumage on the sides of the face. Crest absent in non-breeding birds. Young birds have brownish upperparts. Sexes are alike.

Cape cormorant

Phalacrocorax capensis

These highly social cormorants generally nest in the southern spring, commencing in September, with pairs occupying cliffs and breeding at very high densities. The largest colonies may consist of over 100,000 pairs. This species is the most common of all cormorants occurring off the coasts of southern Africa. However, in the past the population has plummeted in some years, due to a collapse in pilchard stocks, which are a major source of food for them. Fortunately, there are now signs that the birds are taking other pelagic fish and invertebrates, and so are less dependent on this one food source. Cape cormorants feed in large flocks, sometimes consisting of hundreds if not thousands of individuals, diving underwater to catch their quarry. In some areas their numbers have increased following the provision of suitable platforms that the cormorants use for nesting. Like their neighbour, the Cape gannet, the bird's droppings, or *guano*, are then collected and processed into fertilizer.

Distribution: From Namibia around the Cape, reaching Algoa Bay. May extend north to Angola on the west coast, and up to Mozambique outside the breeding period.
Size: 65cm (25¹⁄₂in).
Habitat: Coastal areas, but rarely inland.
Nest: Made from seaweed and flotsam.
Eggs: 2-5, chalky-white.
Food: Predominantly fish.

Identification: Black overall, with distinctive bright blue eyes and a short tail. The skin at the base of the bill is a bright shade of yellow, while the bill itself is greyish. Legs are dark grey. Non-breeding adults have greyer plumage, with paler head feathering. Sexes are alike.

COASTAL WANDERERS

Some wading birds undertake regular migrations from Europe to Africa, usually following the land rather than flying across the ocean. Others occasionally crop up unexpectedly, typically having crossed the Atlantic from North America, perhaps having been blown off course. Such individuals are described as vagrants, since their presence cannot be guaranteed.

Red-necked phalarope

Northern phalarope *Phalaropus lobatus*

Distribution: Circumpolar, breeding throughout the Arctic, with the European population overwintering further south in the Arabian Sea region.
Size: 20cm (8in).
Habitat: Tundra and shore.
Nest: Scrape on the ground.
Eggs: 3-4, buff-coloured with brown spots.
Food: Mostly plankton and invertebrates.

These long-distance migrants fly north to breed in the Arctic region from late May onwards, frequently choosing sites well away from the coast. The ground here is boggy at this time of year, since only the top layer of soil thaws out and the meltwater is unable to drain away. Insects reproduce readily in these standing pools, providing a ready source of food for the phalaropes on which they can rear their chicks. Unusually, both incubation and rearing are undertaken by the male alone. Having laid their eggs, the hens depart the breeding grounds soon afterwards, followed by the males about a month later, once the chicks are independent. The young will be the last to leave. Red-necked phalaropes head south across Europe to their wintering grounds, breaking their journey by stopping off in Kazakhstan and around the Caspian Sea, where they can be observed feeding on lakes, before flying on through the Gulf of Oman to the Arabian sea.

Identification: Cocks duller than hens, with reduced chestnut-orange to the chest and whiter throat. Underparts whitish, grey barring on the flanks. Dark wings (less streaked in cocks). Long, pointed bill. Blackish legs and feet. Young birds have brown rather than black crowns.

Red phalarope

Grey phalarope *Phalaropus fulicarius*

Identification: Breeding hens have reddish underparts, black on top of head, and white cheek patches. Cocks are less vivid. In winter, the head is mainly white with black near the eyes, and the back is grey with a black strip reaching to the tail. Young have orangish chest band.

This phalarope is tied very closely to the ocean, but may be seen on inland water after severe storms. Unlike all other waders, it always migrates over the oceans rather than land. In its North American range it occurs predominantly along the Pacific coast, with peak numbers being seen here in the fall. They are often sighted in the company of whales, feeding on the skin parasites of these marine mammals. Red phalaropes congregate in areas where plankton is present, which provides them with rich feeding. They feed close to the water surface, sometimes dipping down with their strong bills to obtain food. In their breeding grounds in the far north the female leaves after egg-laying, sometimes seeking another partner. Male red phalaropes hatch and rear the young alone.

Distribution: Breeds in Iceland. Migrates south with other populations from Greenland and eastern North America, either to the west African coast or right down to the south-western coast.
Size: 22cm (8¹/₂in).
Habitat: Arctic tundra, coast and ocean.
Nest: Scrape on the ground.
Eggs: 2–4, buff-olive with dark spots.
Food: Invertebrates and fish.

Slender-billed curlew (*Numenius tenuirostris*): 41cm (16in) (E)
Now extremely rare, possibly due to changes in habitat. Formerly overwintered in north-western Africa, having migrated there from Siberia. Now occasionally sighted in Morocco, although vagrants are appearing in Italy. Shorter in stature than the curlew, with more evident white plumage on the underparts. A white stripe may also be present on the head. Characteristic short, slender bill. Young birds have mottled, rather than streaked, flanks. Sexes are alike.

Lesser yellowlegs (*Tringa flavipes*): 27cm (10¹/₂in)
Typically breeds in the far north of North America, wintering in Florida and further south in Central America, but vagrants are recorded annually off the British Isles. Narrow black bill, with dark streaking on the chest and white underparts. The back and wings are mottled and the flight feathers are dark. Characteristic yellow legs. Young birds have buff spotting on brown upperparts. Sexes are alike.

Greater yellowlegs (*Tringa melanoleuca*): 36cm (14in)
Another northern American vagrant sighted around the British Isles, usually during the winter. Larger than the lesser yellowlegs, with a longer, darker bill that curves slightly upwards towards its tip. More barring also evident on the underparts in breeding plumage. Young birds have darker backs. Sexes are alike.

Whimbrel

Numenius phaeopus

The relatively large size of the whimbrel makes it conspicuous among smaller waders. Although it may probe for food, it often snatches crabs scampering across the sand. In their tundra nesting grounds whimbrels have a more varied diet, eating berries and insects too. Both adults help to incubate and raise the young. They begin their migration journey south in July, when they can often be seen flying over land, seeking out inland grassy areas, such as golf courses, in search of food. Unusually, some whimbrels may avoid land, flying directly from Iceland to Africa over the Atlantic Ocean. It is not uncommon for young birds to remain here for their first year, before returning north again.

Distribution: In Europe, breeds mainly in Iceland and Scandinavia. Overwinters from the western Mediterranean and around the coast of Africa, including Madagascar, and on smaller islands in the Indian Ocean.
Size: 45cm (17¹/₂in).
Habitat: Tundra and shore.
Nest: Grass-lined scrape.
Eggs: 4, olive-coloured with dark blotches.
Food: Mostly invertebrates and berries.

Identification:
Brown crown with lighter central stripe. Fainter brown line through eyes. Brown streaks on silvery background on rest of body. Back and wings darker brown. Long, down-curving bill. Sexes are alike. Young have shorter, straighter bill.

Curlew

Eurasian curlew *Numenius arquata*

The distinctive call-note of the curlew, which gives rise to its name, is audible from some distance away. This wader's large size and its long, narrow bill also help to distinguish it from other shorebirds, and its legs are so long that the toes protrude beyond the tip of the tail in flight. Curlews are most likely to be seen in coastal areas outside the breeding season, where they feed by probing in the sand with their bills. They return to the same wintering grounds each year, and can live for more than 30 years.

Identification: Streaked plumage, with lighter ground colour on the throat and buff chest. Larger dark patterning on the wings. Underparts and rump are white. Cocks have plain-coloured heads, but hens' heads usually show a trace of a white stripe running down over the crown. Hens are also distinguished by their longer bills, which can be up to 15cm (6in) in length. When not breeding, the curlew has grey rather than buff plumage.

Distribution: Present throughout the year in the British Isles and adjacent areas of northern Europe. Also breeds widely elsewhere in Europe and Asia, migrating south to the Mediterranean and Africa in winter.
Size: 57cm (22in).
Habitat: Marshland, moorland and coastal areas.
Nest: Scrape on the ground concealed by vegetation.
Eggs: 4, greenish-brown with darker spots.
Food: Omnivorous.

NORTHERN WADERS

Many waders that breed in northern parts of Europe are only temporary residents. They fly south in the winter, when their nesting grounds are likely to be covered in snow. Having bred inland in many cases, this is when they can be sighted on the shoreline. Some however, such as the crab plover, choose to move within their more southerly ranges without being subjected to climatic pressures.

Crab plover

Dromas ardeola

This aberrant plover is the only member of its family, and displays a number of unusual habits. It uses its heavy bill to catch the crabs that form the bulk of its diet, often grabbing them out of their burrows and killing them with blows from its bill. The bill has another important function: it is also used as a digging tool to construct their underground nesting burrow. The tunnel sometimes extends back as far as 2.5m (8ft) before widening into the nesting chamber. Crab plovers are the only waders to nest underground. Young crab plovers remain dependent on the adults for food, not only while they are in the nest but also for some time after leaving. This is probably a reflection of their very specialized diet. Adults have to be very adept at catching crabs, and this is a skill that the young have to learn if they are to survive. This level of parental care helps to explain why they usually lay only a single egg.

Identification: White body with an area of black down the back, even when the wings are closed. Flight feathers also black. Long legs are greyish, and the large, heavy bill is black. Young birds are brownish on the head and over the wing coverts. Sexes are alike.

Distribution: African distribution centred on the continent's east coast, breeding as far south as Tanzania, in coastal areas of Madagascar and on smaller islands. Also present to the Red Sea region and western India, migrating eastwards as far as Thailand.
Size: 40cm (16in).
Habitat: Coastal areas.
Nest: Underground tunnel.
Eggs: 1-2, white.
Food: Crustaceans, but particularly crabs.

Ringed plover

Greater ringed plover *Charadrius hiaticula*

In spite of their relatively small size, these waders have strong migratory instincts. They are most likely to be seen in Europe during May, en route to their breeding grounds in the far north, and then again from the middle of August for about a month, before finally leaving European shores to make their way south to Africa for the winter. Ringed plovers typically breed on beaches and on the tundra, the mottled appearance of their eggs and the absence of an elaborate nest providing camouflage. They can be seen in reasonably large flocks outside the nesting season, often seeking food in tidal areas.

Identification: Black mask extends over the forehead and down across the eyes. There is a white patch above the bill and just behind the eyes. A broad black band extends across the chest.The underparts are otherwise white. The wings are greyish-brown and the bill is orange with a black tip. In winter plumage the black areas are reduced, apart from the bill, which becomes entirely blackish. White areas extend from the forehead to above the eyes. Cheek patches are greyish-brown, and there is a similar band on the upper chest. Sexes are alike.

Distribution: Along most of western and northern coastal Europe, and North America. Winters around much of continental Africa. Also recorded in parts of Asia.
Size: 19cm (7½in).
Habitat: Coasts and tundra.
Nest: Scrape on the ground.
Eggs: 4, stone-buff with black markings.
Food: Freshwater and marine invertebrates.

Terek sandpiper

Xenus cinereus

From April onwards, these small sandpipers can be seen on their northern breeding grounds, where the ground is boggy and there is an abundance of midges which form the bulk of their diet. Pairs normally produce a single clutch of eggs, with their offspring developing rapidly and becoming independent just two weeks after hatching. The exodus south to their winter coastal areas begins in July. It is thought that the Finnish population, at the western edge of their breeding range, fly directly to the south-western coast of Africa. Here, Terek sandpipers are to be seen darting around the shoreline, and enjoying a much more varied diet. They use their bills both to grab and to probe for invertebrates, on land and in shallow water, preferring to feed when the tide is out. They are very agile, able to move quickly to snap up prey before it can escape. Their unusual name derives from the Terek River, which flows into the Caspian Sea.

Identification: Brownish head and back, darker streaking on the breast. Underparts white, with contrasting black markings on the wings. Greyer tone to the upperparts in non-breeding. Bill long, brownish and upturned. Legs and feet slightly orange, more yellowish in young birds. Sexes are alike.

Distribution: Isolated population in Finland. Winters around much of coastal Africa and Madagascar, extending to parts of Asia and Australia. Also breeds throughout Asia.
Size: 25cm (10in).
Habitat: Inland and coasts.
Nest: Scrape on the ground lined with vegetation.
Eggs: 2–5, greenish-brown with dark spots.
Food: Midges and other invertebrates.

Black-winged stilt (*Himantopus himantopus*): 36cm (14in)
Southern Europe, overwinters in Africa. Top of the head to the nape is blackish. Ear coverts are black. Back and wings jet black, underparts are white. Long black bill. Legs are very long and red. Sexes are similar, but hens lack dark head markings and the back is more brownish.

Sanderling (*Calidris alba*): 20cm (8in)
Breeds in the Arctic. Seen in Europe on migration and during the winter. Breast is rufous with black speckling. Underparts white. Back and wings are grey with black and buff markings. In winter, rufous markings less evident, but a broad wing bar with black edging is seen in flight. Sexes alike.

Knot (*Calidris canutus*): 25cm (10in)
Breeds in the Arctic, migrates south to northern Africa. Distinctive rufous underparts, with black and rufous speckling on the wings offset against areas of grey. Black legs and grey upperparts. In winter, has streaking on the head, chest and flanks, greyish-white underparts and grey-green legs. Sexes are alike.

Purple sandpiper (*Calidris maritima*): 22cm (9in)
Iceland to Scandinavia and further north. Winters around the British Isles and from Scandinavia to the Iberian peninsula. Whitish stripe above each eye, with a dark brown area behind. Chestnut and brown markings on the dark wings. Brown streaking extending down the neck and over the underparts, which become whiter. Slightly down-curving, dark bill and yellowish legs. Young birds have brownish-grey breast with spots. In non-breeding, distinctive purplish suffusion over the back. Sexes are alike but hens are larger.

Stone curlew

Thick knee *Burhinus oedicnemus*

The stone curlew is a wader that has adapted to a relatively dry environment, and its mottled plumage enables it to blend in well against a stony background. When frightened, it drops to the ground in an attempt to conceal its presence. These birds are frequently active after dark, when they will be much more difficult to observe. However, their loud call-notes, which sound rather like "curlee", are audible over distances of 2.5km (1.5 miles) when the surroundings are quiet. Occasionally, stone curlews living close to coastal areas fly to mudflats, feeding when the flats are exposed by the sea.

Distribution: Breeds in various locations throughout western and southern Europe, but not as far as Scandinavia. Ranges into southern Asia and south to parts of northern Africa.
Size: 45cm (18in).
Habitat: Open and relatively dry countryside.
Nest: Scrape on the ground.
Eggs: 2, pale buff with dark markings.
Food: Invertebrates, typically caught at night.

Identification: Streaked plumage on the neck, upper breast and wings, with prominent white stripes above and below the eyes. White wing bars edged with black are also apparent on the wings. Abdomen and throat are whitish. Long, thick yellowish legs. Bill is mainly blackish, but yellow at the base. Sexes are alike. There is variation among races, with some having a greyer tint to their feathers.

OYSTERCATCHERS AND OTHER WADERS

Identifying waders is not always straightforward since a number of species moult into breeding plumage, transforming their appearance. While it may be possible to determine the sexes visually during the nesting period, it may be very difficult after a further moult. The situation becomes even more confusing as the young typically have different plumage from the adult birds.

Eurasian oystercatcher

Haematopus ostralegus

Their large size and noisy nature ensure these waders are quite conspicuous. The Eurasian oystercatcher's powerful bill is a surprisingly adaptable tool, enabling the birds not only to force mussel shells apart but also to hammer limpets off groynes and even prey on crabs. When feeding inland, the oystercatchers use their bills to catch earthworms in the soil without any difficulty. Individuals will defend favoured feeding sites such as mussel beds from others of their own kind, although they sometimes form large flocks numbering thousands of birds, especially during the winter.

Distribution: Shores of Europe, especially Great Britain, extending to Asia and down the north-western and Red Sea coasts of Africa.
Size: 44cm (17in).
Habitat: Tidal mudflats, sometimes in fields.
Nest: Scrape on the ground.
Eggs: 2–4, light buff with blackish-brown markings.
Food: Cockles, mussels and similar prey.

Identification: The head, upper chest and wings are black. Underparts are white, and there is a white stripe on the wings. It has a prominent, straight orangish-red bill, which may be shorter and thicker in cock birds. Legs are reddish. In winter plumage, adults have a white throat and collar, and pale pink legs. Sexes are alike.

Avocet

Pied avocet *Recurvirostra avosetta*

The unique shape of the avocet's long, thin, upward-curving bill enables these birds to feed by sweeping the bill from side to side in the water, locating their prey predominantly by touch. Pairs can display very aggressive behaviour when breeding, and in some areas may gather in very large numbers, nesting at high densities. Although they usually move about by wading, avocets can swim well and will place their heads under water when seeking food. On migration, avocets fly quite low in loose lines. Birds from western areas tend to be quite sedentary, while those occurring further east will usually overwinter in Africa as well as the Mediterranean region.

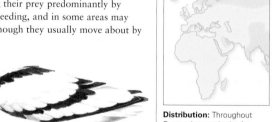

Distribution: Throughout Europe (except in the far north) and northern Africa, often close to the coast. Range extends into western Asia. Some winter in Africa.
Size: 46cm (18in).
Habitat: Mostly lagoons and mudflats.
Nest: Scrape on the ground lined with vegetation.
Eggs: 4, pale brown with faint markings.
Food: Small crustaceans and other invertebrates.

Identification: Slender, with long, pale blue legs. White overall, with black plumage on the top of the head extending down to the nape of the neck. Black stripes extend over the shoulder area and around the sides of the wings. Flight feathers are black. Long, thin black bill curves upwards at the tip. Hens often have shorter bills and a brownish tinge to their black markings.

Black-tailed godwit

Limosa limosa

Grassland areas are favoured by these godwits for breeding. Egg-laying begins in April, with established pairs returning to the same nesting sites, which are out in the open rather than concealed in tall grass. The adults share incubation, which lasts about three weeks, but the chicks are largely brooded by the female. They fledge within five weeks, after which the godwits migrate to their winter quarters, where the young may remain until their second year. Black-tailed godwits can adapt to habitat change, and in the 20th century returned to breed in Britain, where they were formerly extinct. When feeding in water they may vibrate their feet to disturb aquatic invertebrates, including larvae, and in muddy water snails may be found by touch. In Africa they often feed mainly on vegetation.

Identification: Dark stripe runs through each eye, with a white streak above. Pale sides to the face. Chestnut on the neck and upper breast, becoming mottled with black streaks on the lower chest. Underparts white, but some regional variation. Wings brownish-grey with individual blackish markings. Long, narrow bill, pinkish at the base and dark at the tip. Legs are black. Chestnut is missing from both sexes in non-breeding plumage. Young birds have no barring across their underparts. Hens are less brightly-coloured than cocks.

Distribution: Breeding range extends from Iceland and southern Scandinavia through much of western and central Europe into Asia. Western population overwinters in parts of the British Isles and the Iberian Peninsula. Others move further south into Africa, Asia and Australia.
Size: 44cm (17in).
Habitat: Coast and marshes.
Nest: Pad of vegetation.
Eggs: 3–5, greenish-brown with dark blotches.
Food: Mainly invertebrates.

African black oystercatcher (*Haematopus moquini*): 45cm (18in)
Lobito Bay, Angola southwards as far as Natal. Jet black, with a bare red area of skin encircling each eye. Long, relatively narrow red bill. Legs and feet also red. Young birds are browner overall. Sexes are alike, but hen's bill is slightly longer.

Common redshank (*Tringa totanus*): 27cm (10¹/₂in)
Iceland, Scandinavia, British Isles and central Europe. Migrates to the Mediterranean. Greyish head and wings, with striations and mottling on the chest, back and wings. White area in front of each eye. Bill is red with a dark tip. Legs bright red. Non-breeding: body a more even shade of brownish-grey. Young birds have yellowish-orange legs and feet. Sexes are alike.

Broad-billed sandpiper (*Limicola falcinellus*): 17cm (7in)
Scandinavia, wintering in eastern Africa. Rare sightings in western Europe. Asian population winters along the southern coast of Asia, reaching Australia. Black spot in front of the eyes, with streaking on the crown. Dark plumage with pale edging on the wings. Triangular-shaped streaking on the sides of the body. Rest of underparts white. In non-breeding, much paler grey. Bill is blackish. Legs and feet yellowish-grey. Sexes are alike. Young birds are brownish on the back.

Bar-tailed godwit

Limosa lapponica

These godwits fly long distances to and from their breeding grounds. Studies have shown that birds observed in western Europe during the winter are most likely to have come from as far east as the Yamal peninsula. Those overwintering in southern Africa will have originated from further into Asia, their journey entailing crossing the Caspian sea. It is estimated that nearly three-quarters of a million bar-tailed godwits undertake this annual journey to Africa, after the end of the breeding season in late July or August. It is possible to gain an insight into the gender of individual birds by watching a flock feeding on an outgoing tide, as hens, with their longer bills, are better equipped to feed in deeper water. The godwits favour estuarine rather than freshwater areas. Young birds remain on the wintering grounds for their first year, while the adult birds head back north again in May.

Distribution: Scandinavia and northern Asia to Alaska. Winters in British Isles and western Europe to Africa.
Size: 16cm (6in).
Habitat: Tundra and coasts.
Nest: Lined scrape.
Eggs: 2–5, greenish-brown with dark blotches.
Food: Mainly invertebrates.

Identification: Chestnut. Back has shades of brown with pale edging. Dark stripe runs through each eye; crown is also dark. Long, up-curved bill, paler at its base. Legs and feet grey. Hens have whitish underparts, with fine brownish striations on the chest and flanks. Both have barred tail and greyer underparts in non-breeding. Females are larger. Young birds have buff suffusion to the neck and upper breast.

DIVERS AND GREBES

*These species are better known from northern latitudes. Loons as a group are not represented in Africa, whereas grebes range right down to the tip of South Africa. They are suited to their aquatic existence, preferring to swim rather than fly. It is not uncommon for them to carry their young on their backs, affording them some protection from predatory fish such as pike (*Esox lucius*).*

Red-throated diver

Red-throated loon *Gavia stellata*

Distribution: Breeds Iceland, Scandinavia and northern Europe and Asia. Overwinters around the British Isles and southern Scandinavia to the Iberian Peninsula. Present in the Black and Caspian seas. Also North America and Asia.
Size: 64cm (25in).
Habitat: Pools, open country.
Nest: Pile of vegetation.
Eggs: 1–3, olive-brown with dark spots.
Food: Mainly fish.

Red-throated divers pair up for life and stay together throughout the year. In May they return to their northern nesting grounds, revisiting the same location each year. Their nest, usually located among vegetation and surrounded by water, is simply a loose pile of plant matter. This is added to during the incubation period, potentially developing into a large mound. Both parents share incubation duties, although the female normally sits for longer than the male. Young red-throated divers can take to the water almost immediately after hatching, but usually remain at the nest for the first few days. Even once the chicks have entered the water they may still occasionally be carried on their parents' backs. Survival rates can be low, but if they make it through the critical early months of life these divers may live for up to 23 years.

Identification: Distinctive red throat patch present in adults of both sexes during the breeding period. The head is grey and the back of the neck is streaked black and white. Upperparts are brown, underparts white. During the winter it has a pale grey crown, with speckling extending down the back of the neck and white spotting on the back; remaining underparts are white. Yellowish-grey bill. Young birds can be identified by their greyish-brown heads.

Black-throated diver

Black-throated loon *Gavia arctica*

This species occurs in slightly more southerly locations than its red-throated relative, preferring the taiga (forested) area of northern Europe rather than the treeless tundra zone. However, it still has a circumpolar distribution, and is present in North America, but absent from Iceland and Greenland. The British Isles marks the southerly extent of the black-throated diver's breeding range. An estimated 150 pairs nest here during the summer, and numbers can rise significantly when they are joined by overwintering birds that have bred further north in Scandinavia. Solitary by nature, these divers seem especially vulnerable to any disturbance on their breeding grounds. As their name suggests, they seek their food largely underwater, diving to depths of up to 6m (20ft) in search of fish, including freshwater species such as sticklebacks and marine species such as herring.

Identification: In breeding condition, has a distinctive grey head and neck, and a black throat with conspicuous white stripes running down the sides of the neck. Underparts are white, with finer black striping on the sides of the upper breast. Back and wings are predominantly black, with prominent areas of white barring and spotting. Bill, legs and feet black. Remaining upperparts are brownish-grey with a white area on the flanks. Young birds resemble adults out of colour. Sexes are alike.

Distribution: Scandinavia and the far north of Europe and Asia. Overwinters to northern Scandinavia, the British Isles and down to northern Spain. Also in the northern Mediterranean, and in the Black and Caspian seas.
Size: 65cm (25¹⁄₂in).
Habitat: Freshwater lakes and sheltered coastal areas.
Nest: Plant matter by water.
Eggs: 1–3, olive-brown with darker spots.
Food: Fish, some invertebrates and vegetation.

Black-necked grebe

Podiceps nigricollis

Black-necked grebes are frequently observed over the winter period on large stretches of water. They are especially social at this time of year, and can often be found in the company of other birds such as black-headed gulls (*Larus ridibundus*). They also associate with their own kind during the breeding season. Although mostly seen on lakes, black-necked grebes also frequent similar habitats with dense aquatic vegetation around the edges of the water, which provides them with nesting cover. Their floating nests afford protection from land-based animals such as foxes (*Vulpes vulpes*), but the young chicks are still vulnerable to other dangers on fledging, including large predatory fish. Their down feathering is particularly dark on hatching, helping to distinguish them from related species. When migrating after the breeding season, black-necked grebes often associate in large groups, and may sometimes be seen in places where they are not regularly observed, such as the Canary Islands and Madeira.

Identification: Unmistakable in summer plumage, with a black head, neck and back and contrasting chestnut underparts. Golden ear tufts adjacent to the red eyes. Much duller in winter plumage, when chestnut areas are replaced by blackish-white coloration. A white area is present on the throat and sides of the neck. Young birds are similar, but have duller eyes and a faint yellowish hue at the rear of the neck. Sexes are alike.

Distribution: Migratory birds breed in Ireland, the Scottish borders and southern Scandinavia, wintering in western Europe. Others are resident further south, and through eastern Europe. Also in North America and Asia.
Size: 34cm (13in).
Habitat: Ponds and lakes, often coastal areas in winter.
Nest: Floating plant material.
Eggs: 3–4, brownish with darker markings.
Food: Invertebrates and fish.

Great crested grebe

Podiceps cristatus

Great crested grebes are primarily aquatic birds, and their flying ability is compromised by their short wings. They can dive very effectively, however, and often disappear underwater when they feel threatened. Rarely observed on land, these grebes are relatively cumbersome since their legs are located far back on the body, limiting their ability to move fast across open ground. Their toes are not fully webbed, unlike those of waterfowl, but they can swim quickly due to their streamlined body shape. They use their ruff-type facial feathers during display.

Distribution: Eastern parts of Europe, overwintering further south. Generally resident in western Europe. Occurs in parts of northern, eastern and southern Africa, and into Asia.
Size: 51cm (20in).
Habitat: Extensive reedy stretches of water.
Nest: Mound of reeds.
Eggs: 3–6, chalky-white.
Food: Fish and invertebrates.

Identification: Black from top of the head to the back. Brownish sides to the body in winter. In summer, has an extensive black crest, with a chestnut ruff at rear of head edged with black. Bill reddish pink. Sexes are alike.

Great northern loon (common loon, *Gavia immer*): 88cm (35in)
Icelandic and British coasts. Also North America and Greenland. Black head, with barring on the neck and throat. The back is patterned black and white, with white spots. Underparts are white. There is less contrast in the winter plumage, with white extending from the lower bill and throat down over the underparts. In winter, the eyes are dark rather than red. Sexes are alike.

Little grebe (*Tachybaptus ruficollis*): 29cm (11in)
Found in most of Europe on a line from southern Scotland southwards. Also in North Africa and the Middle East. Black head, chestnut patches on the neck and a yellow gape at the corners of the bill. Dark feathering on the back and wings, with brown flanks. In the winter, light buff plumage replaces darker areas. Sexes are alike.

Red-necked grebe (*Podiceps grisegena*): 46cm (18in)
Breeds in eastern Europe, and as far west as parts of Scandinavia. Overwinters primarily in coastal areas around the North Sea, and in the eastern Mediterranean. Black extends over the top of the head to the hind neck, forming a small crest. There is a narrow white band below this, with a prominent grey area on the throat. Sides of the neck and chest are chestnut-red. Back and wings blackish. Grey flanks and underparts. Bill black, yellow at the base. Out of colour, reddish plumage is greyish-white, with the grey of the throat reduced. Young birds display blackish streaking here. Sexes are alike.

LARGER WATERBIRDS

Although generally considered to be among the most spectacular of all of Africa's avifauna, the flamingos and pelicans found on this continent have distributions that actually extend further north into parts of Europe. They are conspicuous birds due to their large size and massive bills, and pelicans in particular have relatively bold natures, happily living alongside people.

Glossy ibis

Plegadis falcinellus

Groups of these ibises can be encountered in a wide range of environments, from rice fields to river estuaries, and they will often undertake extensive seasonal movements. They prefer to feed by probing into the mud with the tips of their sensitive bills, enabling them to grab prey easily even if the water is muddy. Occasionally they will dip their head under water when feeding. These birds may also use their long legs to pursue prey, such as snakes, on the ground. Glossy ibises nest colonially. The nest site is located low over the water, and fledglings sometimes fall victim to crocodiles lurking nearby as they leave the nest.

Identification: Dark brown overall, but with some white streaking on the head. The wings and rump are green. Legs and bill are dark. They are duller in colour when in non-breeding condition. Sexes are alike.

Distribution: Ranges over much of Africa. Extends from the Red Sea via northern India to eastern Asia. Also present in Australia, the Philippines and Indonesia.
Size: 66cm (26in).
Habitat: Shallow water.
Nest: Platform of sticks, built above water.
Eggs: 2–6, deep green to blue.
Food: Invertebrates, small vertebrates and crustaceans.

Sacred ibis

Threskiornis aethiopicus

These ibises are relatively bold by nature, and are not uncommonly seen in areas close to humans. During the breeding season, large numbers of sacred ibises may congregate in suitable locations, building their bulky, platform-shaped nests in trees, often in the company of other birds. In more remote areas with dense vegetation they may occasionally nest on the ground. They are adaptable feeders, able to probe the mud in search of worms or seize small mammals running through the grass. They may even help to control plagues of locusts. Flocks of sacred ibises may be observed scavenging on rubbish dumps, and will even raid the nests of crocodiles to feed on the eggs of these reptiles. Populations tend to be fairly sedentary, with breeding occurring during the wet season. In Egyptian mythology they were reputed to save the country from plagues and serpents.

Identification: Bare black head and neck. White body with fine black plumes extending over the lower back. Depending on race, flight feathers may have black tips and eye colour may vary. Legs, feet and bill black. Young birds are mottled black and white on the head. Sexes are alike.

Distribution: Most of Africa south of the Sahara, except for parts of the south-west. Also present on the Aldabra and Madagascar.
Size: 75cm (29$^{1}/_{2}$in).
Habitat: Usually found close to water.
Nest: Made of vegetation off the ground.
Eggs: 2–3, greenish-white.
Food: Invertebrates, small mammals and carrion.

Greater flamingo

Phoenicopterus ruber

Occurring in huge flocks, these flamingos provide one of the most spectacular sights in the avian world. Even in flight they are unmistakable, flying in lines with their long necks and legs held horizontally (such groups are often referred to as "skeins"). At this time their calls are similar to the honking notes of geese. Flamingos feed by sieving microscopic crustaceans from the salt water using plates in their bills. It is this food source that gives the birds their distinctive reddish coloration. Greater flamingos breed communally on these salt pans, with the female constructing the raised, cone-shaped nest above the water. Their young hatch covered in greyish down, and are chaperoned in groups by the adult birds. Although usually seen wading, flamingos are able to swim if necessary. To get airborne, they run on the water's surface while beating their wings.

Distribution: Range extends from parts of France and southern Spain down through suitable habitat in Africa and the Red Sea region, and eastwards into Asia.
Size: 145cm (57in).
Habitat: Saline lagoons.
Nest: Built of mud.
Eggs: 1–2, white.
Food: Tiny crustaceans and other plankton.

Identification: The tallest of all flamingos. Relatively pale pink overall, with a pinkish bill with a dark tip. Flight feathers are of a more pronounced pinkish shade. Young birds change from brown to pink plumage over approximately three years. Hens are significantly smaller, with shorter legs.

Great white pelican

Pelecanus onocrotalus

Large and sociable, these pelicans are found on open stretches of water where they can fish easily. Each individual needs to catch about 1.2kg (2.6lb) of fish per day. The largest colony, comprising 80,000 birds on Tanzania's Lake Rukwa, requires approximately 35,000 tonnes per annum from this lake alone. The great white pelican is migratory in northern areas, breeding in Europe and overwintering in Africa. Pairs arrive in the Danube Delta from March, departing again by November. About 7,000 pelicans make this journey. They are vulnerable to pollution and overfishing, but may regularly fly long distances in search of food.

Distribution: Breeds from northern to eastern Europe. Present through much of eastern Africa, and south of the Sahara, but absent from south-eastern parts of the continent. Also present in parts of Asia.
Size: Males 175cm (69in); females 145cm (57in).
Habitat: Freshwater and brackish lakes.
Nest: Pile of vegetation on the ground.
Eggs: 1–2, chalky-white.
Food: Mainly fish.

Identification: Large stature. White plumage with black flight feathers. Yellow tinge to the breast when breeding, and a pinkish suffusion overall. Bare eye skin also becomes more pinkish in the male, and orange in the hen. Upper bill dark, yellow pouch beneath. Young birds are mostly greyish-brown.

Spot-breasted ibis (*Bostrychia rara*): 50cm (20in)
Central-western Africa, found in Liberia, Cameroon, Gabon and extending to Zaire and north-eastern Angola. Three very distinctive bluish areas adjacent to the base of the upper and lower bill and behind the eyes. Characteristic cinnamon-buff streaking, from the neck down to the underparts. The remaining plumage is dark, with a greenish iridescence over the wings. Relatively narrow red bill, legs and feet. Hen similar, but with a less brightly-coloured bill and facial spots. Young birds are similar to hens, but duller.

Olive ibis (*Bostrychia olivacea*): 70cm (27½in)
Scattered localities right across Africa, on each side of the Equator, from Sierra Leone and Liberia to Kenya and Tanzania. Distinctive black facial skin coloration, extending around the eyes to the base of the bill. Remainder of the head and neck greyish, with a shaggy crest at the back of the head, which is less prominent in young birds. Prominent iridescent green wing patches, with olive coloration evident here as well. Relatively short reddish bill, legs and feet. Sexes are alike.

RARER WETLAND BIRDS

In Europe especially, there has been increasing pressure over the years to drain marshland areas for agriculture or housing. This has had a severe effect on the avian species found in this habitat, greatly curtailing their numbers, and explains why such species are now often rarer in western rather than eastern Europe, where their habitat remains more intact.

White stork

Ciconia ciconia

Distribution: Summer visitor to much of mainland Europe. Winters in western and eastern parts of North Africa, depending on the flight path. Also occurs in Asia.
Size: 110cm (43in).
Habitat: Wetland areas.
Nest: Large platform of sticks off the ground.
Eggs: 3–5, chalky-white.
Food: Amphibians, fish, small mammals and invertebrates.

Considered a harbinger of good fortune, these birds often return each year to the same site, adding annually to their nest, which can become bulky. The return of the storks in April from their African wintering grounds helped to foster the widespread myth of the link between storks and babies. Their migration – over the Strait of Gibraltar and further east over the Bosphorus – is a spectacular sight. They fly with necks extended and legs trailing behind their bodies. The journey back to Africa begins in August.

Identification: Large, tall, mainly white bird with prominent black areas on the back and wings. Long red bill and red legs. Sexes are alike. Young birds are smaller and have a dark tip to the bill.

Great bittern

Eurasian bittern *Botaurus stellaris*

Bitterns are shy by nature, more likely to be heard than seen, thanks to the loud booming calls of cock birds at night as they try to attract mates. They are very patient hunters, relying on stealth to avoid detection before striking fast once their quarry is within reach. Great bitterns are largely solitary by nature and form no strong pair bond, only coming together to mate. The female is solely responsible for incubating the eggs and rearing the chicks. Hatching takes 26 days, with the chicks fledging after eight weeks. In freezing weather northern bitterns will head to warmer latitudes, where they may be more conspicuous. The isolated South African race (*B. s. capensis*) is slightly darker in colour than its northern relative.

Identification: Relatively light, yellowish-brown colour overall, with variable black markings. A white streak is present under the throat, with dark areas on the top of the head and along the sides of the bill, which is yellowish, as are the legs and feet. Markings of young birds are less defined on the upperparts. Adult hens are paler than cocks.

Distribution: Breeds widely in eastern Europe, and is present in various parts of western Europe where suitable habitat exists. Also found in north-east and central Africa, with a separate population in southern Africa.
Size: 80cm (31in).
Habitat: Reedbeds.
Nest: Mat of vegetation in the reeds.
Eggs: 4–5, pale blue.
Food: Fish and other aquatic creatures.

Hamerkop

Scopus umbretta

The hamerkop's nest is an amazing structure. Usually built in a sturdy tree (although it may sometimes be located on the ground) it consists of up to 8,000 different components, all of which the birds collect locally. The construction process averages three to six weeks. Almost anything may be used for building the nest, including rubbish, plastic and discarded pieces of clothing. It is assembled very carefully, beginning with a platform that is then domed over with sticks and held in place by mud, acting rather like cement. A further covering of vegetation on top ensures that the inner chamber is largely impregnable. The hamerkops enter through a tunnel. Even more remarkably, studies have revealed that pairs routinely build three to five such nests every year. The reason is unclear, but other birds, especially waterfowl such as the African pygmy goose (*Nettapus auritus*), will often adopt the sites.

Identification: Greyish or brownish-grey overall, with a shaggy crest at the back of the head. Slight iridescence on the wings. Stocky, pointed black bill with similarly coloured legs and feet. Sexes are alike.

Distribution: Throughout the whole of Africa south of the Sahara, with the range extending to the south-west Arabian peninsula. Also present on Madagascar
Size: 56cm (22in).
Habitat: Wetland areas with nearby trees.
Nest: A massive mound of vegetation.
Eggs: 3–6, white.
Food: Primarily amphibians such as frogs, but also other aquatic creatures.

African openbill (*Anastomus lamelligerus*): 94cm (37in)
Occurs across Africa south of the Sahara, but absent from central-western and southern parts. Present on western Madagascar. Dark, greyish-black overall, with a greenish suffusion across the mantle and on the breast, appearing more purple or brown in some cases. Distinctive gap between the upper and lower bill can measure up to 6mm (0.2in) in adults, but not apparent in young birds. Dark greyish bill, legs and feet. Sexes are alike but cock birds larger.

Woolly-necked stork (*Ciconia episcopus*): 85cm (33¹/₂in)
Tropical Africa south of the Sahara. Absent from Madagascar. Dense white plumage on the neck, with a black area on top of the head. Grey sides to the face. Underparts, back and wings are blackish, with a purplish gloss. Bill dark at the base, red towards the tip. Legs and feet partially or wholly dark, depending on race. Young birds dull brown. Sexes alike, but males are larger.

Black stork (*Ciconia nigra*): 100cm (39in)
Breeds on the Iberian Peninsula and through eastern Europe to Asia. Overwinters in a band across Africa south of the Sahara, and also in southern Africa, where there is a resident population. Predominantly black, with purplish-green iridescence. White chest and underparts. Bare skin around the eyes; bill, legs and feet are red. Young birds have greenish bill, and are browner. Sexes alike, but cock birds are larger.

African jacana

Actophilornis africanus

The African jacana's long toes enable it to walk across aquatic vegetation. Unusually, it is the male that incubates the eggs and cares for the young. Hens mate and lay in the nest of one partner, before moving on to the next. The reason for this is unclear, but it may help to maximise the number of chicks reared. The jacanas' nests are at risk from flooding and predators during incubation, which lasts just over three weeks. The young will begin feeding themselves soon after hatching; however, it may be about seven weeks before they fly. During this time, they may be carried under the wing of the male parent, as shown here.

Distribution: Range extends throughout Africa south of the Sahara, although absent from the Horn.
Size: 30cm (12in).
Habitat: Wetlands such as lakes and ponds; occasionally the banks of sluggish rivers.
Nest: Platform made from floating vegetation.
Eggs: 2–5, tan-coloured with black markings.
Food: Invertebrates.

Identification: Chestnut body with a yellow area on the breast. The neck is white with a black streak running from the base of the bill to the crown and then down the back of the neck. Brilliant blue bill and frontal shield. Legs and feet are greyish. Young birds have white underparts and no frontal shield. Hens are larger than cocks.

SHY AND LONG-LIVED WATERBIRDS

Although waterbirds such as herons feed in a similar fashion to waders, probing with their bills, their larger size allows them to wander into deeper water in search of food. This affords them greater feeding opportunities, as well as enabling them to prey on larger fish. They are opportunistic feeders, however, and will take amphibians just as readily as fish.

Great white egret

Egretta alba

Great white egrets were once heavily hunted for their plumes, which were used to decorate women's hats. They are adaptable birds, found on farmland and even in pasture some distance from water. Here they feed on rodents and other small mammals, insects, and reptiles such as snakes. Breeding occurs in colonies of up to several hundred pairs. Nests are built on the ground, or in a tree high over water. Mortality can be high in young birds, but adults may survive in the wild for 20 years.

Identification: Tall. Snow-white, with plumes over the back and on the chest of breeding birds. Skin in front of the eyes is blue. Bill yellowish with bluish hue on top. Legs and feet black. Sexes are alike. Birds lack plumes and blue coloration in winter.

Distribution: In Europe, occurs largely around the eastern Mediterranean. Extends to much of Africa, with small numbers also present in Asia.
Size: 99cm (39in).
Habitat: Marshland and flooded areas.
Nest: Made of sticks.
Eggs: 3–5, pale blue.
Food: Fish, small mammals and invertebrates.

Eurasian spoonbill

Platalea leucorodia

Distribution: Breeds in northern temperate parts of Europe and Asia, as far east as China. Winters further south in tropical parts of Africa and South-east Asia. Indian birds are sedentary.
Size: 93cm (37in).
Habitat: Mudflats, marshes and shallow water.
Nest: Platform of sticks off the ground.
Eggs: 3–4, white with brown markings.
Food: Fish, other aquatic creatures and vegetation.

The enlarged surface area of these birds' bills enables them to feed more easily as they move their heads from side to side in the water. Young spoonbills, however, have a much narrower, light-coloured bill with no enlargement at the tip. They can also be identified in flight by the black tips to their outer flight feathers. It may be up to four years before they start nesting. Spoonbills can swim if they need to, but usually prefer to inhabit calm, shallow stretches of water. When resting, they may perch on one leg and tuck their bills over their backs, while in flight they will extend their necks. Spoonbills can live for nearly 30 years.

Identification: Highly distinctive and enlarged, yellow-edged, spoon-like tip to the black bill. Crest of feathers on the back of the neck, longer in the male, and an orange patch on the chest at breeding time. The rest of the feathering is white. Black legs.

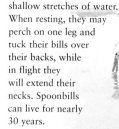

Grey heron

Ardea cinerea

These large, opportunistic hunters are often shy on the ground and can be difficult to spot. They are usually seen in flight, with their long necks tucked back on to their shoulders and their legs held out behind their bodies. They fly with relatively slow, quite noisy wing beats. Grey herons are very patient predators. They stand motionless, looking closely for any sign of movement in the water around them, then lunge quickly with their powerful bills to grab any fish or frog that swims within reach. During the winter, when their freshwater habitats are frozen, grey herons will often move to river estuaries in search of food. These birds frequently nest in colonies, and some breeding sites may be used for centuries by successive generations.

Identification: Powerful yellow bill. White head, with black above the eyes extending to long plumes off the back of the head. Long neck and chest are whitish with a black stripe running down the centre. Grey wings and black shoulders. Underparts are lighter grey. Long yellowish legs. Sexes are alike.

Distribution: Throughout most of Europe into Asia, except for the far north. Also in Africa, but absent from the Sahara and the Horn.
Size: 100cm (39in).
Habitat: Water with reeds.
Nest: Platform of sticks built off the ground.
Eggs: 3–5, chalky-blue.
Food: Fish and any other aquatic vertebrates.

Little egret (*Egretta garzetta*): 65cm (26in)
Southern Europe, overwintering mainly in Africa and the Middle East. White plumage, with blue-grey area at the base of the bill. Long, white nuptial plumes when breeding. Legs blackish, with very unusual yellow toes. Sexes are alike.

Black egret (Black heron, *Egretta ardesiaca*): 52cm (20¹/₂in)
Eastern Africa south of the Sahara. Present on Madagascar. Jet black. Long plumes on the nape of the neck and chest. Narrow black bill, yellow irides. Legs black. Feet yellow, becoming red at the start of the breeding period. Young birds brownish, with no long plumes. Sexes are alike.

Black-crowned night heron (*Nycticorax nycticorax*): 64cm (25in)
Breeds in southern Europe, overwintering in Africa, where there are resident populations. Present on Madagascar. Also occurs in Asia and the Americas. Predominantly grey. Black crown and black plumage extending down the back. Bill is black. Legs and feet yellow, becoming redder at the onset of breeding. White plumes at the back of the neck. Young birds have brownish streaking. Females are smaller than males.

Madagascar pond heron (*Ardeola idae*): 48cm (19in)
Migrates from central and eastern Africa to its breeding grounds on Madagascar and Aldabra. Pure, snow white coloration. Sky blue bill with a black tip. Legs and feet pinkish, the latter becoming green in the breeding season. Eyes yellow with surrounding bare bluish-green skin. Outside the breeding period, has a black ground and nape. Young birds have brown coloration on their tail and flight feathers. Sexes are alike.

African rail

Rallus caerulescens

Like others of its kind, the African rail is a very shy bird, relying on its slim body shape to slip undetected through reeds and similar vegetation. Its toes are sufficiently agile to enable it to climb reed stems in search of insects, but it will also feed on aquatic creatures such as tadpoles, often emerging into the open in the process. African rails have a distinctive, jerky gait, and their short tails twitch constantly as they move. Pairs become very territorial when breeding, calling repeatedly to reinforce their claim to their chosen nesting area. The nest is often built directly above the water. Both adults share the incubation, which lasts about three weeks. Although the young are able to follow the adults as soon as they hatch, they remain dependent on them for food for up to two months. It will be at least a year before the young rails nest for the first time.

Distribution: Centred mainly on the eastern side of Africa, south of the Sahara, but species is also occasionally sighted in western parts of the continent.
Size: 35cm (14in).
Habitat: Wetlands with aquatic vegetation.
Nest: Cup-shaped, made from vegetation.
Eggs: 2–6, pinkish-cream with darker markings.
Food: Mainly invertebrates.

Identification: Back and wings are dark brownish. Grey plumage extends from the head down to the breast, except for a white area on the throat. Prominent white barring on the flanks. Long red bill and legs. Young birds are recognizable by the brown coloration of their breast and bill. Sexes are alike.

CRAKES

This group of birds can often be observed out in the open, but when frightened will usually scuttle away to the safety of the reeds or vegetation along the water's edge. They can all be recognized by their relatively long legs and toes, short stubby tail and narrow body shape, which enables them to slip easily and quietly through their waterside habitat.

Water rail

Rallus aquaticus

Being naturally very adaptable, these rails have an extensive distribution, and are even recorded as foraging in tidal areas surrounded by seaweed in the Scilly Isles off south-west England. In some parts of their range they migrate to warmer climates for the winter. Water rails survive in Iceland during the winter thanks to the hot thermal springs, which never freeze. They are very territorial when breeding and, as in other related species, their chicks hatch in a precocial state.

Identification: Prominent, long, reddish bill with bluish-grey breast and sides to the head. Narrow brownish line extending over the top of the head down the back and wings, which have black markings. Black-and-white barring on the flanks and underparts. Short tail with pale buff underparts. Sexes are alike.

Distribution: Extensive, from Iceland throughout most of Europe, south to northern Africa and east across Asia to Siberia, China and Japan.
Size: 26cm (10in).
Habitat: Usually reedbeds and sedge.
Nest: Cup-shaped, made from vegetation.
Eggs: 5–16, whitish with reddish-brown spotting.
Food: Mainly animal matter, but also some vegetation.

Coot

Eurasian coot *Fulica atra*

Open stretches of water are important to coots, enabling them to dive in search of food. During the winter, these birds may sometimes assemble in flocks on larger stretches of waters that are unlikely to freeze over. Coots may find their food on land or in the water, although they will dive only briefly in relatively shallow water. Pairs are very territorial during the breeding season, attacking the chicks of other coots that venture too close and even their own chicks, which they grab by the neck. Such behaviour is often described as "tousling". The young usually respond by feigning death, and this results in them being left alone.

Identification: Plump, sooty-grey body with a black neck and head. Bill is white with a white frontal plate. The iris is a dark brownish colour. White trailing edges of the wings evident in flight. Long toes have no webbing. Sexes are alike.

Distribution: From Great Britain eastwards throughout Europe, except the far north, south into northern Africa and east to Asia. Also present in Australia and New Zealand.
Size: 42cm (16¹⁄₂in).
Habitat: Slow-flowing and still stretches of water.
Nest: Pile of reeds at the water's edge.
Eggs: 1–14, buff to brown with dark markings.
Food: Various kinds of plant and animal matter.

Spotted crake (*Porzana porzana*):
22cm (9in)
Found in western and central parts of Eurasia as far east as southern Siberia and north-west China. Winters in northen Africa and south-wards from Ethiopia. Has a distinctive, heavily white-spotted breast, although the abdomen is more streaky. Prominent brown ear coverts, with a bluish-grey stripe above, and black markings on the wings. The undertail area is pale buff and whiter at the tip, but may show dark spots in some cases. The bill is yellow, although red at the base. Sexes are alike.

Little crake (*Porzana parva*): 19cm (7¹/₂in)
Present in areas of Spain and Portugal, the range extending eastwards through Europe to China. Overwinters in southern Asia and northern parts of Africa. Slaty-blue head and underparts. Black markings are found predominantly across the top of the wings. The remainder of the back is brown. Has a black-and-white speckled undertail area. The bill is yellow with a red base. Adult hens are easily distinguished by their white chest area, which turns buff on the underparts. Sexes are alike.

Baillon's crake (*Porzana pusilla*): 18cm (7in)
Has a sporadic distribution through Europe and overwinters in North Africa. Also occurs further south, in Africa and on Madagascar. Ranges through Asia to parts of Australia and New Zealand. Slaty-blue head and underparts. Can be distinguished from little crake by the far more extensive barring on the flanks and heavier white speckling on the wings. The bill is dull with no red area. Hens may have paler plumage on the throat.

Moorhen

Common moorhen *Gallinula chloropus*

Although usually found in areas of fresh water, moorhens are occasionally seen in brackish areas – for example, on the Namibian coast in south-western Africa. Their long toes enable them to walk over aquatic vegetation. These birds feed on the water or on land and their diet varies according to the season, although seeds of various types make up the bulk of their food. If danger threatens, moorhens will either dive or swim underwater. They are adept divers, remaining submerged by grasping on to underwater vegetation with their bills. In public parks, moorhens can become quite tame, darting in to obtain food provided for ducks.

Distribution: Very wide, from Great Britain east throughout Europe except for the far north. Occurs through much of Africa, especially southern parts, and also through much of South-east Asia and parts of the Americas.
Size: 30cm (12in).
Habitat: Ponds and other areas of water edged by dense vegetation.
Nest: Domed structure hidden in reeds.
Eggs: 2–17, buff to light green with dark markings.
Food: Omnivorous.

Identification: Slate-grey head, back and underparts. Greyish-black wings. A prominent white line runs down the sides of the body. The area under the tail is white and has a black central stripe. Greenish-yellow legs have a small red area at the top. The bill is red apart from a yellow tip. Sexes are alike.

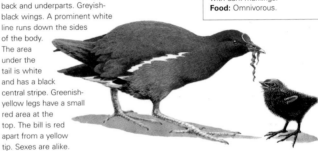

Purple swamp hen

Porphyrio porphyrio

The European population of the purple swamp hen has become more scarce over recent years due to changes in its habitat, specifically drainage of wetland areas. In some other localities, however, such as the Nile Valley of Egypt, the species has expanded its range thanks to the greater availability of suitable habitat created by irrigation schemes. Purple swamp hens are most likely to be observed late in the day, when they venture out in search of food. These birds are rather clumsy on short flights, literally running across the surface of the water to take off, and flying with their legs hanging down rather than being held against the body. They are unable to fly when moulting.

Identification: Relatively large, with vivid blue and purplish shades predominating in the plumage, and prominent white undertail coverts. The wings especially may have a greenish hue in some cases. Bill is dull red with brighter frontal plate. Long legs are pinkish red. Sexes alike.

Distribution: Southern parts of Europe. Sporadic locations in northern Africa and southern parts of that continent. Also present in Asia and Australasia.
Size: 50cm (20in).
Habitat: Reedy lakes and marshes, river banks.
Nest: Platform of vegetation just above the water.
Eggs: 2–7, whitish to green with dark spots.
Food: Mostly vegetarian.

FEEDERS OF WOODLANDS AND WETLANDS

A variety of birds have adapted to living and breeding in close proximity to water. Some, such as the water pipit, are from families normally associated with other types of terrain. Not all actually venture onto the water, but are instead drawn by the availability of food, seeking not fish but rather the host of invertebrates that are associated with the aquatic environment.

Great painted snipe

Rostratula benghalensis

These waders feed in water by moving their bills from side to side, and may also probe the earth in search of worms or pick up seeds from the ground. They are shy by nature, only emerging to feed at dusk, when they may venture into fields. Breeding is frequently triggered by rainfall. The incubation period may last only 15 days, and the young are dependent on their parents for just the first few days after hatching, enabling the adult pair to start nesting again soon afterwards. Hens have been recorded as laying up to four clutches of eggs in rapid succession, when conditions are favourable. If scared, great painted snipe freeze in position, and an incubating bird will slip quietly into the vegetation rather than fly away and reveal the nest site. These painted snipe can swim well from an early age.

Identification: Male has a white streak around each eye. Remainder of the head is greyish with white speckling. A white band extends around the sides of the neck, and the underparts are white. Yellowish-grey sides to the wings, grey elsewhere broken with spots and barring. Yellow V-shaped area on the mantle. Long yellow bill with a dark tip. Young birds resemble adult males. Hens have dark brown rather than grey head and neck.

Distribution: Found in various locations throughout Africa, notably in western and south-eastern parts of the continent. Also present on Madagascar. Range extends to Asia and Australia.
Size: 28cm (11in).
Habitat: Swampy areas.
Nest: Hidden on the ground.
Eggs: 2–5, pale yellow.
Food: Invertebrates, seeds.

Water pipit

Anthus spinoletta

These pipits undertake regular seasonal movements, nesting at higher altitudes in the spring, where they often frequent fast-flowing streams. Pairs nest nearby, choosing a well-concealed location. Subsequently they will retreat to lower altitudes for the winter months, and are not averse to moving into areas of cultivation, such as watercress beds in southern Britain. These aquatic pipits are lively birds, and are sometimes encountered in small flocks. They can often be observed on the ground, searching for invertebrates, and will readily make use of cover to conceal their presence should there be any hint of danger. Their song is attractive, and rather similar to that of the closely related rock pipit (*A. petrosus*), with studies of their song pattern revealing regional variations between different populations. Water pipits, like others of their kind, often utter their song in flight, and this is most likely to be heard at the start of the nesting period.

Identification: In breeding plumage, has a white stripe above the eye, a white throat with a distinctly pinkish tone to the breast, and a white abdomen. Slight streaking evident on the flanks. The head is greyish and the back and wings are brownish. During winter, the breast becomes whitish with very obvious streaking. Wings are lighter brown overall. Regional variations apply. Sexes are alike.

Distribution: Southern England and much of western Europe, extending to the northern African coast and into South-east Asia.
Size: 17cm (7in).
Habitat: Marshes, still water areas. Nests by streams.
Nest: Made of vegetation.
Eggs: 3–5, greenish with darker markings.
Food: Largely insectivorous.

African finfoot

Podica senegalensis

Few birds show greater variation in appearance than the African finfoot. Its name stems from the lobes on its feet, likened to fins, which undoubtedly enhance this species' swimming ability. They are equally adept out of the water, able to climb around in branches. Another unusual feature is their stiffened tail, which is held flat when swimming. Even more surprising, however, is the presence of a claw at the end of each wing, located on a mobile first digit. This may help prevent finfoots from losing their grip when clambering in vegetation. They are solitary birds and difficult to observe, often remaining close to the shore, especially alongside waterways overgrown by vegetation. If disturbed in open water they will freeze, lowering their body down in the hope of avoiding detection. Even when breeding, African finfoots are unusual in having a remarkably short incubation period of just 12 days.

Identification: Considerable variation in appearance through its range, with the Cameroon race (*P. s. camerunensis*) having blackish upperparts and chest, brown feathering edged with white on the lower underparts, and a brown rump. Other forms have a white stripe down each the side of neck, speckling on the wings, and variable barring across the underparts. Males are much larger in size. Red bill, legs and feet.

Distribution: Africa south of the Sahara, largely absent from much of the south-west of the continent.
Size: 39cm (15in).
Habitat: Forested stretches of water.
Nest: Mass of vegetation.
Eggs: 2–3, cream-coloured with dark streaks.
Food: Mainly invertebrates.

Pacific golden plover (*Pluvialis fulva*):
25cm (10in)
Iceland and the far north of Europe, wintering as far south as northern Africa. Black sides of the face extend to the chest and underparts, bordered by white feathering and barring from above the bill down the sides of the body. Coarse, mottled pattern of brown, black and white over the wings. Very upright stance on grey legs. In winter, underparts become mottled with black-and-white feathering. Sexes are alike.

Little ringed plover (*Charadrius dubius*):
18cm (7in)
Southern Scandinavia across Europe, wintering in northern Africa. Also in Asia. Broad black lines across the top of the forehead and from the bill back around the eyes, with a broader black band across the chest. Brown crown edged white. White neck collar. Underparts entirely white. In winter the entire head is brownish, with a pale buff area from the bill to above the eyes, and the black chest band turns brownish-grey. Legs pinkish-brown, bill black. Sexes are alike.

Snipe (common snipe, *Gallinago gallinago*):
28cm (11in)
Iceland eastwards through Europe into Asia, and often into northern Africa in winter. Pale buff streak down the centre of the crown, with buff stripes above and below the eyes. Dark mottled chest and wings. White underparts. White stripes run down the wings, with a white border to the rear of the wings. Long bill, often larger in hens. Sexes otherwise alike.

Egyptian plover

Crocodile bird *Pluvianus aegyptius*

Despite its name, this plover is no longer present in Egypt, where it was common along the River Nile until the early 20th century. Egyptian plovers have bold natures, but there is little evidence to confirm the belief that they will pick food morsels from the open mouths of resting crocodiles. Their prey normally consists of small aquatic creatures, hunted by careful stalking or probing in the sand. Pairs nest on their own on sandbars, where their eggs can be partly buried if the adult birds are away from the nest. The incubating bird will soak its breast feathers if the eggs are in danger of overheating. Even the chicks may be buried until almost a month old, to help conceal their presence, although they can begin feeding themselves when a week old.

Distribution: Ranges in a broad band across the whole of central Africa south of the Sahara, extending as far as northern Angola.
Size: 20cm (8in).
Habitat: Sandy river banks.
Nest: Scrape on a sandbank.
Eggs: 1–4, cream-coloured with dark markings.
Food: Invertebrates.

Identification: Black head and back, with a white streak above each eye. Black extends down the sides of the neck to form a band across the chest, bordered below by a white band. Throat is white, becoming buff on the chest. Underparts are buff. Grey wings. Bill is black, legs and feet grey. Young birds have brownish edges to the feathers on their backs.

HABITAT SPECIALISTS

The adaptability of birds as a group is reflected by the diversity which exists among those associated with freshwater areas. While the dipper is at home by a fast-flowing mountain stream, aquatic warblers and a number of similar species thrive in a more sluggish aquatic environment where reedbeds proliferate, although observing them in this habitat can be difficult.

Eurasian dipper

Cinclus cinclus

The dipper's name comes from the way in which it bows, or "dips" its body, often on a boulder in the middle of a stream, rather than describing the way it dives into the water. Dippers are very adept at steering underwater with their wings, and can even elude birds of prey by plunging in and disappearing from view, before surfacing again further downstream. They feed mainly on aquatic invertebrates caught underwater, sometimes emerging with caddisfly larvae and hammering them out of their protective casings on land. Pairs work together to construct their nest, which may be concealed in a bridge or a hole in a rock. The hen usually sits alone, and the youngsters will fledge after about three weeks. Norway's dipper population is increasing as streams in the southern mountains remain free of ice, possibly due to global warming.

Identification: Prominent white throat and chest. Brown on head extends below the eyes, rest of the plumage is dark. Young birds are greyish with mottling on their underparts. Some regional variation, usually relating to the extent of chestnut below the white of the chest. Dark bill, legs and feet. Sexes are alike.

Distribution: Present in much of Scandinavia but only irregularly through the rest of Europe. Absent from central and eastern England and much of north-west Europe. Range extends south to parts of northern Africa. Also present in Asia.
Size: 20cm (8in).
Habitat: Stretches of fast-flowing water.
Nest: Domed mass made from vegetation.
Eggs: 1–7, white.
Food: Aquatic invertebrates and small fish.

Aquatic warbler

Acrocephalus paludicola

Distribution: Mainland Europe. Few remaining strongholds in eastern Europe, notably in Poland, ranging into Asia. Migrates south to western Africa.
Size: 13cm (5in).
Habitat: Waterlogged areas, with sedge.
Nest: In tussocks of sedge.
Eggs: 4–6, greenish-coloured with dark markings.
Food: Invertebrates.

Identification: Black areas on the head, with a central yellow-buff streak and broader areas above the eyes. Similar markings also at the top of the wings. The remaining wing plumage is brownish with black markings, with marked streaking over the lower back. Underparts are paler and have variable fine streaking. Young birds less brightly coloured. Sexes are similar.

The aquatic warbler's range has contracted significantly over recent years, as the sedgeland areas that these birds favour have been increasingly drained for agriculture. However, they are seen more widely on migration, when they take a westerly route down over the Strait of Gibraltar. During the autumn in particular, they can even be seen in southern parts of England. They remain in Africa from November through to April, before heading north again, where they occur in a number of scattered locations in areas of suitable habitat, including flooded grassland. Aquatic warblers may be difficult to observe since they tend not to utter any calls away from their breeding grounds. When nesting, they will usually sing most frequently towards dusk, from a suitable perch rather than in flight. They are shy birds by nature, and prefer to search for food near the base of reedbeds. They are also very agile, often perching on two adjacent reeds rather than grasping the same stem with both feet.

Grauer's swamp warbler (*Bradypterus graueri*):
15cm (6in) (E)
Eastern Africa, confined to the Albertine Rift
region centred on Rwanda, where it is
endangered by drainage of its habitat. Prominent
white stripe above the eye, with a dark stripe
running through the eye beneath. Whitish
underparts, heavily streaked especially on the
throat and upper breast, becoming browner on
the sides of flanks and lower underparts.
Upperparts dark. Sexes are alike.

Eurasian reed warbler (*Acrocephalus
scirpaceus*): 13cm (5in)
Southern parts of Scandinavia and the British
Isles. Also in northern Africa, overwintering
south of the Sahara, particularly in parts of East
Africa. Brown head, back and wings, with a
rufous suffusion to the plumage on the rump.
There is a paler brown streak above each eye.
Lower cheeks, breast and underparts are
whitish, with a brown suffusion across the chest
and on the flanks. Pointed bill, darker on the
upper bill and paler beneath. Legs and feet are
pinkish-grey. Sexes are alike.

European marsh warbler (*Acrocephalus
palustris*): 13cm (5in)
Central Europe into Asia, north to southern
Scandinavia. Rare in the British Isles. Winters
through much of East Africa. Similar to Eurasian
reed warbler, but with a slightly greyer tone to
the brown upperparts. Underparts also whitish,
with brownish suffusion on the chest and flanks.
Identified by its shorter bill and longer wings, the
tips of which clearly extend behind the rump
when the bird is perched. Sexes are alike.

Great reed warbler

Acrocephalus arundinaceus

Great reed warblers return to their northern
breeding grounds from April onwards, with
their distinctive and sometimes harsh calls
betraying their presence in the reedbeds.
However, they are notoriously difficult to
spot, due to the colour of their plumage.
They sing from the tops of reed stems, and
this provides the best opportunity to spot
them. They are very agile, able to clamber
between the reed stems with ease. In flight,
great reed warblers stay close to the water's
surface, with their tail feathers held out. The
female constructs the nest in May, which is
suspended from several adjacent reed
stems, about half-way up their
length. Incubation lasts around
two weeks and is shared by
both members of the pair,
as is the rearing of the
young. They leave the
nest after about 12
days. Both young
and adult birds
migrate south
as early as
September.

Distribution: Most of Europe,
but restricted to the extreme
south in both Scandinavia and
the British Isles. Overwinters
in Africa south of the Sahara,
except the far south and the
Horn of Africa. Resident
population in northern Africa.
Size: 20cm (8in).
Habitat: Reedbeds.
Nest: Vegetation woven into
a basket shape.
Eggs: 4–6, bluish-green with
dark markings.
Food: Invertebrates.

Identification: Upperparts are
dark brown, with darker areas
on the wings and a pale stripe
running through the eyes. Whitish
underparts, becoming more buff
in colour on the flanks. Some
greyish streaking evident across
the breast. Bill is blackish, lighter
below, while the legs and feet
are typically greyish. Young birds
are rusty-brown above, with buff
underparts. Sexes are alike.

Bearded reedling

Bearded tit *Panurus biarmicus*

This species' distribution is directly affected by the availability of marshland with extensive
reedbeds. Contrary to their name they are members of the babbler family, rather than tits,
although their lively nature and jerky tail movements, coupled with their overall appearance,
are more suggestive of the latter group. In addition to providing a source of insects, the
reeds also produce seeds which the bearded reedlings eat over the winter, when invertebrates
are less common. Nevertheless, these small birds can suffer a high mortality rate when the
weather is harsh. They are more social at this time of year, and may associate in groups of
up to 50 individuals. Pairs breed alone, and the male is
largely responsible for nest-building, choosing a well-
concealed site hidden in the reeds. Both birds incubate
and care for the chicks, which may fledge at just nine
days old. Pairs may rear up to three broods in a year.

Identification: Reddish-brown overall, with a relatively long tail which
tapers to its tip. Some white patches on the wings. Cocks have a mainly
grey head, with a prominent black area beneath each eye, and a white
throat. Hens have a brownish head, with a greyish-white throat. Young
birds similar to hens, but with a distinctive black area on their backs.
Bill is yellowish-orange, legs and feet are black.

Distribution: Localised
distribution from southern
parts of Scandinavia and
England through areas of
Europe and parts of Asia.
Size: 15cm (6in).
Habitat: Reedbeds.
Nest: Made of vegetation.
Eggs: 5–7, white with
dark markings.
Food: Invertebrates, seeds.

DUCKS

Waterfowl are generally conspicuous birds on water, but their appearance and distribution can differ markedly through the year. Drakes often resemble hens outside the breeding season, when their plumage is much plainer. Some species are migratory, heading south to escape freezing conditions, while others are to be found on stretches of water that may at times be covered in ice.

Mallard

Anas platyrhynchos

Distribution: Occurs throughout the northern hemisphere and resident through western Europe. Also occurs in north Africa.
Size: 60cm (24in).
Habitat: Open areas of water.
Nest: Usually a scrape lined with down feathers.
Eggs: 7–16, buff to greyish-green in colour.
Food: Mostly plant matter, but some invertebrates.

These ducks are a common sight, even on stretches of water in towns and cities, such as rivers and canals. They may congregate in quite large flocks, especially outside the breeding season, but they are most evident in the spring, when groups of unpaired males chase potential mates. The nest is often constructed close to water and is frequently hidden under vegetation, especially in urban areas. These birds feed both on water, upending themselves or dabbling at the surface, and on land.

Identification: Metallic green head with a white ring around the neck. Chest is brownish, underparts are grey, and a blackish area surrounds the vent. Bluish speculum in the wing, most evident in flight, bordered by black-and-white stripes. Hen is brownish-buff overall with darker patterning, and displays the same wing markings as drake. Hen's bill is orange, whereas that of male in eclipse plumage (outside the breeding season) is yellow, with a rufous tinge to the breast.

Ruddy shelduck

Tadorna ferruginea

Although ruddy shelducks are resident throughout the year in some parts of their range, they are more often migratory. Occasionally, they may be encountered well outside their natural range, and there have been verified sightings reported from countries as far apart as Iceland, Oman and Kenya. They are quite noisy birds by nature, and the calls of drakes are of a higher pitch than those of hens. These shelducks favour stretches of water surrounded by open countryside, allowing them to graze on the surrounding vegetation. After the breeding season, huge flocks may assemble in areas where conditions are favourable for feeding.

Identification: Cinnamon shade to the head, with paler whitish area around the eyes. Black neck ring. Remainder of the body is orange-brown. Greenish gloss to black feathering on the rump. Tail and flight feathers are black. Bill, legs and feet are also black. White plumage under the wings. Hens lack the neck collar, which is less apparent in drakes outside the breeding season.

Distribution: North-western Africa, south-eastern Europe extending into Asia. Over-winters in eastern Africa.
Size: 70cm (27¹/₂in).
Habitat: Inland, can be some distance from water.
Nest: Under cover, lined with down feathers.
Eggs: 8–15, creamy-white.
Food: Aquatic creatures and plant matter.

Shoveler

Northern shoveler *Anas clypeata*

The broad bills of these waterfowl enable them to feed more easily in shallow water. They typically swim with their bill open, trailing it through the water to catch invertebrates, although they also forage both by upending and catching insects on reeds. Shovelers choose wet ground, often some distance from open water, as a nesting site, where the female retreats from the attention of other drakes. Like the young of other waterfowl, young shovelers take to the water soon after hatching.

Identification: Dark metallic green head and orange eyes. White chest and chestnut-brown flanks and belly, with a black area around the tail. Both back and wings are black and white. The remainder of the body is predominantly white. Broad blue wing stripe, which enables drakes to be recognized even in eclipse plumage, when they resemble hens. Very broad black bill. Hens are predominantly brownish but have darker blotching, yellowish edges to the bill and paler area of plumage on the sides of the tail feathers.

Distribution: Widely distributed throughout the northern hemisphere, overwintering as far south as central Africa.
Size: 52cm (20¹/₂in).
Habitat: Shallow coastal and freshwater areas.
Nest: Down-lined scrape.
Eggs: 8–12, green to buff-white in colour.
Food: Aquatic invertebrates and plant matter.

Teal (green-winged teal, *Anas crecca*): 38cm (15in)
Found throughout Europe. Resident in the west, migrating south to parts of northern Africa. Also found in Asia and North America. Brown head with broad green stripes running across the eyes and yellow stripes above and below. Chest is pale yellow with black dots. Body and wings are greyish with a yellow area under the tail, and a white edge to the sides of the wings. Hens are mottled brown, with a pale whitish area beneath the tail and a green area on the wing. Bill is dark. Drakes in eclipse plumage resemble hens.

Garganey (*Anas querquedula*): 41cm (16in)
Ranges from England and France eastwards across Europe, overwintering south of the Sahara. Present in Asia. Prominent white stripe from the eyes down along the neck. Remainder of the face and breast area are brown with black barring. Greyish area on the body. Wings are greyish-black. Brown mottling over the hindquarters. Hens have mottled plumage with a distinctive buff-white area under the chin. Drakes in eclipse plumage resemble hens but with greyish areas on the wings.

Ferruginous duck (*Aythya nyroca*): 42cm (16¹/₂in)
Occurs throughout much of eastern Europe and into Asia, overwintering around the Mediterranean and further south in Africa, as well as in parts of South-East Asia. Chestnut plumage, lighter on the flanks than the back, with white eyes. Very obvious white wing stripe. Whitish belly, underwing and undertail area. Greyish bill, black at the tip. Hens are similar but have a pale band across the bill and brown eyes (which distinguishes them from drakes in eclipse plumage).

Pintail (northern pintail, *Anas acuta*): 62cm (24in)
Throughout the Northern Hemisphere, migrating south for the winter to central Africa. Long, narrow black tail. Head is blackish, with white stripes on the neck down to the breast and underparts. Grey flanks. Wings are greyish with prominent wing stripes. Hens are brown, with darker patterning on the plumage and a long, pointed tail with a white edge to the wings in flight.

Pochard

Aythya ferina

These ducks are most likely to be found on open water, where they can often be seen diving for food. Islands are favoured as breeding grounds since they provide relatively secure nesting sites, particularly where there is overhanging vegetation. Pairs will stay together for the duration of the nesting period. Subsequently the pochards form large flocks, sometimes moving away from the lakes and other still-water areas to nearby rivers, especially in winter when ice is likely to form on the water's surface.

Distribution: Resident in parts of western Europe, extending eastwards into Asia. Overwinters further south, in parts of western and central Africa.
Size: 49cm (19in).
Habitat: Marshland, lakes.
Nest: Under cover, lined with down feathers.
Eggs: 6–14, greenish-grey.
Food: Aquatic creatures and plant matter.

Identification: Chestnut-brown head and neck, with black chest and a broad grey band encircling the wings and body. Black feathering surrounds the hindquarters. Eyes are reddish. Black is replaced by a greyish tone in eclipse plumage. Hens are significantly duller in coloration, having a brownish head with buff areas and a noticable stripe extending back from the eyes. Brown also replaces the drake's black plumage.

WATERFOWL

Waterfowl are occasionally sighted well outside their natural range, suggesting the bird in question may be an exotic escapee from a wildfowl collection. Some endemic African waterfowl, which are found nowhere else in the world, appear to have no close European relatives, while a number, for example the Hottentot teal, are clearly related to European species.

African black duck

Anas sparsa

These ducks are often encountered in wooded upland areas, on fast-flowing stretches of water, although sometimes they may also be found in more open countryside at lower altitudes. The breeding period varies through their extensive range, but usually takes place during the dry season. The nest site is well-hidden among rocks or debris left by flooding. Incubation lasts approximately four weeks, and the young hatch covered in black down with pale buffy-white underparts. The dark coloration of these ducks makes them difficult to spot in the relative gloom of the forest, particularly as they will remain stationary if disturbed, rather than fly off immediately. When they do fly in this terrain they instinctively follow the path of the waterway, skimming low over the surface. African black ducks feed by dabbling, upending and even occasionally diving beneath the surface of the water.

Identification: Dark, blackish-brown coloration with relatively broad, lighter barring on the wings, back and tail. Bill is completely or partially black, depending on the race. Legs and feet are pinkish-red. Young have narrow barring and a white abdomen. Ducks are smaller than drakes.

Distribution: Two separate populations exist. The most widespread extends from near the Red Sea in East Africa to much of the southern region, while a smaller one is present in western equatorial Africa.
Size: 58cm (23in).
Habitat: Flowing and still stretches of water.
Nest: Vegetation lined with down feathers.
Eggs: 4–8, buffy-grey.
Food: Aquatic plants, invertebrates, small fish.

Comb duck

Knob-billed duck *Sarkidiornis melanotos*

Distribution: Occurs widely throughout Africa south of the Sahara, and is also present on Madagascar. Occurs in South America and southern Asia.
Size: 76cm (30in).
Habitat: Fairly open country with lakes and rivers.
Nest: Made of vegetation.
Eggs: 6–20, yellowish-white.
Food: Grass and vegetation, some invertebrates.

It is unusual for waterfowl to occur naturally both in Africa and South America, although this species is more common in Africa than elsewhere. Comb ducks are likely to be found in relatively open countryside, where they can leave the water and graze on grasses and other vegetation, but they also seek out aquatic invertebrates in the shallows. They may associate in groups of 40 individuals or more, which will disperse at the start of the breeding season. The comb on the bill of the drakes becomes much more conspicuous at this stage. Comb ducks are tree-nesting by nature, but may also adopt large nests abandoned by birds such as hamerkops (*Scopus umbretta*), or even abandoned buildings. Incubation lasts a month. The young can take to the water almost immediately but must first tumble down from the nest site, since it will be nearly 10 weeks before they are able to fly well.

Identification: Black area on the head extending down the back of the neck, with speckling on the sides of the face and throat. Nape of the neck is white, underparts predominantly white. Back and wings are metallic green. Only the drake has the massive, comb-like protrusion on the upper bill, along with a slight yellowish suffusion on the head, grey flanks and a black area around the vent. Hen in contrast has some relatively faint brownish barring on the flanks.

Young birds are brownish in colour.

Goosander

Common merganser *Mergus merganser*

Like many waterfowl of the far north, the goosander occurs at similar latitudes in Europe and Asia. Diving rather than dabbling ducks, they are also called sawbills because of the small, sharp projections running down the sides of their bills, which help them to grab fish more easily. Seen in wooded areas close to water, pairs will nest in a hollow tree or even a nest box, lining it with down to insulate the eggs and prevent them rolling around. Outside the breeding period, common mergansers form large flocks numbering thousands of birds on lakes and similar stretches of fresh water. They may, however, prefer to fish in nearby rivers, returning to the lake at dusk. Common mergansers tend to remain in their nesting location until the water starts to freeze over, whereupon they head south. They pair up mainly over winter, returning north to breed the following spring.

Distribution: Ranges from Iceland and Scandinavia south through northern Europe, including the British Isles, but does not extend to the Iberian peninsula.
Size: 64cm (25in).
Habitat: Lakes and rivers.
Nest: Hole in a tree.
Eggs: 6–17, ivory or pale buff in colour.
Food: Predominantly fish.

Identification: Narrow body. Drake has dark green head and neck, with green on the primary flight feathers. Underparts white, back is greyish. Ducks have chestnut-brown head and white under the throat. Bill and legs red. Drakes in eclipse plumage have a white front to the wings.

Maccoa duck (*Oxyura maccoa*): 51cm (20in)
Two separate African populations exist, one in the central-eastern region and one in the south. The drake in breeding plumage is chestnut overall, with a black head and a broad blue bill. The tail, which is very stiff and is often held just above the water, distinguishes this species from all other African ducks. Ducks and males out of colour are dark brown overall, with a paler stripe below each eye. The throat is also paler, and the bill is a much duller yellowish-black shade. Young birds are similar in colour to hens, but can be easily identified by the narrower shape and more spiky appearance of their tail feathers.

Cape shoveler (*Anas smithii*): 53cm (21in)
Distribution is restricted to southern Africa. The plumage of the drake is a much paler grey than that of the duck, and this coloration is especially apparent on the head and neck. Sky blue wing pattern with a white band behind, which is most apparent in flight. The iris in the drake is pale yellow, darker in ducks. Ducks and young birds are much browner overall, with a slightly lighter black bill. Legs and feet are orange-yellow, but brighter in drakes.

Hottentot teal (*Anas hottentota*): 35cm (14in)
Distribution extends from central-eastern parts of Africa southwards, and is also present on Madagascar. Black area on top of the head, encompassing the eyes, with a white area beneath, broadening out over the hind neck. Creamy cheek patches. Black speckling across the chest and down the sides of the body. The sides of the lower neck and the wings are predominantly blackish. The bill is bluish, and the brighter green wing speculum of the male is very evident in flight.

Canada goose

Branta canadensis

There are a number of different races of Canada goose which all vary in plumage and size. This species has proved to be highly adaptable. Its numbers have grown considerably in Europe, especially in farming areas, where the geese descend in flocks to feed on crops during the winter once other food has become more scarce. When migrating, flocks fly in a clear V-shaped formation. In common with many waterfowl, Canada geese are not able to fly when moulting, but they will readily take to the water at this time and can dive if necessary to escape danger. These geese prefer to graze on land, returning to the relative safety of the water during the hours of darkness.

Identification: Distinctive black head and neck. A small area of white plumage runs in a stripe from behind the eyes to under the throat. A whitish area of feathering at the base of the neck merges into brown on the chest. The wings are dark brown and there is white on the abdomen. The legs and feet are blackish. Sexes are alike.

Distribution: Present in the British Isles and southern Scandinavia, and other parts of north-western Europe. Also throughout the far north of North America, wintering in the southern USA.
Size: 55–110cm (22–43in).
Habitat: Very variable, but usually near water.
Nest: Made from vegetation, on the ground.
Eggs: 4–7, whitish.
Food: Vegetarian.

SWANS AND GEESE

Many of these large, unmistakable birds regularly fly long distances to and from their breeding grounds. They also rank among the longest-lived of all waterfowl, with a possible life expectancy of 20 years or more. Young birds are unlikely to breed until they are three or four years old. Both geese and swans can be aggressive, so caution is advised when observing them.

Snow goose

Anser caerulescens

Although considered a vagrant rather than a regular visitor to north-western parts of Europe, snow geese are a relatively common sight in some areas during the winter months. They are especially attracted to farmland, where grazing opportunities are plentiful, and this appears to be helping the birds to extend their range. As with all waterfowl, however, there is always the possibility that sightings of snow geese are in fact escapees from waterfowl collections rather than wild individuals. The calls of snow geese have been likened to the barking of a dog.

Above: Blue snow geese are much less common than their white counterparts.

Identification: Blue-phase birds (above) are dark and blackish, with white heads and white borders to some wing feathers. Young birds of this colour phase have dark heads. White-phase birds (left) are almost entirely white, with dark primary wing feathers. Young of this colour phase have greyish markings on their heads. Sexes are alike.

Distribution: The far north of North America, Greenland and north-eastern Siberia. Frequently overwinters in Great Britain and nearby coastal areas of north-western Europe.
Size: 84cm (33in).
Habitat: Tundra and coastal lowland agricultural areas.
Nest: Depression on the ground lined with vegetation.
Eggs: 4–10, whitish.
Food: Vegetarian.

Mute swan

Cygnus olor

These graceful birds can be seen in a wide range of habitats and may occasionally even venture out on to the sea, although they will not stray very far from the shore. They prefer to feed on aquatic vegetation, but can sometimes be found grazing on short grass. In town and city parks mute swans often eat a greater variety of foods, such as grain and bread provided for them by people. They rarely dive, but instead use their long necks to dabble under the surface of the water to obtain food. Pairs are very territorial when breeding and the male swan, known as a cob, will actively try to drive away people with fierce movements of its wings if they venture too close.

Identification: Mainly white, with a black area extending from the eyes to the base of the orange bill. A swollen knob protrudes over the upper part of the bill. The legs and feet are blackish. Hens are smaller with a less pronounced knob on the bill. Traces of staining are often evident on the head and neck. Young birds are browner.

Distribution: Resident throughout the British Isles and adjacent areas of western Europe, often living in a semi-domesticated state. Also occurs in the north-west Black Sea area and in parts of Asia. Localized introduced populations also found in other areas including South Africa, the eastern USA, Australia and New Zealand.
Size: 160cm (63in).
Habitat: Larger stretches of fresh water and estuaries.
Nest: Large pile of heaped-up aquatic vegetation.
Eggs: 5–7, pale green.
Food: Mainly vegetation.

Whooper swan

Cygnus cygnus

Although some Icelandic whooper swans are sedentary throughout the year, the majority of these birds undertake regular migrations, so they are likely to be observed in southern Europe only during the winter months. At this time they often frequent areas around inland waterways, such as the Black and Caspian seas. Pairs nest on their own, and the young chicks fly alongside their parents on the journey south. In the winter, whooper swans may sometimes invade agricultural areas, where they eat a range of foods varying from potatoes to acorns, although generally they prefer to feed on aquatic vegetation.

Identification: Body plumage is white, although sometimes it may be stained. The base of the bill is yellow, extending as far as the nostrils, and the tip is black. Legs and feet are grey. Hens are a little smaller, while young birds have pinkish rather than yellow bases to their bills.

Above left: These swans fly in a V-shaped formation when migrating. Huge numbers may congregate together at their wintering grounds.

Distribution: Iceland and north-western parts of Europe. Northern Scandinavia eastwards to Siberia. Overwinters further south.
Size: 165cm (65in).
Habitat: Wooded ponds and lakes. Winters near the coast.
Nest: Mounds of plant matter, often moss.
Eggs: 3–7, pale green.
Food: Vegetation.

Pink-footed goose (*Anser brachyrhynchus*): 75cm (29½in)
Found in eastern Greenland, Iceland and Spitzbergen. Overwinters in northern Britain and Denmark southwards. Has a brown head with white streaking on the neck, and more prominent markings on the wings and underparts. Bill is pinkish but dark at its base. Legs and feet are pinkish. Sexes are alike.

African pygmy goose (*Nettapus auritus*): 33cm (13in)
Most of Africa, south of the Sahara, except for the south-west. Present on Madagascar. Face and throat are white in the male, with an extensive green patch on the back of the head, edged with black. Central area of the underparts is white, with chestnut on the remainder, except for dark feathering around the vent and on the undertail coverts. Bill bright yellow with a dark tip. Legs and feet black. Hens and young birds lack the prominent green neck patch, having a mottled whitish head and a much duller bill.

Blue-winged goose (*Cyanochen cyanoptera*): 75cm (29in)
Restricted to the highland region of Ethiopia, where these geese are found near to lakes and rivers at altitudes above 1800m (6000ft). Grey coloration overall; browner on the underparts, with a white area surrounding the vent. White edging is apparent on the down covering the flanks. Distinctive light blue upperwing coverts, which are evident in flight when the wings are open. Young birds are similar to adults, but lack the glossy sheen on the flight feathers.

Bewick's swan

Tundra swan *Cygnus bewickii*

Bewick's swan is sometimes regarded as a separate species from the tundra swan (*C. columbianus*), which occurs at similar latitudes in North America. They differ most noticeably on the bill, since Bewick's has more yellow coloration, but share identical lifestyles. Both breed in the Arctic during the brief summer, taking advantage of the pools of water that form above the permafrost. Breeding starts in May, with the life-long pairs heaping up vegetation to form their bulky nests. The eggs hatch after about a month, and the young cygnets are able to fly when six weeks old. They travel with their parents on the southward migration during September, but it may be four years before they are ready to nest themselves. If they can avoid the hunters, Bewick's swans may live for over 20 years.

Distribution: Breeding grounds extend along the north Russian coast to Siberia. Overwinters in southern British Isles and parts of north-western Europe, and also in Asia south of the Caspian Sea across to Japan.
Size: 127cm (50in).
Habitat: Pools, marshland.
Nest: A heaped-up pile of aquatic vegetation.
Eggs: 3–5, pale greenish.
Food: Mainly vegetation.

Identification: White overall with a restricted area of yellow on the bill that does not extend as far as the nostrils. Cobs (male swans) are larger than females (known as pens). Young birds are greyish with a pinkish bill.

KINGFISHERS AND WETLAND OWLS

Although renowned for catching fish, a number of kingfisher species do not actually venture near standing water on a regular basis, preferring instead forests or more open areas of country and feeding on invertebrates. Conversely, owls as a group are better-known for hunting rodents, but in Africa several species have adapted to catching fish with their talons.

Kingfisher

Common kingfisher *Alcedo atthis*

These birds are surprisingly difficult to spot, as they perch motionlessly while scanning the water beneath them for fish. Once its prey has been identified, the kingfisher dives down in a flash of colour. A protective membrane covers its eyes as it enters the water. Its wings provide propulsion, and having seized the fish in its bill the bird darts out of the water and back onto its perch with its catch. The whole sequence happens incredibly fast, taking just a few seconds. The kingfisher then stuns the fish by hitting it against the perch, before swallowing it head first. It regurgitates the bones and indigestible parts of its meal later.

Left: Kingfishers dive at speed into the water, aiming to catch their intended quarry unawares.

Identification: Bluish-green extending over the head and wings. The back is pale blue, and a blue flash is also present on the cheeks. The throat area is white, and there are white areas below the orange cheek patches. The underparts are also orange, and the bill is black. In hens, the bill is reddish at the base of the lower bill.

Distribution: Occurs across most of Europe, but absent from much of Scandinavia. Also present in northern Africa, ranging eastwards through the Arabian peninsula and South-East Asia as far as the Solomon Islands.
Size: 18cm (7in).
Habitat: Slow-flowing water.
Nest: Tunnel excavated in a sandy bank.
Eggs: 6–10, white.
Food: Small fish. Also preys on aquatic insects, molluscs and crustaceans.

Giant kingfisher

Megaceryle maximus

These large kingfishers are shy by nature, and are not often seen in the open. They perch quietly, often as high as 4m (13ft) above the water, looking for potential quarry beneath them. They may even occasionally fish out over the sea. Their diet varies through their range, with crabs proving more significant than fish in some parts of South Africa. The breeding season is also variable. A tunnel is excavated in a suitable bank, which can be some distance from water, although mostly it is located in a riverbank, and constructed high enough to avoid any risk of flooding. The tunnel is usually around 2m (6½ft) long, but can sometimes be up to 8.5m (28ft). The young emerge when about five weeks old and are able to dive soon afterwards, although they will not be fully independent for at least a further three weeks.

Distribution: Present across much of Africa south of the Sahara, except for the south-west of the continent. Also absent from the Horn of Africa and a large part of adjacent eastern Africa.
Size: 43cm (17in).
Habitat: Wooded waterways, rivers and estuaries.
Nest: Long tunnel excavated in a suitable bank.
Eggs: 2–3, white.
Food: Mainly fish and crabs.

Identification: Black head with some white markings, notably below the large black bill. Speckled black-and-white patterning on the wings, back and tail. Rufous chest, with white lower underparts. Shaggy crest on the back of the head. Young cocks have black-and-white speckled chest, with rufous areas on the flanks, while females have a white chest. In the adult female, the chest is streaked and the underparts are rufous.

Pel's fishing owl

Scotopelia peli

Like many owls, this species is not easy to observe since it is largely nocturnal. Perching directly above the water, and recognizing the presence of fish below by the ripples they create at the surface, the owl glides down as quietly as possible and scoops up its quarry with its sharp talons. Such is their overall strength that Pel's fishing owls can lift fish weighing as much as 2kg (4.4lb). Only rarely do they enter the water directly, such as when seeking relatively immobile prey like mussels, or seizing crabs in the shallows. These owls favour old forests because they provide plenty of large tree hollows, which make suitable nesting sites. Egg-laying is closely co-ordinated with the seasons, so that when the eggs hatch after about 32 days the water level is falling back. The young owls thus hatch during the dry season, and the declining water level makes it easier for their parents to hunt for food.

Identification: Considerable variation exists in the markings of these owls. Reddish-brown overall, with paler, buff-coloured underparts displaying darker, tear-like droplets. These contrast with the barring evident elsewhere on the body. Bill is blackish. Young birds are paler overall. Sexes are alike. Females have a higher-pitched call.

Distribution: Has a variable distribution in Africa, mostly in western-central and south-eastern regions, but also in other parts where suitable habitat exists.
Size: 60cm (24in).
Habitat: Swamps and old riverine forests
Nest: Tree hollow.
Eggs: 1–2, white.
Food: Fish, crabs, amphibians and invertebrates.

São Tomé Kingfisher (*Alcedo thomensis*): 14cm (5½in)
Restricted to the island of São Tomé, in the Gulf of Guinea, off Africa's west coast. Blue plumage extends over the top of the head and down over the neck, with rows of black feathers across the crown. A series of vertical black stripes are present at the base of the bill, on the orange-fawn plumage there. Throat area white, as is the nape of the neck, and the remainder of the underparts are orange-fawn. Wings and short tail are blue. Sexes are alike. Young birds are much duller, with prominent blue streaking on the chest and a black rather than a reddish bill.

Pied kingfisher (*Ceryle rudis*): 25cm (10in)
Widely distributed across much of Africa south of the Sahara. Prominent black area on the sides of the head and also extending partially across the chest, while the remainder of the underparts are white. Males can be distinguished by the additional presence of a narrower black band across the lower chest. Back and wings are mottled black and white, while the underside of the wings are pure white.

Shining blue kingfisher (*Alcedo quadribrachys*): 16cm (6in)
Restricted to western and central parts of Africa. Brilliant cobalt blue, with a white area on the neck and under the throat. The remainder of the underparts are rufous, apart from a small blue area at the top of the wings. Bill is black, legs and feet red. Young birds display light barring on the chest. Sexes are alike.

Marsh owl

Asio capensis

These owls are unusual since they rest on the ground during the daytime, rather than perch in a tree. This probably reflects their countryside habitat, where few trees are available. Even when hunting, marsh owls swoop low over the ground in search of likely prey. They are opportunistic feeders, prepared to eat whatever is available, and have been observed catching insects attracted by street lamps at night. The nest site is chosen carefully and is screened by vegetation on all sides, while the hen conceals her presence even further by propping up a layer of overhead vegetation from below. She sits alone, and is fed by her mate during this period. The young hatch after about four weeks, and may sometimes leave the nest within 10 days. They are found and fed individually by their parents, who track them by their calls. The young owls will be able to start flying when they are five weeks old.

Distribution: Main African distribution is in the eastern-central region southwards, but several other isolated populations occur, notably in the north-west, west, south-west and on Madagascar.
Size: 38cm (15in).
Habitat: Open country, including marshland.
Nest: Made from vegetation, on the ground.
Eggs: 2–6, white.
Food: Invertebrates and vertebrates.

Identification: Buff face with black edging to the facial disc and eyes. Dark, rufous-brown body, paler underparts broken by barring. Bill and feet greyish. Young greyish. Sexes are alike. Regional variation.

WETLAND HUNTERS

A number of large birds of prey hunt fish and small vertebrates in wetland areas, but being at the top of the food chain has resulted in some populations suffering a build-up of pollutants in their bodies, which have been passed on from their prey. However, most birds of prey are opportunistic hunters rather than specialists, and this has aided their survival.

Eurasian marsh harrier

Western marsh-harrier *Circus aeruginosus*

The Eurasian marsh harrier is a truly opportunistic hunter. It raids the nests of other birds, as well as catching the birds themselves, and also hunts mammals such as rabbits by swooping down on them in the open. It has a varied diet, partly dependent on its range, that may change throughout the year. This adaptability is reflected by the terrain in which the harriers are to be found. Although they favour wetland areas they are not an uncommon sight over farmland, especially when migrating, while the resident northern African race even ventures into quite arid areas of woodland.

Identification: Plumage varies according to race. Head is brownish with white streaks. Darker streaking on a buff chest. The abdomen is entirely brown. Wings are brown with rufous edging to the feathers, and white and grey areas are also apparent. Tail is pale greyish. Hens are larger, with a yellowish-cream suffusion on the head, throat and shoulders. Young birds resemble hens but have darker shoulder markings.

Distribution: Occurs across Africa in a band south of the Sahara, but does not reach the Horn, with a population also in the north-west. Present throughout much of Europe from southern Scandinavia, and eastwards through much of Asia.
Size: 48–56cm (19–22in).
Habitat: Marshland and nearby open country.
Nest: Pile of reeds in a secluded reedbed.
Eggs: 2–7, pale bluish-white.
Food: Birds, small mammals.

Osprey

Pandion haliaetus

The distribution of the osprey extends to all inhabited continents, making it one of the most wide-ranging of all birds. It has adapted to feeding on stretches of fresh water as well as on estuaries and even the open sea, swooping down to grab fish from just below the water's surface using its powerful talons. Ospreys are capable of carrying fish weighing up to 300g (11oz) without difficulty. In many areas, especially in Europe, ospreys are migratory, and the birds will head south to Africa for the duration of the northern winter. Populations occurring in Scotland and Scandinavia will fly south of the Sahara, rather than joining the resident osprey population in north Africa.

Distribution: Found right around the globe. European ospreys range from the British Isles to the Iberian Peninsula and other areas, and from parts of Scandinavia eastwards into Asia. Widely distributed throughout Africa south of the Sahara during the winter.
Size: 58cm (23in).
Habitat: Close to stretches of water.
Nest: Platform of sticks built in a tree.
Eggs: 3, white in colour with darker markings.
Food: Fish.

Identification: Brown stripes running through the eyes and down over the back and wings. The eyes are yellow. Top of the head and underparts are white. Brown striations across the breast, most marked in hens. Tall, upright stance, powerful grey legs and talons. Hens are significantly heavier than cocks.

African fish eagle

Haliaeetus vocifer

These large eagles are fearsome predators. Although fish feature most prominently in their diet they take a wide range of aquatic life, even killing birds up to the size of a flamingo. They also feed on bullfrogs, young crocodiles and monitor lizards (*Varanus* species), and monkeys caught in or near the water. They only rarely feed on carrion, usually when migrating across dry country or in the case of young birds who have not fully mastered the necessary hunting skills. African fish eagles can fly with prey weighing up to 1¹/₂kg (3.3lb), but will tackle heavier creatures, which they drag up on to the shore. Noisy and conspicuous, these eagles are not easily overlooked, particularly when they swoop down over the water with talons outstretched, hoping for a catch. On average, they are successful only once in every eight attempts.

Identification: White extends from head to neck and on to the breast. Tail feathers also white, with the remainder of the underparts brown. The wings are black, with prominent brown shoulder patches. Prominent area of yellow at the base of the bill, which is black at the tip. Young birds have dark brownish markings on the crown, and similar streaking on the white of the back and chest. Cock birds have a higher-pitched call than females and may also display more prominent white on the breast.

Distribution: Occurs south of the Sahara, except in the east towards the Horn and throughout much of south-west and central Africa.
Size: 73cm (29in).
Habitat: Prefers stretches of open water.
Nest: Constructed from sticks and reeds.
Eggs: 2–3, whitish.
Food: Fish and any other aquatic creatures.

Western banded snake eagle (Smaller banded snake eagle, *Circaetus cinerascens*): 60cm (24in)
Occurs across much of Africa, especially in western and central parts, not overlapping with the southern species (see below). Darker and heavier, with a greyish chest and abdomen. Broad white band across the tail. Young birds are dark brown, with streaking on the head down to the breast and the tail band becoming grey. Hens may display more prominent barring on the lower underparts, and are a darker shade of brown overall.

Southern banded snake eagle (East African snake eagle, *Circaetus fasciolatus*): 60cm (24in)
South-eastern areas of Africa, typically close to water in wooded countryside. Greyish head and breast, with barring extending across the remaining underparts and the undersides of the wings. Barred tail, darker on the upper surface. Back and wings dark brownish with some paler edging. Young birds have dark brown upperparts, with paler underwing patterning. Sexes are alike.

African marsh harrier (*Circus ranivorus*): 50cm (20in)
Restricted largely to central-eastern parts of the continent. Similar to the Eurasian marsh harrier, which overlaps in some parts of its range, but distinguishable by the barring extending across both the flight feathers and the tail, which is clearly apparent when viewed from below. Head is also darker, and there is more white speckling across the wings. Young birds have a white band across the lower breast. Sexes are alike.

White-tailed fish eagle

White-tailed sea eagle *Haliaeetus albicilla*

The white-tailed fish eagle is reviving once again after human persecution and pollution contracted its range significantly in the 20th century. Successful reintroductions have now established 15 pairs in Scotland, where it formerly occurred. They are highly effective predators, with both members of a pair hunting co-operatively to achieve a kill, although carrion also features prominently in their diet. These sea eagles will harry other predatory species, including otters and even other birds of prey such as ospreys, into giving up their catches.

Identification: Brown, lighter and creamier on the head and upper body. Darker wings and rump; tail is white. Pale yellow bill, legs and feet. Young are darker, with white on the tail confined to the centre and a blackish bill.

Distribution: From Iceland east to northern Scandinavia and across Russia. Various other countries, particularly in eastern Europe.
Size: 92cm (36in).
Habitat: Large stretches of water, often coastal.
Nest: Bulky, made of sticks.
Eggs: 1–3, whitish.
Food: Vertebrates and carrion.

INSECT HUNTERS

While trees provide birds with fruits, berries and seeds, they also attract a wide range of invertebrates. Different species have developed different hunting techniques in order to locate and catch these insects. Many simply comb the trees, but others use the branches as vantage points, from where they can swoop down directly and seize their prey in flight.

Common scimitarbill

Scimitar-billed woodhoopoe *Rhinopomastus cyanomelas*

Distribution: Ranges from Kenya and parts of Somalia southwards in a broad band across much of southern Africa, reaching central parts of South Africa and extending as far as Namibia in the south-west.
Size: 25cm (10in).
Habitat: Dry woodland areas.
Nest: Tree holes.
Eggs: 3–4, blue.
Food: Mainly invertebrates.

Restricted to Africa, scimitarbills were formerly grouped with woodhoopoes but are now usually regarded as a separate entity. This is based partly on their habits, since they occur in individual pairs rather than in flocks, although they can sometimes be encountered in family parties once the breeding season has ended. They probe into nooks and crannies with their curved bills, extracting grubs and insects lurking in the bark of trees. Common scimitarbills will also occasionally descend to the ground in their search for invertebrate prey, and here they will often raid ants' nests, using their bills to break into the nest. Their breeding period starts towards the end of the dry season, with the hen locating a suitable cavity in a tree, which may have been created by another bird such as a barbet. The chicks hatch after an incubation period of around 16 days. The male continues to roost on his own, but both members of the pair will feed their growing brood.

Identification: Cock bird is dark in colour, with white bands across the outer edges of the open wings and white tips to the undersides of the shorter tail feathers. Glossy purple suffusion over much of the body, with greenish hues apparent also, especially on the sides of the head. Distinctive, narrow, curved black bill is longer in the male. Young birds and hens have brownish coloration on the head.

Bar-throated apalis

Apalis thoracica

These warblers vary in coloration through their range, although the basic patterning of their feathers remains constant. More than 20 different races are recognized in eastern-southern Africa, with upperparts ranging from greyish-brown to green and underparts ranging from white to greenish-yellow. A number of these subspecies are very localized, such as *A. t. spelonkensis*, which occurs in the northern Transvaal. Originating from the Soutpansberg and Woodbush region, this most colourful race of bar-throated apalis has green upperparts contrasting with extensive yellow plumage on the underparts. Their breeding season also varies depending on location, and usually extends over a longer period in more northerly parts of their range. Once paired, the adults generally stay together throughout the year. Bar-throated apalis often hunt insects in the company of other small birds, either catching them among the vegetation or on the wing, but they rarely feed at ground level.

Identification: Upperparts dark greyish-brown. Greyish-white throat and underparts, broken by a prominent black band across the chest. Greenish-yellow flanks. Black bill, dark pinkish legs. White outer tail feathers. Young birds resemble adults but underparts often more buff. Hen less brightly coloured, often with a narrower breast band.

Distribution: Present in parts of eastern to southern Africa, extending from Kenya southwards through Tanzania, Zambia, Malawi and Zimbabwe right down to South Africa. Absent from coastal areas except in South Africa.
Size: 12cm (4³⁄₄in).
Habitat: Forest and thickets.
Nest: An oval dome made from vegetation.
Eggs: 2–4, bluish-white with reddish markings.
Food: Invertebrates.

Eurasian treecreeper

Brown creeper *Certhia familiaris*

These treecreepers can be distinguished from the southerly short-toed species (*C. brachydactyla*) by their longer hind toes, which assist them in climbing vertically up tree trunks. Having reached the top of the trunk, the treecreeper flies down to the base of a neighbouring tree and begins again, circling the bark, probing likely nooks and crannies with its bill. The pointed tips of the tail feathers provide extra support. Pairs start nesting in the spring, with the cock bird chasing after his intended mate. They seek out a small, hidden cavity where a cup-shaped nest can be constructed. The hen incubates mainly on her own for two weeks, and the young fledge after a similar interval. It is not uncommon, especially in southern parts of their range, for pairs to breed twice in succession.

Left: Small crevices in a trunk may be used as a nesting site.

Identification: Mottled brownish upperparts, with a variable white stripe above the eyes, depending on race. Underparts whitish. Narrow, slightly curved bill. Young birds similar to adults. Sexes are alike.

Distribution: Much of northern Europe, except for the far north of Scandinavia. Sporadic distribution through France and northern Spain, not occurring further south on the Iberian peninsula. Not present in northern Africa, but extends into Asia.
Size: 14cm (5½in).
Habitat: Dense woodland.
Nest: Small hollow.
Eggs: 5–7, white with reddish-brown markings.
Food: Assorted invertebrates.

Violet woodhoopoe (*Phoeniculus damarensis*): 40cm (15¾in)
Restricted to south-western Angola and north-western Namibia. Metallic violet coloration overall, with white areas on the wings and on the underside of the shorter tail feathers. Long, slightly down-curving red bill, tapering along its length. Pinkish legs and feet. The hen is distinguishable by its shorter, duller and less curved bill. Young birds have dark bills and either brown throat patches (males) or black throat patches (females).

Green woodhoopoe (*Phoeniculus purpureus*): 36cm (14in)
Ranges widely in a band across Africa south of the Sahara, extending down the eastern side and across southern parts of the continent. Dark greenish head and underparts, with bright blue on the wings and tail. White patches apparent on the open wings, and close to the tips of the shorter tail feathers. Bill strongly down-curved and bright red in the cock, shorter and less curved in the hen. Young birds recognizable by their black bills in their first year.

Chapin's apalis (chestnut-headed apalis, *Apalis chapini*): 12cm (4¾in)
Restricted to eastern Africa, occurring in the forests of southern Tanzania and extending to Malawi and Zambia. Distinctive chestnut-red plumage runs from the base of the bill just above the eyes, down across the breast to the centre of the abdomen. The lower underparts are light grey. Chin is white in the northern race. Upperparts are dark brownish-grey. Young birds resemble adults. Sexes are alike.

Tree pipit

Anthus trivialis

Tree pipits sing with increasing frequency at the start of the breeding period. Their nest is constructed close to the ground in open countryside, well-hidden from predators. This need for camouflage may explain the variable coloration of their eggs. These long-distance migrants overwinter in Africa, reaching southern parts towards the end of October. Tree pipits feed on the ground, moving jauntily and pausing to flick their tails up and down, flying to the safety of a nearby branch at any hint of danger. As well as invertebrates they may also eat seeds. Solitary and quiet, these pipits are not easily observed away from their breeding grounds. They begin returning to Europe in April.

Distribution: Occurs widely through much of Europe up into Scandinavia and eastwards into Asia. Overwinters across Africa south of the Sahara, continuing down the eastern side of the continent, with isolated populations in Namibia and South Africa.
Size: 15cm (6in).
Habitat: Woodland.
Nest: Made of grass.
Eggs: 4–6, greyish with variable markings.
Food: Mainly invertebrates.

Identification: Brownish upperparts with dark streaking. White edging to the wing feathers. Buff stripe above each eye, darker brown stripes through and below them. Throat whitish. Underparts pale yellowish with brownish streaking. Bill dark, especially at the tip. Legs and feet pinkish. Young birds are more buff overall. Sexes are alike.

FOREST FINCHES

Many seed-eating birds are to be found in open country, but a number prefer to live in woodland, at least for part of the year in temperate areas. Here the trees offer a reliable source of food, especially during the winter, when fruit and berries are in short supply. Some species, such as the crossbills, have evolved very distinctive bills to enable them to extract their seeds more easily.

Forest weaver

Ploceus bicolor

Unlike many weavers, this species is quite solitary, usually encountered in individual pairs rather than in flocks. Studies of their song pattern have revealed not only regional differences but that members of a pair learn to attune their song patterns exactly, so that they sound identical. Their subsequent duetting is believed to help reinforce the bond between them, and may also enable the birds to keep in touch with each other in the dense woodland. Forest weavers construct a fairly typical weaver nest suspended off a branch, with both members of the pair collecting material, although it is thought the cock bird alone is responsible for building the structure. Another point of distinction is that male forest weavers do not moult into breeding plumage at the onset of the nesting season.

Identification: Chocolate-brown head, back, wings and tail. The throat is brownish with yellow markings, and the underparts are a rich shade of golden-yellow. Bill is brownish, especially on the upper bill, and pinkish-brown below. Legs also pinkish-brown. Young birds have paler throats. Sexes are alike.

Distribution: From northern Angola across Africa to Tanzania and Mozambique. Extends down the eastern coast to South Africa, and as far as Somalia in the north. Isolated populations also in Cameroon, Gabon and islands in the Gulf of Guinea.
Size: 16cm (6¹⁄₄in).
Habitat: Forest areas, often near streams.
Nest: Suspended, made out of vegetation.
Eggs: 2–4, pinkish-white with brownish markings.
Food: Invertebrates, nectar.

Red-faced crimson-wing

Cryptospiza reichenovii

These colourful forest waxbills are shy by nature, and their small size makes them difficult to observe in the dense undergrowth. They fly relatively short distances, rarely emerging out into the open, although occasionally small groups may be spotted in fields of ripening millet. Red-faced crimson-wings often associate with other finches in mixed flocks, feeding mainly on the ground. The seeds of pine cones are a significant source of food in Zimbabwe. Little is known about their breeding habits, but it is thought that invertebrates feature more prominently in their diet when they are rearing young. The nest is a large and untidy structure, with the birds going back and forth through a side entrance. Young cock birds soon develop the characteristic red facial feathering after fledging. Pairs appear to favour the same tree for nesting, and there are often nests from previous years alongside the current one.

Identification: Cock bird easily distinguishable by the presence of prominent red patches around the eyes. The body plumage is mainly olive, slightly lighter at the base of the bill. Back and rump are reddish, with red areas also on the lower flanks. Flight and tail feathers are black. Hens are similar, but with yellowish-buff patches surrounding the eyes. Young birds are a dull shade of olive-brown, with no distinctive facial patches, and a brownish-green shade on the wings. Bill is black, legs and feet grey.

Distribution: Separate areas of distribution occurring in Uganda, Kenya and Tanzania, Mozambique and Zimbabwe, Angola, and south-western Nigeria and neighbouring islands in the Gulf of Guinea.
Size: 12cm (4³⁄₄in).
Habitat: Dense forest.
Nest: Ball of vegetation.
Eggs: 3–5, white.
Food: Mainly seeds.

Common crossbill

Loxia curvirostra

The crossbill's highly distinctive bill can crack the hard casing of conifer seeds, enabling the bird to extract the inner kernel with its tongue. These finches also eat the pips of various fruits, and will prey on invertebrates, particularly when they have young to feed. The breeding season varies through their wide range, starting later in the north. Both members of the pair build the nest, which is constructed in a conifer, sometimes more than 18m (60ft) high. Common crossbills only rarely descend to the ground, usually to drink, unless the pine crop is very poor. When faced with a shortage of food, they move to areas far outside their normal range. This phenomenon, known as an irruption, occurs once a decade in Europe.

Identification: Males are reddish with darker blackish feathering on the top of the head, more evident on the wings. Underparts reddish, paler towards the vent. Upper and lower parts of the distinctive blackish bill are curved at the tip. Hens are olive-green, darker over the back and wings, and have a paler rump. Young birds resemble hens, but have evident streaking on their bodies.

Distribution: Resident throughout much of Scandinavia and northern Europe, extending into Asia. Found elsewhere in Europe, usually in areas of coniferous forest, extending as far as northern Africa.
Size: 15cm (6in).
Habitat: Coniferous forests.
Nest: Cup-shaped, made from vegetation.
Eggs: 3–4, whitish-blue with reddish-brown markings.
Food: Mainly the seeds of pine cones.

Scottish crossbill (*Loxia scotica*): 17cm (6³/₄in)
Restricted to the pine forests of the Caledonian region of northern Scotland. Similar to the male common crossbill (*Loxia curvirostra*) but with a larger head. The bill is also bulkier and the lower bill is not so pronounced. Hens and juveniles also resemble this species, except for the differences in their bills.

Dusky crimson-wing (*Cryptospiza jacksoni*): 12cm (4³/₄in)
Restricted to a small area of eastern Dem. Rep. Congo, extending to Rwanda and south-western Uganda. Cock has a predominantly red head, with a grey collar extending up the hindneck. Back and rump are also red, and there are some red markings on the flanks. Remainder of the body is dark grey. Wings, tail and bill blackish. Legs and feet greyish. Hens are similar, but the red on the head is restricted to the area surrounding the eyes. Young birds display no red on their head or flanks, and the red on their back is reduced in extent.

Black-bellied seedcracker (*Pyrenestes ostrinus*): 15cm (6in)
Central Africa, ranging from the Ivory Coast east to Uganda and south to northern parts of Angola and Zambia. Red head and chest, extending to the flanks. Rump and tail are also red, and the remainder of the body is black. Stocky greyish-black bill. Legs and feet pinkish. Hens have red restricted to the head and upper breast, as well as from the rump to the tail. Remainder of the body is olive-brown. Young birds are duller, with red only on the rump and tail.

Brambling

Fringilla montifringilla

After breeding in northern parts of Europe, the harsh winter weather forces bramblings to migrate to more southerly latitudes in search of food. Here they can be seen in fields and other open areas of countryside. These finches feed largely on beech nuts, relying heavily on the forests of central Europe to sustain them over the winter period. Although normally occurring in small flocks, millions of individuals may occasionally congregate in the forests. Bramblings have a rather jerky walk when on the ground, sometimes hopping as well when searching for food. Their diet is much more varied during the summer months, when they are nesting. Caterpillars of moths in particular are eagerly devoured at this time and used as a rearing food for their young. Bramblings have a relatively rapid breeding cycle. The hen incubates the eggs on her own, and they will hatch after about a fortnight. The young birds leave the nest after a similar interval.

Distribution: Breeds in the far north of Europe, through most of Scandinavia into Russia, extending eastwards into Asia. Overwinters further south throughout Europe, extending to parts of north-western Africa.
Size: 18cm (7in).
Habitat: Woodland.
Nest: Cup-shaped, made from vegetation.
Eggs: 5–7, a dark greenish-blue colour.
Food: Seeds and nuts.

Identification: Black head and bill. Orange underparts, white rump and white wing bars. Underparts whitish, blackish markings on the orange flanks. Duller in winter, with pale head markings and yellowish bill. Hens like winter males, but have greyer sides to the face and duller scapulars. Young birds like hens but are brown, with a yellowish rump.

WOODLAND-DEPENDENT FINCHES

Many finches associated with woodland in northern latitudes have a wide area of distribution, extending not just into Asia but also sometimes to North America. Conversely, there are other species that have very localized distributions. What links them all is that they are dependent on woodland, with large-scale deforestation posing a severe threat to their survival, locally and globally.

Blue chaffinch

Fringilla teydea

The blue chaffinch is found almost exclusively in the Canarian pine (*Pinus canariensis*) forests of Tenerife and Gran Canaria. The shape of their bills allow these finches to easily crack conifer seeds, but they also hunt invertebrates, seeking beetles and caterpillars as well as butterflies, which are caught in flight. Their breeding period begins in May, with pairs usually only rearing one brood per year. The young remain with the adults after fledging, forming family parties through the autumn. Flocks may sometimes be seen at lower altitudes during the winter, if the weather is especially severe. Inter-island movements appear unlikely, although there is a reliable record of one blue chaffinch being sighted in north-western Lanzarote. On Tenerife, large areas of the pine forest were replanted during the 1950s, and since the chaffinches are legally protected their future seems reasonably assured there, although the population on Gran Canaria appears to be less secure.

Distribution: Restricted to the western Canary Islands, off north-west Africa.
Size: 17cm (6¹/₂in).
Habitat: Pine forests.
Nest: Cup-shaped, made from vegetation.
Eggs: 4–5, bluish-brown with darker markings.
Food: Mainly pine seeds, some invertebrates.

Identification: Cock bird is slaty-blue, slightly darker over the head and wings. Pale bluish-white wingbars and white undertail coverts, with a bluish-grey bill. Hens are brown with pale buff wingbars, greyish underparts and a brownish bill. Young birds resemble adult hens but are a darker shade of brown.

Forest canary

Serinus scotops

Distribution: Restricted to South Africa, occurring from eastern Transvaal to Natal and into Cape Province.
Size: 13cm (5in).
Habitat: Upland forest.
Nest: Cup-shaped, made from vegetation.
Eggs: 3–4, whitish-blue with reddish speckling.
Food: Mainly seeds, but also some fruit.

The relatively dark, streaked plumage of these canaries helps them to blend in with their woodland habitat. Other, similar species are to be found further north in Africa, extending as far as Ethiopia. The song of cock birds, uttered largely just before and during the breeding season, is quite musical, but does not compare to that of domesticated canaries – it is not as loud, although sufficiently distinctive to draw attention to their presence. Forest canaries are not especially social by nature. Cocks are quite territorial, and are most likely to be encountered in pairs or family groups rather than in flocks. The breeding season varies through their range, depending on location and other factors including rainfall. The nest is concealed in a tree or brush, and the hen lines the cup with insulating material such as feathers or wool. She sits alone, with incubation lasting approximately two weeks. The young birds fledge after a similar period.

Identification: Cock birds have a variable blackish area on the sides of the face, extending from the sides of the bill, with a yellow streak above the eyes. Yellow bib and small wingbars. The head, back and wings are otherwise greenish with dark streaking, becoming more yellow on the underparts and rump. Hens have greyish rather than black faces. Young birds are paler than adult hens, with more pinkish feet.

Hawfinch

Coccothraustes coccothraustes

With their characteristic stocky, powerful bills, hawfinches are able to crack open cherry stones and the hard kernels of similar fruits and feed on the seeds within. They usually feed off the ground, but may sometimes descend to pick up fallen fruits. In the spring they will also eat emerging buds, as well as feeding on invertebrates, with their bill strength enabling them to prey on even hard-bodied beetles without difficulty. Pairs are formed during the spring, with the cock bird harrying the female for a period beforehand. She will then start to build the nest, which can be located in the fork of a tree more than 22m (75ft) above the ground. The incubation period lasts approximately 12 days, and the young leave the nest after a similar interval. Hawfinches are most likely to be observed in small flocks over the winter period, with populations occurring in more northern areas usually moving southwards at this time.

Identification: Adult male in breeding condition has a black area around the bill and eyes, with a brown crown and grey around the neck. Whitish area on the wings and black flight feathers. Underparts are brownish. Bill is black, paler in non-breeding, as is the head. Hens have paler and greyer heads, and greyer secondary flight feathers. Young birds have distinct streaking on their underparts.

Distribution: Resident in most of Europe, although absent from Ireland. Breeds in the south of Scandinavia and further east into Asia, where these populations are only summer visitors. Some reported sightings on various Mediterranean islands and parts of northwestern Africa.
Size: 16$\frac{1}{2}$cm (6$\frac{1}{2}$in).
Habitat: Mixed woodland.
Nest: Cup-shaped, made of plant matter.
Eggs: 3–6, bluish-white to green, with dark markings.
Food: Seeds, invertebrates.

Warsangli linnet (*Carduelis johannis*): 13cm (5in)
Juniper forest and upland in northern Somalia. White area above the bill, forming a streak above the eyes, with white extending to the sides of the face and on to the breast and underparts. Head and back greyish. Wings are blackish with a white wing bar. Rufous-brown flanks extending to the rump. Bill silvery-grey, as are the legs and feet. Hens are similar but with streaking on the grey upperparts, especially on the back. Young are browner with more definite streaking, which extends to the underparts.

Grant's bluebill (*Spermophaga poliogenys*): 14cm (5$\frac{1}{2}$in)
North-central Dem. Rep. Congo east to western Uganda. Red head and breast, narrowing to the sides of the flanks, with the rump also red. Remainder of plumage is black. Bill red with bluish markings at its base. Legs and feet blackish. Hens have red restricted to the breast and rump, and the head, back and wings are greyish-black. Underparts spotted with white. Young birds have red restricted to the rump and are darker overall, with more blue on the bill.

Grey-headed negro-finch (*Nigrita canicapilla*): 15cm (6in)
Guinea east to Sudan, Kenya and Tanzania, and south to Dem. Rep. Congo and Angola. Grey on the rear of the head, extending over the back, and black on the face, underparts and across the wings. Narrow white line often apparent on the head, depending on race, with white spots on the wings. Yellow iris, black bill and greyish legs. Young are dark grey overall. Sexes are alike.

Pine grosbeak

Pinicola enucleator

These northern grosbeaks may sometimes be encountered further south, particularly in years when food is scarce. They were first recorded in France as recently as 1992, and have been observed in countries bordering the Mediterranean, including Spain and Italy. The pine grosbeak's song is quite loud, although they are not especially conspicuous birds, particularly when perched – their coloration actually helps them to merge into the shadows. Agile by nature, they feed by climbing around in branches or hopping along on the ground. Various invertebrates including mosquitoes feature in their diet during the summer, while seeds are more significant in the winter.

Distribution: The extreme north of Scandinavia and Russia, extending into Asia. Moves south in the winter, sometimes well away from their usual haunts. Also present in North America.
Size: 25cm (10in).
Habitat: Coniferous forest.
Nest: Bulky, cup-shaped, made from vegetation.
Eggs: 2–5, pale bluish-green.
Food: Seeds, fruit and invertebrates.

Identification: Cock is pinkish with grey on the face, wings and underparts, and white on the wings. Greyish-black bill. Hens are olive-green and grey, with a pale base to the bill. Young similar to hens but greyer, buff not white on their wings.

CUCKOOS AND SHRIKES

Predatory by nature, these two groups of birds also display unusual breeding behaviour. They typically rely on other birds, either of a different species or helpers of their own kind, to raise their chicks. However, although well-known for their parasitic habits, not all cuckoo species neglect their parental duties – some do raise their own offspring.

Cuckoo

Common cuckoo *Cuculus canorus*

The distinctive call of the cuckoo, heard when these birds return from their African wintering grounds, has traditionally been regarded in Europe as one of the earliest signs of spring. Typically, they are only resident in Europe between April and September. Adult cuckoos have an unusual ability to feed on hairy caterpillars, which are plentiful in woodlands throughout the summer. Common cuckoos are parasitic breeders – the hens lay single eggs in the nests of smaller birds such as hedge sparrows (*Prunella modularis*), meadow pipits (*Anthus pratensis*) and wagtails (*Motacilla* species). The unsuspecting hosts hatch a monster, with the cuckoo chick ejecting other eggs or potential rivals from the nest in order to monopolize the food supply.

Right: The young cuckoo lifts eggs on its back to eject them from the nest.

Identification: Grey head, upper chest, wings and tail, and black edging to the white feathers of the underparts. In hens this barring extends almost to the throat, offset against a more yellowish background. Some hens belong to a brown colour morph, with rufous feathering replacing the grey, and black barring apparent on the upperparts.

Distribution: Throughout the whole of Europe, ranging eastwards into Asia. Also present in northern Africa. Populations in Northern Europe overwinter in eastern and southern parts of Africa, while Asiatic birds migrate as far as the Philippines.
Size: 36cm (14in).
Habitat: Various.
Nest: None – lays directly in other birds' nests.
Eggs: 1 per nest, resembling those of its host.
Food: Mainly invertebrates, including caterpillars.

Great spotted cuckoo

Clamator glandarius

These lively cuckoos hunt for invertebrates in trees and on the ground, hopping along in a rather clumsy fashion. Great spotted cuckoos are bold birds by nature. When breeding, they parasitize the nests of magpies and similar corvids, and in Africa will sometimes lay in the nests of starlings. The hen usually removes any eggs already present in the host bird's nest before laying, but if any do remain and hatch, the nestlings are reared alongside the young cuckoo. Their relatively large size and noisy nature make these cuckoos quite conspicuous, particularly after the breeding period, when they form flocks.

Identification: Silvery-grey top to the head, with a slight crest. Darker grey neck, back and wings, with white spots over the wings. Pale yellow plumage under the throat extending to the upper breast. The remainder of the underparts are white. Sexes are alike, although their song notes are different. Young birds are much darker in colour – black rather than grey, with rusty-brown flight feathers.

Distribution: Southern Europe, from Spain to Turkey and into Asia as far as Iran. Migrates to Africa, mainly south of the Sahara.
Size: 39cm (15in).
Habitat: Prefers relatively open country.
Nest: None – lays directly in other birds' nests.
Eggs: 1 per nest, resembling those of its host.
Food: Invertebrates.

Black cuckoo (*Cuculus clamosus*): 30cm (12in)
Much of Africa south of the Sahara. Absent from
southern Dem. Rep. Congo, eastern Tanzania
and much of the south-east. Occurs in Cape
Province. Black overall, with relatively long
wings. The Gabon race (*C. c. gabonensis*) is
more colourful, with a rufous-brown upper
breast, white on the lower breast and abdomen,
and black barring on the underparts. Undertail
coverts are yellow.

Senegal coucal (*Centropus senegalensis*):
40cm (16in)
Senegal to Sudan and Tanzania. Also present in
Egypt and southern Africa. Strong bill. Black over
the head and down the neck. Lemon underparts.
Back is dark brown, wings are rusty-brown and
the tail is long and black. Sexes are alike.

São Tomé fiscal shrike (Newton's fiscal, *Lanius
newtoni*): 23cm (9in)
Restricted to São Tomé, in the Gulf of Guinea.
Slightly glossy black head, back, wings and tail.
Underparts are whitish-yellow, paler on the
throat. Distinctive whitish-yellow patches across
the top of each wing. Bill, legs and feet are
black. Sexes are alike.

Red-eyed puffback (black-shouldered puffback,
Dryoscopus senegalensis): 18cm (7in)
Parts of western and central Africa. Distinctive
red irides. Cock is white below and glossy black
above, with the rump also white. Hens have
more greyish upperparts, and a distinctive white
streak from the upper bill to each eye. Young
birds are duller. Bill, legs and feet blackish.

Magpie shrike

Long-tailed shrike *Corvinella melanoleuca*

The calls of the magpie shrike consist of a
series of noisy whistles, some of which may
reflect the dominance of an individual
within a flock. These shrikes are very social
by nature, even during nesting, when the
members of a breeding pair may have up to
three helpers to assist in collecting food for
their growing brood. Older hens rank
highest in the social structure, which may
explain why the helper birds are normally
males. The eggs are laid in a large nest
usually constructed in a thorn tree, its
branches holding the structure together as
well as affording some protection from
would-be predators. When hunting, magpie
shrikes rely heavily on their keen eyesight,
remaining alert to movement around them
before quickly swooping to seize their
quarry. They will also sometimes catch
invertebrates in flight.

Distribution: Two African
populations. One is centred
on Tanzania, while another
extends from southern
Angola to Mozambique and
northern South Africa.
Size: 50cm (20in).
Habitat: Woodland.
Nest: Cup-shaped, made
from vegetation.
Eggs: 3–5, buff with
brownish spotting.
Food: Small
vertebrates,
insects.

Identification:
Mainly black. White area
across the top of the
wings, creating a broad band. A
white area is also largely hidden
in the folded wing, on the outer
flight feathers. Feathers adjacent
to the back also edged white.
Long, elegant tail, shorter in the
Tanzanian (*C. m. aequatorialis*)
race. Bill, legs and feet black.
Hens have white on the flanks.
Young browner with shorter tails.

White-crested helmet shrike

White-helmeted shrike *Prionops plumatus*

The white-crested helmet shrikes' nest-building skills are highly developed. Instead of
assembling a jumble of material, they use a combination of grass and bark to make a very
tidy cup. Spiders' webs are placed on the outside to bind the structure together, and to the
branch, serving to anchor it firmly in place. A variety of trees may be chosen
for the nesting site, but the positioning of the nest is of more significance.
It is normally located around 5m (16ft) off the ground, usually at some
distance along a branch, rather than adjacent to the main trunk. Pairs
may nest on their own, but frequently have several non-breeding
helpers assisting them in finding food. Occasionally, two hens may
lay in the same nest, but the dimensions of the cup mean that a
number of the eggs will be lost over the rim if piled on top of
each other, falling to the ground below. The young
subsequently join the group once they are three weeks old.

Identification: Distinctive white crown and forehead, with blackish
stripes on the sides of the neck and variable grey plumage on
the hindneck. Underparts are whitish. Young birds have
whiter faces, lack the dark plumage on the hindneck and
have brownish rather than black bills. Sexes are alike.

Distribution: Across Africa
south of the Sahara, from
Senegal to Ethiopia. Ranges
down the eastern side of the
continent to northern South
Africa, and across to Angola.
Size: 25cm (10in).
Habitat: Dry woodland.
Nest: Cup-shaped, usually
anchored to a branch.
Eggs: 2–5, creamy-white with
dark markings.
Food: Invertebrates, fruit.

TOURACOS AND FLYCATCHERS

Touracos are now confined to Africa, although fossilized remains unearthed in Bavaria, Germany indicate that these birds once occurred in Europe. Greens, blues and purples predominate in their plumage, although go-away birds (so called because of their calls) and certain plantain-eaters are grey in colour.

Lady Ross's touraco

Musophaga rossae

These touracos have adapted well to living in trees, and are able to run and jump among the branches with great agility. Their toes are flexible, enabling them to grip the perch either with three toes pointing forward or with two forward and two gripping from behind. Lady Ross's touracos feed on a variety of fruit and berries, congregating in small groups of up to a dozen birds where such food is plentiful. At other times, especially when breeding, they are territorial and surprisingly aggressive, and will even harry birds of prey. The nest site is usually secluded, often hidden by creepers, and both members of the pair work together to build it. This takes just over a week on average. Incubation is also shared, with the birds swapping over several times during the day. The young hatch after about 25 days, and are initially covered in thick, dark brown down feathering.

Identification: Predominantly purplish-blue, with characteristic crimson-red primary flight feathers and a red crest. Yellow bill and frontal shield, with a bare yellow area around the eyes. Legs and feet black. Young birds duller, with no frontal shield and a blackish bill. Sexes are alike.

Distribution: Centred on Dem. Rep. Congo, extending to adjacent countries including Angola, Zambia, Malawi and Tanzania. Believed to occur in isolated areas to the north, including north-eastern Gabon and parts of Cameroon.
Size: 52cm (20¹/₂in).
Habitat: Dense forest.
Nest: Platform of twigs.
Eggs: 1–2, creamy-white.
Food: Berries, plant matter.

Great blue touraco

Blue plantain-eater *Corythaeola cristata*

Distribution: Range extends from Guinea on the western coast of Africa across through Nigeria and Cameroon to southern Sudan, Dem. Rep. Congo and south as far as parts of Angola.
Size: 75cm (29¹/₂in).
Habitat: Forest.
Nest: Platform of sticks.
Eggs: 1–3, whitish or pale bluish-green.
Food: Vegetarian.

This is the largest member of the touraco family, and is most likely to be seen in small groups. Great blue touracos are not powerful fliers but they are agile, and able to climb easily among the branches. Along with fruits and berries, leaves feature prominently in their diet, as do flowers. Where possible, small fruits that can be swallowed whole are preferred. Members of a group leave a fruiting tree individually rather than flying off as a flock, flapping their wings to get airborne and gliding to another nearby tree. At dusk they return to their roosting site, which is normally a tall tree – such sites are known to be used consistently by the same group of birds for more than a decade. Pairs separate from the rest of the flock at the start of the breeding period, which varies markedly through their range, and may be accompanied by a youngster from a previous clutch, whose task is to aid the adult touracos in providing food for their new offspring.

Identification: Predominantly turquoise-blue, with a curved black crest extending right across the top of the head. Underparts are greenish-yellow, lower underparts and vent area are brownish. Prominent black area at the ends of the tail feathers. Bill is yellow, becoming red at the tip. Legs and feet are greyish. Young birds have shorter crest feathers, and are greyer on the breast. Sexes are alike.

Hartlaub's touraco

Tauraco hartlaubi

The brilliant red coloration present in the flight feathers of these and most other touracos is the result of a copper-based colour pigment called turacin, which is unique to this group of birds. Although agile in the trees, Hartlaub's touracos drop significant numbers of fruits when feeding. They can eat fruits that are known to be toxic, and suffer no apparent side effects as a result. In some areas they have adapted to take food from non-native plants, and may also prey on invertebrates such as moths. They are rarely seen on the ground, however, usually descending only to drink. Hartlaub's touracos are opportunistic breeders, nesting repeatedly under favourable conditions. Incubation is quite short, lasting a maximum of 18 days. In common with other touracos, the parent massages the chick's vent area until it produces a dropping, which the adult swallows, keeping the nest clean.

Identification: Metallic blue head and comb-like crest. White area in front of and white stripe below each eye. Underparts and upper back are greenish, becoming bluish-purple on the wings and lower back. Tail also dark bluish-purple. Crimson-red on the flight feathers. Bare red skin encircles each eye. Bill orange-red, darker on the upper bill. Legs and feet blackish. Sexes are alike. Young birds resemble adults.

Distribution: Restricted to an area in eastern Africa, occurring in Tanzania, Kenya and Uganda.
Size: 43cm (17in).
Habitat: Forested areas.
Nest: Platform-type, made of sticks.
Eggs: 1–2, whitish.
Food: Wide variety of berries and fruits, and some other plant matter. Will occasionally take invertebrates.

Bannerman's touraco (*Tauraco bannermani*) (E): 40cm (15.75in)
Restricted to south-western Cameroon, in the Bamenda highlands. Very distinctive, short reddish-orange crest, with dark grey patches on the sides of the face. Lighter green on the hindneck and down on to the chest. Darker green underparts, back and tail, with red patches evident in the wings. Bill yellow, legs and feet grey. Sexes are alike.

Ruspoli's touraco (*Tauraco ruspolii*): 40cm (15.75in)
Confined to southern parts of Ethiopia. Mostly green, darker on the back and lower upperparts. Low creamy-pink crest, with a red patch behind. Bill reddish, legs and feet greyish. Young birds resemble adults. Sexes are alike.

Grey go-away bird (*Corythaixoides concolor*): 48cm (19in)
From parts of Angola and Namibia east to southern Tanzania and northern South Africa. Entirely grey, with a tall, fairly broad crest. Young birds are more buff and have a small crest. Sexes are alike.

Western grey plantain-eater (*Crinifer piscator*): 50cm (20in)
From Senegal to the Central African Republic. Also an apparently isolated population in south-western Dem. Rep. Congo. Greyish, with pale edging on the upperparts and spotting on the white underparts. Tall, shaggy crest, shorter in young birds. Yellow bill. Legs and feet grey.

Black-and-white crested flycatcher

Vanga flycatcher *Bias muscicus*

These flycatchers are very lively birds. There is a strong bond between pairs and they stay together throughout the year, becoming increasingly territorial at the start of the breeding season. Cocks start to sing more frequently at this time, especially in flight, and a male will challenge a rival by raising his crest and extending his neck. Females may also drive off other hens venturing into their territory. Their breeding period tends to begin during March in western Africa, but does not commence until October in more southerly areas. The cup-shaped nest is shallow but well constructed, and may be bound by the sticky protein of spiders' webs. The hen sits alone, while the cock remains nearby, deterring potential nest raiders, such as monkeys. Young birds fledge at about 18 days old.

Identification: Cock has a black head with a crest at the rear, and black plumage extending down over the back and wings. Black feathering is also present on the upper chest. Tail feathers are black, as is the bill, and the legs and feet are yellow. Blackish plumage in hens is largely restricted to the head, with chestnut plumage on the back, wings and tail, and mottling the flanks. Young birds are duller, and tend to have more brownish heads.

Distribution: Ranges down the western coast of Africa, in Kenya in the centre, and down the south-east coast to Mozambique.
Size: 15cm (6in).
Habitat: Forested areas.
Nest: Open, made of vegetation.
Eggs: 2–3, whitish with dark markings.
Food: Mainly Invertebrates.

TROGONS, PITTAS AND BROADBILLS

Trogons are colourful birds, but even their bright hues merge into the gloom of the forest. Three species occur in Africa, although the family is more widespread in Asia. African trogons differ from their Asiatic relatives in having more powerful bills and feet, which may be linked to their predatory lifestyle. Pittas and broadbills are also widespread in Asia, particularly in the south-eastern region.

Narina trogon

Apaloderma narina

Narina trogons are not easily observed, since their sedentary nature helps them to blend in against the forest background. They are most likely to be seen at the forest edge, perched quietly with their heads drawn down, resting on their shoulders. They remain watchful for potential prey, however, and will dart off to seize invertebrate quarry such as spiders and tree grasshoppers, but especially butterfly caterpillars. Occasionally, small vertebrates such as lizards, including young chameleons, may also be caught, but as far as is known narina trogons never eat fruits or berries of any kind. They breed through much of the year, certainly in the Kenyan part of their range. The incubation period lasts for approximately 18 days, with the young leaving the nest once they are a month old. They remain dependent on the adults to provide them with food for at least a further month, until they are able to fly well themselves.

Identification: The head, breast, shoulders, back and rump are a vivid deep green colour. Wings are otherwise greyish, while the underparts are bright red. Hens have brownish-red on the face and breast, with green encircling each eye. The bill is pale yellow with a darker tip. Young resemble hens but are paler.

Distribution: Extends across Africa from Sierra Leone in the west to Ethiopia and Somalia in the east, although not to the Horn of Africa. Ranges down as far as the eastern coast of South Africa, but largely absent from Namibia, Botswana and the rest of South Africa.
Size: 34cm (13in).
Habitat: Rainforest and gallery forest.
Nest: Tree hollow, no lining.
Eggs: 1–4, white.
Food: Mostly invertebrates.

Bar-tailed trogon

Apaloderma vittatum

Distribution: Scattered populations in various parts of Nigeria and adjacent areas of Cameroon. Also present in western Angola and eastern Africa, mainly in Tanzania, Kenya and Uganda.
Size: 30cm (12in).
Habitat: Mountainous areas of woodland.
Nest: Hollow tree.
Eggs: 2–3, white.
Food: Invertebrates.

Quiet by nature, these trogons usually roost in pairs in the forest for much of the day. Occasionally however, they can be detected by the sound of their wings as they hunt insects, darting in among foliage and seizing caterpillars from the leaves of trees. Bar-tailed trogons are highly arboreal and rarely descend from the upper layers of the forest. Resident in Africa throughout the year, there appears to be no mixing of the populations through their widely-scattered range. Pairs choose a small cavity for nesting, often located in a dead tree, and the hen simply lays on the floor of the chamber. This is the only stage at which the "wup"-like call of these birds, which is uttered repeatedly and grows to a crescendo, will be heard, as they stake their claim to the surrounding territory. Any intruders will be fiercely driven away. Incubation is shared, with the cock bird sitting for much of the day.

Identification: Cock bird has a blackish head and chest, with green shoulders, back and rump, and two bare yellowish areas below the eyes. Head and upper breast are dark green. The breast is a bluish bar, and the remaining underparts are bright red. Wings are dark, as is the upper surface of the tail, which has fine, horizontal black-and-white barring underneath. Hens are similar but duller, with a brownish head and rose-coloured underparts. Young birds resemble adult females, but with some spotting on the wings.

African pitta

Angolan pitta *Pitta angolensis*

These dumpy, short-tailed birds spend most of their time on the forest floor, although they will fly up and perch on a branch if disturbed, remaining frozen until the danger has passed. Populations in western Africa are sedentary, but pittas occurring elsewhere in their range migrate, sometimes ending up in areas far outside their normal distribution. They fly at night, and for reasons that remain unclear are attracted to lights in buildings, sometimes being killed after attempting to fly through the windows. When breeding, the display of the male African pitta is quite unusual in that it is accompanied by a purring sound made by the wings. The pitta flutters up to a perch, then simply jumps down to the ground in free fall. At this stage the short tail feathers are raised to display the red lower underparts. Their bulky, domed nest is built off the ground and measures about 20cm (8in) in height and diameter, with the pittas entering the site through a side entrance hole.

Identification: Black cap on the crown and a broad black streak running through each eye, with an area of buff plumage between. Underparts also buff, becoming reddish on the lower abdomen. Back and wings predominantly green, with bluish rump and areas on the wings. Remainder of the wings are black, with white patches evident when open. The bill is blackish (orangish in younger birds) and the legs and feet are brownish-yellow.

Distribution: Sporadic distribution through western parts of Africa as far south as Angola, with the major range extending from the Central African Republic down to Tanzania and Mozambique. Also reported from various locations outside the normal range, including Ethiopia and South Africa.
Size: 22cm (8³/₄in).
Habitat: Forested areas.
Nest: Dome-shaped, made from vegetation.
Eggs: 2–4, whitish with darker, reddish markings.
Food: Invertebrates.

Bare-cheeked trogon (*Apaloderma aequatoriale*): 34cm (13in)
Western Africa, from Nigeria to Gabon. An isolated population is present in north-eastern Dem. Rep. Congo; also recorded once in the south of this country. Cock has green upperparts and breast, with bare yellowish areas of skin close to the eyes. Underside of the tail is white. Hen has green restricted to the top of the head, and the area above the bill and the underparts are rufous-brown, becoming redder below. Young cock birds have brown on the upper breast, while young hens are duller than adults.

Green-breasted pitta (*Pitta reichenowi*): 20cm (8in)
From Cameroon and Gabon eastwards through Dem. Rep. Congo to western Uganda. Head entirely black, except for buff-coloured stripes above the eyes, joining at the back of the head. Throat is white with a small black area beneath. Chest and back are dark green, and the underparts are red. Wing patterning similar to that of the African pitta (*Pitta angolensis*).

African green broadbill (Grauer's broadbill, *Pseudocalyptomena graueri*): 12cm (4³/₄in)
Found in eastern Africa, in the Albertine Rift area, centred on Rwanda and Burundi. Predominantly bright grass-green, with a short tail. Pale buff on the head, with dark speckling which extends down to below the eye. The throat is whitish, and the chest is pale blue. Bill is black, as are the legs and feet. Sexes are alike. Young birds are duller overall.

African broadbill

Smithornis capensis

African broadbills construct a distinctive, bag-like nest, hung off a young tree or bush and typically no more than 2.5m (8ft) above the ground. The nest varies depending on location and the availability of material, but is held together using strands of a fungus. Spiders' webs may also be incorporated. In southern parts of its range it is often made from a type of lichen. Once complete, the nest is about 9cm (3¹/₂in) deep. Both sexes undertake specific, elliptical display flights, particularly just prior to nesting, with the cock bird fluffing up white feathers on his back. The breeding season varies, but egg-laying generally begins just before the onset of the rainy season. African broadbills' nests may be parasitized by barred long-tailed cuckoos (*Coucou montagnard*).

Distribution: Various parts of western Africa, from Sierra Leone to Ghana, and also sporadically from Cameroon to northern Angola. More extensive distribution on the eastern side, from Uganda and Dem. Rep. Congo down as far as South Africa.
Size: 14cm (5¹/₂in).
Habitat: Forested areas.
Nest: Made of vegetation, suspended off a branch.
Eggs: 2–3, white.
Food: Invertebrates.

Identification: Black cap and brown lores. Brown back, with some streaking, and white rump. Throat is whitish. Underparts are buff, becoming whiter lower down, with dark brown streaking evident here too. Bill, legs and feet are blackish. Hens have a dark brown rather than black cap, with some streaking. Young birds resemble hens.

WOOD DOVES AND FOREST PIGEONS

Numerous pigeons and doves inhabit woodland. The islands lying off the south-eastern coast of Africa are home to some of the most unusual pigeons in the world, although habitat destruction still threatens their future, in spite of determined conservation efforts. Fruit figures prominently in the diets of those birds occurring in tropical areas, since it is readily available throughout the year.

Bruce's green pigeon

Treron waalia

Distribution: Range extends right across Africa south of the Sahara Desert, from Senegal in the west through to Sudan, Ethiopia and Somalia in the east. Also present on the adjacent part of the Arabian peninsula.
Size: 30cm (12in).
Habitat: Woodland.
Nest: Platform of twigs.
Eggs: 1–2, white.
Food: Mainly fruit, but especially figs.

Bruce's green pigeons congregate in relatively large numbers where trees are fruiting, which can sometimes be quite close to settlements. They are arboreal by nature, being sighted on the ground only very rarely, usually when seeking water. Their grey-green coloration helps them to blend in against the wooded background. In some parts of their range, where their distributions overlap, they may associate with African green pigeons (*Treron calva*), but there is no evidence that these two species hybridize. The breeding season varies widely through their range, and is most extensive in western Africa, where nesting has been recorded from December right through until the following September. The choice of nest site also varies according to location – date palms are used on Socotra, while in the sub-Saharan region acacia trees are favoured. Both members of the pair share the task of incubation.

Identification: Grey head, neck and breast, with a yellow abdomen and a green area around the vent with white markings. Lesser wing coverts are mauve, and the remainder of the back and wings are green, except for the black flight feathers. Tail is mauvish towards its tip. Bill pale grey, reddish at the base, with legs and feet also reddish. Young birds are less brightly coloured, especially on the purple wing patches. Sexes alike.

Blue-spotted wood dove

Turtur afer

These doves do not form large flocks, preferring instead to associate as pairs or in small groups. Although they are naturally woodland inhabitants, blue-spotted wood doves have adapted to areas where tree cover has been reduced. They will readily venture down to the ground in search of grass seed, which forms the basis of their diet, although they will sometimes feed on invertebrates too. In some parts of their range the doves are migratory – this depends on rainfall, since they generally prefer more humid habitats. Their breeding season varies. The male engages in a head-bobbing display, and also preens the hen's head as part of the courtship ritual. They construct a typical platform nest, which may measure up to 20cm (8in) in diameter, although occasionally pairs have been known to take over the abandoned cup-shaped nests of thrushes. Both the incubation and rearing periods last approximately 13 days. In addition to the blue-spotted there are four other related wood doves, all of which occur in Africa.

Identification: Bluish-grey crown. Reddish-brown underparts. Wings darker brown with blue spots. Two black bands on the rump. Bare whitish-grey skin surrounds each eye. Bill reddish-black, legs and feet pinkish. Young are duller, with small wing spots. Sexes are alike.

Distribution: Much of Africa south of the Sahara Desert, extending as far as Ethiopia. Ranges south to Angola in the west and down as far as South Africa on the eastern side of the continent.
Size: 22cm (9in).
Habitat: Woodland.
Nest: Platform made from small twigs.
Eggs: 2, whitish.
Food: Mainly seeds.

Madagascar blue pigeon

Madagascar blue fruit dove *Alectroenas madagascariensis*

The distinctive blue pigeons are confined to islands in the Indian Ocean, off the eastern coast of Africa. Today there are only four surviving species – a fifth is now extinct. They appear to share a common ancestry with the fruit-eating pigeons and doves found in Asia, rather than those birds occurring on the African mainland. The Madagascar blue pigeon is a typical representative of the group. Like others of its kind it remains vulnerable to forest clearance on its native island, although fortunately it is relatively common within the boundaries of Madagascar's national parks, which should help to safeguard its future. These blue pigeons are normally seen in pairs, but will sometimes associate in larger groups numbering up to a dozen individuals. Their breeding season extends from October to December, and the nest is built in the fork of a tree often well above the ground, at heights of up to 20m (66ft). However, virtually nothing else is currently known about the breeding behaviour of these unusual pigeons.

Distribution: Range extends along the eastern side of Madagascar, off the south-east coast of Africa.
Size: 28cm (11in).
Habitat: Rainforest.
Nest: Platform of twigs.
Eggs: 1, white.
Food: Mainly fruits.

Identification: Dark bluish feathering on the head extending down the back of the neck, with a loose crest here. Rest of the head, and sides of neck and chest, are silvery bluish-grey. Back, wings and upperparts dark blue. Red undertail coverts and tail feathers. Red skin around the eyes. Legs and feet also red. Dark greenish bill with a lighter tip. Young birds have darker facial skin and are duller overall. Sexes are alike.

African green pigeon (*Treron calva*): 30cm (12in)
Ranges largely south of Bruce's green pigeon (*T. waalia*), although absent from much of the southern area. Also islands in the Gulf of Guinea, including Principe. Predominantly green overall, with dull mauve wing coverts, yellow edging on the black flight feathers, and yellow-and-white barring under the tail, which is greyish above. Base of the bill coral-red, the tip pale horn. Legs and feet vary from red to yellow, depending on race. Young birds are duller, less purple on the wings. Hens smaller, with less prominent ceres.

Blue-headed wood dove (*Turtur brehmeri*): 25cm (10in)
From Sierra Leone and Liberia to north-west Angola and east across Dem. Rep. Congo. Cock bird has a bluish head, with rich chestnut-red plumage on the remainder of the body. Browner on the wings, with greenish wing spots. Bill has a dark reddish base and lighter tip. Legs and feet purplish. Young birds have barring on the back of the neck, and are duller overall. Sexes are alike.

Afep pigeon (Congo wood pigeon, *Columba unicincta*): 30cm (12in)
Isolated areas of western Africa, the main range extending from Cameroon and Gabon to Dem. Rep. Congo. Cock is predominantly greyish, darker on the wings, where the plumage is edged with white. Breast has a slight pinkish wash. A prominent, broad greyish band extends across the tail. Bill dark at the base, pale yellow at the tip. Legs and feet greyish. Hens lack the pinkish breast suffusion. Young birds are darker overall, with browner underparts.

Pink pigeon

Columba mayeri (E)

Pink pigeon numbers have plummeted over the past century, partly due to deforestation and hunting. More recently, cyclone damage on Mauritius has further reduced their numbers, and introduced animals such as monkeys and rats have interfered with their nesting. In 1976, with the population having fallen to just 18, the Jersey-based Durrell Wildlife Conservation Trust began a captive-breeding project, which has grown to involve more than forty zoos worldwide. The wild population is now estimated at around 250, with a breeding stock of 180 in zoos, reflecting a remarkable transformation in its fortunes. Furthermore, in the wild these pigeons now favour the introduced Japanese cedar (*Cryptomeria japonica*), which has sharp needles and a very sticky resin that deters rats from preying on their nests.

Distribution: Restricted to the south-west of Mauritius, in the Indian Ocean. Formerly occurred over almost the entire island.
Size: 40cm (16in).
Habitat: Montane forest.
Nest: Platform, made from twigs.
Eggs: 2, white.
Food: Fruits, and seeds.

Identification: Pinkish head, back and underparts, with brown wings and a rufous-brown tail. Bare red skin around the eyes and at the base of the bill, as well as the legs and feet. Young birds are duller, with ashy-brown wings and a greyish suffusion to the pink areas; red skin also more purplish. Sexes are alike.

BARBETS AND TINKERBIRDS

These dumpy, short-tailed birds, all with fairly stumpy bills, are restricted to Africa, with none occurring in Europe. Other members of this group can be found in Asia and the Americas, and appear similar in profile to their African relatives. They use their stubby bills to bore into tree trunks in order to excavate their nesting cavities, rather like woodpeckers. Many have quite loud calls.

Green barbet

Stactolaema olivacea

Distribution: Occurs in isolated areas of eastern Africa, including Kenya and northern Tanzania, and Malawi and Mozambique. Isolated population also present in South Africa.
Size: 17cm (6³⁄₄in).
Habitat: Forested areas.
Nest: Tree hollow.
Eggs: 3–6, whitish.
Food: Fruits, particularly figs, and some invertebrates.

Green barbets are lively birds. They are often to be encountered in small groups, particularly in the vicinity of fig trees, the fruits of which feature prominently in their diet. They will also hunt invertebrates, regurgitating the indigestible harder parts of their bodies, along with fruit stones. The breeding period is variable through their range. A dead tree is often chosen as the nesting site, and the barbets use their powerful, stocky bills to tunnel into the rotten wood, removing any material they excavate in their bills. The chamber itself extends down as much as 60cm (2ft) into the tree. These hollows are also used for roosting outside the breeding season, and can accommodate as many as eight birds at a time. During the breeding season, other barbets may act as helpers to the breeding pair. They will collect food for the young once they have hatched, but it is unlikely that they take part in incubating the eggs. The young birds leave the nest when they are about a month old.

Identification: A number of races are recognized, varying largely in head coloration. Mainly olive-green overall, and lighter below. Blackish plumage on the top of the head extends to the breast in subspecies Thyolo green barbet (*S. o. belcheri*), distinguishing it from Woodward's barbet (*S. o. woodwardi*), which also has greenish-yellow ear coverts. The Tanzanian race (*S. o. rungweensis*) may have either buffy ear coverts or a uniform head, as in the nominate race from the north. Bill, legs and feet are black. Young birds are less brightly coloured. Sexes are alike.

Naked-faced barbet

Gymnobucco calvus

The lack of feathering on the heads of these barbets may help to prevent their plumage from becoming stained and matted by fruit juices. Young birds leave the nest with their heads almost fully feathered, but this plumage is shed as they grow older and not replaced. Social and noisy by nature, naked-faced barbets are very conspicuous birds, encountered predominantly in lowland areas. They nest in colonies, often seeking out dead trees since in these the nesting chambers are more easily created. Using their powerful bills, they excavate chambers that typically extend 23cm (9in) below the entrance. As many as 30 pairs have been reported occupying a single tree.

Identification: Predominantly brown, with significantly darker upperparts and tail. Underparts are light brown. Large, powerful bill, with beard of longer brown feathers at its base. Bare blackish-brown skin on the head. The bare ear holes at the back of the head are clearly evident. Sexes are alike.

Distribution: Range extends from Guinea in western Africa eastwards and southwards following the coastline, reaching as far as northern Angola.
Size: 18cm (7in).
Habitat: Wooded areas.
Nest: Tree hollow.
Eggs: 3, white.
Food: Invertebrates and fruit.

Double-toothed barbet

Lybius bidentatus

The unusual coloration of these barbets, along with shape of their bills, aids identification in the field. The notch on the bill, which looks like a tooth, may help the birds to grasp their food. Double-toothed barbets have a reputation for attacking ripening bananas, and their diet may feature more fruit than barbets inhabiting more open areas of country. They are most likely to be seen in pairs, rather than in larger groups, and may breed throughout much of the year in some parts of their range. They use their strong bills to excavate a nesting site in a tree by hammering at the trunk. Even so, a dead tree or branch is usually preferred since the wood is softer and easier for tunnelling.

Identification: Predominantly black upperparts and red underparts. The rump and an area on each side of the body are white. There is a blackish area around the eyes, and a red wing bar. The prominent, toothed bill is whitish. Sexes are alike.

Distribution: Western-central Africa, from Senegal around to Angola and eastwards to parts of Sudan, Ethiopia, Kenya and Tanzania.
Size: 23cm (9in).
Habitat: Woodland, although not rainforest.
Nest: Tree hollow. Nesting chamber usually lined with wood chips.
Eggs: 3–4, white.
Food: Invertebrates, fruits and berries.

Banded barbet (*Lybius undatus*): 18cm (7in)
Restricted to highland areas of Eritrea and Ethiopia. Races quite variable in coloration. Red plumage from the base of the bill to above the eyes, with a white streak extending back from behind each eye. Remainder of the head and breast blackish, browner over the back, with the plumage often having a slight silvery edging. Underparts white becoming yellow towards the vent, with black barring. Irides yellow. Large bill is black, as are the legs and feet. Sexes are alike.

Black-collared barbet (*Lybius torquatus*): 20cm (8in)
Southern Africa from Tanzania southwards. Absent from much of Namibia and Botswana, except the far north, and the neighbouring area of South Africa. Bright red face and upper breast, with a black band beneath extending up to the back of the head and encircling the neck. Lower underparts yellowish-white. Back and wings brownish, with yellowish edging to the flight feathers. Stocky bill is black, as are the legs and feet. Young birds have a brown head and throat with orangish-red streaks. There is also a rare yellow morph, which has a yellow rather than a red face. Sexes are alike.

Green tinkerbird (*Pogoniulus simplex*): 10cm (4in)
Eastern coastal forests of Africa, from Kenya to Mozambique. Dull green upperparts, greyer on the underparts. Rump yellow, with some yellow edging to the wing feathers. Bill is black with black whiskers. Young birds have a paler base to the bill. Legs and feet black. Sexes are alike.

Red-fronted tinkerbird

Pogoniulus pusillus

These are noisy tinkerbirds, producing a variety of calls from trills to croaking notes that have been likened to the sound of snoring. They are seen individually or in pairs rather than groups, frequently on the bark of trees hunting for invertebrates. They also catch insects in flight, darting down from a perch, but rarely emerge into the open for long, keeping out of sight as far as possible. When foraging separately, both members of the pair will call frequently to each other. Singing is used as a preliminary to courtship by the male, who also retains fruits or berries in his beak that he passes directly to the hen. The well-concealed nest can be up to 55cm (22in) deep, with the entrance hole often measuring no more than 2.5cm (1in) in diameter. It is thought that the incubation period lasts about 12 days, with the young leaving the nest for the first time when they are just over three weeks old.

Distribution: Two widely-spaced populations, one in eastern Africa, from Ethiopia to Tanzania, and another in eastern South Africa.
Size: 10cm (4in).
Habitat: Forest and more open woodland.
Nest: Tree hollow.
Eggs: 2–4, white.
Food: Invertebrates, fruits and berries.

Identification: Characteristic red forehead, with a black stripe in front running through each eye. Parallel white band, and another black stripe from the base of the bill. Largely white behind the eyes, except for another black stripe. Rest of the head, back and wings black with yellowish streaking, and more evident golden-yellow barring above the flight feathers. Underparts pale lemony-white. Bill, legs and feet black. Young birds lack the red on the head. Sexes are alike.

HORNBILLS

This family of rather unusual, often large birds has a distribution that extends from Africa through the forests of Asia. It is thought that they may assist the spread of forest plants, by passing the seeds out of their bodies or by regurgitating them. Hornbills are vulnerable to forest clearance, as they require large territories in order to obtain sufficient food, and mature trees that can be used as nesting sites.

Long-tailed hornbill

White-crested hornbill *Tockus albocristatus*

Distribution: Western Africa, from Sierra Leone to Dem. Rep. Congo. Apparently absent from the border district between Rep. Congo and Dem. Rep. Congo.
Size: 75cm (29¹/₂in).
Habitat: Forested areas.
Nest: Tree hollow.
Eggs: 2, white.
Food: Mainly invertebrates, some fruit.

The distinctive calls of these hornbills echoing through the forest have been likened to the sound of wailing hyenas. Long-tailed hornbills often associate with bands of monkeys moving through the trees, pouncing to seize any prey disturbed by the troupe's presence. This is not only a one-way relationship however, since the hornbills' sharp alarm calls in turn alert the monkeys to approaching danger and they can react accordingly, taking evasive active. These hornbills hunt large invertebrates such as mantids and cicadas, but they will also catch small vertebrates including rodents and lizards, and raid the nests of other birds. Occasionally, they may descend to the ground to feed on fallen fruit. A pair will choose a nest site in a tree hollow, usually around 10–15m (32–48ft) above the ground. Here the hen will seal herself in, using her droppings to plaster over the entrance to the nesting chamber. She will leave a small hole, through which the male can pass her food for the duration of her incarceration.

Identification: Black overall. White crest with black markings. Long tail feathers tipped with white. Coloration around the eyes grey or whitish, depending on race. Blackish bill, pink at the base of the lower mandible. The casque is more prominent in males. Young birds have a greenish bill and no casque, with pale blue rather than cream eyes.

Black-casqued wattled hornbill

Ceratogymna atrata

The braying calls of these hornbills are audible from 2km (1¹/₄ miles) away, with cocks having a deeper tone than hens. The noise of their wings in flight may also help them to keep in touch with each other. Black-casqued wattled hornbills live mainly in pairs, although they can be observed in family groups. They seek food in the canopy, but may descend to the ground to feed on seeds fallen from ruptured seed pods. The nuts of oil palms feature prominently in their diet, but these hornbills will occasionally take invertebrates and have been recorded raiding the nests of village weavers (*Ploceus cucullatus*). However, they are less predatory than many hornbills. Pairs nest in suitable trees, at heights of up to 20m (66ft).

Identification: Predominantly black overall, with white areas on the tips of the tail feathers. Dark greyish area of bare skin around each eye, with a blue area under the lower bill. Iris red. Bill is black, with a very tall, long casque. Hens easily distinguished by their brownish head and much smaller casque. Young birds have no casque or blue throat wattles, and the bill is olive-coloured rather than black.

Distribution: Main area of distribution is from southern Nigeria to Angola eastwards to Dem. Rep. Congo. Also further west in Liberia, Ivory Coast, Ghana and Togo.
Size: 80cm (31¹/₂in).
Habitat: Forested areas.
Nest: Tree hollow.
Eggs: 2, white.
Food: Mainly fruit.

African crowned hornbill

Tockus alboterminatus

These hornbills establish territories, although in some parts of their range, notably South Africa, drought forces them to migrate. Pairs have a number of roosting sites, which are well screened from birds of prey, and their chosen nesting site is often used for a number of years. The female begins to seal the nest from the outside, then retreats inside to continue until only a slit remains. This is believed to protect the occupants from snakes. She will spend about nine weeks confined to the nest, during which she will moult while incubating the eggs and raising her brood. The young birds reseal the entrance after her departure, and remain inside for a further two weeks, with both the adult birds feeding them. They will start to develop their casques at around four months old.

Identification: Predominantly dark brown in colour, with paler scalloping on the wings and similar streaking over the head and neck. White underparts and tip to the tail. Bill red, with cock birds displaying a pronounced casque running along the top of the upper bill. Hens have a greatly reduced casque and turquoise-blue rather than black facial skin. Young birds have orange bills with no casque. Legs and feet blackish.

Distribution: Present mainly in eastern-central Africa, from Kenya down as far as the southern coastal region of South Africa. Extends to Rep. Congo and Angola in the west. There is also an isolated northern population in Ethiopia.
Size: 54cm (21in).
Habitat: Forested areas.
Nest: Tree hollow.
Eggs: 2–5, white.
Food: Invertebrates and fruit.

Brown-cheeked hornbill (*Bycanistes cylindricus*): 75cm (29$\frac{1}{2}$in)
Restricted to the forested area from Sierra Leone to Ghana in western Africa. Black head, neck and top of the wings, with a black band across the tail feathers. The back, flight feathers and tip of the tail are white. Bare reddish skin encircling the eyes. Bill and casque are yellowish, ivory in young birds. Young also have much smaller casques than cocks, as do hens.

Piping hornbill (white-tailed hornbill, *Bycanistes fistulator*): 50cm (20in)
Senegal in western Africa around to northern Angola and eastwards to the Central African Republic and Dem. Rep. Congo. Black and white, with white on the underparts extending down from the lower breast. White also evident in the wings and tail. Cocks have a small yellow casque, and the tip of the bill and its base are yellowish. Hens have darker bills with a smaller casque. Young birds distinguishable by their black bills and the absence of any casque.

Yellow-casqued wattled hornbill (*Ceratogymna elata*): 90cm (35$\frac{1}{2}$in)
Coastal area of western Africa extending from Guinea Bissau to Cameroon. Predominantly black, except for the mostly white tail feathers, which have a central area of black, and the cream streaks evident on the neck, adjacent to the blue wattle. Iris is red, with an area of grey skin around the eyes. Bill blackish, with a prominent yellow casque. Hens have brown heads and a much smaller casque. Young birds similar to adult hens, but have darker brown plumage on the neck.

Silvery-cheeked hornbill

Bycanistes brevis

Groups of 100 or more silvery-cheeked hornbills congregate where food is plentiful, pursuing plagues of locusts, for example. They are agile in the treetops, bouncing from branch to branch in pursuit of prey. More commonly, they are observed in pairs. At the start of the breeding period the nest opening is reduced to a narrow slit by the hen, from pellets of mud mixed with saliva regurgitated by the cock. He collects the food, regurgitating small fruits for the hen. During this period he will collect around 24,000 fruits from some 1,600 forays. Usually only one chick is reared successfully, breaking out of the nest with its mother when 11 weeks old.

Distribution: Restricted to the eastern African region, occurring in several distinct populations. The northerly population occurs in Ethiopia, while the others are found in Kenya and Tanzania, and in Mozambique and Zimbabwe.
Size: 75cm (29$\frac{1}{2}$in).
Habitat: Prefers upland and coastal forests.
Nest: Tree hollow.
Eggs: 1–2, white.
Food: Mainly fruit.

Identification: Predominantly black, but with white on the back, lower underparts and the tip of the tail. There is also a white area on the underwing coverts. The feathers on the sides of the face are tipped with silver. Cocks have a very tall, curved casque that extends along much of the bill. Hens have much shorter, lower casques, as do young birds.

PARROTS OF THE FOREST

Although there are fewer parrot species in Africa than in Asia or the Americas, their ranges extend to many of Africa's offshore islands. These are home to some of the most unusual parrots in the world, such as the vasa parrot (Coracopsis vasa). *Like many other forest birds, parrots do not occur naturally in Europe, since the climate would restrict their food supply.*

Grey parrot

Psittacus erithacus

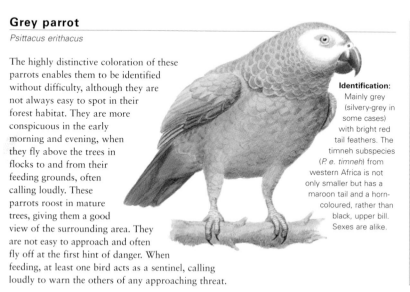

The highly distinctive coloration of these parrots enables them to be identified without difficulty, although they are not always easy to spot in their forest habitat. They are more conspicuous in the early morning and evening, when they fly above the trees in flocks to and from their feeding grounds, often calling loudly. These parrots roost in mature trees, giving them a good view of the surrounding area. They are not easy to approach and often fly off at the first hint of danger. When feeding, at least one bird acts as a sentinel, calling loudly to warn the others of any approaching threat.

Identification: Mainly grey (silvery-grey in some cases) with bright red tail feathers. The timneh subspecies (*P. e. timneh*) from western Africa is not only smaller but has a maroon tail and a horn-coloured, rather than black, upper bill. Sexes are alike.

Distribution: Ranges across much of central Africa, from Guinea eastwards to Ethiopia and Somalia, extending south to Namibia.
Size: 33cm (13in).
Habitat: Woodland areas, including rainforest, savanna and mangroves.
Nest: Tree hollow, often 10m (33ft) or higher.
Eggs: 2–3, white.
Food: Fruits, nuts and seeds, often sought in trees.

Vasa parrot

Coracopsis vasa

These unusual parrots have a very drab appearance, quite unlike that of other members of the family. Another characteristic is their habit of sunbathing, lying at an unusual angle on a perch with one or both wings raised, in similar fashion to pigeons. Although they occur primarily in woodland, vasa parrots also venture into open country, and have come into conflict with farmers on their native islands due to the damage they cause to growing crops, especially rice. The breeding period, which extends from October to December, also brings changes to the parrots' appearance. As well as their bills turning pink, cock birds also develop pronounced swellings adjacent to the vent area, while hens often lose some or all of their head plumage. Exposed to light, the hens' skin becomes yellowish or even orange, but the plumage regrows after the breeding season.

Identification: Unusually drab brownish-black coloration overall, with grey skin around the eyes and dark brown legs. The bill becomes pinkish in the breeding season. Sexes generally alike. Young birds are paler, with little if any bare skin around the eyes.

Distribution: Range extends throughout Madagascar, off the south-east coast of Africa. Also present on Grand Comoro, Anjouan and Moheli in the nearby Comoros Islands, located mid-way between the northern tip of Madagascar and the northern coast of Mozambique.
Size: 45cm (18in).
Habitat: Forested areas.
Nest: Tree hole.
Eggs: 2–3, white.
Food: Seeds and fruit.

Cape parrot

Brown-necked parrot *Poicephalus robustus*

The classification of the Cape parrot is controversial. In addition to its South African range there are populations in western and south-central Africa, each of which are distinctive in appearance and thus often regarded as separate species. Cape parrots cause crop damage in some areas, but usually feed on *Podocarpus* fruits, and favour these trees as nesting sites. They may be semi-nomadic, wandering widely through their range, but are not encountered in large groups. Some areas have large roosts, but these divide into smaller groups that may fly over 80km (50 miles) in search of food. Cape parrots also have regular early morning drinking sites. Their breeding season in South Africa is between August and October. The hen sits alone, and the eggs hatch after 28 days. The young leave the nest after a further two months.

Identification: Brownish mottled head, with green underparts and rump. Wings are dark blackish-green, with the plumage here having lighter green edging. The flight and tail feathers are dark. Prominent reddish-orange area on the shoulders and at the tops of the legs (young birds lack these red areas). Hens are red on the forehead, although this is a variable feature.

Distribution: The species illustrated here is restricted to South Africa, occurring from north-eastern Transvaal down to the eastern Cape Province. **Size:** 35cm (13³/₄in). Other populations occur in west and southern-central Africa. **Habitat:** Forest. **Nest:** Tree hollow. **Eggs:** 2–4, white. **Food:** Seeds and fruit.

Black parrot (*Coracopsis nigra*): 40cm (15³/₄in) Madagascar. Grand Comoro and Anjouan in the Comoros Islands, and Praslin in the Seychelles. Blackish-brown, smaller and darker than the vasa parrot (*Coracopsis vasa*). Bill greyish, lighter in the breeding season. Young birds have a paler bill and paler undertail coverts. Sexes are alike.

Yellow-fronted parrot (*Poicephalus flavifrons*): 25cm (10in) Central Ethiopia. Greenish. Bright yellow head with an an occasional orange suffusion. Yellow on the leading edges of the wings and on the thighs. Young birds duller, with an olive-green head suffused with yellow. Sexes are alike. Bill, legs and feet are black.

Red-fronted parrot (*Poicephalus gulielmi*): 27cm (11in) Several forms. Discontinuous distribution from Ivory Coast to northern Angola, east to Kenya and Tanzania. Dark green, blackish on the head and wings. Reddish-orange above the bill and over the crown, and on the leading edges of the wings and the tops of the thighs. Young birds lack the red coloration. Sexes are alike.

Black-collared lovebird (*Agapornis swindernianus*): 13cm (5in) Isolated areas from Sierra Leone to Gabon and Dem. Rep. Congo. Green head. Black collar, with a similar orangish area below broadening out to the chest. Underparts green, with darker upperparts. Rump is mauve. Bill, legs and feet are black. Young birds duller. Sexes are alike.

Madagascan lovebird

Grey-headed lovebird *Agapornis cana*

Unlike most parrots, lovebirds use nesting material, carrying the leaves and grass to the nest site in the bill, rather than in among the feathers of the rump. Their nest is not an elaborate structure, and consists of a simple lining in the nesting hollow on which the eggs are laid. Incubation lasts 23 days, and the chicks leave the nest at about six weeks old. Madagascan lovebirds are normally observed in flocks, and generally seek their food on the ground. They will often attack rice crops when the seed is ripening, in the company of Madagascar fodies (*Foudia madagascariensis*), a native weaver finch. Not all attempts to introduce these lovebirds to other Indian Ocean islands have proved successful, with the species having failed to establish itself on Mauritius and Zanzibar, but they are now numerous on the Comoros Islands.

Distribution: Naturally occurs on the island of Madagascar, off the south-eastern coast of Africa. Introduced to various neighbouring islands, such as the Comoros. **Size:** 15cm (6in). **Habitat:** Forest and surrounding open country. **Nest:** Tree hole. **Eggs:** 3–6, white. **Food:** Seeds and fruit.

Identification: Grey head and upper breast. Dark green wings and lighter underparts. Dark band on the short tail. Hens entirely green. Bill, legs and feet are greyish. Young birds as adults but with a yellowish bill, and the heads of cocks are suffused with green.

FOREST WOODPECKERS

Few groups of birds are more closely associated with trees than woodpeckers. They are well-equipped to thrive in these surroundings, with their powerful bills serving as tools to obtain food and also to create nesting chambers. Many species occur in dense woodland. However, not all are exclusively arboreal, since a number of species forage for food on the ground.

Great spotted woodpecker

Picoides major

Great spotted woodpeckers can be found in both coniferous and deciduous woodland, especially in areas where the trees are mature enough for the birds to excavate roosting and nesting chambers. Their powerful bills enable them to extract grubs hidden under bark and to wrest the seeds from pine cones – the birds use so-called "anvils", which may be existing tree holes, as vices to hold the cones fast, so as to gain more leverage for their bills.

Identification: Black top to the head. Black areas also from the sides of the bill around the neck, linking with a red area at the back of the head. Wings and upperside of the tail are predominantly black, although there is a white area on the wings and white barring on the flight feathers. Underside of the tail mostly white. Deep red around the vent. Hens are similar but lack the red on the hindcrown.

Distribution: Throughout most of Europe except for Ireland, the far north of Scandinavia and much of south-eastern Europe. Also found in North Africa. Ranges eastwards into Asia.
Size: 25cm (10in).
Habitat: Woodland.
Nest: Tree hollow.
Eggs: 5–7, white.
Food: Invertebrates, eggs and seeds.

Black woodpecker

Dryocopus martius

Distribution: Throughout most of Europe, from parts of Spain, the Pyrenees and France up into much of Scandinavia and eastwards across Asia. Absent from Italy and the British Isles, but present in Greece.
Size: 55cm (21³/₄in).
Habitat: Mature forest.
Nest: Tree hole.
Eggs: 3–5, white.
Food: Mostly invertebrates, some seeds.

Black woodpeckers are found in a range of forest types, especially areas with dead trees. They forage on the trunks, but also seek out the nests of wood ants on the ground, which they raid regularly. Territorial by nature, they rely on their ability to find the ants' nests even under a blanket of snow. Seeds of various kinds, such as beech mast, also help to sustain them over the winter, and they may even attack bees' nests too. Breeding behaviour is evident as pairs are formed at this time of year, but egg-laying will not occur until the spring. They often excavate a new nest hole, rather than reuse an old site. Incubation is shared and, unusually, the cock bird sits through the night. The chicks hatch after two weeks, and the young emerge from the nest when they are about a month old.

Identification: Cock birds are predominantly black, with prominent crimson-red plumage extending over the top of the head. Bill is greyish, as are the legs and feet. Iris whitish. Hens easily distinguished by the much reduced red on the top of the head, which is restricted to a band on the nape. Young birds are duller, less glossy overall, and are more of a sooty-black shade.

Lesser spotted woodpecker (*Dendrocopos minor*): 16cm (6in)
Most of Europe. South to Algeria and Tunisia, and east into Asia. Buff above the bill. Males have a red area on the crown, hens black. Black tail, white barring on the wings. Barring on the underparts, with a reddish area around the vent. Black stripes on the sides of the face.

Stierling's woodpecker (*Dendropocos stierlingi*): 18cm (7in)
Confined largely to Mozambique. Cock has a bright red area extending over the back of the head; back, wings and tail are olive. Barred underparts. Area behind the eyes is dark, and the remainder of the face is whitish. Young birds are duller overall.

African piculet (*Sasia africana*): 8cm (3in)
Cameroon to Dem. Rep. Congo and Angola, and isolated areas in western Africa. Small. Greyish overall. White stripe above the eyes and bare red skin around the eyes. Cock has a rufous area on the forehead. Back and wings olive-green. Young birds have a rufous hue to the underparts.

Mombasa woodpecker (*Campethera mombassica*): 20cm (8in).
Mainly coastal Kenya, including Mombasa. Red over the head to the neck, with red stripes from the base of the bill. Back and wings greenish, with spotting. Tail barred. Sides of the face and breast greyish with black markings, yellower on the abdomen. Hens red only on the hindcrown, with a white-spotted black top to the head. Young like hens, but are more heavily marked.

Grey-headed woodpecker

Dendropicos spodocephalus

This species is closely related to the grey woodpecker (*D. goertae*), which ranges in a band across Africa south of the Sahara. They can be distinguished by their belly colour, which in the grey-headed is more extensive and always red, never orange or yellow as in its near relative. However, both species have very similar calls, particularly the drawn-out rattle used to indicate territory. They become especially vocal prior to breeding, although they are rarely heard drumming at the nest site. This is always located in a dead tree, sometimes close to the ground but more usually up to 20m (66ft) high. The chamber extends down about 30cm (1ft). Both adults incubate the eggs, changing over at least once every 30 minutes during the day, although the cock sits alone through the night.

Distribution: Two distinct populations in eastern Africa, one occurring largely in western Ethiopia, the other present on the border of Kenya and Tanzania.
Size: 20cm (8in).
Habitat: Forest areas, often near rivers.
Nest: Tree hollow.
Eggs: 2–4, white.
Food: Invertebrates.

Identification: Cock bird has a bright red area of plumage on the crown, with red in the centre of the underparts extending down to the vent. Rump is also red. Remainder of the body is grey except for the back and wings, which are yellowish-green, with spotting on the flight feathers and barring on the tail. Hens have grey heads. Young birds are duller, usually with some barring on the underparts, and have greyish-brown irides.

Three-toed woodpecker

Picoides tridactylus

Largely arboreal by nature, three-toed woodpeckers rarely descend to the ground. Cocks forage on trees at lower levels than hens, often venturing quite near to the base. These woodpeckers rely on their pointed bills both to probe into crevices for invertebrates and also as a chisel to strip off bark, especially from dead trees. Their diet consists mainly of beetles and their larvae, although they also bore into the bark to create "sap wells", which offer an additional source of nutrients. Although not easily spotted in the forest, their slow drumming will confirm their presence. They nest in a dead tree, with the incubation period lasting about 12 days. The young fledge after a further four weeks, and will be fed by their parents for another month.

Distribution: Range extends through Scandinavia and across to the eastern coast of Asia. Populations also found in south-eastern Europe. Present in a broad band across North America.
Size: 24cm (9¹/₂in).
Habitat: Conifer woodland.
Nest: Tree hollow.
Eggs: 3–6, white.
Food: Mainly invertebrates.

Identification: Cock bird is predominantly black and white, except for a yellow area on the crown. Black stripe running back from each eye, bordered by white stripes. Wings are black with white markings, as is the tail. Underparts are white with black markings on the flanks. Bill, legs and feet greyish. Hens lack the yellow area on the crown. Young birds are brownish-black, and duller overall. A number of distinctive races of this species are recognized through its wide range.

FLYCATCHERS, BOUBOUS AND SHRIKES

These predatory birds benefit from the insect life that thrives in the woodland. Shrikes will even hunt small vertebrates as well. Many of these often shy species have relatively subdued coloration, which helps them to merge into the background. Others moult into display plumage prior to the breeding season, but observing them in these surroundings can still be difficult.

African paradise flycatcher

Terpsiphone viridis

African paradise flycatchers are summer visitors to South Africa, migrating closer to the equator during April and not usually returning until September. In suburban gardens, the increased planting of trees has provided them with additional habitat, and they may even breed close to buildings. A site up to 6m (20ft) off the ground is usually chosen, and the nest is made from vegetation and spiders' webs. Lichens are added around the outside by way of disguise. Both members of the pair incubate the eggs. Hatching takes 13 days, with the young fledging at just 11 days old. It is not uncommon for African paradise flycatchers to breed twice or even three times over the summer. The cock then moults his tail plumes, which can measure 30cm (12in) or more.

Identification: Cock birds are quite variable in appearance, but usually have greyish underparts and a distinctive crest. The back is rufous in some cases, occasionally with white wing bars and dark flight feathers. Tail is rufous as well, with very long tail plumes during the breeding period. There is also a white form, which may have white wing bars in addition to long white tail feathers. Young birds are less brightly coloured. Hens lack the long tail streamers, and have a paler blue bill and periophthalmic skin.

Distribution: Ranges widely throughout Africa south of the Sahara, but absent notably from the Horn of Africa and from parts of the south-west.
Size: 20cm (8in).
Habitat: Forest, woodland.
Nest: Cup-shaped, made from vegetation.
Eggs: 1–4, creamy with reddish spots.
Food: Invertebrates.

Wattle-eyed flycatcher

Black-throated wattle-eye *Platysteira peltata*

Distribution: Eastern Africa, from Somalia to South Africa. Range extends westwards to Angola, but absent from Namibia, Botswana and much of South Africa.
Size: 18cm (7in).
Habitat: Coastal forests and near rivers.
Nest: Cup-shaped, made from vegetation.
Eggs: 2, cream-coloured with brown spotting.
Food: Invertebrates.

Wattle-eyed flycatchers are very agile birds, able to seize insects both in flight and directly off trees and bushes. They are generally seen in pairs, and in family groups after the breeding period, which in southern parts of their range extends from September to November. Their nest, usually located close to the ground in the fork of a bush, is firmly anchored in place and bound together with spiders' webs. The incubation period lasts about 18 days, and the chicks leave the nest when they are just two weeks old. However, they will not be fully independent of their parents for another three months, and will not develop the characteristic red wattles above their eyes until approximately six months old. Young birds may breed the following year, by the time they are 12 months old. Wattle-eyed flycatchers are relatively quiet by nature, but they have a rapid alarm call that is employed as a warning when they encounter snakes lurking off the ground.

Identification: Named after the red wattles of skin above the eyes. Cock bird has black upperparts, with a black band extending across the chest. Remainder of the underparts are white. Hens have a largely black chest. Young birds have brown mottling on their throats.

São Tomé paradise flycatcher (*Terpsiphone atrochalybeia*): 18cm (7in)
Found only on the island of São Tomé, in the Gulf of Guinea, off the western coast of central Africa. Cock bird is bluish-black, with glossy plumage and tail plumes measuring about 11cm (4¹/₄in) long. The bill is blackish, as are the legs and feet. Hens have chestnut upperparts and a similarly-coloured short tail, with greyish underparts. Young birds are duller.

Bedford's paradise flycatcher (*Terpsiphone bedfordi*): 20cm (8in)
Restricted to lowland rainforest on the north-eastern Dem. Rep. Congo border. Entirely grey, usually slightly darker on the head and back. The skin around the eye is bluish, as is the bill. Young birds are browner. Sexes are alike.

Mountain sooty boubou (*Laniarius poensis*): 20cm (8in)
Found in the Albertine Rift area, like the preceding species (*Terpsiphone bedfordi*). There is also a separate population in the south-west of Cameroon. Entirely black, with a relatively stocky bill. Young birds are more brownish-black. Sexes are alike.

Slate-coloured boubou (*Laniarius funebris*): 20cm (8in)
Range restricted to north-east Africa, from Ethiopia and Somalia to Tanzania. Dark grey overall, and more of a matt shade than glossy shade. Young birds are browner, with barred underparts. Sexes are alike.

Woodchat shrike

Lanius senator

These migratory shrikes return to their European breeding grounds in the spring. Established pairs choose a nest site in a tree or bush, within 5m (16ft) of the ground. Their nest can be built in four days, but egg-laying may not occur for several weeks. The hen sits alone, with incubation lasting about 15 days. Once hatched, she broods the chicks for another 10 days, while the male continues to bring food to the nest. The young leave the nest at nearly three weeks old, remaining with their parents through the summer, and only become fully independent just before their southward migration. Woodchat shrikes leave their breeding grounds relatively early, typically between July and August, arriving back in Africa between August and October.

Identification: Pale yellow area above the bill, with a black mask above encompassing the eyes. Top of the head is a rich brown, extending back to form a collar. Underparts whitish with a hint of orange on the flanks. Wings mainly black with white wing bars. Greyish rump. Hens less vividly coloured, with a greyer back and often a slight barring on the flanks. Bill, legs and feet blackish. Young birds have brownish upperparts, greyish underparts and evident markings on the flanks.

Distribution: Breeds through much of southern Europe bordering the Mediterranean. Overwinters in a broad band across Africa south of the Sahara, with an isolated population in Tanzania.
Size: 19cm (7¹/₂in).
Habitat: Wooded areas in the breeding season.
Nest: Cup-shaped, made of vegetation.
Eggs: 1–8, olive-green or yellowish with dark markings.
Food: Largely invertebrates.

Southern boubou

Laniarius ferrugineus

Identification: Jet black head, back and tail, with narrow white wing bars. The throat area is pure white, becoming rusty-orange on the lower underparts. Bill, legs and feet are black. Hens have greyer upperparts and more rufous underparts. Young birds buff-brown above, with barring on their underparts.

Relatively shy by nature, southern boubous are difficult shrikes to observe, typically remaining hidden in the undergrowth, although their song helps to confirm their presence. Members of a pair duet with each other in close unison, and it can sometimes sound as if one bird is singing from two separate places. Their song pattern is highly individual, even varying between neighbouring pairs. The frequency of singing increases with the advent of the rainy season, which usually also marks the start of the breeding period. The nest, constructed by both members of the pair, is a relatively loose structure often anchored together with spiders' webs. Incubation is also shared by both birds, and lasts approximately 16 days, with the young birds leaving the nest after a similar interval. Adult southern boubous hunt for food among trees and bushes as well as on the ground. The nests of other birds may be raided too, and small lizards and similar creatures are also occasionally caught and eaten.

Distribution: Range extends from Mozambique down along eastern and southern parts of South Africa, as far as Cape Province. Present also in parts of Botswana and Zimbabwe.
Size: 22cm (9in).
Habitat: Wooded areas.
Nest: Generally a loose, bowl-shaped platform.
Eggs: 2–3, greenish-white with darker speckling.
Food: Mainly invertebrates.

WOODLAND INSECT-EATERS

Many birds rely on invertebrates to form a significant part of their diet. Those species resident in Europe may be forced to fly south to warmer climes for the winter, where such food will be more readily available. In Africa however, members of such families are largely resident through the year, although they too may occasionally undertake seasonal movements.

Woodlark

Lullula arborea

The attractive whistling call of these larks, characterized by a distinctive yodelling tone, is mainly heard at sunrise or even on a starry night, rather than during the daytime. They are not easy birds to spot, since their plumage provides them with excellent camouflage. Woodlarks spend long periods on the ground, but sometimes fly up to perch, and this is when they are most conspicuous. Nesting also often occurs on the ground, with both members of the pair building the nest in a suitable hollow, although they may prefer to utilize a shrub or young sapling. The hen sits alone, and the chicks hatch about two weeks later. The young woodlarks develop quickly, and may leave the nest at only 10 days old, emerging on foot since they are not able to fly well at this stage. In the autumn, those birds occurring in more easterly parts head to south-west Europe to overwinter. Some fly further afield, over the Strait of Gibraltar to north-western Africa.

Identification: A white stripe above each eye. Top of the head streaked black and brown, ear coverts brownish. Streaked back, white tip to short tail. Underparts streaked, white on the abdomen. Yellowish-brown bill, yellowish legs and feet. Young have blacker crown, more spotted underparts. Sexes are alike.

Distribution: Range extends throughout much of Europe, but resident only in more westerly areas. Restricted to the south in England. Breeds right across the continent as far as southern parts of Scandinavia. Also extends to north-west Africa.
Size: 15cm (6in).
Habitat: Open woodland.
Nest: Deep and cup-shaped, made of vegetation.
Eggs: 1–6, white with some brown speckling.
Food: Mostly invertebrates, seeds in winter.

Terrestrial bulbul

Phyllastrephus terrestris

Identification: Upperparts dark brown, underparts whitish. Young birds paler, with a yellowish tone to the underparts and a rufous rump and tail. Sexes are alike, but males larger. Dark bill, grey legs and feet.

As their name suggests, terrestrial bulbuls spend their lives close to the forest floor. Social by nature, these brownbuls are usually observed in small, noisy groups, calling almost constantly to each other while on the move. Their main feeding technique consists of flicking over dry leaves with their bills as they comb the forest floor, seizing any invertebrates that are uncovered, although they will also eat fruit and berries. An unusual breeding characteristic of the terrestrial bulbul is that every year a pair will return to the vicinity of their previous nest, although they will construct a new nest here each time. In southern Africa, breeding occurs during the summer months, but it is likely to be more variable in other parts of their range. The nest itself, which may be located in branches or disguised among creepers, is made using a variety of vegetation ranging from leaves to seed pods. The incubation period lasts for around two weeks, with the young bulbuls leaving the nest after a similar interval.

Distribution: Isolated populations in southern Somalia, Kenya and southern Angola. Main range largely centred on Zimbabwe, extending from Tanzania down to Cape Province.
Size: 19cm (7½in).
Habitat: Forest.
Nest: Loose, cup-shaped.
Eggs: 2–3, greenish-white with dark streaks.
Food: Mostly invertebrates.

Yellow white-eye

Zosterops senegalensis

Some taxonomists recognize more than a dozen different subspecies of yellow white-eye through its wide range, which differ from each other in their depth of coloration. Groups of yellow white-eyes wander through the forest, seeking insects among the foliage, often squabbling between themselves. A dominant individual will challenge one of its companions by opening its bill and crouching on the perch. The weaker individual stays still and fluffs up its plumage, keeping its eyes partially closed as well. This causes the surrounding white feathering to form an oval, and also makes it more conspicuous. Such is their natural agility that yellow white-eyes can forage successfully both above and below the leaves, in rather tit-like fashion. They will also take nectar, along with fruit and berries. Pairs nest on their own, choosing a well-hidden site. The hen is largely responsible for incubation, and hatching takes 11 days. The young birds leave the nest when they are just two weeks old.

Identification: Upperparts are dark olive-yellow, with the underparts a pure shade of yellow. Distinctive white band of feathering encircles each eye, with a thinner, darker streak connecting from here to the base of the bill. Slender blackish bill, dark grey feet and legs. Young birds resemble adults. Sexes are alike.

Distribution: Occurs in a band across Africa south of the Sahara, from Senegal to Ethiopia. Also ranges south to northern Namibia and southern Mozambique, but largely absent from Rep. Congo and Dem. Rep. Congo.
Size: 12cm (4.75in).
Habitat: Woodland areas.
Nest: Cup-shaped, made from vegetation.
Eggs: 1–4, whitish-turquoise.
Food: Mainly invertebrates, some nectar.

Cape white-eye (*Zosterops capensis*): 12cm (4³/₄in)
Restricted to eastern and southern parts of South Africa. Dark olive-green upperparts, with a characteristic yellow area on the throat and under the tail. Two distinctive forms, varying in colour on their underparts: *Z. c. capensis* from the south-west has grey underparts, whereas those of *Z. c. virens* are green. Young birds are duller, developing white feathering around the eyes at about five weeks old. Sexes are alike.

Kulal white-eye (*Zosterops kulalensis*): 12cm (4³/₄in)
Range is restricted to northern Kenya, found only in the forested region of Mount Kulal. Dark olive-green above, with yellowish areas above the bill extending below the eyes and on the underparts. Flanks and lower underparts are grey. Relatively broad white eye ring. Young birds resemble adults. Sexes are alike. Bill, legs and feet black.

Johanna's sunbird (Madame Verreaux's sunbird, *Cinnyris johannae*): 14cm (5¹/₂in)
Various isolated locations from Sierra Leone in West Africa. Cock bird has a metallic green head and upper back, while the throat area is purplish, merging into red, with some barring. Wings and lower underparts are black. Rump dark blue. Hens have dark olive-green upperparts, with a pale whitish streak extending above the eye and from the base of the lower bill; underparts becoming more yellowish, heavily streaked overall with green. Bill, legs and feet blackish-grey. Young birds resemble adults, with young cocks having heavier grey streaking.

Superb sunbird

Cinnyris superba

These colourful sunbirds are surprisingly difficult to spot in the gloomy forest. They also forage high up in the canopy, where the trees flower in the sunlight. As well as nectar, superb sunbirds will also feed on invertebrates such as spiders or midges, taking them off leaves or even seizing them in flight. They are also attracted to banana plantations, not only for food but also for breeding. Their nest is suspended off a branch, anchored in place largely by grass. A distinctive tail extends beneath which, along with pieces of lichen attached to the exterior, may help to disguise its presence. The hen builds the nest alone, which can take from a day to a month to complete.

Distribution: Western-central Africa. Range extends from Sierra Leone across central Africa to Uganda, Kenya and Tanzania, and down as far as western Angola.
Size: 15cm (6in).
Habitat: Areas of forest.
Nest: Suspended from a tree branch.
Eggs: 1–2, creamy-white with darker markings.
Food: Mostly nectar, and invertebrates.

Identification: Metallic blue crown, with green sides to the face and back. Throat is metallic purple, with dark red underparts. Wings and tail are black. Hens have olive-green upperparts, a pale stripe above the eyes, dusky yellow throat and golden yellow underparts. Long, down-curved blackish bill. Black legs and feet. Young as adult females, but young cocks have a greenish suffusion on their back.

WOODLAND TITS AND WARBLERS

These small, lively birds are quite bold and aggressive by nature, often associating in mixed groups which forage for food through the woodland. Tits frequently construct elaborate nests, with hens laying relatively large clutches of eggs, and they sometimes nest more than once in a season. While tits remain resident in northern climes through the winter, warblers generally migrate to Africa.

Long-tailed tit

Aegithalos caudatus

The tail feathers of these tits can account for nearly half their total length. Those birds occurring in northern Europe have a completely white head and underparts. The Turkish race (*A. c. tephronotus*) in contrast displays more black feathering, including a bib, with evident streaking on its cheeks. Long-tailed tits are lively birds, usually seen in small parties, and frequently in the company of other tits. They are often most conspicuous during the winter, when the branches are without leaves. Long-tailed tits will roost together, which helps to conserve their body heat – sometimes as many as 50 birds may be clustered together. Groups can be quite noisy when foraging during the day. Their breeding period starts early, in late February, and may extend right through until June.

Identification: Dumpy and long-tailed. Black stripe above each eye extends back to form a collar. Head and upper breast otherwise whitish. Underparts rose-pink. Reddish-brown shoulders, white edges to the flight feathers. Young birds are duller, with brown on their heads. Sexes are alike.

Long-tailed tits build a large nest with a side entrance.

Distribution: Resident throughout virtually the whole of Europe, but absent from central and northern parts of Scandinavia. Extends into Asia, but not found in Africa.
Size: 15cm (6in).
Habitat: Deciduous and mixed woodland.
Nest: Ball-shaped, usually incorporating moss.
Eggs: 7–12, white with reddish speckling.
Food: Invertebrates, seeds.

Crested tit

Parus cristatus

Although these tits can lower their crest feathers slightly, the crest itself is always visible. This makes crested tits easy to distinguish, even when they are foraging with other groups of tits, which happens especially during the winter period. They rarely venture high up, preferring to seek food on or near the ground. Invertebrates such as spiders are preferred, although they often resort to eating conifer seeds during the winter. Crested tits frequently create food stores, particularly during the autumn, to help them survive through the harsher months when the ground may be blanketed with snow. Seeds are gathered and secreted in holes in the bark, and among lichens, while invertebrates are decapitated and stored on a shorter-term basis. Nesting begins in March, with a pair choosing a hole, usually in rotten wood, which they can enlarge before constructing a cup-shaped lining for their eggs. In more southerly areas, two broods of chicks may be reared in succession.

Identification: Triangular-shaped, blackish-white crest. Sides of the face are also blackish-white, with a blackish line running through each eye and curling round the hind cheeks. Black collar joins to a bib under the bill. Upperparts brownish. Underparts paler buff, more rufous on the flanks. Young as adults but have brown rather than reddish irides. Sexes are alike.

Distribution: Resident from Spain across to Scandinavia (although not the far north) and Russia. Present in the British Isles only in northern Scotland. Absent from Italy.
Size: 12cm (4³/₄in).
Habitat: Conifer woodland.
Nest: In a rotten tree stump.
Eggs: 5–8, white with reddish markings.
Food: Mainly invertebrates, seeds in winter.

Grey penduline tit

African penduline tit *Anthoscopus caroli*

These small birds can be hard to spot in their woodland habitat, thanks to their inconspicuous coloration, although they are relatively common through their range, with five separate races now recognised. These tits are most likely to be observed in pairs or family groups, keeping in touch with each other via their calls. Agile by nature, they will comb branches in a typical tit-like fashion, searching for invertebrates and sometimes venturing down very close to the ground. They build distinctive nests, which are so carefully constructed that they remain intact long after being vacated. Suspended off a branch, the nest is made of plant fibres and has the texture of felt. The pair enter through a disguised horizontal slit on the side, which they prize apart with their foot.

Identification: Variable through its range. May have pale buff patches on the sides of the face, extending above the bill, with a faint black stripe running through the eyes. Back, wings and tail are grey, sometimes greyish-green. Throat, chest and underparts are buff. Narrow, pointed greyish bill. Sexes are alike.

Distribution: Occurs in southern and central parts of Africa, centred mainly on eastern Angola, extending east and southwards to northern South Africa. Also found in Uganda.
Size: 9cm (3^1/$_2$in).
Habitat: Woodland areas.
Nest: Hanging pouch of plant matter.
Eggs: 4–6, white.
Food: Mainly invertebrates.

Dusky tit (*Parus funereus*): 14cm (5^1/$_2$in)
Patchy distribution through numerous parts of western and central Africa. Guinea south to Angola and east to Sudan and Uganda. Cocks completely black, with a black bill, legs and feet. Red eyes. Hens are similar but greyer, especially on the underparts. Young birds have white wing bars (white tips to the wing coverts).

White-backed tit (*Parus leuconotus*): 14cm (5^1/$_2$in)
Highland forest areas of Ethiopia. Cock birds are predominantly black, except for a triangular-shaped white area on the mantle. Hens have a more creamy patch here. Bill, legs and feet are black. Young birds are similar to hens.

Stripe-breasted tit (*Parus fasciiventer*): 14cm (5^1/$_2$in)
Confined to the border area of western Uganda known as the Albertine Rift. Black head and upper chest, with a black stripe extending down the centre of the abdomen. Belly whitish, with more buff coloration on the flanks. The back is greenish-grey. Black wings with a prominent white wing bar. Bill is black, legs and feet grey. Young birds are duller. Sexes are alike.

Cape penduline tit (*Anthoscopus minutus*): 8cm (3in)
Southern Africa, mainly Namibia, Botswana, Zimbabwe and western South Africa. Greyish upperparts, with a black area around the bill, extending to the eyes. White on the cheeks and pale yellowish below. Bill, legs and feet black. Young have paler underparts. Sexes are alike.

Icterine warbler

Hippolais icterina

These warblers reach the southernmost parts of their winter range in November, where they are most likely to be found in acacia woodland. Solitary by nature, they remain hidden in vegetation, although will venture into the open to catch flying insects. Small berries and larger fruits are also eaten. Icterine warblers leave their wintering grounds from late February, after moulting. Most head north over the Strait of Gibraltar, rather than crossing further east as occurs on their southward passage. Prior to setting off, male icterine warblers begin to sing more frequently in anticipation of the breeding season, which starts in May. The nest is often built in a bush, and the hen sits alone. The eggs hatch after 12 days, with the young fledging after a similar interval.

Distribution: Ranges widely across much of central and northern Europe into Asia. Overwinters in Africa south of the Sahara, although absent from parts of western Africa, some easterly regions, and the far south.
Size: 14cm (5^1/$_2$in).
Habitat: Woodland.
Nest: Cup-shaped, made out of grass.
Eggs: 4–5, pinkish with darker spots.
Food: Invertebrates, fruit.

Identification: Upperparts olive-green, with blackish wings. Sides of the face, underparts and flanks mainly yellowish, while the abdomen is white. In brown morph, underparts are white and upperparts brownish-grey. Bill is brown, greyish legs and feet. Sexes are alike. Young birds have paler underparts.

THRUSHES AND ORIOLES

The attractive song of these birds forms part of the dawn chorus in woodland areas, and is especially conspicuous in spring when the birds are on their breeding grounds. A number of the more common species are actually migratory, nesting in Europe but overwintering in Africa, where food is more plentiful. Some African species have very restricted areas of distribution.

Common redstart

Phoenicurus phoenicurus

This member of the thrush family seeks cover when building its nest. It is often constructed inside a tree hollow, but sometimes an abandoned building or even an underground tunnel is chosen. The hen incubates alone for two weeks until the eggs hatch, with both parents subsequently providing food for their growing brood. Fledging takes place around two weeks later. The pair may sometimes nest again, particularly if food is plentiful. When migrating south, birds from much of Europe take a westerly route through the Iberian Peninsula, whereas those passing further east through Libya and Egypt are believed to originate from Russia. The return journey back north begins in late March. Males generally leave first, enabling them to establish their breeding territories by the time they are joined by the hens.

Identification: Cock birds have a prominent white area above the bill extending back above the eyes. Remainder of the face is black, and the head and back are grey. Chest is rufous, becoming paler on the underparts. Hens are duller, with a greyish-brown head and buff-white underparts. Young birds have brown heads and rufous tails.

Distribution: Breeding range extends across virtually the whole of Europe, including Scandinavia, and eastwards into Asia. Absent from Ireland. Also occurs in parts of north-west Africa, and overwinters in a band south of the Sahara.
Size: 15cm (6in).
Habitat: Woodland.
Nest: Built in a suitable hole.
Eggs: 5–7, bluish with slight red spotting.
Food: Mainly invertebrates and berries.

Natal robin

Red-capped robin chat *Cossypha natalensis*

Opportunistic hunters, these robin chats will follow ant columns, darting in to seize fleeing invertebrates, as well as seeking food under leaves on the forest floor. Males are talented mimics and determined songsters – one individual was revealed as mimicking the calls of 17 other birds while singing continuously over a period of 20 minutes. They have even been recorded yapping like dogs. Having mastered an unusual call, other cock birds in the vicinity start to mimic the sound, creating regional song variants. Natal robins are highly territorial by nature, and pairs nest in their own territory. In addition to the more typical materials such as leaves and grasses, they have even been recorded smearing hippopotamus dung on their nests, which are constructed on or close to the ground. Their eggs are surprisingly variable in colour – the majority are an olive shade, but some are bright blue.

Identification: Rufous face and underparts, becoming reddish-brown over the crown and down to the nape. Back and wings slaty-blue, and the tail is dark on its upper surface. Bill, legs and feet are blackish. Sexes are alike. Young birds have black upperparts and wings coverts with rufous spotting.

Distribution: Isolated northern populations in Nigeria, Central African Republic and Ethiopia. The main area of distribution ranges across Africa from Angola to Tanzania and down to eastern South Africa.
Size: 18cm (7in).
Habitat: Forested areas.
Nest: Cup-shaped, close to the ground.
Eggs: 2–4, variable in colour, but usually olive.
Food: Mainly invertebrates, some fruit.

Eurasian golden oriole

Oriolus oriolus

Despite their bright coloration, golden orioles are quite inconspicuous birds, preferring to hide away in the upper reaches of the woodland, although they will sometimes descend to the ground in search of food and water. Their diet varies, consisting mainly of invertebrates from spring onwards, with fruits and berries more significant later in the year. Migrants arrive at the southern tip of Africa by November, and by March will have set off on the long journey back to Europe. It is unclear where the small north-west African population disperses to after breeding, but they head south also, returning by the middle of April. Males establish territories on arrival at their breeding grounds. There is no lasting pair bond between orioles.

Identification: Yellow. Black wings with a yellow patch. Red bill. Hens have greenish-yellow upperparts, streaked underparts mainly white, yellow flanks and blackish wings. Young are more greyish-green, white underparts only slight yellow.

Distribution: Breeds right across mainland Europe, to the southernmost parts of Scandinavia, extending east into Asia. In the British Isles, restricted to eastern England. Also present in north-west Africa, overwintering throughout the continent.
Size: 25cm (10in).
Habitat: Prefers deciduous woodland areas.
Nest: Cup-shaped.
Eggs: 3–4, creamy-buff with dark spotting.
Food: Invertebrates, berries and fruits.

Snowy-crowned robin chat (*Cossypha niveicapilla*): 22cm (8¹⁄₂in)
Senegal to Kenya and Tanzania. Also in Ethiopia and southern Dem. Rep. Congo. White crown, black patches on the sides of the head. Rufous throat, underparts and sides of the neck. Back and wings are blackish. Black bill, legs and feet. Young birds are duller. Sexes are alike.

Western forest robin (*Stiphrornis erythrothorax*): 11cm (4¹⁄₄in)
Sierra Leone to Togo. Also in southern Nigeria. Blackish-brown sides to the face, with a white spot in front of each eye. Olive-brown back, a bright orange chest and white underparts. Young birds have spotted plumage, and fledge without the eye spots. Sexes are alike.

East Coast akalat (Gunning's akalat, *Sheppardia gunningi*): 12cm (4³⁄₄in)
Three populations, occurring in Kenya, Malawi and Mozambique. Brownish head and back, with greyer tone on the sides of the face, and a white spot in front of each eye. Underparts orange, white on the lower abdomen. Bill is black, legs and feet pinkish-grey. Young birds have spotted plumage. Sexes are alike.

Somali thrush (Somali blackbird, *Turdus ludoviciae*): 23cm (9in)
Highland forests of northern Somalia. Black head and breast, with greyer underparts and slightly darker wings. Hens have blackish streaking on the throat. Bill is yellow. Young birds are more brownish and have dark bills.

Eastern black-headed oriole

Oriolus larvatus

Often seen individually or in pairs, these orioles also congregate in larger numbers where food is plentiful. They eat a range of berries and small fruits, and will take nectar and pollen from flowers. Invertebrates such as caterpillars may be caught on the ground. Their nest is relatively large, usually built towards the end of a main branch where it forks into several side-branches. Plant fibres such as lichens are used to anchor it tightly in place, a task that is undertaken by the female. It is a slow process that takes at least three days and can last for over a fortnight. Having laid her eggs the hen will incubate alone, with the chicks hatching after two weeks. Both parents feed their brood, and the cock continues to provide food to his mate. The young will leave the nest when they are 18 days old.

Distribution: Ranges down through most of east Africa, from Somalia southwards to South Africa. Also extends westwards through Zambia, Zimbabwe and Dem. Rep. Congo to Angola.
Size: 20cm (8in).
Habitat: Broad-leafed forest.
Nest: Cradle-shaped.
Eggs: 1–3, pinkish-buff with darker markings.
Food: Invertebrates and fruit.

Identification: Black head and chest, with red eyes and bill. Yellow collar and underparts, becoming more yellowish-green across the back and the tail. Wings blackish with white tips to the outer secondary feathers. Young have brownish-black streaking extending from the throat to the chest, and a dark bill. Sexes are alike.

CORVIDS

Studies suggest that corvids rank among the most intelligent of avian species. Many of these birds display an instinctive desire to hoard food such as nuts, to help sustain them through the winter months. Their plumage is often predominantly black, sometimes broken with grey and white areas. Corvids are generally noisy and quite aggressive by nature, but are often quite social as well.

Siberian jay

Perisoreus infaustus

The appearance of these jays varies through their range, essentially in depth of coloration. They are opportunistic feeders, and in some locations will leave the woodland to seek scraps at picnic sites. Virtually anything edible is likely to be eaten, including carrion. They will raid the nests of other birds, seizing their eggs and chicks, and will prey on small mammals and invertebrates. Siberian jays have salivary glands, which enable them to produce food balls for storing over the winter when food is scarce, especially if the ground is covered by snow. Their breeding season starts in March, and chicks may hatch before the spring thaw is complete. They will leave the nest when just over three weeks old, but the young jays may remain with their parents almost until the start of the following breeding season.

Identification: Brownish-black head. Upper breast greyish, back greyish-brown. Rust-red rump, wing patches and tail (central feathers grey). Blackish bill, legs, feet. Sexes are alike.

Distribution: The far north of Europe, ranging from Scandinavia eastwards through Russia right across Asia to the Pacific coast.
Size: 30cm (12in).
Habitat: Coniferous forest.
Nest: Platform of twigs.
Eggs: 3–5, greenish with darker markings.
Food: Omnivorous.

Carrion crow (*Corvus corone*): 51cm (20in)
Western and south-western parts of Europe. Black overall, sometimes slightly glossy. Broad, blunt bill is curved on its upper surface, with no bare skin at the base and feathering around the nostrils. Young birds duller overall, less glossy than adults. Sexes are alike.

Piapiac (black magpie, *Ptilostomus afer*): 36cm (14in)
Western and central Africa south of the Sahara, from Senegal to Ethiopia and Uganda. Glossy black, with unusually long tail feathers that taper slightly along their length. Stout black bill. Relatively long legs and feet are black. Reddish iris, often a deeper shade in hens. Young birds have a pinkish bill and dark irides.

Stresemann's bush crow (*Zavattariornis stresemanni*): 30cm (12in)
Restricted to southern Ethiopia. Predominantly grey on the top of the head and back, with blackish wings and tail. Underparts paler grey, virtually whitish, but sometimes may appear reddish owing to staining by the soil. Prominent area of pale blue skin extending from the bill, encompassing the eyes. Bill, legs and feet are blackish. Young birds duller, with the plumage on the upperparts a more brownish-grey shade. Sexes are alike.

Jay

Eurasian jay *Garrulus glandarius*

Throughout their wide range, there is some local variation in the appearance of these jays, both in the depth of colour and the amount of black on the top of the head. However, their harsh call, which resembles a hoarse scream, coupled with a flash of colour, help to identify them. Jays are shy by nature and rarely allow a close approach. In the autumn they store acorns and other nuts and seeds, with these caches helping to sustain them through the winter, when the ground may be covered in snow and other feeding opportunities limited. During the summer, jays may raid the nests of other birds, taking both eggs and chicks.

Distribution: Range extends throughout the whole of Europe, except for Scotland and much of Norway. Also present in north-western Africa and Asia.
Size: 35cm (14in).
Habitat: Woodland.
Nest: Platform of twigs.
Eggs: 3–7, bluish-green with dense speckling.
Food: Omnivorous.

Identification: Pinkish-brown, with a greyer shade on the wings and streaking on the head. Broad, black moustachial stripe, and a whitish throat. White rump and undertail area. Tail is dark. White stripe on the wings, with black-and-blue markings on the sides of the wings. Sexes are alike.

Raven

Common raven *Corvus corax*

The croaking calls of the raven are a foolproof way of identifying this bird, and its size is also a good indicator. Ravens are the largest members of the crow family occurring in the Northern Hemisphere. The impression of bulk conveyed by these birds is reinforced by their shaggy throat feathers, which do not lie sleekly. There is a recognized decline in size across their range, with ravens found in the far north larger than those occurring further south. Pairs occupy relatively large territories, and even outside the breeding season ravens do not usually associate in large flocks. When searching for food, they are able to fly quite effortlessly over long distances, flapping their wings slowly.

Distribution: From northern Africa and south-western Europe to Scandinavia, and eastwards throughout most of northern Asia. Also present in North America, Greenland, Iceland and the British Isles.
Size: 67cm (26in).
Habitat: Prefers relatively open country.
Nest: Bulky, made of sticks.
Eggs: 3–7, bluish with some darker spots.
Food: Carrion.

Identification: Very large in size, with a powerful, curved bill. Entirely black plumage. Wedge-shaped tail in flight, when the flight feathers stand out, creating a fingered appearance at the tips. Males often larger than females.

Nutcracker

Spotted nutcracker *Nucifraga caryocatactes*

As their name suggests, nuts feature prominently in the diet of these distinctive corvids, particularly hazel and pine nuts, although they will take other items such as invertebrates and berries when available. They use their powerful bills to crack open hard-shelled nuts without difficulty, holding them with their feet or wedging them in a convenient hollow. Nutcrackers lay down large food stores in the autumn, to sustain them through the winter months. In years when the nut crops fail, however, they are forced to leave their traditional winter haunts and seek food elsewhere, often moving much further into western Europe. These irruptions typically occur on average about once every ten years, and usually involve those birds of the Siberian race (*N. c. macrorhynchos*), which are generally restricted to a region east of the Ural Mountains. Thousands of nutcrackers can be involved, with some of them flying as far as the Iberian Peninsula and North Africa. Subsequently, these birds are likely to be encountered in a very wide range of habitats, including gardens, and will prove to be quite bold visitors.

Distribution: Range is generally restricted to central and south-eastern parts of mainland Europe. Also found in southern parts of Scandinavia and through the Baltic region into Asia.
Size: 35cm (13³/₄in).
Habitat: Prefers mainly coniferous forest.
Nest: A well-constructed platform of sticks.
Eggs: 2–5, bluish with some brown speckling.
Food: Omnivorous. Mostly nuts, also invertebrates and some berries.

Identification: A dark brown cap extends across the top of the head. The back, sides of the face and underparts are heavily spotted with white markings. Wings are a dark blackish-grey, as is the rump. The vent area is white, as are the tips of the tail feathers. The dark greyish bill is thick and pointed, and the lores behind are white. Legs and feet are also greyish. Young birds are similar to adults. Sexes are alike, but males may be slightly larger.

HUNTERS OF THE NIGHT

Most owls become more active after dark, and so are more likely to be heard than seen. They are predatory birds, and it is possible to determine their diet by examining their pellets, which are the indigestible remains of their prey regurgitated after a meal. These pellets are often found near their nests or at favoured roosting sites, indicating their presence.

Tawny owl

Strix aluco

The distinctive double call notes of these owls reveal their presence, even though their dark coloration makes them difficult to spot. Tawny owls prefer ancient woodland, where trees are large enough to provide hollow nesting cavities. They will, however, adapt to using nest boxes, which has helped to increase their numbers in some areas. Nocturnal by nature, these owls may nevertheless occasionally hunt during the daytime, especially when they have chicks in the nest. They usually sit quietly on a perch, waiting to swoop down on their quarry. Young tawny owls are unable to fly when they first leave the nest, and at this time the adults can become very aggressive in protecting their offspring.

Identification: Tawny-brown, with white markings across the wings and darker striations over the wings and body. Slight barring on the tail. Distinctive white stripes above the facial disc, which is almost plain brown. Some individuals have a greyer tone to their plumage, while others are more rufous. The bill is yellowish-brown. Sexes are similar, although females are generally larger and heavier. Females are also distinguished by their higher-pitched song.

Distribution: Across Europe (not Ireland) to Scandinavia and eastwards into Asia. Also occurs in North Africa.
Size: 43cm (17in).
Habitat: Favours ancient temperate woodland.
Nest: Tree hole.
Eggs: 2–9, white.
Food: Small mammals, birds and invertebrates.

African wood owl

Woodford's owl *Strix woodfordii*

These owls can be encountered in a range of different woodland types, from mountainous areas right down to coastal forests, and can also be observed in agricultural plantations. They are relatively common throughout their range, although their nocturnal nature ensures they are inconspicuous. African wood owls take a wide variety of prey, but typically hunt in a similar fashion irrespective of location. They perch on a relatively low branch, often no more than 2m (6.5ft) off the ground, and proceed to drop down on their unsuspecting target from above, although occasionally they will also catch insects in flight. As well as invertebrates, numerous small vertebrates may also be caught, ranging from amphibians and reptiles to small mammals such as shrews. Breeding pairs will establish their own territory and choose a nest site, which is likely to be reused annually. The hen sits alone, with incubation lasting approximately 31 days, and the young will leave the nest after a similar interval, before they are able to fly well.

Identification: Pale whitish area above and beneath the eyes, with fine brown barring over the face. Variable dark brown head and back, with white spotting. Spotting especially evident on the wings, extending in a line from the shoulders. White and brownish barring on the underparts. Alternating dark and light barring across the tail too. Some individuals are a more russet shade. No ear tufts. Dark irides and yellow bill. Young birds paler with white barring. Hens are larger in size.

Distribution: From Senegal in western Africa eastwards across central Africa to Kenya and southern Somalia. Also extends north into Ethiopia and down the east coast to South Africa, but absent from Namibia and surrounding areas of the south.
Size: 34cm (13in).
Habitat: Forested areas.
Nest: Tree cavity.
Eggs: 1–3, white.
Food: Mainly invertebrates.

Long-eared owl (*Asio otus*): 37cm (14.5in)
Ranges through Europe and across Asia. Found
also in north-western Africa and North America.
Characteristic tufts on the head are only raised
when the owl is alert. Facial area is an orangish-
yellow, with a white central area extending
between the orange eyes and around the bill.
Underparts are pale yellow with black streaking.
Hens have more rusty-buff faces, otherwise
sexes are alike.

Shelley's eagle owl (*Bubo shelleyi*):
60cm (24in)
Restricted to West Africa, notably Sierra Leone,
ranging to Gabon and Dem. Rep. Congo. Large
and dark, with brown patches surrounding the
characteristic dark eyes. Underparts are blackish-
brown, with alternating white barring. Tall ear
tufts and brown barring on the tail. Females are
larger. Young birds are paler than adults, with
more evident white areas of plumage.

Maned owl (Akun scops owl, *Jubula lettii*):
40cm (15.75in)
West Africa, from Liberia to Ghana, with a
separate population between Cameroon and
Gabon extending eastwards across Dem. Rep.
Congo. Distinctive shaggy feathers, creating a
mane-like appearance on the nape. White
eyebrows edged with black, and a rufous area
around the eyes. Characteristic rufous chest,
becoming buff with streaks on the underparts.
Back also rufous, with some white markings.
Light and dark barring on the wings and tail.
Eyes and bill yellow. Hens are darker and more
heavily marked. Young birds are paler.

Ural owl

Ural wood owl *Strix uralensis*

Ural owls often hunt on the fringes of the
woodland, occasionally straying near to
villages, particularly in winter. Here they are
able to catch birds such as pigeons and
sparrows more easily. Traditionally, small
mammals such as voles are their main prey.
Hunting at night, these owls rely largely on
their keen sense of hearing, and can even
detect quarry under 30cm (1ft) of snow.
Their breeding season begins in February.
A tree cavity is normally chosen, but
the abandoned nests of other birds
of prey may be used. They will
also adopt nest boxes, which
has helped to increase their
numbers in some areas.
Mature when three
years old, banding
studies reveal
Ural owls may
live for over
20 years.

Distribution: Ranges through
the Baltic region, Finland and
much of Sweden into Russia,
and across Asia to Japan.
Also occurs in separate
locations in central and south-
eastern Europe.
Size: 60cm (24in).
Habitat: Prefers
lowland forest.
Nest: Tree cavity.
Eggs: 2–4, white.
Food: Mainly small
mammals and birds.

Identification: Relatively
plain greyish facial disc.
Remainder of the plumage
is white, heavily streaked on
the underparts, with a greyer
tone barred with brown
markings over the back and
tail. Bill yellowish, irides
dark brown. Young birds
paler, with white markings
on the head. Hens larger.

Northern hawk owl

Surnia ulula

Distribution: Ranges from
northern parts of Scandinavia
eastwards through Russia,
extending as far as the Pacific
coast of Asia. Also present at
similar latitudes
in North America.
Size: 40cm (15³/₄in).
Habitat: Coniferous forest.
Nest: Tree hole.
Eggs: 5–13, white.
Food: Small mammals.

Occurring in the far north, where day length varies
significantly through the year, northern hawk owls can
be encountered at any time. They are solitary by nature
outside the breeding season. Males call to attract a mate
in late spring. A pair may choose from a variety of
nesting sites, for example making use of a hole created
by a woodpecker, taking over an abandoned stick nest,
or simply choosing a site on top of a tree whose crown has snapped
off, creating a depression. They make no attempt at nest-building
themselves. Eggs are laid at two-day intervals, with the hen sitting alone
and the male bringing food to her. Lemmings usually predominate in their diet,
but in years when the lemming population plummets, other prey – even small fish –
may be caught. Breeding success is directly related to the availability of food. The
young fledge at four weeks old, but it will be a further two weeks before they can fly,
and they remain dependent on their parents for food for a further month.

Identification: Prominent white eyebrows and white cheeks, with whitish spotting on the dark head and
wings. European birds appear whiter overall than those from North America. Broad black bars on each side of
the neck. More brownish on the barred underparts and tail. Eyes and bill pale yellow. Eyes are brighter yellow
in young birds. Sexes are alike.

DAYLIGHT PREDATORS

Numerous birds of prey whose relatives are more commonly seen over open country have adapted to living and hunting in forests. They range from large eagles to the smaller, more agile goshawks and sparrowhawks. Some hunt in the forest understorey, while others glide above the canopy, ever watchful for movements of prey in the trees beneath them.

Goshawk

Accipiter gentilis

Goshawks are opportunistic hunters. In the far north, birds such as grouse (*Tetraonidae*) are significant in their diet, but in central Europe they prey more on pigeons and rabbits. The Spanish population hunts lizards, although larger quarry is preferred. Appearance is equally variable through their range, with birds from the far north paler than those further south. Breeding starts in April, with pairs seeking out tall trees as nesting sites, each occupying a large territory. The bulky nest is made from sticks with a softer lining of leaves. Incubation lasts five weeks. Young cock goshawks leave the nest after a similar interval, about a week before their female siblings.

Identification: Dark cap, pale around the eyes. Grey ear coverts, lighter wings. White underparts finely barred with grey. Broad, light-and-dark grey tail banding. Iris orange. Yellow cere, dark tip to the bill. Hens slaty-grey, cocks bluish-grey. Young brownish above, with brownish streaking on buff-coloured underparts.

Distribution: Throughout mainland Europe, except for the far north of Scandinavia and southern parts of the Iberian Peninsula. Localized in British Isles (absent from Ireland). Small population present in north-west Africa, opposite the Strait of Gibraltar. Extends across Asia. Also found in North America down to Mexico.
Size: 68cm (26³/₄in).
Habitat: Forested areas.
Nest: Platform made from sticks and leaves.
Eggs: 1–5, bluish-white.
Food: Mammals and birds.

African cuckoo hawk

Aviceda cuculoides

Cuckoo hawks are so named not because they prey on cuckoos but simply because their barred patterning is similar to that of many cuckoos (*Cuculidae*). They are shy birds by nature, perching quietly for long periods before darting down to seize prey such as a chameleon climbing along a branch, or taking quarry directly from the ground. African cuckoo hawks have even been recorded as catching fish and crabs, and they may also catch flying insects. The breeding period varies through their range, but is usually linked to the onset of the rainy season. The nest is located as high as 30m (100ft) above the ground, and measures up to 30cm (1ft) in diameter. The young hatch after about 30 days, and will fledge up to six weeks later. After the breeding period, African cuckoo hawks disperse and may be recorded in areas where they are not normally seen. They themselves can also fall victim to larger birds of prey.

Identification: Bluish-grey head and chest, becoming darker grey over the wings. A paler streak is present above the eyes. Small crest at the back of the head. The tail has alternating bands of dark and light grey, and the underparts are white with rufous bands. Cocks have reddish-brown irides, while hens have yellow. Young birds have brown upperparts and brown mottling on the breast.

Distribution: Roughly south of a line from Senegal in western Africa to Kenya in the east, although absent from much of Tanzania. Absent also from much of Namibia, Botswana and western South Africa.
Size: 40cm (15³/₄in).
Habitat: Woodland.
Nest: Platform of sticks.
Eggs: 2–3, greenish-blue with darker markings.
Food: Mostly invertebrates and lizards.

Palmnut vulture

Gyphohierax angolensis

Up to two-thirds of the diet of these raptors consists of palmnuts and similar food such as dates, although they are not entirely frugivorous. They will also catch fish and crabs, especially in the eastern part of their range. In more typical vulture-style, they will scavenge on carrion, frequently being attracted to road kills. Usually quite solitary birds, palmnut vultures occasionally associate in groups, particularly where food is plentiful, and will drive away birds such as hornbills (*Bucerotidae*) as well as monkeys attracted to the palm trees. Pairs become very territorial when breeding. The nest is large and bulky, measuring up to 90cm (3ft) in diameter, although only a single egg is laid. Their chick grows slowly, and will not fledge until it is approximately three months old. Both adults share the incubation and rearing.

Identification: Black and white, with the black plumage extending over the back and wings, and also at the base of the tail, which is short and rounded. Bare reddish-pink areas of skin on the face. Large horn-coloured bill, and yellowish legs. Young birds are brownish and black, with greyish skin on the face and a dark bill and legs; white plumage only evident as a band in front of the black flight feathers under the wings. Hens are significantly heavier than cocks.

Distribution: Western and central Africa, from Senegal to southern Sudan, south to Angola and northern Zambia. Occasionally reported further south. Also occurs in some eastern coastal areas from Kenya to Mozambique.
Size: 60cm (23¾in).
Habitat: Forested areas, often close to palms.
Nest: Large platform made from sticks.
Eggs: 1, white with dark brown and lilac markings.
Food: Mainly fruit, some animal food.

African crowned eagle (*Stephanoaetus coronatus*): 98cm (38¾in)
Western-central Africa, and down the eastern side to South Africa. Dark grey upperparts. Whitish lower chest and abdomen heavily barred with black, with a rufous suffusion. Barring on the tail. Iris, legs and feet yellow, bill black. Slight crest at the back of the head. Hens have fewer wing bars. Young have white head and underparts, dark iris, and speckling on the legs.

Forest buzzard (*Buteo trizonatus*): 50cm (19¾in)
Southern South Africa. Also from Zimbabwe to Lesotho. Brownish head, back and wings, whitish above the eyes and on the cheeks. Tail rufous with darker brown barring. Whitish breast band, with brown streaking on the underparts and rufous markings around the thighs. Wings dark at their tips when seen from beneath, with brown markings, especially on the leading edge. Rest of the wings white. Cere yellow, bill dark at its tip. Young birds lack the broad sub-terminal tail band, and have paler underparts.

Red-thighed sparrowhawk (*Accipter erythropus*): 30cm (12in)
Sierra Leone to Dem. Rep. Congo. Population in Senegal. Dark greyish-black upperparts and tail. White rump, white spots on the tail underside. Whitish throat, greyer underparts. Rufous suffusion on the flanks. Hens have browner upperparts and barring on the breast. Iris and cere orange-red, bill black. Young have brown upperparts, dark rump, yellow iris and often barring on the breast.

Lesser spotted eagle

Aquila pomarina

Lesser spotted eagles catch a wide variety of prey, from amphibians to small mammals, depending on location. In Greece they take snakes, whereas in Africa they prey on red-billed weavers (*Quelea quelea*) and termites. Pairs return annually to their chosen nest site. The youngest chick fails to survive since it is deprived of food by its older sibling, which fledges after eight weeks. It can be five years before the young bird attains full plumage. European birds head to Africa during September, flying east over the Bosphorus and Israel.

Distribution: Breeds in eastern and central parts of Europe, reaching the Caspian Sea. Overwinters in eastern and southern parts of Africa. Also occurs in India.
Size: 65cm (25½in).
Habitat: Forested areas.
Nest: A platform made from sticks.
Eggs: 1–2, dull white with variable dark markings.
Food: Takes a wide range of prey.

Identification: Brown body and dark greyish flight feathers. Slightly paler head and neck. Relatively small bill, yellow at the base and dark at the tip. Feet yellow with black claws. Young birds usually display white edging to the flight feathers, often with a rufous patch at the back of the head. Hens are larger.

GIANTS OF THE PLAINS

The spread of open grassland afforded some birds the opportunity to grow much larger. Although this left them unable to fly, their pace, physical stature and lethally-strong legs meant they could defend themselves against predators. The ostrich is the only member of this ancient group surviving in Africa today, but other large birds live in groups on the plains too.

Ostrich

Struthio camelus

The ostrich is the tallest and one of the heaviest birds in the world, with males weighing up to 150kg (330lb). They have just two toes on each foot, and can run at 50kph (31mph) – even faster over short distances. They will eat almost anything, from plant matter and carrion to lizards and even small tortoises. Ostriches live in groups, headed by a dominant male. He pairs with one of the females, known as the major hen, who lays her eggs in a scrape. Other hens also lay here, but the major hen concentrates on her own eggs, rolling any surplus out of the nest. The young ostriches will all hatch six weeks later.

Identification: Blackish, with a white tail, white wing feathers and white neck band. Hens smaller and greyish-brown, with no white. Legs dark pink. Young are smaller, light brown and striped.

Distribution: Ranges across Africa in a band south of the Sahara, and also through much of eastern Africa. Separate population found in the south of the continent.
Size: 275cm (108in).
Habitat: Open country, including semi-desert.
Nest: Scrape on the ground.
Eggs: 7–10, glossy white.
Food: Omnivorous.

Secretary bird

Sagittarius serpentarius

Distribution: Found in a broad band across Africa south of the Sahara, through eastern Africa, and across the south of the continent.
Size: 140cm (55in).
Habitat: Open grassland.
Nest: Platform of sticks.
Eggs: 1–3, whitish to bluish-green in colour.
Food: Invertebrates, snakes, small animals.

These unusual birds of prey have no close relatives. Although capable of soaring on their large wings like vultures, secretary birds spend most of the time walking across the plains on the look-out for prey, covering about 20km (12¹/₂ miles) a day. Their long legs are useful for tackling venomous snakes, which they will literally stamp to death, without being bitten. They may catch small birds, and raid their nests, and have been observed trying to eat golf balls thinking they are eggs. Inedible items are, however, ejected as pellets after a meal.

Pairs build a large, bulky platform nest, sometimes over several months, and both adults incubate and raise their offspring. Chicks spend about 10 weeks in the nest, although their growth is influenced by the food supply.

Identification: Whitish head, with prominent red skin around the eyes. Darker, trailing crest. Chest, neck, upper back and wings, rump and tail are all grey. Flight feathers and the rest of the wings are black, as are the thighs. Black tip to the tail. Long, yellowish legs and grey bill. Young birds have yellow skin and a short tail. Sexes are alike.

Northern crowned crane (black crowned crane, *Balearica pavonina*): 100cm (39in)
Range is restricted to a band across Africa south of the Sahara (more patchily distributed in western parts and more common in Sudan and Ethiopia). Golden crown on the head, with a reddish area beneath. Predominantly dark grey, with white on the wings and a golden area towards the brown tail. Prominent reddish throat wattle. Bill, legs and feet are blackish. Sexes are alike. Young birds display brown mottling on their plumage.

Blue crane (*Anthropoides paradiseus*): 100cm (39in)
Range is mainly confined to eastern and southern parts of South Africa, with a separate population in northern Namibia. White cap over the broad head. Remainder of the plumage is greyish, darker on the back, flight feathers and tail. The bill and legs are yellowish-grey. Sexes are alike. Young birds are paler overall, especially on the head.

Demoiselle crane (*Anthropoides virgo*): 90cm (35in)
Distribution extends from Egypt southwards, to Chad in the west across to eastern Ethiopia. Greyish-black head and upper neck, with a light grey patch extending from behind the eyes to form a tuft of feathers at the back of the neck. Dark plumage otherwise restricted to the underside of the throat and the flight feathers. Young birds easily recognized by the absence of blackish markings on the head and throat. Sexes are alike.

Grey crowned crane

Balearica regulorum

With a population estimated at 90,000 individuals, these are the most common cranes in Africa. They have adapted well to increased farming, moving into agricultural areas, especially adjacent to wetlands. Crowned cranes will sometimes associate with herds of grazing herbivores, such as zebras, looking for insects and small animals disturbed by the herd. In wetland areas, amphibians such as frogs form a significant part of their diet. Frequently quite solitary, grey crowned cranes may form large flocks during the dry season. Their breeding period is closely linked to rainfall. Incubation lasts about a month, and the young birds, which are brownish at first, may remain in the nest for nine weeks or more. They become sexually mature during their second year.

Identification: Prominent golden crown, with a black area in front. White skin on the cheeks with a thin black line behind, and a red wattle on the throat. Grey neck and upper breast. Back and underparts dark grey, with prominent white and golden areas on the wings. Tail brown. Bill, legs and feet greyish. Young birds have small cheek patches, with a less prominent crown.

Distribution: Eastern Africa, from Kenya to Mozambique and westwards to southern Angola and northern Namibia. Also present in the eastern part of South Africa.
Size: 110cm (43in).
Habitat: Grassland and agricultural areas.
Nest: On the ground, made from vegetation.
Eggs: 1–4, dirty white with brown spots.
Food: Omnivorous.

Wattled crane

Grus carunculatus

These cranes are most likely to be encountered in wetland areas. They use their large bills to dig in the wet soil for the tubers of water-lilies and other roots. They also feed on amphibians and invertebrates such as water snails, and will forage over agricultural land. Their breeding period is linked to the rainy season. Wattled cranes construct a bulky nest from vegetable matter, normally surrounded by about 4m (13ft) of water, which protects them from predators. Incubation can last nearly five weeks, and the young cranes develop slowly. They are unlikely to leave the nest before three months of age, and sometimes not until they are 4¹/₂ months old. Development is influenced by the available food supply.

Identification: Tall, elegant bird with a prominent area of red skin at the base of the bill, and an adjacent wattle. Bare greyish-black crown. Hind part of the head and the neck are white, while the underparts are black. Back and wings grey. Bill is light grey, legs and feet darker. Sexes are alike. Young birds have a whitish crown.

Distribution: Isolated populations in Ethiopia, Angola and Namibia, and South Africa. Main range is centred on Zambia and surroundings countries. Also occasionally recorded from elsewhere in Africa.
Size: 120cm (47in).
Habitat: Grassland adjacent to wetlands.
Nest: Pile of vegetation.
Eggs: 1–2, sandy-cream, with darker markings.
Food: Mainly vegetation, some invertebrates.

STORKS AND IBISES

While some large African birds have moved into grassland areas, storks still retain a close affinity with water. Different species have developed distinctive feeding habits suited to their particular diet and environment, perhaps none more so than the unmistakable shoebill. Ibises are smaller, but they too are most likely to be encountered near water.

Shoebill stork

Whale-headed stork *Balaeniceps rex*

Identification: Unmistakable. Huge greyish-yellow bill. Plumage greyish overall, slightly darker on the back and wings, with a slight crest on the back of the head. Blackish legs and feet. Young darker grey, with a pink tip to the bill. Sexes are alike.

These bizarre storks are very distinctive thanks to their massive bill, which measures nearly 20cm (8in) long and almost as wide. This enables them to catch larger fish and other aquatic prey such as small crocodiles. Quarry is decapitated using the sharp ridges along the edge of the bill. The shoebill's hunting technique is also quite distinctive. It relys primarily on stealth, waiting with head pointing downwards and seizing prey that comes within reach, toppling forwards as it lunges. It has just a single opportunity to strike, since its intended prey is likely to be out of reach once it has regained its balance. Such is the difficulty of feeding in this fashion that shoebills may have to wait several days to make a catch. They are solitary birds by nature, even when breeding.

Distribution: Eastern Africa, from Ethiopia and Sudan to Uganda. Scattered distribution in Tanzania, Dem. Rep. Congo and Zambia.
Size: 120cm (47in).
Habitat: Open country, close to water and swampland.
Nest: Platform of vegetation.
Eggs: 1–3, a chalky bluish-white colour.
Food: Aquatic vertebrates, especially fish.

Saddle-billed woodstork

Saddlebill *Ephippiorhynchus senegalensis*

Distribution: Ranges in a narrow band across Africa south of the Sahara, up to north-eastern Sudan. Also occurs south across much of the continent, except for the far south.
Size: 145cm (57in).
Habitat: Open country, close to water.
Nest: Tree platform of sticks.
Eggs: 2–3, dull white.
Food: Small vertebrates.

Like other storks, saddlebills are found near wetland and feed mainly on fish, but they also prey on other aquatic creatures, including water beetles and amphibians, as well as small birds. They will usually seize their quarry directly, but in muddy water or among reeds will probe with their long bills to detect prey. Unlike most storks, however, the saddlebill and other members of its genus display clear sexual dimorphism. Nesting generally begins towards the end of the rainy season, so that water levels will be falling once the young have hatched, making it easier to find food for them. Pairs of saddlebills are normally solitary by nature and often choose an isolated nesting site, occasionally adopting a cliff-face rather than a tree. The young are unlikely to reach maturity until they are at least three years old, and have a potential life expectancy of 30 years or more.

Identification: Cock has a black head and neck, with a small wattle, and a white area encircling the upper body, extending down on to the underparts. Central areas of the wings are black, as is the tail. Multi-coloured bill, maroon at the base with a yellow area on top, black in the middle, and the terminal half dull red. Brown irides. Legs black with prominent red joints and feet. Bills of young birds are greyish, with a black band down their length. Hens are smaller, with yellow eyes and no wattle.

Marabou stork

Leptoptilos crumeniferus

These storks are frequent scavengers, often to be seen seeking scraps near human habitation, and drawn to road kills of animals too. They will also hunt for their food, both on land and in water. Marabous sometimes mingle with herds of herbivores, seizing snakes and other animals flushed out into the open by the presence of the herd. They will wade into water to hunt fish and other aquatic creatures, both by probing in the shallows and by watching and waiting. Here, they can be seen in groups. Marabou storks breed in colonies, often nesting in association with other storks, and in suitable locations there can be thousands of nesting pairs. They may sometimes nest colonially on the fringes of towns, where there are good opportunities for scavenging on nearby rubbish dumps. However, the majority of birds do not breed on an annual basis, and this may be linked to their long life expectancy – marabous can live for several decades.

Identification: Largely unfeathered reddish head, with a white area behind and on the underparts. Back and wings dark greyish-black. Very prominent, pendulous, pinkish wattle hangs down over the chest. Large, dull-coloured bill. Young birds have a covering of down on their heads. Legs and feet greyish. Sexes are alike, but males larger.

Distribution: Ranges across Africa south of the Sahara, from Senegal in the west to north-eastern Sudan and Ethiopia. Extends southwards through much of eastern and central parts of the continent, reaching the west side in Rep. Congo and Gabon, and again in southern Angola and northern Namibia.
Size: 150cm (59in).
Habitat: Grassland, especially near wetlands.
Nest: Platform made from sticks, in a tree.
Eggs: 1–4, white.
Food: Vertebrates, carrion.

Abdim's stork (white-bellied stork, *Ciconia abdimii*): 80cm (31in)
Across most of Africa south of the Sahara, except for the western coastal region, much of Mozambique, Namibia and the far south. Predominantly blackish, with a dark bluish face. White plumage on the lower underparts extends beneath the wings, and the lower back and rump are also white. Greenish-grey legs, with pinkish feet. Young birds are duller, especially on the face. Sexes are alike, but male larger.

Wattled ibis (*Bostrychia carunculata*): 80cm (31in)
Restricted to the highland areas of Ethiopia and southern Eritrea. Plumage of the head is greyish, with faint white edging to the untidy crest at the back of the head. Wings are darker, with more prominent white patches running down from the shoulders. Bill reddish, with a wattle at the base. Feet also reddish. Young birds are duller, with no wattle. Sexes are alike.

São Tomé ibis (dwarf olive ibis, *Bostrychia bocagei*): 62cm (24in)
Found only on the island of São Tomé, in the Gulf of Guinea off Africa's west coast. Dull greenish head and underparts, with traces of white edging to the crest at the back of the head. The area around the eyes is dark, with a whitish streak extending a short distance back from here. Metallic green coloration on the wings. Iris orangish. Bill, legs and feet reddish. Young birds have shorter crests. Sexes are alike.

Southern bald ibis

Geronticus calvus

These ibises hunt for invertebrates in short grass grazed by livestock. Their breeding cycle is linked to the grassland fire season, which results from lightning strikes. The young leave the cliff-face colony at eight weeks, but fledging success depends on rainfall. Unlike the northern bald ibis (*G. eremita*), which is critically endangered, this species is relatively common and has a population of up to 5000 individuals. A few new colonies have also been discovered in recent years.

Distribution: Restricted to southern Africa, ranging from north-east Botswana down to South Africa and eastwards to Lesotho and the coast.
Size: 80cm (31in).
Habitat: Grassland.
Nest: Platform of sticks.
Eggs: 1–5, bluish-white with dark markings.
Food: Mainly invertebrates.

Identification: Glossy blackish overall, with coppery-purple patches on the shoulders. Top of the bare head has a reddish crown, and the face itself is pinkish. The bill, legs and feet are pinkish-red. Young birds are significantly duller, lacking the coppery feathering on the wings; head has a covering of brownish feathers, and the bill, legs and feet are mainly greyish.

ADAPTABLE INSECT-HUNTERS

Open countryside can take a number of forms, ranging from huge expanses of grassland to inaccessible upland areas where trees are largely absent. Birds have adapted to living in both types of terrain. For example, rock nuthatches nest and hunt for invertebrates on exposed crags and hillsides, whereas all other species of nuthatch are at home in woodland areas.

Rock nuthatch

Western rock nuthatch *Sitta neumayer*

Distribution: Resident in south-eastern parts of Europe into Asia, from along the eastern Adriatic down to Greece and through much of Turkey into Iran.
Size: 15cm (6in).
Habitat: Rocky country.
Nest: Made of mud.
Eggs: 6–9, white with heavy dark markings.
Food: Largely invertebrates.

Ranging to altitudes of around 900m (3,000ft), these nuthatches occur most commonly in limestone areas, and are quite at home on steep slopes. They hunt avidly for small invertebrates such as spiders, probing into crevices and among vegetation in search of food. Their breeding season starts in the spring, and the nest is made from wet mud hardened into a bottle-shaped chamber. It is well-hidden, out of sight at the base of a cliff overhang or in a cleft in the rocks. The interior of the nest is lined with soft material including feathers and plant matter. The hen incubates the eggs on her own, with the chicks hatching after about two weeks. Both members of the pair will forage for food for their offspring, who fledge when they are 25 days old.

Identification: Narrow black eye stripe from the base of the bill back through each eye and down the sides of the neck. The cheeks and remainder of the underparts are pure white, but with a very indistinct buff suffusion on the lower underparts. Upperparts are grey. Bill, legs and feet are all blackish-grey. Young birds are similar to adults. Sexes are alike.

Wallcreeper

Tichodroma muraria

Grouped together with nuthatches, wallcreepers are similarly agile, able to climb vertical surfaces and dart up rock faces without difficulty, although they are very rarely observed in trees. However, wallcreepers also spend a significant amount of time foraging for food on the ground. They are lively birds, with a fluttering flight pattern not dissimilar to that of a butterfly. Even when sedentary, they often flick their wings repeatedly. In the Alps they reach altitudes of 2,300m (7,500ft), but may venture to more than double this height in the Himalayas. They move to lower altitudes during the winter. In Europe, breeding begins in May. A variety of material gathered by both adults is used to make the nest, which is hidden in a small hole in a cliff face, although they have also been found in buildings.

Identification: In summer, cocks have a black throat and black sides to the face, with dark grey underparts and upperparts. Wings have very evident reddish patches, with white tips to the darker feathers here and on the tail. Hens have a pale greyish-white throat and chest, with the grey on the wings lighter; they also develop a blackish patch on the throat during the summer. Young birds are duller. Narrow, slightly curved black bill. Legs are also black.

Distribution: Resident in southern parts of Europe, from northern Spain and the Pyrenees through to parts of Italy and along the eastern Adriatic to Greece. Also present in Asia.
Size: 17cm (6³/₄in).
Habitat: Rocky areas.
Nest: Made of vegetation.
Eggs: 4, white with reddish-brown markings.
Food: Invertebrates.

Eastern rock nuthatch (*Sitta tephronota*): 18cm (7in)
Extreme south-eastern Europe, into Asia. Broad black stripe through and behind the eyes. Grey upperparts. Sides of the face and breast are whitish, with the abdomen showing a very clear buff suffusion. Grey bill, legs and feet. Young birds are similar to adults. Sexes are alike.

Black-headed lapwing (*Vanellus tectus*): 25cm (10in)
Across Africa south of the Sahara, from Senegal to Somalia. Head is black above, with a white stripe through the eyes and black below, on to the chest. Buff back and wings, with white and black areas. Rump white, tail black. Pale buff underparts. Reddish wattles at the base of the black-tipped bill. Legs and feet reddish. Young birds duller, with small wattles. Sexes are alike.

Senegal lapwing (*Vanellus lugubris*): 25cm (10in)
Senegal to Nigeria. Also across central-eastern Africa to South Africa. Isolated population in Angola. Dull whitish forehead and throat, with greyish-black over the head and breast; a black band separates this from the white underparts. Wings and back dark brownish-grey. Rump and back of the wings in flight are white. Tail black. Reddish skin encircles the eyes. Bill is greyish, as are the legs and feet. Young birds browner on the back, with buff fringes. Sexes are alike.

Eurasian wryneck

Jynx torquilla

Wrynecks return to their breeding grounds by April, when pairs are very territorial. They seek a suitable hollow, which may be in a tree, on the ground or in a bank. When displaying, pairs face each other and shake their heads, opening their bills to reveal pink gapes. The two-week incubation is shared, and both adults care for their young, who fledge after three weeks. They are independent in a further two weeks. Two broods may be reared. If disturbed on the nest, a sitting adult will stretch out its head and neck, before suddenly withdrawing it, hissing like a snake. Wrynecks use their long, sticky tongues to rapidly pick up ants, and will eat other invertebrates such as spiders.

Identification: Mottled grey on the upperparts, browner over the wings. Broad, tapering tail. Dark stripe through each eye, narrower adjacent white stripe above. Throat and chest are buff with streaking. Abdomen barred, mainly white with buff near the vent. Young birds are duller. Sexes are alike.

Distribution: Breeds through most of mainland Europe, extending eastwards into northern Asia. Absent from Ireland, and the only British breeding population is in Scotland. Overwinters in Africa in a broad band south of the Sahara, with a resident population also in the north-west.
Size: 16.5cm (6¹/₂in).
Habitat: Open country.
Nest: Suitable hole.
Eggs: 7–10, white.
Food: Mainly ants.

Blacksmith plover

Vanellus armatus

Identification: White crown. Head black, extending over the breast and on to the back. White back to the neck, underparts also white. Wings greyish with black flight feathers. Lower back and rump white, with black on the tail. Bill, legs and feet black. Young have a brownish head, with greyish-brown flight feathers. Sexes are alike.

These plovers are named after their calls, which sound like a hammer hitting a blacksmith's anvil. They are usually found in small groups, but larger numbers may be seen where food is plentiful – such flocks are often mainly immature birds. Their breeding period varies, starting in April in the north but sometimes not until September in the south. They nest near water, and both adults share the incubation, which lasts about a month. The dark markings apparent on the eggs are mirrored in the chicks when they hatch. The young blacksmith plovers fledge when they are six weeks old, but will not breed themselves until their second year. Breeding pairs can become surprisingly aggressive, dive-bombing people who venture too close to the nest site.

Far right: Blacksmith plovers seek invertebrates disturbed by herds

Distribution: Range extends from Kenya on the eastern side and Angola in the west down across virtually the whole of southern Africa. Largely absent from the south and the eastern coastal area of Tanzania, and almost all of Mozambique.
Size: 30cm (12in).
Habitat: Grassland with nearby wetland.
Nest: Scrape on the ground lined with vegetation.
Eggs: 2–4, buff-brown with darker markings.
Food: Invertebrates.

BEE-EATERS AND ROLLERS

Colourful and athletic in flight, these birds are well-known migrants between Europe and Africa. Some Asian populations also head to Africa for the winter, and within Africa itself there are more sedentary species occupying relatively restricted ranges throughout the year. Bee-eaters do hunt bees, carefully removing the stings before swallowing their prey.

Bee-eater

European bee-eater *Merops apiaster*

In spite of their name, European bee-eaters hawk a much wider range of prey in the air than simply bees. More than 300 different invertebrates have been identified in their diet, including dragonflies and butterflies. They have even been known to swoop on spiders, seizing the arachnids from their webs. Although individual birds hunt on their own, European bee-eaters nest in colonies of up to eight pairs. Sandy cliffs, where they can excavate their breeding tunnels with relative ease, are favoured nesting sites. Outside the breeding season, groups roost huddled together on branches.

Identification: Whitish band above the black bill, merging into blue above the eyes. Black band extends from the bill through each eye. The throat is yellow, with a black band separating it from the bluish underparts. Chestnut-brown extends from the top of the head, over the back and across the wings. Golden scapulars and rump. Hens have more green on their wings and scapulars.

Distribution: Ranges across much of southern and south-eastern Europe, extending into adjacent parts of Asia and into North Africa. Overwinters in western and southern Africa.
Size: 25cm (10in).
Habitat: Open country.
Nest: Tunnel in a bank or cliff.
Eggs: 4–10, white.
Food: Flying invertebrates.

Blue-cheeked bee-eater

Merops persicus

These social and predominantly Asiatic bee-eaters may migrate alongside European bee-eaters, flying at high altitude to their African wintering grounds. They head over north-west Somalia and the Rift Valley region of Ethiopia, with those birds travelling right down to South Africa arriving here from November. Large numbers may be observed in some locations – as many as 1,500 bee-eaters were observed in a single tree in Mauritania. When seeking flying insects, they will often use vantage points in the open, such as telegraph poles, and so are relatively conspicuous. In direct contrast to their arid breeding habitat, however, blue-cheeked bee-eaters favour wintering grounds close to water, where they are able to catch dragonflies, an important item in their diet. They may even trawl large invertebrates on the water's surface, flying back to a perch to hammer the unfortunate creature before eating it.

Identification: Broad black stripe running through each eye, edged with a border of white, with light blue stripes above and below. Throat yellowish-orange. The back of the head and wings are green, as is the tail, which terminates in narrow streamers. Chest greenish, underparts blue. Reddish undersides to the wings. Young birds are duller. Hens have shorter tail streamers.

Distribution: Breeds in north-west Africa, and the extreme south-east of Europe through into Asia. Winters in western Africa, from Senegal to Central African Republic, and also through central and eastern parts of the continent south to northern Namibia and northern South Africa.
Size: 25cm (10in).
Habitat: Open country.
Nest: Bank or ground burrow.
Eggs: 4–8, white.
Food: Bees, flying insects.

European roller

Coracias garrulus

European rollers may occupy an old woodpecker nest site, and will even tunnel into a suitable bank. The hen sits alone during incubation, which lasts 18 days, and the young fledge after a further month. Although solitary at this stage, the European roller's northward migration in early April is a spectacular sight. Tens of thousands of birds can be observed flying in massive columns more than 2km (1¼ miles) wide through the coastal regions of Tanzania and Kenya. They leave Africa via Somalia and head to Oman, which is used as a staging post before they continue northwards to their breeding grounds. The journey covers some 10,000km (6,250 miles) and lasts just over three months. Their southerly migration is less evident, and takes even longer.

Identification: Vivid turquoise-blue head and breast, with more lilac stripes around the sides of the head. Underparts slightly greener. Wings also vivid blue on the edges, and the back and inner area are reddish-brown. Mainly black flight feathers. Tail bluish, with greyish central feathers. Young are much duller and paler, with pale blue streaked underparts and brown on the wings. Sexes are alike.

Distribution: Summer visitor to Europe, breeding through much of the Iberian peninsula and the Mediterranean region into Asia, and through much of eastern Europe north to the Baltic. Also breeds in north-west Africa. Migrates mainly to eastern and southern parts of Africa, but also western Africa.
Size: 30cm (12in).
Habitat: Arid open country.
Nest: Usually a tree hole.
Eggs: 2–6, white.
Food: Largely invertebrates.

Red-throated bee-eater (*Merops bulocki*): 22cm (8¾in)
Extends across western Africa, from Senegal to Chad. A separate population ranges from Ethiopia to northern parts of Uganda and Dem. Rep. Congo. Bright green head with a broad blackish eye stripe. Red throat, with an orange breast becoming yellower on the abdomen. Undertail coverts and rump are blue. Dark black edging along the flight feathers. Narrow, slightly down-curved dark bill. Black legs and feet. Young birds are duller. Sexes are alike.

Little green bee-eater (*Merops orientalis*): 20cm (8in)
Range extends across Africa south of the Sahara. Also present in the Middle East. Predominantly green overall, lighter and decidedly more yellowish on the cheeks, throat and underparts. A black stripe passes through each eye, with blue beneath. Narrow black stripe across the throat. The flight feathers are greenish-brown with black tips. Young birds lack the throat marking and are less brightly coloured overall. Long tail streamers. Black bill, legs and feet. Sexes are alike.

Somali bee-eater (*Merops revoilii*): 15cm (6in)
Restricted to Somalia and neighbouring parts of Ethiopia and Kenya. Black eye stripe, with a blue line above. Prominent area of white plumage on the throat. Pinkish-buff collar and underparts. Blue lower back and rump, the upperparts otherwise greenish. Blue undertail coverts. Bill, legs and feet are black. Young birds are slightly duller. Sexes are alike.

Racket-tailed roller

Coracias spatulatus

As with related species, male racket-tailed rollers have a dramatic display flight. This entails them flying vertically to 10m (33ft) and tumbling down with wings closed, calling loudly, then rolling as they begin to fly up again. Unlike many rollers, however, these birds are sedentary, although they may undertake local movements outside the breeding season. Racket-tailed rollers often rest on and hunt off low perches, darting down to the ground to grab a range of invertebrates. Nesting occurs between September and December. Pairs seek out a bare chamber, which may have been created by a woodpecker or a barbet, around 7m (23ft) off the ground. Here they are very territorial, but outside the breeding season may be seen in small groups – possibly family parties – of up to seven birds.

Distribution: Range extends through part of southern Africa, from southern Angola on the western side of the continent across to northern Tanzania and southern Mozambique in the east.
Size: 30cm (12in).
Habitat: Open country.
Nest: Tree hollow.
Eggs: 2–4, white.
Food: Invertebrates.

Identification: Black stripe runs through each eye, with white above and brown on the crown extending back over the wings. Sky blue cheeks and slightly greenish underparts. Violet-blue shoulders, rump and flight feathers. Dark upper tail feathers with a pair of enlarged "rackets" at their tips, which are absent in young birds. Young are duller overall, as are moulting adults. Bill, legs and feet black. Sexes are alike.

SMALLER BIRDS OF THE PLAINS

Camouflage is an important element of survival in the grassland, since there is much less natural cover here for birds. It is no coincidence that shades of brown, black and white are very common in the coloration of birds occurring in this type of habitat, rather than the vibrant reds and purples typically associated with ground-dwelling species found in forested areas.

Small buttonquail

Kurrichane buttonquail *Turnix sylvaticus*

Identification: Cock bird has a speckled head, with a whitish throat and a rufous-brown chest. Black spots evident on the sides of the breast, and the underparts are a buff shade. Upperparts brownish-black with white edging to the plumage. Hens are larger, with buff around their eyes extending down and around the throat, and are more brightly coloured overall. Young birds are spotted and speckled, and have white abdomens.

In spite of their similarity both in appearance and behaviour to true quail, buttonquail as a group are anatomically more closely related to rails – in lacking a hind toe, for example. The hen's call is noticeably louder than that the cock bird. Having mated with a particular male she will leave him to incubate the eggs and rear the chicks on his own, moving on to find other partners to mate with. Breeding can take place throughout the year, but is most common during the summer months. The chicks hatch after a period of two weeks, and have developed sufficiently to fly by the time they are 10 days old. Kurrichane buttonquail favour dry conditions for breeding, and in years when rainfall is excessive they will irrupt westwards in search of drier terrain. The unusual name of this species – which is pronounced "currycane" – is derived from a place known as Kaditshwene, in the western Transvaal, where it was originally documented by Sir Andrew Smith in 1834.

Distribution: In Europe, a small population is present in southern Spain. Main range extends across Africa south of the Sahara, though largely absent from Somalia and much of Ethiopia, the central area from southern Nigeria to Dem. Rep. Congo, and southern Namibia to western South Africa. Extends to Asia.
Size: 15cm (6in).
Habitat: Grassland areas.
Nest: Scrape on the ground.
Eggs: 3–4, cream-coloured with darker speckling.
Food: Seeds, invertebrates.

Whinchat

Saxicola rubetra

Whinchats hunt for food largely on the wing, catching their insect prey in the air or swooping low over the ground. They arrive in Europe by April, and in agricultural areas can be seen perching on field fences in the open. They often flick their tail feathers upwards when they land on a perch. These chats have a protracted song which is often audible at night, although it is not as fluid as those of true thrushes. The female builds the nest on her own, choosing a site which is relatively hidden. She uses a variety of material to create the basic structure, including grass, and lines the inside with softer material such as feathers. The hen also incubates alone, while her partner remains in attendance nearby. The eggs hatch about two weeks later and both members of the pair will feed their young chicks, who grow rapidly and may leave the nest when they are just 12 days old. Pairs often rear two broods. They begin the southbound migration to their African wintering grounds by October.

Identification: Cock bird has a white stripe above each eye. Another white stripe separates the blackish cheeks from the reddish-orange breast, while the abdomen is whitish. Upperparts have brown and black speckling, and the tail has a prominent black tip. Black bill, legs and feet. Hens have buff rather than white eye stripes, and buffy cheek markings. Young birds resemble hens but have black spotting on the breast.

Distribution: Breeds through most of Europe including Scandinavia, except for parts of Ireland, southern England and much of the Iberian Peninsula. Overwinters in western Africa to Cameroon, and from Sudan to Zambia. Present across Asia to Japan.
Size: 14cm (5¹/₂in).
Habitat: Breeds in open, uncultivated areas.
Nest: Close to the ground.
Eggs: 5–6, pale blue with reddish-brown markings.
Food: Invertebrates.

Stonechat (*Saxicola torquata*): 13cm (5in)
Resident in western Europe, the northern Mediterranean and north-west Africa. Migratory populations breed further east, across Asia to Japan. Overwinters in northern, south-eastern and central Africa. Black head, white collar. Dark wings with a white streak. Underparts reddish-orange, with white around the vent and spotting on the rump. Hens are brownish rather than black, with paler underparts. Young birds have lighter, more buff upperparts.

Blackstart (*Cercomela melanura*): 15cm (6in)
South-eastern Europe. Overwinters in Africa, from eastern Mali and Niger across to Somalia. Whitish throat, with an ash-grey head, chest and wings, and white underparts. Lower back, rump and tail are black. Relatively slender bill is black, as are the legs and feet. Young birds resemble adults. Sexes are alike.

Cream-coloured courser (*Cursorius cursor*): 23cm (9in)
Across Africa, from Mauritania to Sudan. Upright stance. Small area of grey on the hindcrown, with a white stripe extending from the bill above the eyes onto the back of the neck. Black lines extend back from behind the eyes. Sandy body, darker on the wings. Black under the wings, with a small white area at the rear, adjacent to the body. Narrow, dark, slightly down-curved bill, and greyish legs. Young birds have mottled upperparts. Sexes are alike.

Black-winged pratincole

Glareola nordmanni

These pratincoles are most active soon after dawn, when the air is cool, and then again towards dusk. Fast runners, they search for insects on the ground as well as hawking them in flight. Pairs breed in large flocks on steppelands close to water, before starting to moult in July. The southward migration to Africa begins the following month, with the birds usually flying directly over Arabia and the Red Sea. Their winter range may extend as far south as the Kalahari region, where they often help to control the plagues of locusts that arise in this part of the continent (although in South Africa locust control may have led to a decline in numbers). These birds are quite nomadic, moving on to new locations quite unexpectedly.

Distribution: Typically breeds around the Black and Caspian Sea area, extending north-eastwards into northern Asia. Migrates to Africa for the winter, to south-eastern Dem. Rep Congo, Zambia, northern Namibia, Botswana and northern South Africa.
Size: 25cm (10in).
Habitat: Grassland.
Nest: Scrape.
Eggs: 2–3, buff to stone-coloured, dark markings.
Food: Invertebrates.

Identification: Breeding: white throat, underparts and rump. Brownish upperparts, buff chest. Bill base reddish. Non-breeding: duller. Upperparts scalloped in young birds. Sexes alike.

Cattle egret

Bubulcus ibis

Distribution: Very wide pan-global distribution. Ranges through most of Africa except the Sahara and a region in the south. Extends into South-east Asia, to parts of Australia and New Zealand.
Size: 56cm (22in).
Habitat: Shallow waters and even relatively dry areas.
Nest: Sometimes in reedbeds, often on a platform above the ground.
Eggs: 2–5, pale blue.
Food: Invertebrates and small vertebrates like amphibians.

The sharp bills of these egrets enable them to catch their quarry with ease, although in urban areas they can often be seen scavenging around markets and in rubbish dumps. The Asiatic race (*B. i. coromandus*) is the largest and tallest of the three subspecies found worldwide. Banding studies have revealed that cattle egrets will fly long distances, with those birds occurring in north-eastern Asia moving south in the winter. Ringed birds have turned up as far afield as the Philippines. This tendency to roam widely has enabled these egrets to colonize many of the more remote islands in the Pacific. Indeed, distinct seasonal movements have even been recorded in Australia.

Below: The egret's buff plumage is replaced largely by white during the breeding period, for displaying.

Identification: Pale buff coloration on the head, throat (extending down to the breast), back and rump. The remainder of the plumage is white. There may be traces of white plumage around the yellow bill. The legs and feet are also yellow. Sexes are alike.

SMALLER THRUSHES

Many thrushes are migratory by nature, breeding in Europe before flying south to overwinter in Africa. This is partly a reflection of their diet, since thrushes consume large numbers of invertebrates, which are more difficult to obtain during the European winter. Some display marked regional variations in plumage from one part of Europe to another, such as the bluethroat.

Bluethroat

Luscinia svecica

Bluethroats have a powerful and mellifluous song. They arrive in their northern breeding grounds from April onwards, with the loud song of the cock bird betraying its presence, although they are quite shy by nature and not easily observed. Bluethroats are also talented mimics, and in some areas may incorporate other birds' song passages into their own song. Breeding starts at the beginning of May in more southerly parts of their range, while further north it usually commences about a month later. The hen builds the nest on her own, which is carefully concealed close to ground level, hidden among the vegetation. She incubates the eggs for about two weeks, but once the chicks have hatched both members of the pair forage for food for their offspring. The young birds fledge around two weeks after hatching. Bluethroats hunt largely on the ground, seeking worms, snails and other invertebrates. They will also eat berries when they ripen in the autumn.

Identification: Blue throat with a red or white spot, black bib and a reddish band beneath. Underparts greyish-white. Broad white stripe above each eye, brownish-grey cheeks. Upperparts greyish. Inner tail rusty, base black. Hens have a white throat. Young birds are spotted. Bill, legs and feet black.

Distribution: Resident in parts of Iberian Peninsula and east of the Caspian Sea. Breeds in parts of western Europe, but mainly in central and north-eastern Europe across into Asia. Overwinters in Africa south of the Sahara, from Senegal to Somalia.
Size: 14cm (5¹/₂in).
Habitat: Breeds in wetlands and sparse woodland.
Nest: Made of vegetation.
Eggs: 4–7, green to reddish-cream, with darker markings.
Food: Mainly invertebrates.

Common wheatear

Oenanthe oenanthe

Distribution: Breeding range extends throughout virtually all of Europe and parts of north-west Africa, although more patchily distributed in western areas. Overwinters across central Africa north to Egypt, joined by populations from North America.
Size: 15cm (6in).
Habitat: Open countryside.
Nest: Built in a hole.
Eggs: 5–6, pale blue.
Food: Invertebrates.

Found throughout the far north but overwintering in Africa, some wheatears undertake a migration journey of around 12,000km (7,500 miles). Young birds head further south than adults, even reaching South Africa. The wheatear's name is derived from the sound of its calls, rather than its feeding habits. Various types of insects as well as spiders make up the bulk of their diet, although they occasionally eat grass seeds too. Pairs start nesting in April. The hen builds the nest on her own, sometimes in a wall but usually well-hidden and close to the ground. She incubates the eggs largely on her own for two weeks, though both members of the pair hunt for food for their chicks. The young fledge after about 15 days in the nest. A pair may breed twice in succession, especially in southern parts of their breeding range, before migrating south for the winter.

Identification: Cock bird has a white stripe above and a black stripe running through each eye. Remainder of the head and back is grey in breeding condition. The wings and tip of the tail are black. Underparts are white, but with a buff suffusion on the throat and chest. Grey areas become much browner in the autumn. Hens easily separated as their wings are brown not black, and they have no black on the head. Young birds are similar to hens.

Black wheatear

Oenanthe leucura

These wheatears are encountered in rocky areas, often with very little vegetation, usually individually or in pairs rather than as larger groups. Cock birds initiate the breeding cycle, and their distinctive song can be heard more frequently from February onwards. The male seeks out potential nesting sites, but the hen subsequently builds the nest and incubates the eggs largely on her own. The nest is a bulky structure, and the birds use stones weighing up to 28g (1oz), not only at the entrance, where they serve as a barrier against predators, but also as a marker outside. Large accumulations of stones, totalling in excess of 2kg (4½lb), have been recorded at some nests, although these may have been built over more than one breeding season. The young leave the nest at approximately two weeks of age, before they are able to fly well, and retreat under larger rocks and other cover. It may be a further two weeks before they are fully independent.

Identification: The cock bird is a dull shade of black, with white plumage restricted to an area behind the legs, including the vent and rump. The base of the tail feathers is black, and the central tail feathers are all black. Hens are a more sooty-brown shade overall, rather than black. Bill, legs and feet also black. Young birds similar to hens, but have dark brown underparts.

Distribution: In Europe, range extends throughout the Iberian Peninsula. Also present through the adjacent region of north-west Africa, extending into Libya.
Size: 14.5cm (5¾in).
Habitat: Arid slopes.
Nest: Built in a hole.
Eggs: 3–5, whitish to greenish-blue, with some reddish spotting.
Food: Mainly invertebrates.

White-crowned wheatear (*Oenanthe leucopyga*): 18cm (7in)
Resident in scattered locations throughout northern parts of Africa, especially in the north-west, in Morocco and Algeria. Predominantly black overall. Prominent white area on the head from just above the bill, extending back over the crown to the nape. The area behind the legs is white, and the tail is also largely white, with a very definite black central stripe. Bill, legs and feet are black. Young birds have blackish crowns, often with just a few white feathers. Sexes are alike.

Cyprus wheatear (*Oenanthe cypriaca*): 15cm (6in)
Breeding range restricted to the Mediterranean island of Cyprus. Overwinters further south in Africa, in southern Sudan and Ethiopia, migrating via the Middle East. Cock in breeding plumage has a white crown that extends from the bill above the eyes and over the nape of the neck. Remainder of head and upper breast is black, as are the wings. Tips of the tail feathers are also black, with a black central tail stripe. Underparts, rump and lower back are white, with a slight buff suffusion on the breast. Hens have duller plumage overall. In the autumn, the white on the head is replaced by grey, with a buff streak above the eye extending down the sides of the neck; the black plumage becomes greyer with buff edging, and the underparts are more yellowish-ochre. Hens have browner upperparts at this stage. Young birds are similar but have browner upperparts.

Desert wheatear

Oenanthe deserti

As their name suggests, desert wheatears are found in arid areas, although not in areas of shifting sand and dunes. Resident pairs occupy breeding territories and are quite conspicuous, running across the ground and perching in the open, often flicking their tails. They are agile in flight, able to hover and dive down on prey. Eurasian birds leave their African wintering grounds by March, as do birds from north-western Africa, having overwintered up to 1,000km (625 miles) further south. The cock bird's song announces their return, and the hen builds a nest for her eggs made largely of dry grass lined with softer material such as feathers.

Distribution: Breeds in the far eastern Mediterranean region, and also in Asia. Overwinters in Africa from northern Senegal and Mauritania across to Sudan and Somalia. A migratory population occurs in north-western Africa, but resident there at lower latitudes.
Size: 15cm (6in).
Habitat: Dry, open country.
Nest: Bulky, in a hollow.
Eggs: 3–5, greenish-blue with reddish-brown markings.
Food: Invertebrates.

Identification: Cock has a buff-brown top to the head and upper back. A white stripe runs back through each eye and around on to the upper chest, separating the black throat and lower face from the adjacent buff-brown feathering. Underparts whitish, with a slight buff suffusion on the chest and flanks. Tail is predominantly black, as are the bill, legs and feet. Hens are duller, with brownish ear coverts and no black on the face or at the top of the wings. Young birds have browner wings.

LARGER THRUSHES

This group of birds is well-known for its song. Cock birds become especially vocal at the start of the breeding period, as they lay claim to their territories. Although their bills are not particularly strong, thrushes are adept ground feeders, able to smash snails out of their shells by banging them on rocks, and sometimes even overpowering small vertebrates in this way.

Cape rock thrush

Monticola rupestris

Strongly territorial throughout the year, Cape rock thrushes are only likely to be seen in groups after the breeding period, before the young birds disperse. They are not always easy to observe, being both rather shy and also relatively inactive by nature. These thrushes usually forage on the ground, although occasionally they will take fruit from trees. Their breeding period extends from September to February. Pairs choose a well-concealed site among boulders for their nest, although occasionally they may prefer the protection offered by the leaves of plants such as large aloes. The cock bird has a special call for alerting the hen to danger while she is on the nest – she will fly off quietly, returning only when the male indicates the threat has passed.

Identification: Cock bird has a bluish-grey head, while the breast and underparts are orangish-red, particularly rich on the breast. Back and wings are rufous-brown. Bill, legs and feet are black. Hens have a brownish head, with a pale throat and a pale white streak on the side of the face; back and wings rufous-brown and underparts orangish-red, but paler than in the cock. Young birds have black scalloping on their underparts and buff spotting above.

Distribution: Range is restricted to eastern and southern parts of South Africa, including Swaziland and Lesotho.
Size: 20cm (8in).
Habitat: Rocky grassland.
Nest: Cup-shaped, made from vegetation.
Eggs: 2–4, bluish-cream with darker markings.
Food: Largely invertebrates.

Groundscraper thrush

Turdus litsitsirupa

Distribution: Found in Eritrea and Ethiopia. Also patchily distributed in southern parts of Africa, from Dem. Rep. Congo, Angola and Tanzania to South Africa.
Size: 24cm (9¹/₂in).
Habitat: Mountain grassland and savanna.
Nest: Cup-shaped, made from vegetation.
Eggs: 1–4, pale bluish with darker markings.
Food: Largely invertebrates.

These thrushes are relatively social by nature, and may be seen in groups for much of the year. Even when breeding, young from a previous brood may remain with their parents and help to feed the new chicks. Groundscraper thrushes hunt for food on the ground. They are often attracted to bushfires, seeking out creatures attempting to escape from the flames, sometimes even preying here on small lizards. More commonly however, groundscraper thrushes seek their food by turning over leaves and other debris, seizing invertebrates lurking beneath. Their breeding season varies according to location, but typically occurs outside the main rainy season. The nest can be located as high as 7m (23ft) above the ground, with the thrushes often nesting in association with fork-tailed drongos (*Dicrurus adsimilis*); this may give the thrushes protection against predators, since these colonial drongos are highly aggressive in defence of their nest sites.

Identification: Upright posture. Greyish head, back and wings. Chestnut wing bars seen in flight. Face and underparts white. Black streaking through and around the eyes, and speckling on the throat becoming larger over the chest, flanks and upper abdomen. Upper bill blackish, lower bill yellowish with a dark tip. Legs and feet yellowish. Young as adults, with whitish speckling on the head and back. Sexes are alike.

Rufous-tailed scrub robin

Rufous bush robin *Cercotrichas galactotes*

Rufous-tailed scrub robins spend much of their time on the ground, hopping rather than flying, often flaring out their tail feathers and fanning them up and down. Cock birds have a very powerful song, usually uttered from a branch, and rivals challenge each other by displaying in intimidating fashion with their wings and tail. The nest is constructed by both members of the pair, and though it is largely made of dry grass, other items, including wool, may also be used. In Tunisia, they often incorporate shed snakeskin, possibly to deter would-be predators. A concealed site is normally chosen, often in a cactus or palm. The hen incubates alone, and the chicks hatch after about thirteen days, with both parents providing food for their offspring. The young birds grow quickly and may leave the nest when just 10 days old, before they can fly well.

Identification: White stripe above and below each eye, with a black stripe running through. Top of the head, sides of the face and neck are a variable shade of brown, as are the wings. Underparts whitish but with a slight brownish suffusion, especially across the chest. Rufous extends from the lower back down to the tail, which terminates in a black and white tip. The upper bill is dark, paler at the base of the lower bill. Young birds are a slightly greyer shade of brown. Sexes are alike.

Distribution: Southern part of the Iberian Peninsula and the southern Mediterranean coast in summer, also in the eastern Mediterranean to Asia. Overwinters largely south of the Sahara, from south-western Mauritania right across Africa to Sudan, Somalia and Kenya.
Size: 15cm (6in).
Habitat: Dry areas of scrub.
Nest: Cup-shaped nest of vegetation.
Eggs: 3–5, whitish or pale bluish with dark markings.
Food: Mainly invertebrates. Some fruit.

Benson's rock thrush (*Monticola bensoni*):
16cm (6½in)
Western-central region of Madagascar, typically in boulder-strewn habitat. Cock has a slaty-grey head and back; wings are darker. Underparts are orange-red. Bill is black, legs and feet are grey. Hen has greyish-brown upperparts, with white on the throat and brown streaking evident on the chest, plus dirty buff-white underparts. Young cocks have grey spotting on the head, whereas hens are completely grey in breeding.

Sentinel rock thrush (*Monticola explorator*):
18cm (7in)
Restricted to eastern and southern parts of South Africa, including Lesotho. Cock has a light, ash-grey head and back, with darker wings. Underparts rufous-orange. Hens have a brown head, back and wings; whitish on the throat and at the base of the bill, with brownish streaks on the sides of the head extending over the breast. Pale rufous-orange on the upper abdomen, with a white area around the vent. Tail is rufous-orange below, brown above. Young have buff spotting on the upperparts.

Black scrub robin (*Cercotrichas podobe*):
20cm (8in)
Western Mauritania and Senegal eastwards in a band across to Eritrea, and down the coast to Somalia. Predominantly black, but with white edging to the feathers of the vent. Long tail feathers have white tips. Rufous area evident on the wings in flight. Bill, long legs and feet are black. Young birds brownish-black. Sexes alike.

Rufous-tailed rock thrush

Monticola saxatilis

These rock thrushes return to their northern breeding grounds in March. They are seen in a wide range of habitats, including ruined buildings. Cliff faces with ledges are often adopted as breeding sites, and nests may be built in walls. The incubation period lasts about two weeks, and the young fledge after a similar interval. Pairs in northern areas tend to reproduce just once a year, and may begin to depart Europe as early as August. In their African wintering grounds, they are encountered in virtually any type of open country, including coastal sand dunes, but not forested areas. These thrushes frequently seek food on the ground, watching for potential prey from a low perch, although they are also adept at catching winged insects in flight.

Identification: Cock in breeding condition has a bluish-grey head, and a white patch on the back. Wings are slate-grey and underparts rufous. Hens and cocks out of colour are similar; brownish overall, lighter on the underparts, with barred markings and a paler bill.

Distribution: Throughout the north Mediterranean and Asia on a similar latitude. Winters in Africa, ranging extensively through northern parts, and to Tanzania in the east.
Size: 20cm (8in).
Habitat: Open rocky areas.
Nest: Cup-shaped.
Eggs: 3–6, pale blue with some speckling.
Food: Invertebrates, fruit and seeds.

HORNBILLS OF OPEN COUNTRY

These hornbills are generally smaller than their forest-dwelling cousins, with the notable exception of the ground hornbills, which have adapted to living terrestrially and foraging in groups. Hornbills have clearly defined social structures, and individuals often work collectively to ensure that breeding is successful. Many male hornbills have a swelling on the upper bill, known as a casque.

Northern red-billed hornbill

Tockus erythrorhynchus

These hornbills are often observed in small groups foraging on the ground. They will seek out the droppings of large herbivores, digging with their bills in search of grubs. They also prey on small reptiles such as geckos, and may raid the communal nests of red-billed weavers (*Quelea quelea*). Pairs become more territorial at the start of the nesting period. A suitable tree hollow is sought, although they may adopt a cavity created by a woodpecker or barbet, and the nest is lined with fresh vegetation. The hen seals herself in the nest with mud, leaving just a slit through which the male will feed her. She remains here until the chicks have hatched and are about three weeks old, before breaking her way out and helping the male to feed their brood. The chicks reseal the nest behind her, emerging when they are approximately six weeks old.

Identification: Blackish stripe running down the centre of the head, from above the bill to the back of the neck. Sides of the head and underparts are whitish. Back and wings blackish, with white spots extending from the shoulders. Upper tail feathers also dark. Bare red skin encircles each eye and also present at the base of the lower bill. Bill reddish, with a darker marking near the base of the lower bill. Young birds have smaller, brownish-yellow bills. Cocks have larger and blacker bills than hens. Blackish legs and feet.

Distribution: Range extends across Africa south of the Sahara, from Senegal to Somalia and south as far as Tanzania. Also further south, from Angola and Namibia eastwards to Mozambique.
Size: 48cm (19in).
Habitat: Savanna.
Nest: Tree hole.
Eggs: 3–5, white.
Food: Invertebrates, fruits, some seeds.

Yellow-billed hornbill

Tockus flavirostris

Distribution: Range is restricted to the eastern side of Africa, from Eritrea in the north down through Ethiopia, Somalia and Kenya as far as northern Tanzania.
Size: 50cm (20in).
Habitat: Savanna.
Nest: Tree hollow.
Eggs: 2–3, white.
Food: Mainly invertebrates, some fruit.

These hornbills hunt invertebrates on the ground, especially locusts and termites. They have a remarkable relationship with the dwarf mongoose (*Helogale undulata*) – these small mammals help the hornbills find food by flushing locusts out of the grass. In return, the hornbills alert the mongooses to birds of prey flying overhead. Their breeding season extends from February to May, although in Ethiopia pairs may nest again in October. Courtship involves the male passing items of food to his partner. Hollows in acacia trees are often chosen as nesting sites, and the floor of the nest is lined with bark chips. The hen is sealed-in for much of the nesting period, with the cock bird feeding her through a vertical slit measuring 1.7cm (7/10in) wide. Incubation lasts approximately 24 days, and the young birds break out when they are around six weeks old.

Identification: Blackish crown stripe and dark ear coverts. Rest of the head and top of the back are white. Underparts also white, with black streaking on the chest. Wings are black, with large white spots and a stripe. Long tail, dark above and white below. Yellow bill, cock is reddish at the base of the lower bill. Hens have shorter bills, with a less evident casque. Young birds have smaller, mottled bills and dark eyes.

Tanzanian red-billed hornbill (*Tockus ruahae*): 48cm (19in)
Central Tanzania. Black stripe across the head, with white spots on the blackish wings. Whitish underparts. Blackish area surrounds the yellow iris. Base of the lower bill blackish. Down-curved bill otherwise red, larger in males. Young birds have smaller, less brightly coloured bills.

Von der Decken's hornbill (*Tockus deckeni*): 47cm (18¹/₂in)
Southern Ethiopia, Somalia, Kenya and Tanzania. Black crown stripe, with another through the eyes. Wings and tail black, with a white patch on the wings evident in flight. Rest of the body whitish. Cock bird has a distinctive casque which is red and yellow, with a dark tip. Hens lack the large casque and have a predominantly black bill. Young birds have paler bills than hens, with spotting on the wing coverts.

Southern yellow-billed hornbill (*Tockus leucomelas*): 55cm (21³/₄in)
Range extends from western Angola and northern Namibia eastwards to the southern tip of Malawi, down to northern parts of South Africa. Black crown, with extensive blackish markings on the neck and breast. Narrow white area extending down the back, and large pale spots on the wings. Characteristic area of red skin around the eyes, with a patch each side of the lower bill too. Cock bird has a bright yellow bill with an evident casque. Hens have pinker skin, with a smaller, often paler bill. Young birds have grey irides and mottled bills.

African grey hornbill

Tockus nasutus

These hornbills catch winged insects such as bees in flight, removing their stings prior to swallowing them. They also hunt tree frogs and reptiles such as lizards, and will raid the nests of weavers. They are can be observed around large herbivores and troupes of monkeys, always watchful for disturbed prey. Grey hornbills may be forced into different areas in times of drought. They can fly quite fast, at speeds of around 30kph (18³/₄mph), and have a distinctive, dipping flight. As with other *Tockus* hornbills, the female will not begin to lay until she is confined to the nesting cavity. She will add to her clutch on alternate days.

Distribution: Range extends across Africa in a band south of the Sahara, from Senegal in the west to Sudan in the east, and down the eastern side as far as northern South Africa. Also extends west to parts of Angola and Namibia.
Size: 50cm (20in).
Habitat: Savanna.
Nest: Tree hollow.
Eggs: 2–5, white in colour.
Food: Various.

Identification: Upperparts grey-brown. White stripe on each side of the crown. Underparts white. Bill is black with a yellowish stripe. Hens' upper bill is white, tip maroon, no casque. Young have grey bill and no casque.

Southern ground hornbill

Bucorvus leadbeateri

These large hornbills live in groups of up to 11 individuals. There is always a dominant pair, and often more than one mature male along with a number of immature birds, but rarely more than one adult female. They can be aggressive, attacking their reflections in windows, smashing the glass with repeated blows of their powerful bills. They can catch hares, snakes, large tortoises and locusts, and will feed on carrion and even take honey from bees' nests. Although terrestrial, members of a group will roost in trees at dusk. Members also assist the breeding pair in finding food. Mating occurs on a branch. The young develop quite slowly and fledge when three months old.

Distribution: South-eastern Africa, from southern Kenya down to eastern South Africa and across to Angola and northern Namibia.
Size: 100cm (39in).
Habitat: Open country near woodland areas.
Nest: Hole in large tree.
Eggs: 1–3, white.
Food: Largely carnivorous.

Identification: Prominent area of red skin around each eye and a red wattle under the throat. Remainder of the plumage jet black, except for the white wing tips (most evident in flight). Cock has a low casque on the upper bill, which is also black. Hens lack the casque, and have blue on the throat and a reduced wattle. The facial skin of young birds is a duller brownish-yellow.

LOVEBIRDS AND PARAKEETS

*Lovebirds occur only in Africa, and are distinguishable by their small size and short-tailed appearance.
In contrast, ring-necked is the only parakeet found on mainland Africa – of its relatives occurring on
islands off the south-east coast, only the echo parakeet (Psittacula echo) still survives, in a critically-
endangered state on Mauritius. Others such as Newton's parakeet (P. excul) are now extinct.*

Black-cheeked lovebird

Agapornis nigrigenis

Distribution: Range is
restricted to an area of
southern Africa, in the south-
west of Zambia.
Size: 14cm (5¹/₂in).
Habitat: Fields with nearby
woodland areas.
Nest: Tree hollow.
Eggs: 3–8, white.
Food: Mainly seeds but also
eats berries.

These small members of the parrot family have a very
restricted area of distribution, which may explain why they
were not discovered until 1904. Their breeding period
extends through November and December. Hens collect
nesting material such as dry grass, which they carry back to
their chosen nest sites in their bills, and make a bulky,
domed nest that they line with softer material such as
feathers. Incubation lasts approximately 23
days, and the young birds fledge after
around five weeks in the nest. The
total population of black-cheeked
lovebirds is estimated at about 10,000
birds, and seems relatively stable.
Luckily, they occur in a region with little possibility
of further agricultural development, since the land is
generally poor. However, drought is a potential
hazard they face, which could have a serious
impact on their numbers, as these lovebirds
rarely stray far from water.

Identification: Blackish-brown
head, white skin around each eye
and at the base of the upper bill.
Throat is orangish, and the back
of the head is brownish-orange.
Back and wings greenish, with
darker flight feathers, green
underparts and a paler yellowish-
green rump. Bill red, legs and
feet greyish. Young
birds have paler
bills. Sexes
are alike.

Abyssinian lovebird

Black-winged lovebird *Agapornis taranta*

Relatively little is known about these lovebirds, although
they will associate in small flocks when not breeding,
particularly in areas where food is plentiful. They are
not always easy to observe due to their small size
and green coloration. Abyssinian lovebirds are
typically encountered in grassland areas with
nearby woodland, although occasionally they
will venture into gardens in Ethiopia's capital,
Addis Ababa. Juniper (*Juniperus communis*)
berries are a favoured item in their diet, and figs
(*Ficus carica*) are also eaten regularly too. Unlike
other lovebirds, they will sometimes use their feet
to hold food. Abyssinian lovebirds also build a less
elaborate nest than other species, often constructing
little more than a pad of feathers on which the hen
lays her eggs. This is usually located in a tree hollow,
but sometimes other locations may be chosen,
including the disused nests of weaver finches and
suitable hollows in walls. They have no fixed breeding
season, with pairs nesting throughout the year.

Identification: Cock birds are
bright green overall, slightly
darker on the back and wings.
Underwing coverts are black.
Evident red plumage above
the bill, which is also red.
Legs and feet are grey.
Hens lack the red
plumage on the
head and also have
green underwing
coverts. Young
have pale bills.

Distribution: Range is
restricted to a small region in
eastern Africa, largely in the
highland areas of Ethiopia
but also ranging north into
neighbouring Eritrea.
Size: 15cm (6in).
Habitat: Savanna.
Nest: Pad of feathers, in a
suitable hollow.
Eggs: 3–8, white.
Food: Various seeds and also
some berries.

Peach-faced lovebird

Rosy-faced lovebird *Agapornis roseicollis*

Living and breeding in flocks, these small parrots are encountered from sea level to altitudes of 1,600m (5,250ft). They may be present in large numbers in agricultural areas when crops are ripening – a time when flocks will join together. For breeding, they may take over the abandoned nests of weaver birds, which enables them to nest in colonies. Peach-faced lovebirds have an unusual way of building their own nests: hens collect strips of nesting material and carry it back to the nest site folded and tucked into the plumage on the rump. The nest may be sited in a range of locations, from cliff-faces to the eaves of buildings.

Identification: Predominantly green, although darker on the wings. Has a blue rump, a reddish forehead and rose-pink facial feathering that extends onto the upper breast. Rosy coloration less pronounced in young birds, who may show traces of darker markings on their bill, when fledging. Sexes are alike, but pinkish coloration may sometimes be paler in hens (this is not usually apparent). The Angolan race (*A. r. catumbella*) is more lightly coloured overall.

Distribution: Ranges from northern Angola southwards to South Africa.
Size: 15cm (6in).
Habitat: Dry woodland and agricultural areas.
Nest: Tree hollow or disused weaver nest.
Eggs: 4–6, white.
Food: Seeds, including cultivated crops such as millet and sunflower.

Masked lovebird (*Agapornis personata*): 14cm (5¹⁄₂in)
Present in northern and central parts of Tanzania. Blackish head merging into a yellow collar and underparts. The wings and abdomen are green. Prominent white areas encircle the eyes. Bill is red, legs and feet greyish. Sexes are alike.

Fischer's lovebird (*Agapornis fischeri*): 14cm (5¹⁄₂in)
Found in eastern Africa, mainly in northern Tanzania. Reddish-orange head becoming paler around the throat and the back of the neck, where there is also a yellowish area. Underparts are light green, wings are dark green and the rump is mauve. Prominent white eye ring of bare skin. The bill is red and the legs and feet are grey. Sexes are alike.

Nyasa lovebird (*Agapornis lilianae*): 14cm (5¹⁄₂in)
Restricted to Zambia, particularly in the south, and also neighbouring Malawi. Orangish-red head with a prominent white eye ring, becoming yellow across the neck and on the chest. Underparts are yellowish-green, and the back and wings are a darker shade. Bill is red. Young birds are duller, have darker bills and lack the eye ring. Sexes are alike.

Red-headed lovebird (*Agapornis pullaria*): 15cm (6in)
Isolated areas of western Africa. Main range extends from Nigeria eastwards to Kenya and Uganda. Also extends to Angola in the west. Cock bird has a bright red face, with green upperparts and more yellowish underparts. Rump is blue, with a dark band across the tail feathers. Bill red, legs and feet greyish. Hens are similar but with more orange facial colouring, whereas young birds are more yellowish.

Ring-necked parakeet

Rose-ringed parakeet *Psittacula krameri*

Distribution: Found across Africa in a band south of the Sahara, from Mauritania and Senegal eastwards to Sudan and Ethiopia. Also extends further eastwards through the Arabian Peninsula and Asia to China.
Size: 40cm (16in).
Habitat: Light woodland.
Nest: Tree cavity high off the ground, sometimes on a rocky ledge.
Eggs: 3–6, white.
Food: Cereals, fruit, seeds.

Identification: The African race (*P. k. krameri*) has black on the bill and is more yellowish-green than the Asiatic form (*illustrated*), which is now established in various locations including parts of England, well outside its natural range. Hens and young birds of both sexes lack the distinctive neck collar seen in cocks, which is a combination of black and pink.

The ring-necked parakeet is the most widely distributed member of the parrot family in the world. It is a naturally adaptable species, commonly occurring both in agricultural areas as well as parks and gardens in cities, although it is usually observed in areas with nearby woodland. The spread of agriculture has led to an increased food supply in many areas of their range, and this in turn has helped them to expand their distribution. Ring-necked parakeets fly quite high, often in small groups, and their distinctive, screeching calls carry over long distances. These are unmistakable parakeets, especially when silhouetted in flight, with their long, tapering tails streaming behind their bodies.

PARROTS

Poicephalus parrots are the most widely distributed group of parrots in Africa, although they are found only on the mainland and not on offshore islands. Some species have quite localized distributions, whereas others range more widely across the continent. They occur most commonly in small groups, sometimes causing crop damage in agricultural areas.

Senegal parrot

Yellow-bellied parrot *Poicephalus senegalus*

These parrots are usually only observed in small groups, although much larger flocks may congregate in areas where food is plentiful, for example agricultural areas when crops are ripening. Groundnuts are a particular favourite food. In some areas seasonal movements have been reported, such as in southern Mali, where the parrots head further south as water becomes more scarce during the dry season. These are shy birds by nature, difficult to observe when perched and ready to fly off rapidly when disturbed; at such times their calls, which frequently consist of whistling notes, become more raucous.

Identification: Greyish head and bill, with a green back and wings. Distinctive V-shaped green area on the chest, with orangish-yellow plumage on the underparts. The distinctive western subspecies (*P. s. versteri*) has more reddish underparts and darker green plumage. Sexes are alike.

Distribution: Ranges from western to central Africa, from Senegal through Nigeria and northern Cameroon to south-west Sudan.
Size: 23cm (9in).
Habitat: Open countryside and forest.
Nest: Tree hollow, typically 10m (33ft) above the ground.
Eggs: 2–4, white.
Food: Fruit, greenery, seeds and cultivated crops, notably groundnuts and millet.

Red-bellied parrot

Poicephalus rufiventris

Unlike their relatives, these *Poicephalus* parrots can easily be sexed from a distance. They occur in arid country, often in the vicinity of baobab trees, and in some areas may be encountered at altitudes of up to 2,000m (6,500ft) in the summer, retreating to lower altitudes in the winter. In Somalia, they seek out ripening figs in the summer, retreating to lower altitudes in the winter. Acacia seeds also feature regularly in their diet, and they will sometimes raid maize fields too.

Red-bellied parrots are normally seen in pairs or small groups, but are not very conspicuous. When breeding, as many as six pairs have been observed using baobab trees (*Adansonia digitata*) in the same area. The nesting period varys widely through their range. Pairs occasionally adopt arboreal termite mounds in preference to tree holes, presumably benefiting from the protection the termites afford.

Distribution: North-eastern Africa, extending from Djibouti through western Somalia, Ethiopia and Kenya to northern Tanzania.
Size: 24cm (9½in).
Habitat: Sparse woodland.
Nest: Tree hole.
Eggs: 1–2, white.
Food: Fruit, seeds.

Identification: Cock bird has brown head, back and wings. The lower chest and upper abdomen are orange, and the lower underparts are green. Irides red. Bill is black, legs and feet dark grey. In hens, underparts are green rather than red. Young birds are similar to hens, but cocks have some orange-red plumage on the abdomen.

Meyer's parrot

Poicephalus meyeri

Meyer's parrot is the most widely distributed member of its genus, with six distinct races recognized through its range. These parrots generally feed on seeds rather than fruit, although they may occasionally also eat caterpillars and other invertebrates. Their habit of invading maize fields and orange groves has led to them being considered serious crop pests in some parts of their range. Meyer's parrots breed during the dry season, with pairs preferring to nest on their own rather than colonially. They often seek out tree holes created by other birds such as woodpeckers, usually at least 3m (10ft) above the ground, although once a suitable site is found it may be reused over a number of years. The interior of the nest is lined simply with wood chips, rather than any material collected by the parrots themselves. The hen sits alone, and the eggs hatch around 30 days after laying. The fledging period can be quite variable, with the young birds leaving the nest between 8½ and 12 weeks of age.

Identification: Variable. Underparts generally bluish-green. Yellow areas on the shoulders and head, which is mainly brownish, as are the back and wings. Dark bill, legs and feet. Young birds are duller, with less yellow. Sexes are alike.

Distribution: Ranges widely across central and southern Africa, from Nigeria to Ethiopia in the north down to the Botswana-South African border in the south. Extends westwards to Angola and northern Namibia.
Size: 23cm (9in).
Habitat: Savanna.
Nest: Tree hollow.
Eggs: 2–4, white.
Food: Seeds and fruit.

Brown-headed parrot (*Poicephalus cryptoxanthus*): 25cm (10in)
South-eastern Africa, from Kenya to northern South Africa. Dark brown head and a green body. Dark flight feathers contrast with yellow underwing coverts, evident in flight. Undertail coverts a yellowish-green shade. Dark upper bill, yellow lower bill. Pale yellow irides. Sexes are alike. Young birds are duller, with dark irides.

Niam-niam parrot (*Poicephalus crassus*): 25cm (10in)
Restricted to central Africa, from Cameroon through the Central African Republic to south-western Sudan. Brownish head and breast, with brownish wings edged green. Lower breast, underparts and rump bright green. Blackish area of bare skin around the eyes. Irides bright red. Upper bill dark, lower bill pale yellowish. Grey legs and feet. Sexes are alike. Young birds have olive-yellow markings on greyish heads.

Grey-headed parrot (*Poicephalus suahelicus*): 36cm (14in)
A close relative of the Cape parrot (*P. robustus*). Mainly south-eastern Africa, extending from Tanzania to northern South Africa. Greyish head with pale edging to the individual feathers, especially over the head and back. Bright orange-red shoulder patches, with similar plumage also at the top of the legs. Chest is greyish and the underparts are green. Large bill is light grey. Legs and feet dark grey. Hens are similar but have a slight reddish suffusion above the bill, absent in cocks. Young birds lack the orange-red coloration seen in adults.

Ruppell's parrot

Poicephalus rueppellii

A rather short, square-tailed and relatively compact appearance is characteristic of Ruppell's and other *Poicephalus* parrots. Although naturally inhabiting dry country, these parrots are most likely to be encountered near water. They can sometimes be observed in small flocks comprising 20 or more birds, particularly in areas where figs are plentiful. They will actually feed on a wide range of vegetable matter, including shoots, buds and flowers, as well as seeking out nectar, especially that of flowering mistletoe. Their main breeding period usually begins in February and extends through until May, though some pairs nest later – this is possibly linked to the onset of the rainy period. Breeding pairs will generally remain together, and favoured nesting sites may be reused in successive years. Ruppell's parrots are not uncommon birds in Angola, while further south in Namibia their population consists of an estimated 9,000 individuals.

Distribution: Range is confined to the western side of southern Africa, occurring from western Angola south to central Namibia.
Size: 22cm (8½in).
Habitat: Dry country.
Nest: Tree hollow.
Eggs: 3–5, white.
Food: Seeds and fruit, also plant matter.

Identification: Greyish overall, more silvery on the ear coverts, with yellow plumage at the shoulders extending under the wings. Lower underparts, back and rump are blue. Irides red. Bill, legs and feet black. Young birds are duller overall. Hens have a larger area of blue on their underparts.

BARBETS, HOOPOES AND OXPECKERS

Barbets found in open country are more insectivorous than those species living in the forest, often probing into ant and termite nests with their strong bills. Hunting techniques of birds living in this type of habitat vary greatly, however, as reflected by the oxpecker, which has formed a remarkable partnership with other animals to obtain its food.

Levaillant's barbet

Crested barbet *Trachyphonus vaillantii*

Distribution: Southern Africa, from northern Angola and Tanzania southwards, though absent from much of southern Angola, Namibia and southern South Africa.
Size: 22cm (9in).
Habitat: Open country.
Nest: Hollow chamber.
Eggs: 3–5, white.
Food: Mainly invertebrates, but also fruit and berries.

Although there are slight variations in the patterning of these barbets, it is not possible to distinguish between the sexes. Levaillant's barbets are quite conspicuous birds, and can be observed perching in trees or searching for food on the ground, often near termite mounds. When breeding, they will sometimes seek the relative security offered by the termite mounds, tunnelling in to create a safe nesting chamber. Their intrusion is apparently not resisted by the insects, who would normally deter potential predators. One advantage of nesting in a termite mound is that the heat generated by their surroundings will keep the eggs warm enough for the adult birds to leave the nest.

Identification: Reddish-orange area on the top of the head and lores. Tall black crest. The wings are predominantly blackish with white markings. A black band with white spots extends across the chest. Underparts are yellowish with some reddish streaks, becoming paler with fewer markings on the abdomen. The rump is yellow, red at the base, and the tail feathers have white tips. The bill is pale greenish-yellow. Sexes are alike.

Hoopoe

Eurasian hoopoe *Upupa epops*

The distinctive appearance of these birds helps to identify them with relative ease, especially as they are most likely to be observed in open country. When in flight, the broad shape of the wings is clearly visible and the tall crest is held flat over the back of the head. Hoopoes often raise their crest on landing, however. They use their long bills to probe for worms in the ground, or to grab prey such as lizards scurrying through the grass. They can also often be observed dust-bathing, which keeps their plumage in good condition. Hoopoes are not especially shy of people, and pairs will sometimes nest in buildings. Their common name is derived from the sound of their "hoo, hoo" call.

Identification: Mainly pale buff, although more orange on the crown and with black edging to the feathers. Alternate bands of black-and-white coloration on the wings. Long, narrow, downward-curving bill. Sexes are alike.

Above: The hoopoe's black-and-white barring is also present on the underside of the wings, shown to best effect in flight.

Distribution: Range extends throughout most of Europe, although usually absent from Scandinavia and the British Isles. Overwinters in Africa south of the equator. Also occurs in parts of north Africa and much of central Africa, extending to the Arabian Peninsula and Asia.
Size: 29cm (11in).
Habitat: Open country.
Nest: Secluded hole.
Eggs: 5–8, whitish to yellowish-olive.
Food: Mainly invertebrates, especially worms.

D'Arnaud's barbet (*Trachyphonus darnaudii*):
17cm (7in)
Ranges in eastern parts of Africa, from Sudan,
Ethiopia and Somalia through Uganda and Kenya to
south-west Tanzania. Black crown that is often
spotted with yellow, although yellow is usually more
evident on the sides of the face. Variable black
markings present on the throat and breast. The
underparts are mainly pale yellow in colour. Undertail coverts are red and the upperparts are brown
with white spotting. Individuals differ from each
other slightly in the pattern of their markings.
Sexes are alike.

Pied barbet (*Lybius leucomelas*): 16cm (6in)
Distributed in southern parts of Africa, where it can
be found in Zimbabwe, Botswana and South Africa.
Deep red forehead with black plumage behind.
Adjacent white stripes with some yellow suffusion
extend to the back of the neck. An irregularly-shaped
black area runs from below the bill down on to the
chest. The remainder of the underparts are white.
The wings are black, except for some white
markings which have a sporadic yellow suffusion.
Sexes are alike.

Red-faced barbet (*Lybius rubrifacies*): 15cm (6in)
Present in only a small area of eastern Africa, in
southern Uganda and north-western Tanzania. An
area of red plumage above the pale greyish bill
extends to the sides of the face, but not on to the
crown or throat. The remainder of the plumage is
blackish, and there is a yellow edging to the wings.
Sexes are alike.

Yellow-fronted tinkerbird

Pogoniulus chrysoconus

These small and relatively slim members
of the barbet family will sit for long
periods during the day on well-concealed
branches, uttering their monotonous-
sounding call. However, it can be
surprisingly difficult to locate them by
their sound alone. Their lively, agile
nature becomes evident when seeking
food. They hover and pick insects off
branches, and hop up tree trunks like
woodpeckers, seeking grubs. They will
also eat fruit, especially the berries of
mistletoe and other similar plants. Once
eaten, yellow-fronted tinkerbirds help to
distribute these plants
around their
environment by
passing the
seeds in their
droppings.

Distribution: Across much of
central and southern Africa,
from Senegal to Ethiopia and
down as far as South Africa.
Size: 11cm (4in).
Habitat: Savanna.
Nest: Tree hole.
Eggs: 2–3, white.
Food: Invertebrates and fruit.

Identification: Prominent yellow
plumage above the upper bill,
appearing almost orange in some
cases, with alternating black-and-
white stripes on the sides of the
head. A similar, mottled colour
combination extends over the
wings, with yellow coloration
evident on the flight feathers.
The rump is sulphur-yellow.
Underparts are whitish with a
yellowish suffusion. Legs and
the long, stout bill are black.
Sexes are alike.

Red-billed oxpecker

Buphagus erythrorhynchus

These starlings have formed a close association with large grazing mammals including
rhinoceroses, elephants, antelopes and buffalo. Perching on their bodies, the oxpeckers hunt
for ticks by scissoring, which entails pushing the bill into the coat
and snapping it open and shut in the hope of locating a
parasite. They also use the animals as
vantage points from which to hawk
insects. As specialist feeders, red-
billed oxpeckers are at risk from
any decline in the number of
large animals, and they are also
threatened by cattle-dipping,
which wipes out parasites.
Not all animals appreciate
their intentions either, and
will shake their bodies to
dislodge the birds. When
breeding, oxpeckers use hair
collected from animals,
especially impala, to make a
soft lining for their nest, with
dung often being added too.

Distribution: From Eritrea
and Ethiopia in eastern Africa
south-westwards to southern
Angola and down to northern
South Africa.
Size: 20cm (8in).
Habitat: Savanna.
Nest: Tree holes.
Eggs: 2–5, creamy-white with
darker markings.
Food: Invertebrates, mainly
ticks and other parasites.

Identification: Olive-brown head,
back and wings. Underparts and
chest paler. Pale skin around red
iris. Stocky bill red. Legs and feet
grey. Young birds duller, irides and
bill brown. Sexes are alike.

GRASSLAND BIRDS

Although grassland birds tend to have relatively subdued coloration, enabling them to blend into the background, larks are well known for their song and the display flight of cock birds, which makes them conspicuous. Less musical, but equally distinctive, are the calls of the corncrake, which was formerly a common summer sound in northern meadows and fields.

Dupont's lark

Chersophilus duponti

Dupont's larks are found in open country, usually with tussocks of grass which provide them with cover and nesting cover. The eastern North African race (*C. d. margaritae*), which extends from southern Algeria to Egypt, is noticeably lighter in colour and more of a cinnamon-brown shade than the nominate race. These larks are shy by nature and difficult to spot on the ground, retreating out of sight by running rather than flying if approached. They extend their necks cautiously above the grass to check for possible danger before emerging from cover. Their song can often be heard after dark, although it is commonly uttered at both ends of the day, especially during the breeding period. The display flight of Dupont's lark is a spectacular sight, with birds flying almost vertically to a height of around 150m (500ft), remaining in the air while singing for up to an hour before dropping straight down to the ground again. They sometimes engage in wing-clapping as part of their display too.

Identification: Birds occurring in Europe and north-west Africa have a whitish area bordering dark brownish ear coverts. The breast is white with dark brown streaking. Top of the head is dark, as are the back and wings, with the wing feathers having pale edging. Lower underparts are white. Relatively long brownish bill, yellowish legs and feet. Young birds are paler overall. Sexes are alike.

Distribution: Ranges through central and eastern parts of the Iberian Peninsula. Also sporadically seen in North Africa, through the southern Mediterranean region.
Size: 18cm (7in).
Habitat: Dry sandy areas, including coastal plains.
Nest: Scrape on the ground.
Eggs: 3–4, pinkish-white with dark spots.
Food: Invertebrates, seeds.

Desert lark

Ammomanes deserti

There are marked differences in the depth of coloration of desert larks – some races are much paler than others, which may be linked to their habitat. They are rarely seen in large groups, and if flushed tend to fly low, weaving from side to side, before returning to the ground some distance away. Invertebrates are caught on the ground and in flight, and animal dung may be broken up as the larks search for undigested seeds. Breeding starts around March. Both members of the pair collect material to build their nest, which is concealed on the ground, often with stones deposited around it. The hen incubates on her own. The young larks may leave the nest before they are able to fly properly, but the birds will remain in family groups for some time. It would appear that desert larks have a low requirement for water, since they are rarely observed drinking and have been spotted as far as 6km (3¹/₄ miles) from the nearest water source. It is thought that they obtain much of their water requirement from their food.

Identification: Dark brownish upperparts, with a paler area around the eye and on the throat, which has slight black streaking. The breast is more prominently streaked with black and the belly is rufous, as is the tail. Bill is pale with a dark tip, and the legs and feet are greyish. Young birds have mottled upperparts. Sexes are alike.

Distribution: North-western Africa, including western Sahara and Mauritania east to Niger, the border of Niger, Algeria and Libya, and northern Chad. Also ranges southwards from Egypt to Somalia and into Sudan.
Size: 15cm (6in).
Habitat: Rocky areas, desert.
Nest: Cup-shaped, made from vegetation.
Eggs: 2–3, white with some dark speckling.
Food: Invertebrates, seeds, plant matter.

Common skylark

Alauda arvensis

The skylark's drab coloration and patterning help it to remain hidden on the ground, where it sometimes freezes to escape detection. If disturbed at close quarters, however, it takes off almost vertically. Skylarks are talented songsters, and frequently reveal their presence by singing. Their distinctive, rounded song can be heard throughout most of the year, even in the depths of winter. Their song flight entails fluttering their wings and rising slowly through the air to a height of 100m (330ft) or so, then hovering before plunging back down, singing the whole time. During the breeding period, a sitting hen may draw attention away from her nest site by feigning injury, dragging one wing along the ground and taking off only as a last resort.

Above: Skylarks build their nests on the ground, hidden in the grass

Identification: Greyish-brown plumage over the back and wings, with speckling becoming paler on the flanks. Underparts are mainly white. Whitish stripe above each eye extends around the ear coverts, which are greyish. Short crest on the crown, not always visible. Hens are similar but lack the crest.

Distribution: Resident throughout much of western Europe from Denmark southwards. Also occurs in northern Africa. Breeding range extends further north to Scandinavia and through eastern Europe into Asia.
Size: 18cm (7in).
Habitat: Open countryside, especially farmland.
Nest: On the ground, hidden in grass.
Eggs: 3–5, greyish in colour and darkly spotted.
Food: Invertebrates, also plant matter

Greater hoopoe lark (*Alaemon alaudipes*): 23cm (9in)
North Africa and the Middle East. A black stripe runs through the eyes, with similar moustached patterning adjacent to the bill. Whiter stripe above each eye. Throat and underparts white, with a darker streaked area on the breast. Back of the head and neck greyish. Wings a browner shade becoming black with white edging; broad central white area bordered by black, evident in flight. Long tail black below, browner above. Bill black, legs and feet grey. Hens are more buffy-grey. Young birds are paler and more yellowish.

Gray's lark (*Ammomanopsis grayi*): 13cm (5in)
Southern coastal Angola to adjacent Namibia. Light sandy brown upperparts. Pale brownish speckling on the breast at the shoulders; throat, sides of the neck and underparts otherwise white. Short dark bill, greyish legs and feet. Northern Namibian race (*A. g. hoeschi*) identical but significantly darker brown. Young birds have slightly mottled upperparts. Sexes are alike.

Cape long-billed lark (*Certhilauda curvirostris*): 24cm (9½in)
Western coastal South Africa. Pale greyish-white streak over the eyes. Upperparts greyish overall, with paler edging to the plumage over the wings. Throat is whitish, with slight dark streaking; remaining underparts are more heavily streaked. The blackish bill is long and curves slightly downwards to a point. Young birds have mottled upperparts, and less streaking on their underparts. Hens have smaller bills.

Corncrake

Crex crex

Similar in appearance to quails, corncrakes are actually members of the rail family. Agricultural practices have led to a fall-off in numbers – entire broods are wiped out when cornfields are harvested. The corncrake's distinctive "crek, crek" call explains its scientific name, and is also the reason why rails are known as "crakes". Corncrakes hide among vegetation, running to escape danger rather than flying. Pairs begin nesting in May. The hen incubates for 14 days, and the young fledge at five weeks old. They will be fully grown three weeks later.

Identification: Bluish-grey sides to the head, with a brown stripe running back through each eye. Rufous flanks with vertical white striping. Flight feathers also rufous. Back brownish with prominent black spotting and streaking. Bill pinkish, legs and feet yellowish. Hens have less bluish-grey on the flanks. Young birds have greyer legs and feet.

Distribution: Breeding range extends across much of central Europe, but absent from the Iberian Peninsula, Italy and most of Scandinavia (except the south). Scarce in England. Overwinters in central and down eastern parts of Africa.
Size: 25cm (10in).
Habitat: Fields, meadows.
Nest: Scrape on the ground.
Eggs: 6–14, greenish-grey to buff, with some darker markings.
Food: Mainly invertebrates, some seeds.

DRY COUNTRY OPPORTUNISTS

Living in areas with low and irregular rainfall creates difficulties for birds, especially during the breeding season, as their young require water as well as food. In areas with few trees for nesting they may even be forced to breed on the ground, where both eggs and chicks will be more vulnerable to predators. Even so, a range of species flourish in such relatively inhospitable surroundings.

Temminck's courser

Cursorius temminckii

Distribution: Western Africa, from Mauritania to Nigeria and Chad. Also over much of southern Africa, reaching as far as northern Ethiopia.
Size: 20cm (8in).
Habitat: Grassland.
Nest: Lays on bare ground.
Eggs: 1–2, yellowish-buff with dense black markings.
Food: Invertebrates, seeds.

Coursers are aberrant waders found in dry country, and Temminck's is the smallest species. They prefer to run on their long legs if disturbed, rather than flying off, although they can fly well if necessary. Their upright stance affords them good visibility, while their coloration helps them to blend in against the background. Temminck's coursers often hunt in areas that are being swept by fire, catching fleeing invertebrate prey, and are rather nomadic in their habits – it is thought that they are drawn to such areas by the smoke. They may also be active after dark, and can usually be encountered in small parties outside the breeding period. Pairs are territorial when nesting, however, and will drive away young from the previous season who have remained with them up until this stage. The eggs blend in very well with the bare soil, and their brown plumage camouflages the adult birds on the nest. Incubation lasts approximately 30 days.

Identification: Broad black stripe through each eye extending to the back of the neck. White stripe above, linking at the back of the head. Top of the head is rufous, as is the belly, with a paler rufous area on the cheeks. Throat is white, with white on the lower underparts. Remainder of the body is brownish, and the flight feathers are black. Sexes are alike. Young birds have dark brown crowns and mottled upperparts, with a brownish-black rather than black patch on the underparts.

Speckled pigeon

Triangular-spotted pigeon, rock pigeon *Columba guinea*

These social pigeons are often seen in flocks comprised of hundreds of individuals. They breed in loose colonies where conditions are favourable, such as rocky cliff-faces or caves. In the extreme south of their range pairs will even nest under boulders on the ground, adjacent to colonies of jackass penguins (*Spheniscus demersus*). They are now becoming more common in cities, breeding on tall buildings, and will sometimes take over nests of other birds such as storks. Incubation is shared, with the cock bird usually sitting for much of the day and the hen taking over at dusk. The chicks hatch just over two weeks later, and are initially reared on a special high-protein food known as pigeon milk, which is produced by glands in the crops of the adult birds. They grow quickly, and may leave the nest at three weeks old.

Identification: Greyish head, with a prominent area of red skin around each eye. Streaked neck. Underparts are grey. Back and wings are vinous, with greyish-black flight feathers and rump. Distinctive, triangular-shaped white markings extend across the wings in rows. Bill blackish, legs and feet pinkish. Tail is blackish with a grey band. Young birds are duller and browner, notably on the breast, where there is no white patterning. Sexes are alike.

Distribution: Two separate populations, the northern one extending in a band across sub-Saharan Africa, east to Somalia and south to Tanzania. The southern Africa population ranges from southern Angola to South Africa, extending north as far as Zimbabwe.
Size: 34cm (13in).
Habitat: Open country, including farmland.
Nest: Platform of sticks.
Eggs: 1–3, white.
Food: Seeds and fruit.

Lichtenstein's sandgrouse

Pterocles lichtensteinii

The barred plumage of these sandgrouse creates what is described as "disruptive camouflage" – breaking up their appearance so they are more difficult to recognize, especially in stony areas. However, they often forage at night to avoid the intense heat of the desert. Their breeding period varies but usually peaks between May and July. A sheltered site is preferred, partly to prevent the eggs being exposed to the hot sun. The hen incubates during the day and the cock bird takes over at dusk, sitting overnight. The young hatch after 23 days and are patterned to blend in with their surroundings. They develop rapidly, eating seeds when just a day old.

Identification: Cock bird has two black bands across the top of the head, reaching down to the base of the upper bill and the eye on each side, with intervening white plumage that extends back towards the neck. Two black bands also extend across the breast, with a sandy-yellow strip of plumage in between and above. The underparts are otherwise yellowish-white, with fine black vermiculations, while the upperparts display similar mottling but on a more prominent yellow background. Hens are plainer, lacking the evident barring on the head and lower breast of cocks, and their bills are brownish rather than brightly coloured. Legs and feet yellowish. Young birds are similar to adult hens.

Distribution: Scattered locations from north-west Africa to Somalia, and along the Red Sea coast to Egypt. Also across southern Arabian Peninsula to Pakistan.
Size: 28cm (11in).
Habitat: Relatively arid areas.
Nest: Scrape on the ground.
Eggs: 2–3, stone-coloured with darker markings.
Food: Largely seeds.

Somali courser (*Cursorius somalensis*): 22cm (9in)
Eritrea, eastern Ethiopia and Somalia to Kenya. Black stripe through each eye, white stripe above joining on the hindcrown. Top of the crown brown. Abdomen white, remainder of the plumage fawn-brown, except for the black flight feathers. Bill blackish, legs and feet yellowish-grey. Sexes are alike. Young birds have mottled upperparts and barring on the tail.

White-collared pigeon (*Columba albitorques*): 32cm (12¹/₂in)
Highland areas of Eritrea and Ethiopia. Brownish-grey overall. Crown and face dark grey, with a white band encircling the back of the head. Whitish edging and longer feathers also on the back of the head, often with green iridescence. Pale grey band across the tail. Black markings across the wings, and white plumage seen when the wings are open. Bill greyish, legs and feet red. Sexes are alike. Young are browner and duller, with lighter edging to the crown feathers.

Yellow-throated sandgrouse (*Pterocles gutturalis*): 30cm (12in)
Sporadically from Eritrea and Ethiopia south via Tanzania. Southern population centred on Botswana. Large. Pale yellow head, greyish crown and a broad black neck collar. Diffuse golden area beneath, merging into grey on the body. Back greyish with some darker markings, and chestnut on the wings and underparts. Hens are heavily mottled and lack the black band. Young birds as hens, but with smaller spots and more intense barring on the upperparts.

Pin-tailed sandgrouse

Pterocles alchata

Male pin-tailed sandgrouse wade into pools of water before flying back to the nest, where the chicks instinctively suck droplets of water from their saturated plumage. (First reported in 1896, it took zoologists until 1960 to become convinced of this behaviour.) However, studies suggest that in spite of their efforts, the nesting success of these birds is poor, with the majority of young chicks falling victim to predators. If eggs are taken, a pair may nest again soon afterwards. Pin-tailed sandgrouse remain relatively common in Morocco and Spain, but elsewhere in Europe their numbers have fallen markedly over recent years.

Identification: Black throat and stripe through each eye. Greyish crown, neck and chest. Orangish breast (bordered black) and sides of the head. Underparts white, yellow spots over the back and wings. Black-and-buff barring on the rump and characteristic long tail. Hens are paler, have a shorter tail and mottled wings, and lack the yellow spots. Young paler too, with no upper black breast line and only a trace of the lower.

Distribution: Resident in south-west Europe and in the Caspian region. Migratory in some parts of Asia. Also found in northern Africa.
Size: 32cm (12¹/₂in).
Habitat: Open, dry country.
Nest: Scrape on the ground.
Eggs: 3, stone-coloured with darker mottling.
Food: Seeds, plant material.

GAME BIRDS AND SONGSTERS

*Game birds as a group are commonly associated with woodland areas, but francolins have adapted
successfully to live in more open country. However, they may not always be resident throughout the year
in these areas, often undertaking regular migrations or sometimes even irregular seasonal movements
influenced by rainfall or the availability of food.*

Red-necked francolin

Red-necked spurfowl *Francolinus afer*

The red-necked francolin's head markings differ markedly
through its range, with the feathering on the sides of the
head sometimes whitish rather than predominantly blackish.
The patterning of the underparts also differs in
the nominate race, *F. afer*, from western
Angola and adjacent parts of Namibia,
which has white underparts with black
markings. In total, there are five distinct races
recognized through its range. Red-necked
francolins are found in areas of higher rainfall
than Swainson's francolin (*Pternistes swainsonii*),
since here there is more vegetation to provide
cover. They are most likely to be encountered in
the early morning and towards dusk, seeking shade
when the sun is at its hottest. Red-necked francolins
rarely fly, although if being chased they may fly low
over the ground for a short distance, before dipping
back down into vegetation and continuing on foot;
they may sometimes take to a tree for a short time.
They also roost in trees.

Identification: Prominent bare
red skin around each eye and on
the throat. Fine white streaking
on the black neck, becoming
longer on the underparts. Back
and wings brown. Bill, legs and
feet red. Sexes are alike. Young
birds are browner, with a dark bill,
yellowish legs and down partly
obscuring the bare
throat skin.

Distribution: Ranges in a
band across southern Africa,
from Rep. Congo and Angola
in the west across to
Tanzania and down the
eastern side of the continent
to southern South Africa.
Size: 41cm (16in).
Habitat: Grassland, often
near scrub.
Nest: Scrape on the ground
lined with vegetation.
Eggs: 3–9, buff to pale brown.
Food: Plant matter.

Swainson's francolin

Swainson's spurfowl *Francolinus swainsonii*

Distribution: Southern parts
of Africa, extending from
Zambia to southern Angola
and northern Namibia in the
west, and down to northern
South Africa.
Size: 38cm (15in).
Habitat: Arid savanna.
Nest: Scrape on the ground
lined with vegetation.
Eggs: 4–8, creamy-buff.
Food: Mainly plant matter.

These francolins can sometimes be observed in small groups, which are described
as coveys, as well as in the company of other related species. They are also
known as spurfowl because of the presence of one or two spurs which are
evident on the legs of cock birds. Pairs nest individually, usually choosing a
site hidden in grass and protected from above by a bush. Hatching typically
takes about 21 days, with the young birds able to fly shortly afterwards.
In some parts of their range they may nest twice during the year. In
agricultural areas, Swainson's francolin will invade freshly-sown
maize fields, digging up the seeds. They often forage in this way,
unearthing edible plant items from the ground, as well as eating
invertebrates. If disturbed in the open, these francolins will fly
off and drop down out of sight in the nearest available cover.
Especially during periods of heavy rainfall, they may also be
seen perching in suitable trees. They have loud, harsh calls
that frequently betray their presence.

Identification: Predominantly dark brown, with black markings
evident on the underparts. Bare red skin around the eyes and under the
throat. Bill, legs and feet are blackish. Young birds are duller, lack the red
on the head and have paler markings on the flanks. Sexes are alike.

Tawny pipit

Anthus campestris

The tawny pipit's breeding season begins in Europe in April, with cock birds engaging in song flights, fluttering upwards almost vertically to a height of around 30m (100ft) before plunging back down, singing especially loudly at this stage. The cock will also chase his mate frantically until egg-laying commences. She constructs the nest on her own, usually hiding it behind a tussock of grass. Incubation lasts about two weeks, with the young pipits leaving the nest after a similar period. It is not uncommon for pairs to rear two broods. Like many young birds however, a significant proportion will die in the first few weeks following fledging, but those which survive will migrate south to their African wintering grounds from September onwards. Tawny pipits may be observed in small flocks of up to 30 individuals when migrating. A relatively small number of pairs also nest in north-west Africa.

Identification: Black stripe through each eye, with a white stripe above. Upperparts mainly plain, slightly greyish, with buff-white underparts. Row of darker markings across the median coverts, and also slight streaks at the sides of the chest. Bill is darker at the tip. Legs and feet are pale pink, with a short hind claw. Young birds display more heavily marked upperparts, with streaking over the head and back. Sexes are alike.

Distribution: Ranges through Europe as a breeding visitor. Absent from the British Isles and Scandinavia (except for the extreme south-west). Overwinters in Africa, from southern Mauritania and Senegal across to Somalia and Kenya. Present in Asia.
Size: 18cm (7in).
Habitat: Sandy areas and gravel pits.
Nest: Cup-shaped, made from vegetation.
Eggs: 4–6, white, spotted.
Food: Largely invertebrates.

Yellow-necked francolin (*Pternistes leucoscepus*): 40cm (15¾in)
Eastern Africa, with an isolated population in Eritrea. Also ranges from Somalia to parts of Ethiopia, Kenya, Uganda and Tanzania. Recognizable by its distinctive bare yellow throat patch and predominantly brown plumage with very evident white streaking, especially on the underparts. Young birds have paler throats. Sexes are alike.

Moorland francolin (*Scleroptila psilolaemus*): 35cm (13¾in)
East Africa, occurring in areas of Ethiopia and Kenya, ranging to Uganda. Mottled brown upperparts, with a white throat. Ethiopian race (*S. p. psilolaemus*) has buff underparts, with wavy black lines across the chest and speckling on the underparts. Underparts become more rufous in the southerly race (*S. p. elgonensis*). Young birds yet to be described. Sexes are alike.

Quail plover (*Ortyxelos meiffrenii*): 13cm (5in)
Sub-Saharan Africa, in a band from Mauritania to Sudan. Also Ethiopia south to Kenya. Isolated areas elsewhere, including Ghana. Looks like a miniature courser, but exact relationship unclear. Cheeks and sides of the neck are pale yellow. Rufous ear coverts. Mottled brownish markings on the back and across the chest. White is evident on the underparts and across the wings, which are predominantly black when seen from above. Bill greyish with a dark tip. Legs yellowish. Young birds are paler, with more intense spotting on the upperparts. Hens have more rufous coloration on the breast.

Grasshopper warbler

Locustella naevia

Difficult to observe, these warblers are very adept at clambering through grass and low vegetation. They may be spotted running across open ground, flying low if disturbed and seeking vegetation as cover. Their song, which is usually heard at dusk, may also betray their presence. They sing in bursts of up to a minute in duration, and their calls incorporate ringing notes that have been likened to the sound of a muffled alarm clock. Grasshopper warblers migrate largely without stopping, and have been observed in West Africa from August onwards. They undertake the return journey to their breeding grounds in Europe and Asia between March and May, flying in a more easterly direction, often crossing the Mediterranean from Algeria. The breeding period extends from May until July, with the bulky nest built close to the ground. The chicks hatch after two weeks, and are reared by both adults before leaving the nest as early as 10 days old.

Distribution: Breeds through central and northern parts of Europe as far as southern Scandinavia. Present in much of the British Isles. Absent from the Mediterranean region. Overwinters in parts of Africa, especially on the western side.
Size: 12.5cm (5in).
Habitat: Marshland and grassland areas.
Nest: Made of vegetation.
Eggs: 6, creamy with brownish-red spotting.
Food: Invertebrates.

Identification: Olive-brown upperparts. Streaked head, back and undertail coverts. Faint eye stripe. Underparts whitish, more yellowish-green on the breast. Variable chest markings. Narrow, pointed bill. Pink legs and feet. Sexes are alike. Young birds have yellowish underparts.

PHEASANTS AND PARTRIDGES

A number of pheasant and partridge species have been selectively bred and released for sport, so that sightings far outside their usual areas of distribution are not unusual. In Europe, these game birds are most likely to be observed during the winter months, when there is less natural cover available and groups may be forced to forage more widely.

Common pheasant

Ring-necked pheasant *Phasianus colchicus*

Common pheasants show considerable individual variation in appearance throughout their European range. This is due to hybridization between races, resulting in the loss of distinguishing characteristics. Even odd black-feathered (melanistic) examples are not uncommon. This situation has arisen largely because of widespread breeding of these pheasants and their subsequent release into the wild for shooting. They occur naturally in Asia. Common pheasants usually live in groups comprised of a cock bird with several hens. They forage on the ground, flying noisily and somewhat clumsily when disturbed, and may choose to roost off the ground.

Right: Its mottled plumage provides the common pheasant hen with good camouflage.

Identification: Cock bird has prominent areas of bare red skin on each side of the face, surrounded by metallic dark greenish plumage. Variable white area at the base of the neck. The remainder of the plumage is predominantly brown, with the underparts a more chestnut shade with dark blotching. Hens are lighter brown overall, with darker mottling, especially on the back and wings.

Distribution: Range now extends throughout most of western Europe, except for much of the Iberian Peninsula, and in a band eastwards through central Asia as far as Japan. Has also been introduced to the United States, Australia, Tasmania and New Zealand.
Size: Cock 89cm (35in); hen 62cm (24in).
Habitat: Light woodland.
Nest: Scrape on the ground.
Eggs: 7–15, olive-brown.
Food: Plant matter including seeds, berries and young shoots, also invertebrates.

Red-legged partridge

Alectoris rufa

The red-legged partridge was brought to England as long ago as the late 1600s for shooting, and its adaptable nature ensured that its range steadily expanded. However, during the 20th century the chukar partridge, which hybridizes with the red-legged variety, was also introduced to the British Isles. Today it can be difficult to determine whether partridges are pure or cross-bred red-legged individuals, even in their natural range, thanks to their similarity in appearance to chukars. Red-legged partridges form individual pairs when breeding. The cock bird chooses and then prepares the nest site.

Identification: Prominent black collar with disctinctive black streaks extending around the sides of the neck to the eye. Black stripe continues through the eye to the bill, with a white stripe above and white below around the throat. Bluish-grey above the bill, and on the breast and barred flanks. Brownish abdomen. Hens are smaller and lack the tarsal spurs on the legs.

Distribution: Found naturally in Europe from the Iberian Peninsula to Italy. Introduced to the rest of Europe.
Size: 38cm (15in).
Habitat: Open countryside.
Nest: Scrape on the ground.
Eggs: 9–12, pale yellowish-brown with dark spotting.
Food: Mainly plant matter, some invertebrates.

Rock partridge

Alectoris graeca

Rock partridges take their name from the rocky slopes on which they can frequently be observed, which in Italy range to altitudes as high as 2,700m (8,850ft). They often move down to lower levels in the winter, when snow collects on the slopes, and they avoid north-facing slopes altogether. Throughout the year, rock partridges are rarely sighted far from water, and are most likely to be seen in flocks. Their coloration provides excellent camouflage when foraging on the ground. When flushed, their flight is quite low and fast, and they will dip down into nearby cover again as soon as they are out of danger. Rock partridges nest as individual pairs, and their chicks will be fully grown when they are three months old.

Distribution: Central southern Europe, from south-east France to Italy and along the eastern Adriatic coast to Greece. Present on Sicily.
Size: 36cm (14in).
Habitat: Rocky alpine areas.
Nest: Scrape on the ground.
Eggs: 8–14, yellowish-brown with some darker spotting.
Food: Mainly plant matter, some invertebrates.

Identification: Grey crown. Thick black stripe running from around the red bill through each eye and down onto the chest, encircling the white lower face and throat area. Breast is greyish-blue, becoming fawn on the underparts, with black-and-white barring on the flanks. Brownish suffusion over the back. Sexes are alike.

Helmeted guineafowl

Numida meleagris

Helmeted guineafowl vary considerably in appearance throughout their wide range. In the past, taxonomists have recognized more than 30 different races, but this figure has now been whittled down to approximately nine. The various subspecies can be distinguished by the shape of their casques and wattles, as well as by the depth of blue coloration on the sides of their head. These guineafowl prey readily on invertebrates, even to the extent of picking off ticks from warthogs. They scratch around on the ground using their powerful toes, searching for seeds, invertebrates and other edible items. Young helmeted guineafowl are able to fly just 14 days after hatching, and family groups link up with the main flock again after a month or so.

Identification: Distinctive, horn-coloured casque on the top of the head, often with an adjoining area of red skin. Blue areas on the sides of the face extending down the neck. The head is largely bare, although traces of fine down feathering may be visible. Plumage is predominantly dark, broken by variable white spots. Sexes are similar, but hens are smaller than cocks.

Distribution: Much of Africa south of the Sahara, except some western and eastern areas. Introduced elsewhere, including Saudi Arabia and the Caribbean.
Size: 53–63cm (21–25in).
Habitat: Open country, especially savanna.
Nest: Scrape on the ground, often hidden in long grass.
Eggs: 6–12, creamy-buff with brown-and-white speckling.
Food: Mostly plant matter and invertebrates.

Chukar partridge (*Alectoris chukar*): 35cm (14in)
Found in southern Europe eastwards to Asia. Introduced to the British Isles and elsewhere. Very similar in appearance to the rock partridge (*Alectoris graeca*) but has a cream rather than white area on the sides of the face and chest, a broader white stripe above each eye, and black only on the side of the lower mandible rather than on the whole bill. Numerous races are recognized through its wide range. Hens lack the tarsal swelling of cocks, and their head patterning is less colourful.

Grey partridge (*Perdix perdix*): 32cm (12½in)
Occurs in a broad band across central Europe, from Ireland eastwards to Asia. Orange-brown face, with faint grey stripes extending back on the sides of the head. Crown, neck and much of the underparts are greyish, with dark edging to the plumage. Prominent dark brown feathering on the belly is largely absent or reduced in size in hens. The flanks are barred with brown, while the wings are brown with black speckling. Tail is reddish brown.

Barbary partridge (*Alectoris barbara*): 35cm (14in)
Natural range is in North Africa. Introduced to southern Spain and also present on Sardinia. Dark stripe on the crown, with a greyish-white area beneath and a lighter fawn stripe extending through each eye. The remainder of the head and throat area are greyish-white. Reddish-brown border to the bib, with black-and-white speckling behind. The chest is otherwise greyish and the abdomen is fawn. Back and wings are greyish with a fawn suffusion. Brown and black markings on the flanks on a whitish background. Sexes are alike.

BUSTARDS AND GROUSE

This group of birds may be encountered in a range of different landscapes, from arid, desert-like terrain to the frozen north, but they all rely heavily on cryptic plumage to avoid detection. Grouse, whose range extends into the tundra region, have plumage that extends right down their legs and over their toes to minimize heat loss and guard against frostbite.

Great bustard

Otis tarda

These massive birds have declined greatly in number over recent years owing to a combination of hunting and habitat change. They still flourish in undisturbed areas, where they are seen in groups throughout the year. The display of the cock is an amazing sight as he bends forwards, raising his wings and inflating his throat sac. His head disappears from view, creating what has been likened to a foam bath. Great bustards are quiet birds by nature, uttering a short call resembling a bark only if alarmed. They will hunt voles, but invertebrates are favoured for rearing the chicks, which is accomplished by the hen alone.

Identification: Grey head and neck, with a rufous area at the base. Black-and-chestnut markings over the wings, with prominent white areas. Underparts and tips of tail feathers are also white. Hens have more extensive but paler rufous coloration on the neck, and less white on the wings.

Distribution: Scattered locations through the Iberian Peninsula and adjacent parts of north-west Africa. Also present in eastern Europe, ranging eastwards into Asia.
Size: Cock 105cm (41in); hen 75cm (29½in).
Habitat: Open steppes and acricultural land.
Nest: Flattened area, made of vegetation.
Eggs: 2–4, greenish or olive-brown in colour.
Food: Invertebrates, plant matter and small mammals.

Black korhaan bustard

Eupodotis afra

Distribution: Southern Africa, extending from the Cape north across much of Namibia and Botswana.
Size: 52cm (20½in).
Habitat: Grassland, savanna.
Nest: Lays on bare ground.
Eggs: 1, olive-green with darker brown markings.
Food: Mostly invertebrates and plant matter.

Male black korhaan bustards are bold and conspicuous by nature, whereas hens are much shyer. Highly territorial, the male's call, from a vantage point such as a termite mound, can travel over 1km (⅝ mile). He will also fly regularly over his territory, and may end up in aerial conflict with one or more neighbouring cock birds. Males display throughout the year, and hens may mate at any stage too, hatching and rearing their offspring alone. The chick follows its mother almost immediately. Some taxonomists believe the black korhaan bustard should be reclassified as two separate species: the northern form (*E. afraoides*) has white centres to its flight feathers and white underwing coverts, while its southern relative (*E. afra*) is characterized by its black underwing coverts.

Identification: Black head, white patches behind the eyes, white neck collar. Underparts black. Brown-and-black mottling on the back. White sides to the wings. Bill is red, tip greyish-black. Legs and feet yellow. Hens have a paler bill and a mottled head and neck; whiter on the lower chest, with black confined to the lower underparts. Young resemble hens.

Willow grouse (red grouse, *Lagopus lagopus*): 35–43cm (14–17in)
Circumpolar distribution, including northern areas of the British Isles (where the race concerned is called red grouse) and Scandinavia. Brownish head and upperparts, and white underparts. Plumage becomes pure white during the winter months. Hens are similar but have much more speckled upperparts, and also become pure white in winter.

Black grouse (Eurasian black grouse, *Tetrao tetrix*): Cock 58cm (23in); hen 45cm (18in)
Present in Scotland and northern England. Extends from Belgium north to Scandinavia and eastwards across northern Asia. Also occurs in the Alpine region. Predominantly jet black, with scarlet combs above the eyes. White wing bar, white undertail coverts and a white spot at the shoulder area. The tail feathers are decidedly curved. The hen is predominantly brown, speckled with black barring, and has a narrow white wing bar.

Hazel grouse (*Bonasa bonasia*): 40cm (16in)
Occurs in north-eastern France, Belgium and Germany north to Scandinavia and eastwards across Asia. Distinctive-looking solid black throat patch, outlined in white, and a tall crest. The back, vent and legs are greyish. Darker abdominal markings are highlighted on a white background. Rufous patches appear on the sides of the chest. Hens have a speckled throat patch and a smaller crest.

Caucasian black grouse (*Tetrao mlokosiewiczi*): 55cm (22in)
Present in parts of Turkey and the adjoining Caucasus mountain range between the Black and Caspian seas. Almost entirely black, except for a small white patch at the shoulder area of the wings and a prominent red stripe above each eye. Relatively long, slightly curved tail. Hens are greyish-brown overall, with fine barring over the body and dark ear coverts.

Capercaillie

Western capercaillie *Tetrao urogallus*

Like New World turkeys (*Meleagris* species), male capercaillies adopt a display pose with tail feathers fanned out in a circle. They display communally to hens at sites known as "leks". After mating with her chosen partner, the hen nests and rears the young alone. The weather in the critical post-hatching period has a major impact on the survival rate of chicks – in wet springs, many become fatally chilled. Hens are about a third of the weight of cocks. Both sexes have strong, hooked bills, which enable them to easily nip off pieces of tough vegetation such as Scots pine (*Pinus sylvestris*) shoots. This helps them to survive when the ground is covered by snow.

Distribution: Present in Scotland and other mountainous regions in western Europe. Range extends through much of Scandinavia and eastwards through northern Asia.
Size: 80–115cm (31–45in).
Habitat: Coniferous and deciduous areas.
Nest: A shallow scrape on the ground.
Eggs: 6–10, yellow with light brown blotches.
Food: Buds and shoots.

Left: Male capercaillies fan their tail feathers when displaying to hens at leks.

Identification: Greyish-black head with an obvious red stripe above each eye. Green area on the chest. Wings are chestnut, the rump and tail blackish. Underparts are variable, ranging from predominantly white to black. Legs are covered with brown feathers, toes are exposed. Hens have an orangish patch on the sides of the face and chest, brown mottled upperparts and whiter underparts.

COLD COUNTRY INHABITANTS

Many birds have adapted to living through the winter period, while some can survive in this kind of habitat throughout the year thanks to their dense plumage, which provides insulation against the cold. Some species also grow larger than close relatives found at lower altitudes, with their increased body mass helping to counter the freezing temperatures.

Snow bunting

Plectrophenax nivalis

This bunting breeds closer to the North Pole than any other passerine. The cock has an attractive display flight, rising to about 10m (30ft) before starting to sing, then slowly fluttering down again. The nest is often sited among rocks, which provide shelter against cold winds. The hen incubates alone for about 12 days, with the young fledging after a similar period. Outside the breeding season, snow buntings are social and can be seen in flocks, searching for food on the ground, often in coastal areas. They are usually quite wary, flying away to prevent a close approach. These buntings have a varied diet comprised of seeds and berries when invertebrates are scarce over the winter.

Identification: Breeding males are mainly white, with black on the back, wings, tail and flight feathers. Bill and legs black. Hens have dark brown streaking on the head, buff ear coverts and brown on the wings. Non-breeding males resemble hens but with a white rump and whiter wings. Young birds are greyish and streaked.

Distribution: Breeds in Iceland, northern Scandinavia and the far north of Europe eastwards into Asia. Overwinters further south in Europe and Asia. Also present in North America. Populations from Greenland often overwinter in the British Isles.
Size: 17cm (6³⁄₄in).
Habitat: Tundra, grassland.
Nest: Scrape on the ground.
Eggs: 4–6, white with reddish-brown spots.
Food: Seeds, invertebrates.

Lapland longspur

Calcarius lapponicus

The nest of the Lapland longspur is set into the ground and lined with feathers, giving the hen some protection against the cold as well as helping to conceal her from predators while she is at her most vulnerable. The breeding period is short, taking advantage of the brief thaw in the tundra ice during the Arctic summer. This leads to a profusion of midges and other insects hatching in the surface meltwater, which cannot drain away because of the permanently frozen soil beneath. This abundance of insect life is available to the young Lapland longspurs once they have hatched. They grow and fledge rapidly, leaving the nest at just ten days old, and then begin to hunt themselves. Longspurs are so called because of their elongated rear claws, which may help them to maintain their balance, since they move either by walking or running instead of hopping on the ground like most birds.

Identification: Breeding males have a black head and upper breast, with white behind each eye extending down along the edge of the wings, bordered by a chestnut collar. Lower underparts are white, with black streaking on the flanks. Wings are a variable blackish-brown pattern. Tail black. Hens are less striking, with black-edged brown ear coverts, a black-streaked rufous collar, and black speckling on the chest. Males in eclipse plumage resemble females, except for a broad brownish area at the back of the neck, while hens gain a brownish suffusion on the chest and flanks. Young birds have distinctive speckling on the face.

Distribution: Breeds in northern Scandinavia and in the far north of Europe, extending eastwards into northern Asia. Overwinters in coastal areas of eastern England and along adjacent coasts of mainland Europe. Also overwinters around the Caspian Sea region and eastwards into Asia.
Size: 16cm (6¹⁄₄in).
Habitat: Tundra, grassland.
Nest: Cup-shaped.
Eggs: 3–7, greenish-buff with dark spots.
Food: Seeds, invertebrates.

White-winged snowfinch (*Montifringilla nivalis*):
19cm (7¹/₂in)
Northern Spain to the Alps and along the
northern Mediterranean to the Red Sea. Main
distribution is in central Asia. Breeding cock has
a greyish head with a black throat, and white
underparts. Brownish-grey back, with white on
the sides of the wings, visible in flight. Tail black
above, white below. In winter, bill is ivory rather
than black. Hens are paler. Young birds resemble
hens, but with buff on the sides of the head.

Caucasian snowcock (*Tetraogallus caucasicus*):
60cm (24in)
Caucasus Mountains. Head and sides of the
face yellowish-grey, with orange encircling the
eye. White throat, with a rufous streak and a
white band behind. Rufous on the back of the
neck. Vermiculations on the neck and breast,
extending over the back and wings, which have
orangish markings. Broad white bands across
the open wings. Underparts have reddish-brown
streaking. Undertail white. Bill greyish, legs and
feet yellowish. Hens have narrower streaking on
the flanks. Young birds are smaller and duller,
with indistinct streaking on the flanks.

Guldenstadt's redstart (*Phoenicurus
erythrogaster*): 15cm (6in)
Breeds in the Caucasus, moving lower in the
winter. Cock has a white crown, with a broad
white area on the wings. Head, throat, upper
back and wings are black, lower back, rump and
rest of the body chestnut-red. Bill, legs and feet
blackish. Hens are greyish, with a yellowish
tinge to the lower parts and slightly rufous on
the tail. Young birds are duller.

Rock ptarmigan

Lagopus mutus

These grouse live in a region where natural
cover is very scarce, and undergo a stunning
transformation in appearance through the
year. Their summer plumage is mottled
brown and their winter plumage is white,
enabling them to merge into the snowy
landscape. When snow is on the ground,
rock ptarmigans feed on buds and twigs of
shrubs such as willow, which manage to
grow in this treeless region. Pairs nest in the
brief Arctic summer, often choosing a site
protected by shrubs. The cock stays nearby
while the hen incubates alone. The chicks
are covered in down and
can move easily, but are
not able to fly until their
flight feathers have
emerged fully, at
about ten
days old.

Distribution: Circumpolar.
Present in Iceland, Scotland,
northern Scandinavia and in
the Alps and Pyrenees. Also
in the far north of Asia, North
America and Greenland.
Size: 38cm (15in).
Habitat: Tundra.
Nest: Scrape on the ground,
lined with vegetation.
Eggs: 6–9, creamy-buff,
heavily blotched and spotted
with blackish-brown.
Food: Buds, leaves, berries
and other plant matter.

Identification: Head is mottled
and brownish, with red above
each eye. Similar patterning
across the body, which
becomes white in the
winter. Blackish
stripes on the
face, lacking
in hens.

Caspian woodcock

Caspian snowcock *Tetraogallus caspius*

This woodcock occurs in mountainous areas and
is the most southerly representative of its genus.
It is normally encountered in pairs or in small
groups. Most active in the early morning,
Caspian woodcocks then hide away among
the rocks until late in the afternoon, when
they venture out to feed again. Seeds form an
important part of their diet, but they will also
dig up bulbs and pull off leaves with their stocky
bills. Unfortunately, in some parts of their range
overgrazing by sheep and goats is depriving them
of food. In the winter they may move down to lower
altitudes, although are still often to be encountered
well above the treeline at this time of year. Their
plumage is very dense – individual feathers have
down at their bases which helps to trap warm
air next to the skin, insulating the birds
against the bitter cold.

Identification: White head and
throat, grey down the sides of
the face. Orange skin encircling
each eye. Back and chest grey,
darker spotting on the chest.
Underparts bluish-grey with
orange streaks. Vent area
white. Wings bluish-
grey with orangish
spotting, and dark
tips to the flight
feathers. Bill is
greyish, legs and
feet orangish.
Hens are
similar but
smaller and
duller. Young
are smaller
and duller
than hens.

Distribution: Extreme south-
east of Europe. Present
around the Caspian Sea area,
in central and eastern parts of
Turkey to north-western Iran,
extending south as far as the
Persian Gulf.
Size: 60cm (24in).
Habitat: Bare mountains.
Nest: Scrape on the ground,
lined with vegetation.
Eggs: 6–9, pale greenish-
brown, with some reddish-
brown markings.
Food: Plant matter.

MOUNTAIN-DWELLERS

Mountainous areas such as the Alps have a harsh climate, particularly during the winter months. In this bleak landscape, birds make use of whatever cover is available, which often means roosting and breeding in caves. Some mountain birds have become surprisingly tame, especially around alpine campsites and similar areas where they are regularly fed.

Alpine chough

Yellow-billed chough *Pyrrhocorax graculus*

Identification: Blackish overall, with a slight gloss to the plumage. Relatively short yellow bill, and red legs and feet. Sexes are alike. Young birds are duller and more brownish, with grey feet and a duller yellow bill.

These choughs eat snails and similar invertebrates, which they dig from the ground with their powerful bills, and from late summer onwards will forage for berries. In areas popular with walkers and skiers, these bold and intelligent corvids have learnt to take scraps from visitors. Alpine choughs are social by nature, and can be seen in flocks of 100 or more birds. They are very agile in flight. They roost communally when not nesting, often in caves, where they will be protected from the worst of the weather. Breeding starts in late spring. Incubation lasts 19 days, and the chicks leave the nest 30 days later. The family party joins a larger flock, and the young choughs are fed by the group until they are fully independent.

Distribution: The Pyrenees, Alps and mountainous areas through the northern and eastern Mediterranean, and into Asia to the Himalayas. Also ranges to parts of north-west Africa.
Size: 38cm (15in).
Habitat: Mountain regions.
Nest: Made of twigs, roots and similar material.
Eggs: 3–6, cream to pale green, with dark markings.
Food: Omnivorous.

White-necked raven

Corvus albicollis

These large corvids weigh as much as 1kg (2¹/₅lb), and have a wingspan of 1.5m (5ft), which enables them to glide effortlessly. They are most often seen in pairs, but flocks of up to 800 individuals may be encountered where food is plentiful. White-necked ravens are primarily scavengers, attracted to road kills, although they are considered a menace by sheep-farmers in South Africa for attacking young lambs and sick ewes. They also catch reptiles and small mammals, and will steal the eggs and chicks of other birds, even those of the Cape vulture (*Gyps coprotheres*), which may share the same nesting cliffs. Their powerful bills can hammer open eggs and even the shells of young tortoises. The breeding period extends from August to December, and the hen incubates alone for three weeks.

Distribution: Range extends through highland areas of eastern and southern Africa, from Kenya and Tanzania right down to the coastal regions of South Africa.
Size: 54cm (21¹/₄in).
Habitat: Mountain regions.
Nest: Bulky pile of sticks.
Eggs: 1–6, greenish with olive spots.
Food: Omnivorous.

Identification: Predominantly black, more glossy on the upperparts, with a very broad white collar around the back of the neck. Occasionally there may be signs of a pale area across the breast as well. Upper bill is broad and down-curved, and the bill overall is black with a white tip. Very short tail. Sexes are alike. Young birds are more of a brownish-black shade.

Rock sparrow (*Petronia petronia*): 17cm (6½in)
Iberian peninsula, southern Italy and the eastern
Mediterranean north-eastwards into Asia. Also
north-west Africa. Broad white stripe from the
eyes down the sides of the neck. Blackish-brown
above, grey central crown. Underparts white
with irregular brown streaks down the sides and
across the chest. Faint yellow spot at the base
of the throat. Upperparts light brown with darker
markings. Bill dull brown, paler on the lower bill.
Pinkish legs and feet. Young birds warmer buff
above and greyer below, with no yellow spot.
Sexes are alike.

Rock bunting (*Emberiza cia*): 15cm (6in)
Northern Mediterranean, including the Iberian
Peninsula. Also north-west Africa. Greyish head
and upper chest, broken with black stripes over
the crown, through the eyes and around the
cheeks. Underparts and back rusty-brown, black
lines down back. Two narrow white wing bars,
the wings blackish and brown. Tail dark at the
tip, white beneath. Hens similar, less black head
patterning. Young have orange-buff underparts.

Grey-necked bunting (*Emberiza buchanani*):
15cm (6in)
Eastern Turkey, overwintering in India. Grey
head, whitish throat patch and moustachial
stripe. Underparts reddish-brown with pale
fringes, becoming whitish near the vent. Grey
shoulders, with an adjacent band of rufous.
Wing feathers blackish with light brown edging.
Hens are duller, with less distinct red wing bars,
and streaking on the breast. Bill, legs and feet
pinkish. Young birds similar to hens.

Crag martin

Eurasian crag martin *Hirundo rupestris*

These martins appear uniformly brown from
a distance. They fly relatively low, usually
alongside the crags and mountainsides
rather than above them, and as with other
related species spend most of their time in
the air. They often remain close to cliff-faces
when these are in sunlight, which may help
them to capture insects in flight, and will
forage as far as 16km (10 miles) from their
roosts. Crag martins have a varied diet
including flying beetles, butterflies and
wasps, and feed almost entirely on the wing,
although very occasionally they will feed on
the ground. Pairs nest on their own or in
small colonies, and are strongly territorial.
Both members of the pair construct their
distinctive nest, which can take up to three
weeks. Caves are traditionally used, but
crag martins may also
breed in buildings.
Their young can
fly at four
weeks old.

Distribution: Through much
of the Iberian Peninsula and
the northern Mediterranean
region to Turkey, and east
into Asia. Also present in
north-west Africa. European
birds overwinter in Senegal
and Gambia, while those in
the east travel through the
Rift Valley, occurring in Egypt,
Sudan and Ethiopia.
Size: 15cm (6in).
Habitat: Craggy landscapes,
sometimes cliffs.
Nest: Cup made of mud,
lined with grass.
Eggs: 1–5, white with slight
red-and-grey spotting.
Food: Invertebrates.

Identification: Dull brown head,
back and upperparts. Lighter on
the cheeks and down over the
breast onto the abdomen. Slight
speckling on the throat. Blackish
underwing coverts. Bill is black,
legs and feet paler. Sexes are
alike. Young birds have pale buff
edging on their upperparts.

Alpine accentor

Prunella collaris

Although only recorded in Europe at altitudes up to 3,000m
(9,850ft), reaching the snowline, Alpine accentors have been
observed as high as 8,000m (26,250ft) in the Asiatic part of
their range. They seek out the warmest areas and forage on
the ground, using their feet to hold on to rocks, probing
small openings for invertebrates such as spiders. They are
also able to catch insects in flight. Males engage in short
display flights to gain the attention of their mates, although
mating itself takes less than a quarter of a second.
Both members of the pair share the incubation,
and the chicks hatch after two weeks. The
adults may be joined by other Alpine
accentors, who act as helpers
in providing food for the
brood. The young fledge
after approximately 16 days, and will be
independent in a further two weeks. They
may subsequently remain with the adult birds,
forming larger flocks over the winter.

Identification: Dark greyish head
with brown ear coverts. Throat is
white with heavy barring. Dull
greyish-yellow underparts, with
evident rufous streaking. Back is
brownish with black streaking.
Two narrow white wing bars, the
area in between
blackish, forming
a distinct band
in flight. Narrow
bill is dark at the tip
and orange-yellow
at the base. Legs
and feet are pinkish.
Young birds have mostly
brown heads. Sexes alike.

Distribution: Range extends
through mountainous areas
of the Iberian Peninsula and
northern Mediterranean,
including the Pyrenees and
Alps, east to the Caucasus
and into Asia. Also present in
north-west Africa.
Size: 17cm (6¾in).
Habitat: Prefers barren and
stony ground.
Nest: Among boulders, or in
a crevice.
Eggs: 3–4, pale blue.
Food: Mainly invertebrates
and seeds.

SWIFTS, SWALLOWS AND MARTINS

This group of birds spend most of their lives in flight. They undertake long journeys, with European populations migrating south to Africa at the approach of winter, and returning to breed the following spring. Pairs frequently return to the same nest site they had occupied previously – a remarkable feat of navigation after a journey covering thousands of kilometres.

Swift

Common swift *Apus apus*

Distribution: Found across virtually the whole of Europe, extending to northern Africa and Asia. Overwinters in southern Africa.
Size: 16.5cm (6½in).
Habitat: In the air.
Nest: Cup-shaped, built under cover.
Eggs: 2–3, white.
Food: Flying invertebrates, such as midges and moths.

Flocks of swifts are most noticeable when uttering their distinctive, screaming calls, flying low overhead in search of winged insects. At other times they may appear little more than distant specks in the sky, wheeling around at heights of 1,000m (3,300ft) or more. Their flight pattern is quite distinctive, consisting of a series of rapid wingbeats followed by gliding into the wind. Their tiny feet do not allow them to perch, although they can cling to vertical surfaces. Except when breeding, swifts spend their entire lives in the air, and are apparently able to sleep and mate in flight too. If hunting conditions are unfavourable, such as during a cool summer, nestling swifts respond by growing more slowly, while the adults can undergo short periods of torpidity to avoid starvation.

Identification: Dark overall, with relatively long, pointed wings and a forked tail. Pale whitish throat. Sexes are alike.

Swallow

Barn swallow *Hirundo rustica*

The swallows' return to their European breeding grounds is one of the most welcome signs of spring. Although pairs return to the same nest site every year, they do not migrate together. Cock birds arrive back before their partners and jealously guard the site from would-be rivals. Cocks fight with surprising ferocity if one of the birds does not back down. Although swallows may use traditional nesting sites such as caves or hollow trees, they more commonly build their nests inside buildings such as barns, choosing a site close to the eaves. It can take up to a thousand trips to collect enough damp mud, carried back in the bill, to complete a new nest.

Identification: Chestnut forehead and throat, dark blue head and back, and a narrow dark blue band across the chest. The wings are blackish and the underparts are white. Long tail streamers. Sexes are alike.

Distribution: Throughout virtually the entire Northern Hemisphere. European populations overwinter in Africa south of the Sahara.
Size: 19cm (7½in).
Habitat: Open country, close to water.
Nest: Made of mud, built off the ground.
Eggs: 4–5, white with reddish-and-grey spotting.
Food: Flying invertebrates.

Alpine swift (*Apus melba*): 23cm (9in)
Found throughout southern Europe and North Africa. Overwinters in southern Africa. Plain brown upperparts, with a black collar around the neck. Throat, chest and upper abdomen are white. Lower underparts brown. Tail is short. Sexes are alike.

Red-rumped swallow (*Hirundo daurica*):
17cm (7in)
Southern Europe, the Mediterranean and North Africa. Overwinters in sub-Saharan Africa. Dark bluish area on the head and back, separated by a wide chestnut collar. Wings are blackish. Pale chestnut rump with narrow streaking; streaking also on the underparts. Sexes are alike.

Rock martin (pale crag martin, *Hirundo fuligula*):
13cm (5in)
Occurs in Africa, except for the central region. Also extends into south-western Asia. Brownish upperparts, rufous-brown underparts. Northern birds are lighter and greyer. Sexes are alike.

Plain sand martin (brown-throated sand martin, *Riparia paludicola*): 12cm (5in)
Sporadic distribution in north-western and sub-Saharan Africa. Also occurs on Madagascar. Predominantly brown overall, with a greyish-brown tinge to the throat and breast. Remainder of the underparts are white. Sexes are alike.

Congo sand martin (*Riparia congica*):
11cm (4¹/₂in)
Confined to three regions of the Congo River, hence its common name. Similar to the sand martin (*Riparia riparia*), but the brown breast band is less defined. Sexes are alike.

House martin

Delichon urbica

The house martin's breeding habits have changed significantly due to an increase in the number of buildings in rural areas. They traditionally nested on cliff faces, but over the past century began to prefer the walls of houses and farm structures as sites, as well as beneath bridges and even on street lamps, where a ready supply of nocturnal insects are attracted to the light. The nest is usually spherical and normally made of mud. The base is built first, followed by the sides. On average, the whole process can take up to two weeks to complete. House martins are highly social by nature, nesting in huge colonies made up of thousands of pairs where conditions are suitable. Even outside the breeding period, they will associate in large flocks comprising of hundreds of individuals.

Identification: Dark bluish head and back. Black wings with white underwing coverts. The underparts and rump are also white. Forked tail is dark blue. Sexes are alike.

Distribution: Throughout the whole of Europe, extending eastwards across much of Asia. Overwinters in Africa south of the Sahara.
Size: 13cm (5in).
Habitat: Open country, close to water.
Nest: Cup made of mud.
Eggs: 4–5, white.
Food: Flying invertebrates.

Sand martin

African sand martin, bank swallow *Riparia riparia*

During the summer, sand martins can usually be observed near lakes and other stretches of water, frequently swooping down over the surface to catch invertebrates. They are most likely to be nesting in colonies nearby, in tunnels excavated in suitable sandy banks. These can extend up to 1m (3ft) into the bank, and the nesting chamber at the end is lined with grass, seaweed and similar material. The eggs are laid on a soft bed of feathers. Once the young martins leave the nest, they stay in groups with other chicks, waiting for their parents to return and feed them. The adults typically bring around 60 invertebrates back from each visit. Parents recognize their offspring by their distinctive calls. If danger threatens, the repetitive alarm calls of the adult sand martins cause the young to rush back into the nesting tunnels for protection.

Identification: Brown on the head, back, wings and tail, with a brown band across the breast. Throat area and underparts are white. Long flight feathers. Small black bill. Sexes are alike. Young birds have shorter flight feathers, and are browner overall.

Distribution: Ranges across virtually the whole of Europe and parts of northern Africa into Asia. Overwinters in sub-Saharan Africa.
Size: 11cm (4in).
Habitat: Open country, close to water.
Nest: Hole in a sandbank.
Eggs: 3–4, white.
Food: Flying invertebrates.

SUNBIRDS AND SUGARBIRDS

These nectar-feeding birds are not encountered north of the Mediterranean, and both sugarbird species occur only in southern Africa. Metallic plumage is a common feature of male sunbirds in breeding condition. Their relatively small size does not indicate a placid nature however – these lively and bold birds can be very aggressive towards their own kind.

Giant sunbird

Dreptes thomensis

Distribution: Found only on the island of Sâo Tomé in the Gulf of Guinea, off the west coast of Africa.
Size: 23cm (9in).
Habitat: Open country and forest areas.
Nest: Pouch-shaped, made from vegetation.
Eggs: 2, white with some red spotting.
Food: Nectar, soft fruit and also invertebrates.

The sole member of its genus, the giant sunbird is the largest sunbird of all. They can usually be encountered in upland areas on their native island, but will also fly further afield and may be found in more open agricultural areas. Giant sunbirds probe flowers – often the flowers of banana trees – with their long bill, but will also clamber over the bark of trees rather like a treecreeper (*Certhia* species), searching for invertebrates in a similar fashion. They catch invertebrates in flight too, and use their bills to suck up the juicy pulp of ripe fruits. Their nesting period on Sâo Tomé extends from September to January, at which time males become very territorial. It is thought that breeding trios comprised of a cock bird and two hens are not unusual in this species, but relatively little is known about their breeding habits. The nest is suspended off the end of a narrow branch, and may be located as much as 10m (32ft) above the ground.

Identification: Predominantly dark, appearing blackish in colour, with greenish-yellow plumage around the vent. The longest tail feathers are entirely black but those beneath have white tips. Bill, legs and feet are black. Hens are similar but smaller. Young birds are also smaller.

Scarlet-tufted malachite sunbird

Nectarinia johnstoni

These distinctive sunbirds can be found in mountainous areas of Africa, such as Mount Kilimanjaro in Tanzania, where the temperature drops considerably at night despite being close to the Equator. These sunbirds seek flowering plants, which provide them with nectar, and are often seen near flowering *Protea* bushes. They usually occur in pairs or small parties, although cock birds are often very aggressive towards each other, particularly during the breeding season. Their bulky nests are constructed from a wide variety of materials bound together with cobwebs, and lined with feathers.

Distribution: Ranges through the eastern side of Africa, from parts of Kenya, Uganda and Tanzania south as far as Malawi and eastern parts of Zambia.
Size: Cock 30cm (12in); hen 15cm (6in).
Habitat: Open country.
Nest: Suspended in bushes.
Eggs: 2–3, cream-coloured with dark streaks.
Food: Mostly nectar and small invertebrates.

Identification: A rich shade of dark green, with red pectoral tufts at the top of the wings. Non-breeding cock's body feathers are blackish-brown. The tail is square, with two much longer narrow tail plumes extending beyond it, accounting for half the bird's total length. Hens are dark brown, paler in the centre of their bellies, and lack the long tail feathers.

Orange-breasted sunbird

Violet-headed sunbird *Anthobaphes violacea*

These sunbirds move from area to area, tracking the flowering periods of the heather on the mountain heathland, the blooms of which provide the nectar that forms the basis of their diet. Unlike many sunbirds, the orange-breasted is often encountered in loose flocks, although cocks become territorial at the start of the breeding season. The nest, which may be reused each year, is built by the hen on her own, although she is often accompanied on her forays to find suitable material by the cock. It is constructed near to the ground and made of roots, pieces of heather and similar items, while the interior is lined with soft material gathered from *Protea* flowers growing alongside the heather. Incubation lasts approximately two weeks, and the chicks spend three weeks in the nest. They are closely supervised after fledging by the hen, and will not be independent for another three weeks.

Identification: Cock has brilliant metallic green plumage on the head and upper back. Purple band across the breast and golden-orange beneath. Olive-brown back and elongated central tail feathers. Plainer in non-breeding condition, with an olive head, purple band more indistinct and the abdomen less brightly coloured; also lacks the longer central tail feathers. Hens are olive-green above and greenish-yellow below, becoming yellow on the abdomen. Bill, legs and feet are black. Young birds resemble hens, but upperparts are browner.

Distribution: Occurs at the southern tip of Africa, in the Cape Province region in southern South Africa.
Size: 15cm (6in).
Habitat: Mountain heathland.
Nest: Made of vegetation.
Eggs: 2, creamy with some dark streaks.
Food: Nectar, invertebrates.

Tacazze sunbird (*Nectarinia tacazze*): 15–22cm (6–8¹⁄₂in)
Eritrea to Ethiopia and parts of Kenya, Tanzania and Uganda. Dull bronzy-green head, with a reddish or purple iridescence across the chest and back, extending over the rump. Tail feathers are black, with long, narrow extensions to the upper pair. Hens lack extensions and have dark upperparts, more yellowish underparts, and yellowish streaks above and below the eyes. Young birds have a black throat, and are greyer above and yellower below.

Pemba sunbird (*Cinnyris pembae*): 10cm (4in)
Restricted to Pemba Island, off the coast of Tanzania. Dark metallic green head and back. Narrow violet breast band extending to the shoulders. Blackish underparts and wings. Bill, legs and feet black. Hens have greyish-green upperparts, pale stripe above the eyes and a greyish-brown tail. Underparts creamy-white. Young birds resemble hens, but have grey mottling on the underparts.

Gurney's sugarbird (*Promerops gurneyi*): 23–29cm (9–11¹⁄₂in)
Eastern Zimbabwe to northern and eastern South Africa. Rufous-brown crown. White stripe below, behind the eyes, and a black streak through the eyes. Ear coverts, back, rump and tail grey. Throat is white. Broad chestnut band across the chest, with darker brown speckling over the white underparts, particularly the flanks. Undertail coverts bright yellow. Bill, legs and feet black. Hens are similar, but have a small tail. Young birds have a dark brown breast and crown, with greenish-yellow undertail coverts.

Cape sugarbird

Promerops cafer

These sugarbirds may sometimes appear to have a yellow crown, but this is just pollen which has rubbed off the *Protea* flowers on which they feed. Consequently, sugarbirds play quite an important part in the pollination of these shrubs. Although there are similarities between sugarbirds and sunbirds, there are differences too, not least in their flight pattern, which in sugarbirds is much more direct. Sugarbirds catch large insects on the wing in similar fashion to flycatchers, battering them against a perch in order to kill them. Pairs remain together throughout the year, becoming more territorial at the start of the breeding period, which extends between March and August. Interestingly, the tail length of males is very important, since this is the major factor in attracting females. Furthermore, these hens lay more eggs per clutch on average than hens mating with cock birds with shorter tails.

Distribution: Occurs at the southern tip of Africa, in the Cape Province region of South Africa, extending up towards Namibia.
Size: 28–44cm (11–17in).
Habitat: *Protea* heathlands: the fynbos.
Nest: Cup-shaped, made of twigs.
Eggs: 1–2, buff with darker spots.
Food: Mainly nectar, but also invertebrates.

Identification: Brown head, back and chest. Brown stripe on white throat. Darker mottling on underparts. Vent area yellow. Back and long tail dark brown. Bill, legs and feet are black. Hens have a white breast, shorter tail. Young greyer, no yellow, and no brown on the breast.

AFRICAN FINCHES

Many finches, particularly members of the waxbill or estrildidae family, live in the more arid regions of Africa. They feed largely on seeds, although also take small invertebrates as well, especially as a rearing food for nestlings. The spread of agriculture has assisted their population growth, with flocks increasingly becoming pests as they raid ripening crops such as millet.

Quailfinch

Ortygospiza atricollis

As their name suggests, these unusual members of the waxbill family spend most of their time on the ground, never normally perching. If flushed, they fly up vertically like a quail, before gliding back down into the grass some distance away. They build their nest on the ground too, using grass to create a well-hidden, ball-like structure with a clear area in front. It is invariably sited carefully, on a well-drained piece of ground to prevent flooding, since quailfinches normally breed during the rainy period. The incubation, which lasts two weeks, is shared by both members of the pair. Invertebrates as well as seeds feature in the diet of the young birds, who leave the nest by the time they are three weeks old. Although they do not live in tight-knit flocks, these finches do form loose groupings, with up to two hundred individuals present in some locations. They are often encountered in South Africa in the grass borders alongside rural airstrips.

Identification: Cock bird has a mostly blackish face and throat, with a white bib under the bill. Top of the head is greyish, and in southern populations there are white spectacles around the eyes; the head is brownish in quailfinches found further north. Black-and-white barring across the breast and down the flanks. The underparts are pale orangish. Bill is red, legs and feet are pinkish-grey. Hens are less brightly coloured, and have a darker upper bill. Young birds have dark bills and very little barring on the flanks.

Distribution: Range extends in Africa south of the Sahara. Various locations in western Africa and across to Ethiopia, extending down through Kenya and Tanzania and over much of the southern half of the continent.
Size: 9cm (3¹/₂in).
Habitat: Grassland.
Nest: Made of vegetation.
Eggs: 4–6, white.
Food: Mainly seeds.

Red-billed firefinch

Common firefinch *Lagonosticta senegala*

Distribution: From the Cape Verde Islands across Africa south of the Sahara, and down the eastern side of the continent to South Africa, reaching Angola and northern Namibia in the west.
Size: 10cm (4in).
Habitat: Grassland.
Nest: Made of vegetation.
Eggs: 3–4, white.
Food: Seeds.

Firefinches are so named because of their red coloration, which is most evident in adult cock birds. Red-billed is the smallest and the most widely distributed species, occurring through most of sub-Saharan Africa. These finches are often encountered in small flocks, and members of a group stay in close contact with each other. They feed on seeds gathered on the ground, and in the vicinity of homes can become quite tame. They may also be seen in agricultural areas, feeding on ripening millet seedheads. Flocks generally split up during the breeding season.
Red-billed firefinches construct the typical, bulky nest associated with waxbills, using mainly dried grasses and lining the interior with softer material. The adult birds enter through a side opening, which may afford some protection from predators. The incubation period normally lasts around 12 days, and the young firefinches will leave the nest after a further 18 days.

Identification: Cock bird has a reddish head, back and breast, becoming browner on the underparts. The wings and tail feathers are also brown, and the lower back is red. There are some faint white spots on the sides of the chest and flanks. Bill, legs and feet are reddish. Hens have spots on their chest and are brownish overall, except for their pinkish-red rump area and lores, between the bill and the eyes; bill is also duller than in cocks. Young birds are plain brown, with a dark bill.

Red-billed quailfinch (black-chinned quailfinch, *Ortygospiza gabonensis*): 9cm (3¹/₂in)
Equatorial Guinea and Gabon to southern Angola and Namibia, east to Uganda. Black around the base of the bill. Ear coverts chestnut-brown, remainder of the head brownish with black flecking, as are the wings. Head blackish in *O. g. fuscata*. Chest barred black-and-white, as are the flanks. Underparts pale orange, becoming whiter beneath. Hens have grey cheeks and no black surrounding the bill. Young birds have dark bills and display little barring on the underparts.

Red-headed finch (*Amadina erythrocephala*): 13cm (5in)
Coast of Angola across Namibia and South Africa. Bright red head. Scalloping on the underparts, becoming reddish-brown on the flanks and paler around the vent. Upperparts brown, with dark edging and white tips creating two wing bars. Bill pale, legs and feet pinkish. Hens have brown heads. Young birds are paler than hens, with faint barring on the rump.

Reichenow's firefinch (Chad firefinch, *Lagonosticta umbrinodorsalis*): 10cm (4in)
Localized, restricted mainly to Chad but also north-east Cameroon. Distinctive greyish crown and nape, reddish on the mantle, becoming rufous-brown over the back and wings. Sides of the face and underparts red, with faint white spotting at the shoulder. Tail reddish, darker towards the tip. Vent and undertail coverts blackish. Bill, legs and feet greyish. Hens have brown upperparts, paler and more orange below. Young birds are browner overall.

Cut-throat

Amadina fasciata

Depth of coloration varies in cut-throats through their range; birds ranging in eastern Africa show more prominent black markings compared with those originating further south. Breeding occurs mainly during the dry season, when pairs will often adopt nests originally built by weavers, which are vacated at the end of the wet season. However, they may sometimes build their own nests in a range of different locations, including among bushes and even in suitable cavities in buildings. There is a tunnel leading into the nest, which is lined with soft material such as feathers. Outside the breeding season, cut-throats may form large flocks, often associating with various weavers and the related red-headed finch (*A. erythrocephala*), where their distributions overlap. They feed on the ground, eating mainly grass seeds, but will also hunt for invertebrates such as termites.

Identification: Distinctive red throat area from the ear coverts, with white above. Head white with black markings. Back brownish with darker brown markings. White wing bars. Underparts warm brown, becoming whiter below, with dark markings. Bill is pale, legs and feet pinkish. Hens lack the red throat area and have completely mottled heads. Young birds resemble hens.

Distribution: Occurs in a band across Africa south of the Sahara, extending down in the east as far as Tanzania. A second population extends from the Namibian-Angolan border region to Mozambique and into northern parts of South Africa.
Size: 10cm (4in).
Habitat: Arid areas.
Nest: Made of grass.
Eggs: 4–9, chalky-white.
Food: Mainly seeds, also eats invertebrates.

Violet-eared waxbill

Common grenadier *Uraeginthus granatina*

Shy by nature and difficult to approach, these colourful dry country waxbills visit waterholes in the middle of morning to drink and forage on the ground. As well as eating seeds, they will hunt for invertebrates, particularly termites, and – unusually for waxbills – will also eat ripe fruits. They breed between December and April, and the nest is made of dry grasses often sited quite low down in a thornbush. Incubation takes around 13 days, with the young waxbills leaving the nest when they are 16 days old. Their distinctive violet facial coloration develops quite rapidly, around three weeks later. Occasionally, shaft-tailed whydah hens (*Vidua regia*) may enter the waxbills' nests and lay, with pairs rearing the young whydah chicks alongside their own.

Identification: Bluish above the bill, violet patches on each side of the head, and a narrow black band from the base of the bill to the eyes. Underthroat area is black. Dark chestnut back and body, browner wings. Blue lower back and rump. Bill is red, legs and feet blackish. Hens have creamy-buff underparts, lighter brown above. Young birds have black bills, and tan-coloured faces.

Distribution: Ranges in southern Africa, extending from southern Angola and northern Namibia across to Zimbabwe and Mozambique, and south to northern parts of South Africa.
Size: 15cm (6in).
Habitat: Savanna.
Nest: Made of grasses.
Eggs: 3–6, white.
Food: Seeds, invertebrates.

WHYDAHS AND WEAVERS

These birds have fascinating breeding cycles, with cocks often undergoing a remarkable transformation
from their dull, sparrow-like non-breeding appearance. Black predominates in the coloration of
whydahs, which is why they are sometimes known as widowbirds. They do not usually rear their own
chicks, although those birds known as indigobirds may do so on occasions.

Eastern paradise whydah

Vidua paradisaea

Distribution: Mainly eastern Africa, extending from Eritrea and Ethiopia down to South Africa, and via Botswana and Namibia to the coastal region of Angola.
Size: 12cm (4³/₄in); breeding cocks 36cm (14in).
Habitat: Savanna.
Nest: Lays in those of the melba finch (*Pytilia melba*).
Eggs: Unknown.
Food: Seeds.

Five paradise whydah species are recognized in Africa, with breeding cocks differing in their nape and chest colouring and in the length and shape of their majestic tail plumes. They perform elaborate, acrobatic flights to attract the attention of the hens, although they come together only briefly to mate. Hens lay in the nests of melba finches (*Pytilia melba*), which is the only host species used by these whydahs. The markings inside the mouths of the hatchling whydahs are identical to those of the young melba finches, so the adults rear them unsuspectingly alongside their own chicks. The whydahs' incubation is slightly shorter, so they hatch simultaneously.

Identification: Breeding cock has a black head and upper breast. Ochre on the breast and neck. Yellowish underparts turning buff on the abdomen. Back and wings blackish, with broad, down-curving central tail feathers. Bill, legs and feet black. Hens have black-and-white striping on the head and greyish-brown streaked upperparts; plain, pale buff below. Non-breeding cocks resemble females. Young birds are brown with a pale belly.

Pin-tailed whydah

Vidua macroura

The finery and display of the cock pin-tailed whydah attracts a harem of hens during the breeding period. After mating however, the females lay individual eggs in the nests of waxbills, rather than constructing their own nests. This species ranks among the most adaptable of all birds displaying parasitic breeding behaviour – as many as 19 different species have been recorded as playing host to a pin-tailed whydah chick. However, unlike the common cuckoo for example, the young whydahs do not kill their fellow nestlings but are reared alongside them. They even develop similar mouth markings on hatching, which fool their hosts into believing the whydah is one of their own.

Identification: Breeding cocks have a black cap, with a white collar, sides of the face and underparts. Remainder of the upperparts are black, except for the white wing bars. Very long tail plumes. Hens and out-of-colour cocks have black stripes from the sides of the bill through the eyes, a black area on the crown, and speckling over the back and wings. Underparts are a lighter shade of fawn.

Distribution: Occurs widely throughout Africa south of the Sahara.
Size: 11cm (4in) excluding male's tail plumes, which reach 25cm (10in).
Habitat: Open country.
Nest: Lays in those of other species, mainly waxbills.
Eggs: 3, whitish.
Food: Mainly seeds, but also some invertebrates.

Straw-tailed whydah (*Vidua fischeri*): 10cm (4in); breeding cocks 28cm (11in)
North-east Africa, extending from Djibouti and Somalia to Ethiopia, Kenya and Tanzania. Cock bird in breeding colour has a buff cap, while the head, chest and wings are black. The lower chest and abdomen are buff, as are the long, slender, straw-like tail plumes. Bill is reddish, legs and feet pinkish. Hens have a broad brownish streak above the eyes, with a pale central area. Back and wings streaked brown, with pale edging to the plumage. Young birds are brown with dark bills.

Quailfinch indigobird (*Vidua nigeriae*): 12cm (4³⁄₄in)
Western Africa, restricted to Nigeria and Cameroon. Cock birds in breeding condition are black, with a greenish suffusion to their plumage. The wings are pale brown, with white edging to the flight feathers. Bill is silvery, legs and feet dark. Males out of breeding colour resemble hens, who have black streaking on the head, and brown plumage over the back with lighter edges. Underparts whitish, with a pale brown suffusion on the breast. Young birds are brown, with a paler abdomen and eye stripe.

Cape weaver (*Ploceus capensis*): 17cm (6³⁄₄in)
Ranges in South Africa, except for the central part of the country. Cock birds have a chestnut suffusion on the face, while the sides of the head and underparts are yellower. Upperparts olive-yellow, with dark plumage on the wings. Pale irides. Long, pointed black bill, and pinkish feet. Hens are a more olive-green shade overall, but have dark eyes, which distinguishes them from out-of-colour cock birds. Young birds are duller overall.

Red-billed weaver

Black-faced dioch, red-billed quelea *Quelea quelea*

This weaver is considered to be the most numerous bird in the world, with the total population estimated at ten billion individuals. It lives in large flocks which can inflict massive damage on ripening crops of millet and other seeds. To reflect this, red-billed weavers are often known as feathered locusts. They are communal breeders – nests are built close together in thorn trees, which helps to deter any potential predators, while the thorns also serve as fixing points for the nests.

Distribution: Ranges widely across Africa in a band south of the Sahara, to Sudan and Ethiopia. Extends down the eastern side as far as South Africa, and in the west to Namibia and western Angola.
Size: 13cm (5in).
Habitat: Often stays close to reedbeds.
Nest: Made of grasses.
Eggs: 2–4, pale blue.
Food: Seeds, invertebrates.

Identification: Both sexes have brown-and-black streaked plumage outside the breeding season. Cocks in breeding colour have a black mask, with pinkish plumage on the head extending across the underparts. Dark brown-and-black wings. The tail feathers are also dark.

Orange weaver

Red bishop *Euplectes orix*

As well as cracking open the seeds that form the basis of their diet, the stocky bills of these weavers also make highly effective needles, enabling the birds to weave their elaborate nests. This is a learnt skill which improves with practice, and young cocks, with their clumsily-constructed nests, are far less likely to attract mates than the more experienced males. Cocks are polygamous, with each mature male mating with several hens and providing each one with a nesting site, although he takes no direct role in hatching the eggs or rearing the chicks.

Above: By weaving their nests, orange weavers can site them in areas where they are more likely to be out of reach of predators.

Distribution: Across Africa south of the Sahara reaching Ethiopia, extending south as far as Zimbabwe.
Size: 13cm (5in).
Habitat: Grasslands.
Nest: Woven from grasses.
Eggs: 3–4, pale blue.
Food: Seeds, vegetation and some invertebrates.

Identification: Orangish-red ruff around the head. Face, lower breast and upper abdomen are black. Blackish-red mantle, orangish-red lower back and abdomen. Brown flight feathers. Hens and out-of-colour cocks (left) have brownish-black streaked upperparts, a pale yellowish stripe above each eye, and buff underparts with light streaking on the breast sides.

MIGRATORY INSECT-EATERS

In temperate areas, obtaining sufficient invertebrate prey throughout the year can be difficult. During the winter, winged insects such as butterflies, bees and flies either hibernate or die, and frozen ground can make it impossible to find food such as earthworms. Not surprisingly, many birds migrate south in the autumn in search of a more dependable food supply.

Nightjar

European nightjar *Caprimulgus europaeus*

Nightjars are regular summertime visitors to Europe. These birds are nocturnal by nature, which makes them relatively difficult to observe. However, they have very distinctive calls, likened both to the croaking of a frog and the noise of a machine, which are uttered for long periods and carry over a distance of 1km (⅝ mile). During the daytime, nightjars spend much of their time resting on the ground, where their mottled, cryptic plumage provides them with excellent camouflage, especially in woodland. Additionally, they narrow their eyes to slits, which makes them even less conspicuous. Nightjars are sufficiently agile in flight to catch moths and other nocturnal invertebrates, flying silently and trawling with their large gapes open. If food is plentiful, pairs may rear two broods in succession, before beginning the long journey south to their African wintering grounds.

Identification: Very small bill and long wings. Greyish-brown and mottled in overall appearance, with some black areas, especially near the shoulders. There are white areas below the eyes and on the wings, although the white spots on the wings are seen only in cock birds.

Distribution: Most of Europe and north-west Africa, east to Asia. Northern European birds overwinter in south-eastern parts of Africa, while southern European birds migrate to western Africa.
Size: 28cm (11in).
Habitat: Heathland and relatively open country.
Nest: Scrape on the ground.
Eggs: 2, buff-coloured, with darker markings.
Food: Invertebrates.

Pied flycatcher

Ficedula hypoleuca

These flycatchers hawk invertebrates in flight, and will also catch slower-moving prey such as caterpillars by plucking them off vegetation. They can frequently be seen in oak woodlands in Europe during the summer, though may range north to the taiga, where mosquitoes hatching in pools of water during the brief Arctic summer provide an almost constant supply of food. Pied flycatchers are closely related to collared flycatchers (*F. albicollis*), and the two species may sometimes hybridize. It is usually possible to identify the male offspring of these pairings by the narrow area of black plumage evident on the nape of the neck.

Identification: Summer plumage is a combination of black and white. White patches are present above the bill and on the wings. The underparts are white, and the remainder of the plumage is black. Hens also have whitish underparts and white areas on the wings, while their upperparts are brownish. Cocks in non-breeding plumage resemble adult hens, but retain the blackish wings and uppertail coverts.

Distribution: Summer visitor to Europe. Breeding range extends throughout virtually the whole of Europe including Scandinavia, although not the far north. Overwinters in Africa north of a line from coastal Nigeria to Djibouti.
Size: 13cm (5in).
Habitat: Most areas where insects are common.
Nest: Hole in a tree.
Eggs: 5–9, pale blue.
Food: Invertebrates.

Greater short-toed lark (*Calandrella brachydactyla*): 16cm (6in)
Breeds in southern Europe and North Africa, sometimes seen as far north as the British Isles. Overwinters in Africa and the Middle East. Largely unmarked white underparts. Dark patch on each side of the throat. Dark wing bar, wings otherwise brownish and streaked. The eye stripes are white and the ear coverts are a darker brownish colour. Sexes are alike.

Bar-tailed desert lark (*Ammomanes cincturus*): 14cm (5¹/₂in)
Extends from north-western Africa into parts of the Middle East. Pale sandy-brown overall, with brownish wings, darker at the tips of the flight feathers. Black bar across the tail feathers, clearly visible in flight. Sexes are alike.

Meadow pipit (*Anthus pratensis*): 15cm (6in)
Resident in the British Isles and neighbouring parts of western Europe east to Denmark. Individuals from more northerly and easterly areas overwinter around the Mediterranean. Brownish head and wings with darker markings. Dark streaking on the breast and flanks, which are a darker shade of buff. Underparts become whiter in the summer. Sexes are alike.

Collared flycatcher (*Ficedula albicollis*): 13cm (5in)
Occurs as a summer breeding visitor in central-eastern parts of Europe, overwintering in Africa. Similar to the pied flycatcher (*F. hypoleuca*), but cocks are usually identified by the white collar encircling the neck and the white area on the rump. Hens have greyer upperparts and a distinct white patch on the edge of the wings.

Lapwing

Northern lapwing *Vanellus vanellus*

These birds are also known as peewits in some areas due to the sound of their calls. Flocks of lapwings are a common sight in farmland areas, where they comb the ploughed soil for invertebrates. They are easily recognized even from a distance by their distinctive crests. Lapwings may breed in loose groups, and their scrapes are lined with what often becomes quite a substantial pile of vegetation. Lapwings may move long distances during prolonged spells of severe winter weather, sometimes congregating in huge flocks in estuaries when freshwater areas become frozen.

Distribution: Occurs from southern Scandinavia south across the whole of Europe to the Mediterranean. Migrates eastwards across Asia as far as Japan. Also occurs in North Africa, and may even be seen in areas further south.
Size: 30cm (12in).
Habitat: Marshland, farmland.
Nest: Scrape on the ground.
Eggs: 4, light brown with dark markings.
Food: Mainly invertebrates.

Identification: Long, narrow, backward-curving black crest, with black on the face which is separated by a white streak in hens. Underparts are white, except for the chestnut undertail coverts. Wings are dark green, with a greyer green area on the neck. The white cheek patches behind the eyes are broken by a black line. Outside the breeding period the facial plumage is buff, and white areas are restricted to the chin and throat.

Dartford warbler

Sylvia undata

These small warblers have been recorded from Sweden, but their most northerly breeding outpost is in southern Britain, where they maintain a tenuous foothold – numbers become severely depleted in harsh winters. They roost in groups, which helps conserve body heat. Dartford warblers forage low down in shrubbery, sometimes venturing to the ground, where they can run surprisingly quickly. Berries feature more significantly in their diet during the winter, certainly in northern areas. Males establish breeding territories in the autumn. They sing more loudly and frequently during the spring, raising the grey feathers on the sides of their faces as part of the courtship ritual. The nest is built by both adults, hidden in a shrub. The hen incubates mainly on her own, for two weeks, and the chicks fledge after a similar interval.

Identification: Cock bird has a greyish head, back and wings. White spots on the throat, reddish chest and a grey central area to the underparts. Red area of skin encircles each eye. The bill is yellowish with a dark tip, and the legs and feet are yellowish-brown. Hens are paler with white throats. Young birds have grey-buff underparts, with no orbital skin and dark irides.

Distribution: Range extends through western parts of Europe, including the Iberian Peninsula, the western Mediterranean region and western parts of North Africa. Also present in southern parts of England.
Size: 14cm (5¹/₂in).
Habitat: Heathland.
Nest: Cup-shaped, made from vegetation.
Eggs: 3–5, whitish with darker markings.
Food: Mostly invertebrates, but some berries.

CORVIDS AND SHRIKES

These two groups of predatory birds frequently associate in flocks with others of their kind, and display relatively well-developed social awareness. Breeding shrikes are often assisted by "helpers" in caring for their young while they are still in the nest. As well as increasing the likelihood of the chicks receiving sufficient food, this may also develop the helpers' nesting skills.

Pied crow

Corvus albus

These corvids are characteristically versatile feeders. They scavenge near human settlements, especially on rubbish tips, and watch for road kills, carrying off surplus food which they store in a cache to be eaten later. Pied crows have even been observed washing dirty food before eating it. Their strong bills are used to crack shells, as well as for digging up crops of grain. Vegetable matter often features in their diet alongside carrion, and the birds will hunt too, catching small birds and even pulling ticks off cattle. Bold by nature, they have profited from the development of towns across Africa, where large numbers often congregate on the outskirts at suitable roosts. Pairs are equally versatile when breeding, nesting not only on cliffs and in trees but also on telegraph poles. The young crows fledge from the age of five weeks onwards.

Identification: Plumage is a glossy black, except for the thick white collar broadening out across the lower breast and abdomen. Bill, legs and feet are black. Sexes are alike. Young birds are duller, with faint black tips to the white areas of plumage.

Distribution: Much of Africa, south of the Sahara, except for central and eastern areas. Isolated locations elsewhere, notably in rainforest. Also occurs on Madagascar.
Size: 50cm (20in).
Habitat: Open country.
Nest: Large pile of sticks.
Eggs: 3–7, bluish-green with darker markings.
Food: Omnivorous.

Brown-necked raven

Desert raven *Corvus ruficollis*

Distribution: Across much of northern Africa and through the Arabian Peninsula into Asia. Separate population in central Asia, to the east of the Caspian Sea.
Size: 56cm (22in).
Habitat: Arid, desert country.
Nest: Pile of sticks.
Eggs: 2–7, bluish with brownish markings.
Food: Omnivorous.

In some parts of the Middle East, brown-necked raven roosts comprise over 1,000 individuals, although typically these birds are seen in small groups. Like the larger birds of prey, they sometimes soar on upcurrents of warm air, known as thermals. Opportunistic feeders, brown-necked ravens will eat locusts as well as carrion, and have even been observed ripping open sacks with their powerful bills to plunder supplies of grain. They will also readily eat dates. Pairs generally breed on their own, seeking out remote locations in the desert rather than nesting near settlements, although they may use abandoned oil drums here as nesting platforms. Material discarded by people, for example rags, may also be collected and used to line the nest. The young ravens leave the nest by the age of six weeks, and will remain as part of the family group with their parents for perhaps a month or more.

Identification: Black back and relatively short wings. Brownish-black head and underparts, the brown suffusion being more pronounced prior to a moult. Bill, legs and feet black. Sexes alike. Young birds similar to adults.

Fiscal shrike (common fiscal, *Lanius collaris*): 23cm (9in)
Two populations, one from sub-Saharan western Africa eastwards, the other over much of southern Africa. Black upperparts with a prominent white bar. The underparts are white. Hens have rufous flanks.

Dwarf raven (lesser brown-necked raven, Somali crow, *Corvus edithae*): 46cm (18in)
From Eritrea to Somalia and Ethiopia, south into northern Kenya. Dark overall, except the base of the neck is white, evident when displaying. Brownish suffusion to the head and underparts, with wedge-shaped tail feathers. Bill, legs and feet black. Sexes are alike. Young birds are duller overall.

Fan-tailed raven (*Corvus rhipidurus*): 47cm (18½in)
Mountainous areas in western and central sub-Saharan Africa, and from Egypt southwards to Uganda and Kenya. Also in parts of the Middle East, especially eastern and southern Arabian Peninsula. Black overall, with a very distinctive short tail, the feathers of which look fan-shaped when spread open. Sexes are alike. Young birds are duller.

Black crow (*Corvus capensis*): 50cm (20in)
One population from Eritrea through parts of Sudan, Ethiopia and Somalia, with scattered populations as far south as Tanzania. Another population from southern Angola right down to the Cape, ranging eastwards to Zimbabwe. Glossy black plumage, with a fairly long, narrow black bill. Sexes are alike. Young birds are less glossy overall.

Red-backed shrike

Lanius collurio

In common with many insectivorous species, the red-backed shrike migrates south each autumn, spending the winter in savanna where food is more plentiful. In some parts of this shrike's breeding range, its nests are parasitized by the common cuckoo. However, unlike many host species, pairs learn to recognize cuckoo eggs laid alongside their own and discard them from the nest. Cock birds often impale their prey during the breeding season, and this behaviour ensures a more constant supply of food for the chicks, although there is always a risk that such stores will be raided by scavengers.

Distribution: Mainland Europe, except for much of the Iberian Peninsula and northern Scandinavia. Extends eastwards to the Caspian Sea. Overwinters in southern parts of Africa.
Size: 18cm (7in).
Habitat: Open country.
Nest: Cup-shaped, in the fork of a bush or tree.
Eggs: 5–9, variable coloration.
Food: Invertebrates.

Identification: Light grey crown. Black stripe extends through each eye from the bill. Underparts pinkish, reddish-brown back and wings. Hens have a brownish area at the front of the crown, grey behind, and dark brown wings; underparts white with darker edging to the feathers, brown patches behind the eyes.

Southern white-crowned shrike

Eurocephalus anguitimens

These shrikes are highly social by nature, and are usually encountered in groups of up to ten individuals, leapfrogging over each other in turn as they move through the branches. They hunt invertebrates, often on the ground and sometimes in the company of other birds, especially *Tockus* hornbills, preferring larger quarry including locusts and termites. Southern white-crowned shrikes show no tendency to cache surplus prey by impaling it on thorns. Breeding is carried out collectively, with nesting pairs frequently being assisted by up to five helpers. The nest is usually constructed on a horizontal branch, using a combination of dry grass and bark anchored together with spiders' webs, which give it a silvery appearance. Occasionally, a second hen may lay here unannounced, but the limited space available in the nest means that a number of the eggs will fall out onto the ground below. The incubation period lasts for up to 20 days, with the young shrikes fledging after a similar interval.

Identification: A black stripe extends from the bill through each eye to the sides of the neck, and the crown above is white. The throat and upper breast are white, and the underparts are pale greyish. A thin white collar is evident on both sides of the neck. The back is completely greyish and the wings are blackish, as is the tail. Bill, legs and feet black. Sexes are alike. Young birds are paler, and mottled on the crown.

Distribution: Ranges in a band across southern Africa, from western Angola and northern Namibia eastwards via Botswana and Zimbabwe to north-eastern parts of South Africa.
Size: 25cm (10in).
Habitat: Arid country.
Nest: Cup-shaped, made of grass and bark.
Eggs: 3–4, white with some darker blotches.
Food: Largely invertebrates.

FALCONS

Agile, aerial predators, these opportunistic birds of prey rely on strength and speed to overcome their prey, which frequently includes smaller birds. In the past, falcon populations were adversely affected by organochlorine pesticides such as DDT, but there has been a resurgence in their numbers in many areas, with populations occasionally even moving into urban areas.

Kestrel

Common kestrel *Falco tinnunculus*

These common birds of prey can frequently be seen hovering at the side of busy roads, largely undisturbed by the traffic thundering close by. Roadsides provide them with good hunting opportunities, and their keen eyesight enables them to spot even quite small quarry such as grasshoppers on the ground. In the winter, they may resort to hunting earthworms drawn to the surface by heavy rainfall. Kestrels also venture into towns, hunting in parks.

Identification: Bluish-grey head, with a black stripe under each eye and a whitish throat. Dense black spotting on the pale brownish chest, extending to the abdomen. Wings are chestnut-brown with black markings. Rump and tail feathers are grey with black tips. Hens are similar but have browner heads and distinct barring across the tail feathers.

Distribution: Range extends throughout western Europe across to South-east Asia and North Africa. Also breeds in Scandinavia.
Size: 37cm (14½in).
Habitat: Open countryside.
Nest: Platform of sticks in a tree or farm building.
Eggs: 3–7, pale pink with dark brown markings.
Food: Invertebrates and small mammals.

Peregrine falcon

Falco peregrinus

Peregrine falcons are powerful aerial predators, swooping down incredibly quickly on unsuspecting birds from above. Indeed, it is thought that they can dive at speeds of up to 350km/h (217mph). The impact made by their feet when they strike is so great that their quarry is frequently killed instantaneously. Pigeons are generally favoured as prey, although they may also hunt waterfowl. Peregrine falcons are highly adaptable hunters and can very occasionally be sighted in cities, where apartment blocks replace the crags from which they would normally fly on hunting excursions.

Identification: Dark grey upperparts. A broad blackish stripe extends down below each eye, and the surrounding white area extends right around the throat. The barring on the chest is lighter than on the abdomen. Darker markings are apparent on the grey feathers of the back and wings. The tail is barred, with paler grey feathering at the base. The legs and feet are yellow. Wings appear relatively narrow when seen in flight. Hens are much larger than male birds.

Distribution: Resident throughout most of western Europe and much of Africa, except for the Sahara Desert and the central rainforest band. One of the most adaptable and widely distributed birds of prey, occurring on all continents.
Size: 38–51cm (15–20in).
Habitat: Usually near cliffs, sometimes open ground.
Nest: Cliff ledges.
Eggs: 3–4, whitish with red-brown markings.
Food: Birds.

Red-footed falcon (*Falco vespertinus*): 34cm (13in)
Eastern Europe and Asia. Sighted in western Europe including the British Isles. Bluish-grey overall, with red lower abdomen and undertail coverts. Legs bright red. Hens are rufous-brown, with white cheeks and throat, blue-grey wings with black barring, and pinkish legs.

Hobby (Eurasian hobby, *Falco subbuteo*): 35cm (14in)
Mainland Europe to southern Scandinavia, east to Asia and south to North Africa. Overwinters in southern Africa. Long, pointed, dark bluish-grey wings. White band around the sides of the face. White underparts with barring. Reddish on the lower abdomen. Barred underside to the tail. Sexes are alike.

Lanner falcon (*Falco biarmicus*): 50cm (20in)
South-eastern Europe, Arabia and much of Africa except the central rainforests. Upperparts slaty- or brownish-grey (North African birds are more bluish). Dark stripe below each eye extends into a whitish area across the cheeks and throat. Underparts white with dark barring. Legs and feet yellow. Sexes are alike but hens larger.

Saker falcon (*Falco cherrug*): 55cm (22in)
Central Europe eastwards across South-east Asia to China. Westerly populations migrate to the eastern Mediterranean and North Africa; also observed in Arabia and eastern Africa. Brown overall, with a paler head. Heavily streaked on the breast, with darker areas on the flanks. Dark underwing coverts broken by whitish markings. Sexes are alike. A rare grey morph also exists.

African pygmy falcon

Polihierax semitorquatus

These small birds of prey are bold and conspicuous, frequently perching in the open. They hunt lizards, including skinks and agamids, as well as larger invertebrates. When a target is spotted from its vantage point, the African pygmy falcon bobs its head then flies down to seize it. Rodents are caught in this way too. The determining factor affecting their distribution is not the availability of prey however, but rather that of suitable nesting sites. These falcons seek out nests built by weavers, such as the social weaver (*Philetairus socius*), occasionally preying not only on the weaver chicks but the adult birds as well. The incubation period lasts four weeks, and the young leave the nest for the first time about a month later. The adult pair may soon nest again, but it is not unusual for the young to remain in the area for up to a year after fledging.

Distribution: Two African populations. One occurs in eastern Africa, from Djibouti, Ethiopia and Somalia south as far as northern Tanzania. The other is in the south-west, from Namibia to northern South Africa.
Size: 20cm (8in).
Habitat: Arid country.
Nest: Adopts those built by weaver birds.
Eggs: 2–4, white.
Food: Mainly lizards and larger invertebrates.

Identification: Cock bird has a greyish head, back and wings. Pale facial area, with a pale area also across the back of the neck. Pale underparts and rump. Black flight feathers and tail with white spots. Bare reddish skin around each eye. The bill is greyish with a dark tip. Legs and feet are pinkish. Hens are easily recognized by the chestnut plumage on the back. Young birds have brown backs.

Gyr falcon

Falco rusticolus

The gyr falcon is the largest member of its genus. It has adapted well to surviving life in the far north, where its coloration helps to conceal its presence, even in areas with little tree cover. These impressive falcons can often be sighted in coastal regions, where they prey on seabirds. They fly low when hunting in open countryside, taking grouse and similar birds as well as small rodents, preferring to catch their quarry on the ground rather than in flight. When breeding, pairs may adopt artificial nest sites, in buildings associated with oil pipelines, for example.

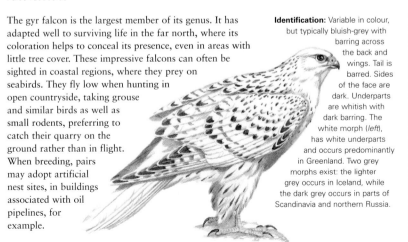

Identification: Variable in colour, but typically bluish-grey with barring across the back and wings. Tail is barred. Sides of the face are dark. Underparts are whitish with dark barring. The white morph (*left*), has white underparts and occurs predominantly in Greenland. Two grey morphs exist: the lighter grey occurs in Iceland, while the dark grey occurs in parts of Scandinavia and northern Russia.

Distribution: Through Iceland and Scandinavia. An annual vagrant in the British Isles.
Size: 63cm (25in)
Habitat: Mainly taiga and tundra regions.
Nest: On cliff ledges.
Eggs: 3–4, buff with dense reddish speckling.
Food: Mostly takes small birds and mammals.

AGILE AERIAL HUNTERS

Aerial agility is a feature associated with birds of prey, particularly those that hunt other birds. Some are equally adept at pursuing terrestrial prey. Many species have developed specialized hunting techniques, and the young of these birds have to remain with the adults for some time after fledging in order to learn the skills they will need to feed themselves.

Red kite

Milvus milvus

Distribution: Range includes Wales, the Iberian Peninsula and the adjacent area of North Africa. Extends north-eastwards across Europe to southern Sweden, and also found in Russia.
Size: 66cm (26in).
Habitat: Light woodland.
Nest: Platform of sticks, built in a tree.
Eggs: 1–4, white with reddish-brown markings.
Food: Small birds, mammals and carrion.

Although very agile hunters, red kites also seek carrion such as dead sheep. This behaviour has resulted in their persecution in some areas because of misplaced fears that the kites actually kill lambs. When seeking prey, red kites circle repeatedly overhead, relying on their keen eyesight to spot any movement on the ground. They will then drop and sweep low, homing in on their target. Up until the 1700s, flocks of red kites were common scavengers on the streets of London, where they were sufficiently tame to swoop down and steal food from children. It was their willingness to scavenge, however, that led to a dramatic reduction in their numbers, since they were easily killed using carcasses laced with poison.

Identification: Predominantly reddish-brown, with a greyish head streaked with darker markings. Darker mottling over the wings, with some variable streaking on the underparts as well. Feet are yellowish with black talons. White areas under the wings and forked tail can be clearly seen in flight. Sexes are alike.

Hen harrier

Northern harrier *Circus cyaneus*

Hen harriers are very distinctive hunters, flying low over moorland, seeking not only small mammals but also birds. Their preference for hunting grouse has led to persecution by gamekeepers in various parts of their range. However, over the winter months these harriers may be forced to feed largely on carrion. Their range extends further north than those of related species, into the tundra region, but they are not resident in far northern areas throughout the year, and will head further south before the start of winter. Hen harriers are unusual in not only roosting on the ground but also breeding on the ground. Once the breeding season is over they will often congregate at communal sites, which may be used for several generations.

Identification: Mainly chestnut overall, streaked with white. Darker over the wings. Narrow white band around each eye, with a solid brown area beneath. Tail is barred. The bill is dark, and the legs are yellow. Hens are larger.

Distribution: Throughout much of the Northern Hemisphere. Extends across most of Europe, including Scandinavia, east to Asia. Often moves south for the winter as far as North Africa.
Size: 52cm (20in).
Habitat: Moorland.
Nest: On the ground, hidden in vegetation.
Eggs: 3–5, whitish.
Food: Mainly small mammals and birds.

Pale chanting goshawk

Melierax canorus

The so-called chanting of these goshawks is only audible during the breeding season, and consists of a series of similar call notes repeated persistently. They breed from June to March, with the nest itself built near the top of a tree or even on a telegraph pole. The hen incubates largely on her own for five weeks, and the young leave the nest when they are two months old. Pale chanting goshawks hunt from a perch, swooping down to the ground, but will also scavenge at road kills. They are adept hunters, and have struck up a remarkable relationship with mongooses (*Galerella*) and honey-badgers (*Mellivora*). They follow these mammals closely, waiting patiently on the ground while they excavate in the hope of catching disturbed rodents or lizards. If necessary, the goshawks are able to run fast across the ground to capture fleeing quarry.

Identification: Grey head, chest and back, with grey barring on a white background on the abdomen. The rump and inner flight feathers are white, outer flight feathers black. Tail dark above, banded grey-and-white below. Red base to the bill, tip dark. Legs and feet reddish. Sexes are alike, but male is slightly smaller. Young birds are distinctive: brown overall, darker on the crown, back and wings, with a white throat; underparts streaked with black above, displaying brown-and-white barring below; bill dark, legs and feet orangish.

Distribution: Range is restricted to south-western Africa. Extends from south-west Angola and northern Namibia through Botswana to western parts of Zimbabwe, and occurs over much of South Africa except for the eastern side.
Size: 54cm (21in).
Habitat: Arid country.
Nest: Pile of twigs, usually built in a tree.
Eggs: 1–2, bluish-white.
Food: Lizards, rodents and other terrestrial vertebrates.

Black kite (*Milvus migrans*): 60cm (24in)
Present on much of mainland Europe to Asia and Australia. Also occurs in North Africa and overwinters south of the Sahara. Mainly brown but darker on the wings. The underparts are decidedly rufous. Barring on the tail. Some grey markings on the head. Sexes are alike.

Common black-shouldered kite (*Elanus caeruleus*): 30cm (12in)
Present in North Africa and widely distributed south of the Sahara. Grey head, extending down the back over the wings. Whitish sides to the face and white underparts. Prominent black area on each wing extending from the shoulders. Sexes are alike.

Montagu's harrier (*Circus pygargus*): 50cm (20in)
Found in Europe and North Africa, east to Asia. Overwinters in central and eastern Africa south of the Sahara. Predominantly grey, with barring on the lower underparts. Narrow white rump. Hens are larger, with brown plumage replacing the grey. In the dark morph, males are blackish and hens are a dark chocolate-brown.

Black harrier (*Circus maurus*): 52½cm (21in)
Restricted to southern Africa, including parts of Namibia and South Africa. Cock is brownish-black, with white feathering on the rump, grey flight feathers and grey bands on the tail, which also has a white tip. Black bill, yellow cere, and yellowish legs and feet. Sexes are alike. Young birds have rufous-brown edging on the wings, and buff underparts also streaked with brown.

Sparrowhawk

Eurasian sparrowhawk *Accipiter nisus*

These hawks favour preying on groundfeeding birds, and males generally take smaller quarry than females, reflecting the difference in their respective sizes. Even females rarely take birds much larger than pigeons, although they will prey on thrushes. Pairs nest later in the year than many songbirds, so there are plenty of nestlings to prey on and feed to their own chicks. Sparrowhawks have short wings and are very agile in flight, able to manoeuvre easily in wooded areas. They approach quietly with the aim of catching their target unawares, seizing their prey using their powerful feet.

Identification: Grey head, back and wings, with darker barring on the grey tail. The underparts are also barred. Bare yellow legs and feet, with long toes. Cock birds are smaller than hens and have pale rufous areas on the lower sides of the face, extending to the chest, while the barring on their underparts is browner.

Left: Young male sparrowhawks fledge several days before their heavier siblings.

Distribution: Resident in most of Europe (except the far north of Scandinavia), North Africa and the Canary Islands. Migratory birds overwinter around the Red Sea. Extends east to Asia.
Size: 28cm (11in).
Habitat: Light woodland.
Nest: Made of sticks.
Eggs: 4–6, pale blue with reddish-brown markings.
Food: Mainly birds.

BUZZARDS

These predatory birds possess sharp, pointed bills and powerful talons. They feed on other birds as well as mammals, while some also resort to eating carrion and invertebrates. Buzzards can sometimes occur in recognized colour morphs, with their plumage being either lighter or darker than usual. Individuals of this type occur alongside those with normal coloration.

Common buzzard

Eurasian buzzard *Buteo buteo*

With its rather broad and stocky appearance, the common buzzard's silhouette in flight helps to confirm its identity. Buzzards are capable of soaring for long periods, before suddenly swooping down to seize a rabbit – their traditional prey, particularly in many parts of Europe. On the other hand, buzzards can sometimes be observed hunting invertebrates, walking purposefully on the ground in search of their quarry. They may occasionally be spotted on roads too, feeding on road kill, even placing themselves in danger from the passing traffic. However, buzzards remain one of the most common raptors in Europe, thanks largely to their adaptable feeding habits.

Identification: Mainly dark brown, with a variable amount of white plumage around the bill and on the underparts. The tail is barred, with paler plumage around the vent. Legs and feet are yellow, and the bill is yellow with a dark tip. White predominates in the pale morph. Hens are often larger.

Distribution: Resident in western Europe. Summer visitor to parts of Scandinavia and across Asia. Migratory European birds overwinter in southern and eastern Africa.
Size: 57cm (22in).
Habitat: Areas with trees.
Nest: Platform of sticks, usually in a tree.
Eggs: 2–4, white.
Food: Small mammals and other prey.

Jackal buzzard

Buteo rufofuscus

Although carrion features in their diet, these buzzards do not scavenge as much as some vultures. Jackal buzzards are active and efficient hunters, scanning the ground below from prominent perches overlooking open ground, which often includes nearby roads. This is a productive strategy for reptile-hunters, since lizards and snakes often bask on warm tarmac in the morning, to raise their body temperature. Jackal buzzards also hunt on the wing, soaring and hovering over the ground. Pairs remain in their breeding territories throughout the year, and will often reuse the same nest annually, lining it with green leaves at the start of the breeding period. A cliff face is often favoured as a nest site, but trees may also be used. According to ringing studies, young birds may disperse over distances of up to 640km (400 miles) from the nest site.

Distribution: Southern Africa, from Namibia in the west and Zimbabwe in the east down across virtually all of South Africa.
Size: 55cm (22in).
Habitat: Grassland.
Nest: Made of sticks.
Eggs: 1–3, white with reddish-brown markings.
Food: Mainly small mammals and reptiles.

Identification: Predominantly black head, back and wings, usually with a chestnut breast. Black underparts, with white edging to the plumage. Prominent white underwing areas, with chestnut undertail coverts and tail. Bill yellow at the base, black at the tip. Legs and feet yellowish. A rare white-breasted morph also exists, with almost totally white underparts. Sexes are alike. Young birds are easily distinguished by their brown coloration, darker on the wings with pale edging; tail lightly barred with darker brown stripes.

Long-legged buzzard

Buteo rufinus

These buzzards vary in depth of coloration, with some a much darker shade of brown than others. European birds migrate south in August, with most heading no further than Kenya, though some are seen in South Africa. They start returning in February, and the male may be joined by his partner in aerial display, rising and circling each other in the sky. The nest measures about 80cm (32in) in diameter, and is usually built on a cliff face or an inaccessible site at ground level. Incubation lasts a month, and the young fledge after six weeks. For a while they may stay together in a family group, but long-legged buzzards are generally solitary birds by nature.

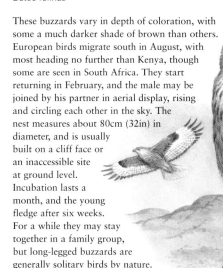

Identification: Whitish head, streaking on the back of the neck and breast. Otherwise brownish, with blackish centres to the plumage on the back and wings. Flight feathers dark at the tips. White areas spotted brown on the undersides of the wings. Tail more rufous. Bill base yellow, tip dark. Legs and feet yellowish. Sexes alike but females larger. Young are browner, especially on the head, and the tail is lightly barred.

Distribution: Ranges through extreme south-eastern parts of Europe, extending into Asia and to the Arabian Peninsula. Migrates across northern parts of Africa, where it is also resident, with a more extensive range in eastern Africa, extending from northern Sudan to Kenya. Also occasionally recorded in other locations in southern Africa.
Size: 65cm (26in).
Habitat: Grassland.
Nest: Bulky pile of sticks.
Eggs: 2–5, whitish with darker markings.
Food: Small vertebrates.

Steppe buzzard (*Buteo vulpinus*): 58cm (23in)
Present throughout Europe, extending to eastern and southern parts of Africa. Overall coloration is brownish, noticeably darker in some individuals than in others. Lightly barred rufous tail. Bill is yellow at the base, dark at the tip. Legs and feet are yellow. Sexes are similar. Young birds have yellow irides.

Grasshopper buzzard (*Butastur rufipennis*): 44cm (17in)
Occurs across Africa south of the Sahara, extending down the eastern coast to northern Tanzania. Greyish head and a white throat, with rufous underparts displaying dark streaking on the breast. Undertail coverts are whitish. Back and wings are greyish, the wings showing distinctive rufous patches in flight. Sexes are alike. Bill is yellow at the base, dark at the tip. Legs and feet yellowish. Young birds have browner upperparts, with grey restricted to the ear coverts.

Augur buzzard (*Buteo augur*): 55cm (22in)
Largely confined to eastern parts of Africa, from Sudan to Zimbabwe, with a separate population extending from southern Angola to northern Namibia. Dark blackish head and back, with black speckling in a band across the wings. Short rufous tail. Largely white when seen from below, with dark edging to the flight feathers. Bill is yellow at the base, black at the tip. Legs and feet are yellow. Young birds are dark brown rather than black above, with a lighter brown barred tail.

Rough-legged buzzard

Buteo lagopus

These buzzards hunt lemmings and voles, but, when rodent populations undergo their regular cyclical collapse, take birds including snow buntings and grouse. In winter, wood pigeons are frequently targeted. Insects and spiders may also be caught, along with fish, and carrion may be scavenged. Pairs return to their breeding grounds in mid-April, reusing a nest built previously, lining the inside with fresh greenery. Like many species nesting in the far north, the number of chicks reared is directly correlated to the availability of food.

Identification: Brownish head and upperparts, with darker brown chest markings and barring on the white underparts. Tail white, with a broad brown tip. Whitish wings edged dark when seen from below. Bill base is yellow, tip dark. Legs are feathered, feet yellow. Sexes similar, but hens heavier with fewer tail bars. Young paler.

Distribution: Circumpolar. Breeds throughout the far north of Europe, extending to Asia. Migrates southwards to eastern England and across much of central Europe and South-east Asia. Absent from much of France, the Iberian Peninsula, Italy and Africa.
Size: 59cm (23in).
Habitat: Open country.
Nest: Pile of sticks.
Eggs: 3–5.
Food: Rodents, birds.

EAGLES

These large predatory birds are most conspicuous when seen in flight. They range over wide areas, although do not occur at high densities unless food is plentiful. A number of species have developed specialized feeding habits, for example snake eagles, but all tend to be relatively opportunistic feeders, prepared to scavenge on carrion of all types.

Bateleur

Terathopius ecaudatus

Bateleur is the French word for tight rope walker, and describes this bird's wings-outstretched display flight. They are adept at locating carrion, but also hunt prey including larger birds such as bustards (*Otididae*) and eagle owls (*Bubo*), and even small antelopes. Bateleurs spend much of the day on the wing, covering distances of more than 500km (300 miles) in search of food. Their young develop slowly, spending nearly 16 weeks in the nest. After fledging, they spend a similar period learning to hunt with their parents. It will take up to eight years to acquire full adult plumage. Bateleurs are usually solitary, but may congregate in larger numbers where food is plentiful.

Identification: Black head and underparts. Brown V-shaped area on the back, edged black. Grey shoulders. Long, narrow wings, white underneath. Short brown tail. Bare red skin around the eyes to the base of the bill, which is black at its tip. Legs and feet red. Hens similar but have another, more silvery area on the wings. Young birds much duller, brown overall, with a brownish-yellow bill and red only on the feet and legs.

Distribution: Occurs in a band across Africa south of the Sahara, and down the eastern side of the continent to northern South Africa. Ranges westwards to Gabon, Angola and Namibia.
Size: 70cm (28in).
Habitat: Savanna.
Nest: Stick platform in a tree.
Eggs: 1, white.
Food: Mainly vertebrates.

Verreaux's eagle

Black eagle *Aquila verreauxii*

Verreaux's eagles are specialist hunters of rock hyraxes (*Heterohyrax* and *Procavia*), which look like guinea pigs but are considered small ungulates, rather than rodents. Studies in the Matobo Hills of Zimbabwe have revealed more than 18,000 are killled every year by these eagles. Their range closely mirrors that of the rock hyrax itself, although the birds also feed on a range of other prey, and carrion too. Pairs establish territories and are resident year-round, staying in close contact even to the point of sharing kills. Usually only one chick is reared successfully, since the younger nestling will be attacked and killed by its older sibling.

Identification: Black overall, white rump. Underwings speckled, whiter nearer the tips. Base of the bill yellowish, tip dark. Legs and feet yellow. Hens similar but slightly larger. Young birds browner, wings edged white, underparts blackish mottled brown.

Distribution: Occurs mainly along eastern and southern parts of Africa. Isolated northern population on the Chad-Sudanese border. Patchily distributed from southern Sudan down to South Africa, and up the western side of the continent to western Angola.
Size: 95cm (37in).
Habitat: Mountainous and rocky country.
Nest: Large pile of sticks.
Eggs: 2, white, sometimes with speckles.
Food: Small mammals.

Short-toed snake eagle

Circaetus gallicus

As their name suggests, snakes feature prominently in the diet of these eagles. They are able to catch snakes measuring over 1.5m (5ft) in length, holding down and overpowering even venomous ones with their powerful feet and sharp bills. Once dead, the reptile is swallowed head first, often on the ground but sometimes in flight, depending on size. Other reptiles, notably lizards, may also be caught occasionally, along with small mammals up to the size of hares. Pairs establish their own breeding territories, becoming more conspicuous during this period, with males especially calling loudly. The single chick grows rapidly, and is capable of eating whole snakes measuring up to 9cm (3½in) long when just three weeks old.

Identification: Dark brownish upperparts, with paler edging to the wing coverts. Tail is banded with four brown bars. Underwings whitish with regular rows of dark brown markings, also running across the body. Head and chest dark brown. Greyish bill, legs and feet. Sexes are alike, but female slightly larger. Young birds have paler underparts, and the undersides of their wings are largely unmarked.

Distribution: Breeds in the Iberian Peninsula and through southern Europe, extending into north-west Africa, the Middle East and Asia. Birds from Europe and North Africa migrate to a fairly narrow band across Africa south of the Sahara, east as far as Sudan, with a number of reports from Kenya.
Size: 67cm (26in).
Habitat: Arid country.
Nest: Stick platform in a tree.
Eggs: 1, white.
Food: Mainly vertebrates.

Martial eagle (*Polemaetus bellicosus*): 85cm (34in)
The largest African eagle. Ranges down eastern and throughout southern Africa, from Dem. Rep. Congo to the Cape. Dark brown head, breast and upperparts, with a short crest at the back of the head. Underparts white with brown spots. Tail is barred, as are the flight feathers when seen from below. Irides yellow, bill black. Legs feathered, feet are yellow. Sexes are similar, but hens often slightly larger, with bigger feet. Young birds are lighter overall, with whitish underparts and sides of the face.

Beaudouin's snake eagle (*Circaetus beaudouini*): 65cm (26in)
Ranges from Senegal to Kenya. Dark blackish upperparts. Whitish area under the bill. Breast is dark, with vermiculated lower underparts and whitish undertail coverts. Banding across the flight feathers when seen from below, and on the tail. Bill is greyish, black at the tip. Legs and feet also greyish. Sexes are alike. Young birds have brown bodies and less distinct barring across the wings.

Bonelli's eagle (*Hieraaetus fasciatus*): 65cm (26in)
Wide range encompasses the Iberian peninsula, southern France, north-west Africa, the Middle East, southern China and parts of Indonesia. Regional variations in colour occur. Has a dark brown head and upperparts. Underparts are white, often with dark brown streaking. Pale grey tail with a broad, black band at tip. Black bill; yellow cere and feet. Hens are a little larger.

Black-chested snake eagle

Circaetus pectoralis

These snake eagles differ from their close relatives by spending longer on the wing searching for food, hovering in flight. In Zimbabwe, large and potentially deadly cobras form a significant part of their diet. Their small nest is built in a tree, on top of the canopy. The chick hatches after seven weeks, and spends long periods alone in the nest while its parents are hunting for food. Returning adults will regurgitate a partially swallowed snake, aided by the youngster, who helps to pull it from its parent's mouth. The chick then swallows the snake while rhythmically rotating its head, which presumably helps to transport the reptile along its digestive system. Fledging takes place once the young snake eagle is about three months of age.

Identification: Blackish upperparts, with the black extending onto the chest. Underparts white. Underwings white with three rows of black barring, and black tips to the flight feathers. Tail is greyish below with black barring. Bill, legs and feet are greyish. Sexes are alike, but hens slightly larger. Young birds are mostly brown overall, with a barred tail and black flight feathers.

Distribution: Eastern and southern parts of Africa. From Sudan down to northern South Africa in the east, and from Rep. Congo southwards in the west.
Size: 68cm (27in).
Habitat: Open areas, woods.
Nest: Platform of sticks.
Eggs: 1, white.
Food: Largely snakes.

OTHER EAGLES AND VULTURES

Soaring overhead, these eagles and vultures are usually quite conspicuous. Unfortunately, they have suffered intense persecution by people due to fears that they will attack domestic stock, and their readiness to feed on carrion has meant they can be easily poisoned. Many species are therefore quite scarce, and are only observed in more remote areas of country.

Golden eagle

Aquila chrysaetos

Identification: Brown overall, with yellowish-brown plumage on the back of the head extending down the nape of the neck. Those eagles inhabiting desert areas, such as the Middle East, are slightly paler overall. The bill is yellow with a dark tip. Feet are also yellow, with black talons. Hens are larger in size than cocks.

These majestic eagles generally inhabit remote areas away from people, where they are likely to be left undisturbed. When seen in flight, the golden eagle's head looks relatively small compared to its broad tail and large, square-ended wings. It has some yapping call notes not unlike those of a dog, but generally its calls are quite shrill. Golden eagles have adapted their hunting skills to suit their environment. For instance, in some areas they take tortoises, dropping the reptiles from a great height in order to smash their shells before eating them; in other areas, they may prey on cats. They prefer to capture their quarry on the ground, swooping down low, rather than catching birds in the air.

Distribution: Ranges sporadically through the Mediterranean region and eastwards into Asia. Present in Scotland and Scandinavia. Also occurs in parts of northern Africa.
Size: 90cm (35in).
Habitat: Mountainous areas.
Nest: Massive cliff nest made of sticks.
Eggs: 2, white with some dark markings.
Food: Birds and mammals.

Imperial eagle

Eastern imperial eagle *Aquila heliaca* (E)

The imperial eagle population declined dramatically during the 20th century due to persecution by humans. However, thanks to effective protection there are now signs that numbers are increasing again in countries such as Hungary. Here they can frequent areas of open countryside, rather than being forced into retreating to the relative safety of the mountain forests. Imperial eagles, like others of their kind, are potentially long-lived birds, having few natural enemies other than people. Their longevity is measured not in years but decades, and is mirrored in the pace of their development: young imperial eagles may not breed for the first time until they are six years old, before they have even attained their full adult plumage.

Identification: Predominantly dark brown. Pale buff on the back of the head extending down around the neck. Patches of white at the shoulders. The bill is yellow with a dark tip. Feet also yellow. Sexes are alike. This species is now regarded as distinct from the Spanish imperial eagle (*A. adalberti*), which has small white shoulder patches.

Distribution: Eastern parts of Europe and Turkey eastwards across much of central Asia. Overwinters in Africa, from Egypt southwards, and also in Arabia and southern parts of Asia.
Size: 84cm (33in).
Habitat: Open country.
Nest: Made of sticks and other vegetation.
Eggs: 2, white with some dark markings.
Food: Small mammals, birds and carrion.

Griffon vulture

Eurasian griffon *Gyps fulvus*

These vultures are most likely to be seen in areas of relatively open countryside with surrounding cliffs, which are used for nesting and roosting. They glide over plains, using their keen eyesight to locate carcasses, although nowadays groups of griffon vultures can often be found scavenging at rubbish dumps. Hot currents of air, known as thermals, enable them to soar with very little effort and remain airborne for long periods. Griffon vultures nest in colonies that have been known to consist of as many as 150 pairs. Their chicks develop slowly, often not embarking on their first flight until they are nearly 20 weeks old. Young birds are unlikely to breed until they are at least four years old.

Identification: Dark brown around the eyes, with the top of the head and neck whitish. Light brown body, back and wings. Darker flight feathers and tail. Relatively elongated horn-coloured bill, curved on the upper tip. Legs and feet grey, whitish on the inner thighs. Sexes are alike. Young birds have a darker brown back and a brown neck collar. Distinguished from African white-backed vulture (*G. africanus*) by its larger size and paler plumage.

Distribution: North-western Africa, the Iberian Peninsula and the Caucasus eastwards into Asia. Young birds may migrate further south to western and eastern Africa.
Size: 110cm (43in).
Habitat: Mountain country.
Nest: Sticks on rocky crag.
Eggs: 1, white with reddish-brown markings.
Food: Carrion.

Ruppell's vulture (*Gyps rueppellii*): 105cm (41in)
Ranges across Africa south of the Sahara in a band to Somalia, extending further south here than in the west, down through Uganda and Kenya to Tanzania. Vagrants also occasionally recorded further south. Blackish, with creamy-white edging to the feathers on the body and wings, creating a scaly appearance. Covering of whitish, down-like feathering on the back of the head; skin is bluish-grey. Bill pale horn-coloured at its tip, grey at the base. Legs and feet grey. Dark flight feathers when viewed from beneath, with white banding evident. Sexes are alike. Young birds are very distinctive: predominantly brown, darker across the wings, with the feathers here having buff edging; bill, legs and feet greyish. Young obtain adult plumage slowly, over the course of successive moults, with this process typically taking seven years.

Black vulture (Eurasian black vulture, *Aegypius monachus*): 107cm (42in)
Range extends from Spain and the Balearic Islands eastwards to the Balkans, and from Turkey across Asia. Some birds overwinter in north-eastern Africa. Pale bluish skin encircles the nostrils. Bald head with a brownish area around the eyes. Plumage is a dark sooty black. Sexes are alike.

Egyptian vulture (*Neophron percnopterus*): 70cm (27½in)
Distributed around the Mediterranean into Asia. Also the Canary Islands and across Africa south of the Sahara to Tanzania and Arabia. Pale whitish plumage with brown markings prominent over the wings and flight feathers. Bald, bright yellow area of skin on the sides of the face and along the bill, which may have a dark tip. Sexes are alike.

Lappet-faced vulture

King vulture *Aegypius tracheliotus*

These massive scavengers have a wingspan of 3m (10ft), weigh 7kg (15½lb) and can carry up to 1.45kg (3lb) of food in their crops. They are dominant at a kill, which is why they are known as king vultures. They also hunt small mammals. Pair stay together for life, and build the largest nest of any vulture – up to 2m (6½ft) in diameter. Hens normally lay a single egg, incubated by both adults, which hatches after 55 days. The chick grows slowly and is unlikely to fledge until it is 18 weeks old. The vultures remain in a family group for over a year, and the young birds are fed by the adults throughout this period.

Distribution: Scattered locations in Africa, largely south of the Sahara. Main range extends eastwards to Somalia. Also down many parts of eastern Africa. Southern range extends from western Angola through Namibia and Botswana as far as northern South Africa.
Size: 115cm (45in).
Habitat: Arid savanna.
Nest: Made of sticks.
Eggs: 1–2, white.
Food: Largely carrion.

Identification: Pinkish and blue skin on the head and throat, which varys depending on distribution. Back is black. Whitish areas extend down the sides of the underparts and the thighs. White markings under the wings, near the leading edge, close to the body. Bill is horn-coloured at its tip, greyish at the base in southern areas but darker further north. Legs and feet greyish. Hens can be larger. Young birds are brown, with whitish streaking on the mantle, pale heads and greyer bills.

OWLS OF OPEN COUNTRY

Although often considered forest birds, a number of owl species are encountered in areas of open country, ranging from the Arctic through temperate latitudes to the tropics. They generally hunt from dusk onwards, having keen eyesight and hearing which enables them to home in on their quarry very accurately. Owls pursue a wide range of prey, catching it on the ground.

Snowy owl

Nyctea scandiaca

The snowy owls' plumage enables them to blend in very effectively with the tundra landscape. In this harsh environment, their numbers are closely correlated to the availability of their main prey: when lemmings are rife, the snowy owl population also rapidly increases. Once the lemming population declines, however, the breeding success of the snowy owls is greatly reduced, and pairs may not even nest at all in some years. At this time, adult birds are forced to abandon their usual territories and fly south in search of other sources of food. Unusually, snowy owls are active during the daytime.

Distribution: Circumpolar in the Northern Hemisphere, moving south in winter.
Size: 65cm (25$\frac{1}{2}$in).
Habitat: From woodland to the tundra.
Nest: Scrape on the ground.
Eggs: 3–11, white.
Food: Mainly lemmings, also birds, invertebrates and fish.

Identification: White with yellow eyes, and feathering down to the claws. Hens have brown barring over the body, but not on the face. Young are similar to hens.

Barn owl

Tyto alba

Barn owls seek out dark places in which to roost, using buildings in various parts of their range. They may be seen in open country, swooping over farmland, with some individuals choosing to pursue bats. Males in particular will often utter harsh screeches when in flight, which serve as territorial markers, while females make a distinctive snoring sound for food at the nest site. They pair for life, which can be more than 20 years. Barn owls have adapted to hunting along roadside verges, but here they are in real danger of being hit by vehicles.

Distribution: Worldwide. Throughout western Europe, Africa (except the Sahara) and the Middle East.
Size: 39cm (15in).
Habitat: Prefers relatively open countryside.
Nest: Hollow tree or inside a building.
Eggs: 4–7, white.
Food: Voles and amphibians, also invertebrates.

Identification: Whitish, heart-shaped face and underparts. In much of Europe, underparts more yellowish-orange. Top of the head and wings greyish-orange with spots. Eyes black. Males often paler than females.

African scops owl

Otus senegalensis

The calls of these small owls, which may be uttered quite frequently, have been likened to those of a frog. African scops owls are difficult to observe during the daytime, since their cryptic coloration proves excellent camouflage. They are often attracted to lights at night, in order to catch the flying insects which feature prominently in their diet. They will also take prey from the ground, as has been revealed by the remains of scorpions found in their pellets, which are regurgitated after a meal and contain the indigestible remains of their prey. These owls may take small vertebrates occasionally too. During the breeding period the hen sits alone, but her partner remains in the vicinity and may alert her to any danger. He will also bring food to the nest for her, although she may occasionally hunt for herself during the incubation, which lasts around 22 days. The young owls will leave the nest when they are about four weeks old.

Identification: Greyish overall, with prominent ear tufts. Some variable brown feathering, with black streaks and white areas too, especially on the wings. A variable blackish border is evident around the facial disc. Irides yellow, bill black. Legs and feet feathered whitish. Sexes are alike. Young birds are similar to adults.

Distribution: Range extends in a band across Africa south of the Sahara, and widely in eastern Africa. Extends down along the Dem. Rep. Congo border to cover most of southern Africa, but largely absent from the coastal areas of southern Angola, Namibia and western South Africa.
Size: 17cm (6³/₄in).
Habitat: Savanna.
Nest: Tree hole.
Eggs: 2–4, white.
Food: Largely insectivorous.

African grass owl (*Tyto capensis*): 38cm (15in) Rep. Congo to Mozambique. Also in eastern and southern South Africa, along the Kenyan-Ugandan border, and in Nigeria. White, heart-shaped face surrounded by dark brown, faintly spotted white over the back of the neck. Underparts pale buff. Bill grey, legs and feet feathered. Sexes alike. Young birds are darker on the underparts, with rufous facial feathering.

Cape eagle owl (*Bubo capensis*): 54cm (21¹/₄in) Eastern Africa, notably in central Ethiopia, Kenya and Zimbabwe. Main range in southern Africa. Grey face with black edging, and a white bib. Prominent ear tufts speckled black-and-brown. White mottling on the wings and underparts. Tail is barred black-and-brown. Irides bright orange, bill blackish. Legs and feet feathered. Mostly whitish underwings, with some rows of darker markings. Sexes alike, females usually larger. Young birds lack ear tufts until six months old.

Southern white-faced scops owl (*Ptilopsus granti*): 28cm (11in) Gabon to Kenya and down to Lesotho. Absent from north-eastern South Africa. Whitish face, greyish around the bill. Black on the sides of the face. Head, back and wings bluish-grey with vertical dark streaking. Oblique white bands across each wing. Chest white, greyer below, streaked black. White vent. Prominent ear tufts. Barred tail feathers. Irides bright orange, bill grey, legs whitish. Sexes alike, but hens heavier. Young birds browner overall, with yellow irides.

Eagle owl

Eurasian eagle owl *Bubo bubo*

The eagle owl's scientific name reflects the sound of its loud calls, which are clearly audible on still nights even from quite a distance. Pairs will call alternately before mating, and the call notes of the female are higher-pitched than the male's. In spite of their large size, these owls fly quietly and may sometimes be seen soaring. Formidable hunters, they will occasionally take large, potentially dangerous quarry such as buzzards and herons. Eagle owls are adaptable in their feeding habits, and may sometimes resort to catching earthworms and fish, as well as eating carrion when hunting opportunities are limited.

Distribution: Throughout southern Europe, Scandinavia and eastwards across Asia. Small populations in parts of western Europe and western North Africa.
Size: 73cm (29in).
Habitat: Rocky areas and relatively open country.
Nest: Cliff ledges, or occasionally on the ground.
Eggs: 1–4, white.
Food: Mammals and birds.

Identification: Brownish with dark markings on the wings. Underparts are buff-brown with streaking, most evident on the breast. Prominent ear tufts. Black bil, orange irides. Hens are often slightly larger. There may be great variation in appearance through their wide range, and at least 13 different races are recognized.

WARBLERS AND OTHER SMALL GARDEN VISITORS

Spotting these birds in a garden is not always easy since their neutral coloration merges in well against the foliage. They generally favour overgrown areas where there will be a good supply of invertebrates. Some are resident in northern latitudes throughout the year, while others migrate to Africa for the winter.

Wren

Troglodytes troglodytes

Although often difficult to spot due to their size and drab coloration, these tiny birds have a remarkably loud song which usually betrays their presence. Wrens can be found in areas where there is plenty of cover, such as ivy-clad walls, scurrying under the vegetation in search of spiders and similar prey. During the winter, when their small size could make them vulnerable to hypothermia, the wrens huddle together in roosts overnight to keep warm. However, populations are often badly affected by prolonged spells of severe weather. In the spring, the hen chooses one of several nests that the male has constructed, lining it with feathers to form a soft base for her eggs. Wrens are surprisingly common, although not always conspicuous, with the British population alone made up of an estimated ten million birds.

Identification: Reddish-brown back and wings with visible barring. Lighter brown underparts and a narrow eye stripe. Short tail, often held vertically, which is greyish on its underside. Bill is long and relatively narrow. Sexes are alike.

Distribution: Resident throughout Europe, except in Scandinavia and neighbouring parts of Russia during the winter. European wrens move south in the winter. Present in northern Africa.
Size: 10cm (4in).
Habitat: Overgrown gardens and woodland.
Nest: Ball-shaped.
Eggs: 5–6, white with reddish-brown markings.
Food: Mainly invertebrates.

Eurasian nuthatch

Sitta europaea

With relatively large, strong feet and very powerful claws, Eurasian nuthatches are adept at scampering up and down tree trunks. They hunt for invertebrates, which they extract from the bark with their narrow bills, but their compact and powerful beak also enables them to feed easily on nuts. The nuthatches first wedge the nut into a suitable crevice in the bark, then hammer at the shell, breaking it open so they can extract the kernel. They will also store nuts, which they will eat when other food is in short supply. The bill is also useful as a tool for plastering over the entrance hole of their nest in the spring. The opening, just small enough to allow the adult birds to squeeze in and out, helps to protect them from predators. Eurasian nuthatches are most likely to be encountered in areas with broadleaved trees, as these provide food such as acorns and hazelnuts.

Distribution: Found throughout most of Europe, except for Ireland, northern England and Scotland. Also restricted to southern parts of Scandinavia. Occurs in northern Africa opposite the Strait of Gibraltar.
Size: 14cm (5¹/₂in).
Habitat: Gardens and parks with mature trees.
Nest: In a secluded spot.
Eggs: 6–9, white with heavy reddish-brown speckling.
Food: Invertebrates, nuts and seeds.

Identification: Bluish-grey upperparts from head to tail. Distinctive black stripes running from the base of the bill down the sides of the head, encompassing the eyes. Underparts vary in colour from white through to a rusty shade of buff, depending on the race. Dark reddish-brown vent area, more brightly coloured in cocks.

Willow warbler

Phylloscopus trochilus

Distribution: Occurs in the summer from the British Isles right across most of Europe. Overwinters in Africa.
Size: 12cm (5in).
Habitat: Wooded areas.
Nest: Dome-shaped, built on the ground.
Eggs: 6–7, pale pink with reddish spotting.
Food: Small invertebrates.

The subdued coloration of these small birds is so effective that, despite being one of Europe's most common species, willow warblers are very inconspicuous. Difficult to observe in their wooded habitat, it is their song, which heralds their arrival in woodland areas in early spring, that usually betrays their presence. In the British Isles, the willow species is the most numerous of all warblers, with a population estimated at around three million pairs. These warblers are typically resident in Europe between April and September. Their nest is hidden among the vegetation and features a low entry point. In late summer, willow warblers can often be seen in loose association with various tits, before they head off to their African wintering grounds.

Identification: Greyish-green upperparts, with a pale yellowish streak running across each eye. Pale yellow throat and chest, with whitish underparts. The yellow plumage is much whiter in birds from more northern areas.

Blackcap (*Sylvia atricapilla*): 15cm (6in)
Resident population is restricted to southern parts of the British Isles (including Ireland), France, the Iberian Peninsula and Italy; also north-western Africa. Jet black area on the crown, extending just above the eye and bordered by grey above the bill. Remainder of the head and breast is greyish. White plumage under the throat. Back, wings and underparts are olive-grey. Sexes are alike. Young birds have a reddish-brown cap.

Spotted flycatcher (*Muscicapa striata*): 15cm (6in)
Occurs throughout Europe during the summer, wintering in Africa. Greyish-brown upperparts, with darker streaking on the head extending to the whitish underparts. Area above the bill is also white. Relatively long wings and long, distinctive, square-tipped tail that can be spread to aid hovering. Bill, legs and feet are blackish. Young birds have dull yellowish markings extending from the head down over the wings, rump and tail. Sexes are alike.

Chattering cisticola (*Cisticola anonymus*) 12.5cm (5in)
This African warbler ranges from Nigeria west across Dem. Rep. Congo, and south as far as the Angolan border. Rufous crown, with a dark stripe from the base of the bill to the eyes, and a narrow dusky white area above and below, extending over the throat. Neck, back and wings are dark brownish. Slender, blackish bill, pinkish legs and feet. Sexes are alike, although cocks may be identified by their song.

Garden warbler

Sylvia borin

Rather dull coloration, coupled with their small size, ensures these warblers are relatively inconspicuous, particularly when darting among foliage. However, their attractive song and call notes may help identify them in the undergrowth. Garden warblers arrive on their breeding grounds from middle of April onwards, and construct a fairly large nest using a variety of plant matter, usually including stems of grass, and lining it with softer material. The hen sits alone through the incubation period, which lasts approximately 12 days, but subsequently both parents will seek food for their rapidly-growing brood. The young quickly leave the nest, sometimes when just 9 days old, and may be forced to scrabble among the vegetation to escape would-be predators until they are able to fly from danger. In more southern parts of their breeding range, pairs of garden warblers may produce two successive broods of chicks. They return to Africa in September.

Identification: Olive-brown head and upperparts, with a greyish area present at each side of the neck. Underparts are greyish-white, buffer along the flanks. Bill and legs are dark greyish. Young birds similar to adults. Sexes are alike.

Distribution: Summer range extends from Scandinavia southwards across virtually all of Europe. Migrates south for the winter, ranging over much of Africa except the Horn and the south-west.
Size: 14cm (5½in).
Habitat: Gardens with trees, also parks.
Nest: Made of vegetation.
Eggs: 4–5, buff with brown spots.
Food: Mainly invertebrates.

TITS

Thanks to their small size, most tits are most likely to be spotted in gardens during the winter months, when the absence of leaves on trees makes these birds more conspicuous. They are also more frequent visitors to bird feeders and tables during this period. Tits are very resourceful when seeking food, clearly displaying their aerobatic skills as they dart about, even feeding upside down.

Coal tit

Parus ater

These tits are often to be seen in gardens feeding on bird tables, sometimes taking food which they will then store in a variety of locations, ranging from caches on the ground to suitable hollows in trees. The urge to store food in this way becomes strongest in the late summer and during the autumn, and helps the birds to maintain a food supply through the coldest months of the year. This hoarding strategy appears to be very successful, since coal tit populations rarely crash like many other small birds following a particularly harsh winter. In fact, these tits have increased their breeding range significantly over recent years, with their distribution now extending to various islands off the British coast, including the Isles of Scilly. During the winter, in their natural habitat of coniferous forest, they may form flocks comprised of many thousands of individuals, yet in gardens they are only usually seen in quite small numbers.

Identification: Jet black head, with white patches on the sides of the face and a similar area on the nape. Greyish-olive upperparts, with white wing bars, and brownish-white underparts, although some marked regional variations. Young birds have pale yellowish cheek patches. Sexes very similar, but the female's head markings may be duller. The bill is black. Legs are greyish.

Distribution: Resident throughout the whole of Europe, although absent from northern parts of Scandinavia. Range extends south to north-western parts of Africa, and spreads right across Asia to Japan.
Size: 11cm (4^{1}/$_{2}$in).
Habitat: Wooded areas.
Nest: Cup-shaped, made from vegetation.
Eggs: 8–11, white with reddish markings.
Food: Mostly invertebrates and seeds.

Great tit

Parus major

Distribution: Found through all of Europe except in parts of northern Scandinavia, and ranges south as far as northern Africa. Also extends widely across much of Asia.
Size: 14cm (5^{1}/$_{2}$in).
Habitat: Woodland.
Nest: Cup-shaped, made from vegetation.
Eggs: 5–12, white with reddish spotting.
Food: Invertebrates, seeds.

There is a marked difference in appearance between great tits throughout their wide range. They form groups after the breeding season, often associating with other small birds, foraging for food through woodland as well as visiting bird tables, where their bold, jaunty nature makes them conspicuous. Although they do not hoard food like some tits, they are able to lower their body temperature significant overnight when roosting, effectively lessening the amount of energy they need. Great tits become much more territorial at the start of the breeding season, which in Europe typically starts during March. They build their nest in a tree hollow, but readily use garden nestboxes where provided. Studies have shown that the male seeks out potential nesting sites within the pair's territory, but it is the female who has the final choice. Pairs may nest twice during the breeding period, which lasts until July.

Identification: Cock has a black head with white cheek patches. Broad band of black feathering extends down the centre of the body, with yellow plumage on either side. Wings are olive-green at the top, becoming bluish on the sides and on the flight feathers and tail. Hens are similar but display a narrower, uneven vertical black band. Young birds significantly paler overall, with yellowish cheeks and little of the vertical band seen in adults.

Blue tit

Parus caeruleus

Distribution: Throughout Europe except the far north of Scandinavia. Also present in north-western Africa.
Size: 12cm (5in).
Habitat: Wooded areas, parks and gardens.
Nest: Tree holes.
Eggs: 7–16, white with reddish-brown markings.
Food: Invertebrates, seeds and nuts.

A common visitor to bird tables, blue tits are lively, active birds by nature, and are welcomed by gardeners because they eat aphids. Their small size allows them to hop up the stems of thin plants and, hanging upside down, seek these pests under leaves. Blue tits are well-adapted to garden life and readily adopt nest boxes supplied for them. Their young leave the nest before they are able to fly properly, and are therefore vulnerable to predators such as cats. Those that do survive the critical early weeks can be easily distinguished by the presence of yellow rather than white cheek patches.

Identification: Has a distinctive blue crown edged with white, and a narrow black stripe running back through each eye. The cheeks are white. Underparts are yellowish, and the back is greyish-green. There is a whitish bar across the top of the blue wings. The tail is also blue. Sexes are similar but hens duller.

White-bellied tit (*Parus albiventris*): 15cm (6in) Occurs eastern Africa, from Sudan to Tanzania. Also in western Cameroon. The cock has a black, slightly glossy, head, back and chest, with a very conspicuous white abdomen and vent area. Also displays white shoulder patches. The bill is black; legs and feet are greyish. Hens are more of a sooty-black shade, with browner colouring on the face. Young birds duller overall.

Marsh tit (*Parus palustris*): 13cm (6in) Widely distributed in a central band across Europe, but largely absent from the Iberian peninsula and much of Scandinavia, as well as areas of the British Isles. There is also a separate Asian population. Black cap extends right over the top of the head, and there is usually a small area of black plumage below the bill. Broad whitish area on the cheeks, while the back and wings are brown. The underparts are paler, being whitish in colour. Bill black, legs greyish. Young birds whiter on the underparts. Sexes are alike.

White-bellied tit (*Parus albiventris*): 15cm (6in) Scattered throughout Cameroon, western Africa, but occurs more consistently in the east, from Sudan southwards to Tanzania. Cock bird has black, slightly glossy plumage over the head, chest and back. A striking white bar extends down across each wing from the shoulders; adjacent feathers, including the flight feathers, and also the tail, are white. Underparts are also white. Bill, legs and feet are dark. Hens are similar, but more sooty-grey than black, with these areas being browner in young birds.

Southern grey tit

Parus afer

These tits are most commonly observed in pairs, or larger family groups after the breeding season, which extends from August through until October. The nest is usually hidden in a tree but can be at ground level in a suitable bank, or even in buildings, with open pipework being especially favoured. The incubation period lasts approximately two weeks. It is thought that the young from a previous brood may assist the adults in rearing their chicks. Southern grey tits hunt a wide variety of invertebrates, including beetles and wasps, as well as various types of insect larvae. Their natural agility means they can obtain food upside down, holding themselves in position with their claws. Although they usually forage on their own they will occasionally join up with other birds, including various warblers, and this may make it easier for them to disturb and catch their prey.

Identification: Prominent jet black cap extending over the top of the head, and a broad black area extending down from the throat on to the breast. Upperparts are dark brown, while the underparts are a more buff shade. Young birds are duller overall. Sexes are similar, but hens have a much smaller area of black on the breast.

Distribution: Two distinct populations are present in southern Africa: one in South Africa, reaching southern parts of Namibia, the other in Namibia, extending into western Botswana.
Size: 13cm (5¼in).
Habitat: Open scrubland.
Nest: Cup-shaped, usually in a tree hole.
Eggs: 3–4, white with reddish markings.
Food: Mainly invertebrates.

FINCHES

By feeding mainly on seeds but adopting different feeding strategies, finches can exploit a wide variety of food sources without competing with each other. Goldfinches, for example, probe for and eat small seeds such as teasel, whereas the stout-billed hawfinch can crack tougher seeds such as cherry, exerting a force equivalent to 50kg (110lb) to reach the kernel within.

Chaffinch

Fringilla coelebs

The behaviour of the chaffinch changes significantly during the year. These birds can be seen in groups during the winter, but at the onset of spring, and the breeding season, cock birds become very territorial, driving away any rivals. While resident chaffinches remain in gardens and similar settings throughout the year, large groups of migrants seeking refuge from harsh winter weather associate in large flocks in farmland areas. Chaffinches usually prefer to feed on the ground, hopping and walking along in search of seeds. They seek invertebrates almost exclusively for rearing their chicks.

Identification: Black band above the bill, with grey over the head and neck. Cheeks and underparts are pinkish. The back is brown, and there are two distinctive white wing bars. Cocks are less brightly coloured in winter plumage. Hens have dull grey cheek patches and dark greyish-green upperparts, while their underparts are a buff shade of greyish-white.

Distribution: Resident in the British Isles and western Europe, and a summer visitor to Scandinavia and eastern Europe. Also resident in the west of northern Africa and at the south-western tip.
Size: 16cm (6in).
Habitat: Woodland, parks and gardens.
Nest: Cup-shaped, usually in a tree fork.
Eggs: 4–5, light brown or blue with dark, very often smudgy, markings.
Food: Mostly seeds, but some invertebrates.

European goldfinch

Carduelis carduelis

The long, narrow bill of the goldfinch enables it to prise kernels out of seeds, and these birds often congregate in the winter to feed on stands of thistle heads and teasel. Alder cones are also a favoured food at this time of year. Goldfinches are very agile birds, capable of clinging on to narrow stems when feeding. They are social by nature, usually mixing in small flocks in areas where food is plentiful, although they are usually shy when feeding on the ground. They have a relatively loud, attractive, twittering song. Pairs usually prefer to build their nest in the fork of a tree rather than concealing it in a hedge.

Identification: Bright red face with black lores. Black area across the top of the crown that broadens to a collar on the neck. White extends around the throat, and a brown necklace separates the white on the throat from the paler underparts. Brown back and flanks, underparts otherwise white. The bill is narrow and pointed. Wings are black with white spotting and yellow barring. Tail is black with white markings. Hens display duller coloration with yellow less apparent.

Distribution: Occurs throughout much of the British Isles and mainland Europe, including Denmark but confined to the extreme south of Scandinavia. Also present in northern Africa.
Size: 13cm (5in).
Habitat: Woodland and more open areas.
Nest: Cup-shaped, made from vegetation.
Eggs: 5–6, bluish-white with darker markings.
Food: Mainly seeds, but some invertebrates.

Syrian serin (*Serinus syriacus*): 13cm (6in)
Occurs north-eastern Africa, and eastern Mediterranean. Cock displays a band of deep yellow plumage above the bill, encircling the eyes and also on the throat. Ear coverts and top of the head are greyish, as are the flanks. Remainder of the underparts have a yellowish suffusion. Bill greyish, legs and feet pinkish-grey. Hens are less colourful on the head, with definite streaking on the grey of the flanks and back. Young birds are pale buff rather than grey.

Common linnet (*Carduelis cannabina*): 14cm (5¹⁄₂in)
Resident throughout western Europe and in parts of north-western Africa. Summer resident in north-eastern Europe, but absent from much of Scandinavia. Grey head with a red crown. Back and wings are brown. The sides of the chest are red, becoming paler on the flanks with a white area on the breast. Hens are much duller with a short grey bill.

Common redpoll (*Carduelis flammea*): 14cm (5¹⁄₂in)
Occurs in northern Europe, including Iceland, moving further south in the winter. Crimson-red cap and black lores contrast with the yellowish bill. The brownish upperparts are quite streaked. Red chest fades to white on the steaked abdomen. White wing bar. Hens are similar but lack the red on the chest.

Common rosefinch (*Carpodacus erythrinus*): 15cm (6in)
Now breeding as far west as southern Scandinavia. Cock has a deep pinkish-red head, breast and rump. Lower underparts are whitish. The lores and area behind the eyes are brown, as are the wings and tail. Dark stocky bill, pinkish-brown legs and feet. Hens are brownish overall, with streaking on the head and back, and on the underparts. Young birds resemble hens, but are a warmer olive brown in colour.

European greenfinch

Carduelis chloris

Greenfinches have quite stout bills that enable them to easily crack open tough seed casings to reach the edible kernels inside. These birds are most likely to be observed in areas where there are trees and bushes, which provide nesting cover. In the winter, European greenfinches visit bird tables, readily taking peanuts as well as foraging in gardens. Groups of greenfinches are also sighted in more open areas of countryside, such as farmland, searching for weed seeds and grains that may have been dropped during harvesting. Pairs will often nest two or three times in succession during the summer, and when there are chicks in the nest the birds consume invertebrates in much larger quantities.

Identification: Greenish head, with greyer areas on the sides of the face and wings. Yellowish-green breast, with yellow also evident on the flight feathers. Relatively large, conical bill. Hen is duller, with greyer tone overall, brownish mantle and less yellow on the wings.

Distribution: Throughout Europe and much of northern Africa, but absent from more northern parts of Scandinavia.
Size: 16cm (6in).
Habitat: Edges of woodland and more open areas.
Nest: Bulky, cup-shaped.
Eggs: 4–6, whitish to pale blue with darker markings.
Food: Largely seeds and some invertebrates.

European serin

Serinus serinus

Although mainly confined to relatively southerly latitudes, these serins are occasionally seen in the British Isles and have even bred successfully in southern England. It appears that serins are slowly extending their northerly distribution, with ornithological records revealing they had spread to central Europe by 1875 and had started to colonize France within another 50 years. Serins often seek out stands of conifers, where they nest, although they also frequent citrus groves further south in their range. Young birds differ from adults in that they are predominantly brown and lack any yellow in their plumage.

Identification: Bright yellow forehead extends to a stripe above each eye, encircling the cheeks and joining with the yellow breast. Back is yellow and streaked with brown, as are the white flanks. Hens are duller in coloration, with a pale yellow rump.

Distribution: Resident in coastal areas of France south through the Iberian Peninsula to northern Africa and around the northern Mediterranean area. A summer visitor elsewhere in mainland Europe.
Size: 12cm (5in).
Habitat: Parks and gardens.
Nest: Cup-shaped, in a tree.
Eggs: 3–5, pale blue with darker markings.
Food: Mostly seeds and some invertebrates.

WAXBILLS AND MANNIKINS

Occurring in Africa rather than Europe, these finches are highly social by nature. They often associate in relatively large flocks, especially in agricultural areas, where they may inflict considerable damage on millet crops. Waxbills are so called because the red coloration of their bills resembles sealing wax. They are also more colourful overall than mannikins (which are sometimes called munias).

Orange-breasted waxbill

Golden-breasted waxbill, zebra waxbill *Amandava subflava*

The striped patterning on the sides of their bodies explain why this species is also known as the zebra waxbill. They are the smallest of all waxbills and have a very confiding nature. They can be observed in areas near reedbeds, since these provide the birds with roosting and breeding sites. Occasionally though, and particularly in southern areas, the waxbills will take over abandoned nests constructed by birds such as the red bishop (*Euplectes orix*).

In open country they are more likely to construct their own nests, usually near the ground. Breeding coincides with the end of the rainy season, commencing in January in South Africa, and pairs often rear two broods. Invertebrates feature more prominently in their diet at this stage. The chicks can fledge just 2¹/₂ weeks after hatching.

Identification: Cock bird has a bright red eye stripe, and yellowish underparts becoming decidedly orange on the breast. Darker greenish-grey barring on the flanks corresponds to the coloration of the upperparts. Rump reddish. Young birds are very plain, greenish-grey with more yellowish underparts and dark bills. Hens lack the red eye stripe and the orange on the underparts.

Distribution: Extends from Senegal in western Africa across to Sudan and Ethiopia in the east, and from here south across much of central Africa down to the eastern side of South Africa.
Size: 10cm (4in).
Habitat: Grasslands, fields.
Nest: Large domed structure made from grass.
Eggs: 4–6, white.
Food: Mostly small seeds, but also invertebrates.

St Helena waxbill

Common waxbill *Estrilda astrild*

A highly adaptable species, these waxbills are commonly encountered not only in Africa but also in other parts of the world, including the island of St Helena, where they have been introduced. Populations are also established on the islands of Rodriquez, Seychelles and Reunion, close to Africa, as well as places further afield such as Hawaii and Brazil. St Helena waxbills are most likely to be observed in flocks in areas where there are relatively tall grasses, although they rarely stray far from water. Grass seeds feature prominently in their diet, and the birds can be seen grasping on to the stems and feeding from the ripening seedheads. They often roost alongside each other. While in proximity to people, whether in gardens or villages, they can become quite tame.

Distribution: Occurs across much of Africa from a line south of the Sahara, although is absent from the more heavily-forested areas
Size: 12cm (4¹/₂in).
Habitat: Grassland, gardens.
Nest: Bulky, pear-shaped structure made from grass.
Eggs: 4–8, pink.
Food: Seeds, invertebrates.

Identification: Grey forehead and prominent red eye stripes. Chest is pale. The wings are dark grey and barred, with heavy barring also on the underparts, including the flanks. Displays faint red markings in the centre of the abdomen. Sexes are alike.

Orange-cheeked waxbill (*Estrilda melpoda*):
10cm (4in)
From Senegal in western Africa down to the
Dem. Rep. Congo, Angola and Zambia. Large
orange cheek patches. The surrounding plumage
is greyish but the head is darker. Wings are
chestnut brown. The rump is reddish. Sexes are
generally alike, although hens may be slightly
paler than the cock.

African silverbill (*Lonchura cantans*): 10cm (4in)
Extends in a broad band across Africa south of
the Sahara, from Mauritania in western Africa
eastwards to Somalia and Tanzania. Also ranges
further east, from Saudi Arabia to Oman. The
top of the head is dark brown, continuing down
over the back and wings. The chest and cheeks
are pale buff, becoming darker on the abdomen.
Silvery bill and black rump. Sexes are similar, but
hens may be a little smaller.

Madagascar munia (*Lonchura nana*):
10cm (4in)
Present only on Madagascar, often in the vicinity
of villages. Black stripe extends from the bill to
the lores. Black bib. Rest of the head is greyish
with blackish speckling, merging into the brown
of the back and wings. Underparts pinkish-buff
with darker speckling, evident also on the rump.
Tail is dark. The bill is black above and greyish
below. Legs and feet are pinkish. Young birds are
brown above, paler brown below. Bill is dark.
Sexes are alike.

Magpie mannikin

Lonchura fringilloides

Mannikins as a group are relatively dull in
colour, with black, brown and white mostly
predominating in their plumage. The magpie
mannikin is no different in this respect from
Asiatic members of the group. It lives in
small flocks, but is not especially common
through much of its range when compared
to other African mannikins overlapping its
area of distribution. Tall grasses, reeds and
bamboos are all favoured for roosting,
feeding and breeding, whether in close
proximity to people or further afield.
Magpie mannikins prefer to
feed on ripening seeds,
and use their spindly
claws to anchor
themselves to
narrow stems.

Distribution: Ranges from
Senegal in western Africa
eastwards across to Kenya,
and down as far as Angola in
the west; also to South Africa
in the east.
Size: 13cm (5in).
Habitat: Grassland and
woodland clearings.
Nest: Ball of dried grass and
similar material.
Eggs: 5–6, white.
Food: Seeds, invertebrates.

Identification: Head is a glossy
bluish-black, with a powerful,
conical greyish-black bill. The
underparts are entirely white
except for black and brown
barring on the flanks. Back and
wings are dark brown, broken by
some lighter markings, especially
on the back. Rump and tail are
black. Sexes are alike.

Bronze mannikin

Lonchura cucullata

These mannikins are common throughout their extensive
range, living in flocks and often being sighted in the
company of other related species. They are opportunistic
breeders, with pairs nesting several times each year under
favourable conditions. The social structure of the group
appears to be reinforced by nest-building activity, in which
most members of the flock participate. The birds may
construct a fresh nest for communal roosting almost on a
daily basis, using sprigs of dry grass and similar material.
Although the sexes are identical in appearance, males are
easily recognisable by the way in which they bob and
display to females, as well as by their singing,
during which performance the male may
sometimes twist his body round towards
his intended mate. He will also initiate
nest building although this task will
ultimately be taken over by his partner. The
bulky nest constructed for breeding is typically
comprised of more than 600 separate strands of
grass, and is lined inside with feathers.

Identification: Dark brown head.
Purplish suffusion on the upper
chest, becoming a lighter shade
of brown over the back and
wings. The underparts are white
with individual dark metallic green
markings on the flanks, and a
more prominent greenish patch at
the top of each wing. Bill greyish,
darker on the upper mandible.
Legs black. Young birds brownish,
with paler underparts and a dark
grey bill. Sexes are alike.

Distribution: Has a similar
range to magpie mannikin.
Distribution extends through
much of central Africa, from
Senegal in the west across to
Ethiopia in the east, though
not as far as the coast, and
down as far as Angola and
eastern South Africa.
Size: 10cm (4in).
Habitat: Open countryside.
Nest: Domed-shaped, made
from grass.
Eggs: 4–8, white.
Food: Mainly seeds, but
some invertebrates.

SPARROWS AND OTHER SEED-EATERS

A variety of sparrows are to be found across Africa. The majority can be easily identified by the predominance of brown, black and grey tones in their plumage, although there are exceptions, typified by the golden sparrows, so called due to the appearance of the cock birds. Yet other small seed-eaters are brightly coloured too, for example the cordon bleus.

House sparrow

Passer domesticus

A common sight on garden bird tables and in city parks, house sparrows have adapted well to living so closely alongside people, even to the extent of nesting under roofs of buildings. These sparrows form loose flocks, with larger numbers congregating where food is readily available. They spend much of their time on the ground, hopping along but ever watchful for passing predators such as cats. It is not uncommon for them to construct nests during the winter, which serve as communal roosts rather than being used for breeding. The bills of cock birds turn black in the spring, at the start of the nesting period. During this time, several males will often court a single female in what has become known as a "sparrows' wedding". In more rural areas, house sparrows will sometimes nest in tree hollows, and may even occasionally construct domed nests.

Identification: Rufous-brown head with a grey area on top. A black stripe runs across the eyes and a broad black bib runs down over the chest. The ear coverts and the entire underparts are greyish, and there is a whitish area under the tail. Hens are a duller shade of brown, with a pale stripe behind each eye and a fawn bar on each wing.

Distribution: Very common, occurring throughout virtually the whole of Europe, and eastwards across Asia. Also present in northern and south-east Africa.
Size: 6in (15cm).
Habitat: Urban and more rural areas.
Nest: Tree hollows and under roofs of buildings.
Eggs: 3–6, whitish with darker markings.
Food: Invertebrates and seeds, but very adaptable.

Cape sparrow

Passer melanurus

Like others of its kind, the Cape sparrow has proved to be a highly adaptable species. These birds are often to be found close to people, and can be frequent visitors to bird tables. As with the house sparrow (*Passer domesticus*), the bill of the cock bird is black only for the duration the nesting period, being brown like the hen's for the remainder of the year. Pairs may sometimes nest communally, in trees or even deserted buildings, but where they choose to establish their own territories the cock bird actively seeks to drive away any would-be rivals. The nest itself is a bulky, untidy pile of vegetation, which may incorporate torn strips of paper and other rubbish, with an entry point near the top. When the young chicks hatch the adult birds raise them largely on invertebrates, until they fledge at about three weeks old. After the breeding season, pairs join together into flocks numbering as many as 200 individuals.

Identification: Cock bird has a black face, crown and chest, with a silvery area behind the eyes forming a collar. Underparts pale brownish-grey. Prominent chestnut area at the top of the wings, with a white band below and similar edging on the wing coverts. The back is dark brown, as are the flight feathers. Bill is black, legs and feet dark grey. Hens are similar, but with much duller facial coloration. Young birds are similar to hens.

Distribution: Southern Africa, reaching up to Angola in the west and Zimbabwe in the east.
Size: 15cm (6in).
Habitat: Scrubland and more open country.
Nest: Bulky, domed mass of vegetation and other material.
Eggs: 2–5, greenish-white with darker markings.
Food: Invertebrates and seeds, also a regular visitor to bird tables.

Tree sparrow (*Passer montanus*): 14cm (5½in)
Present in Europe except for northern Scandinavia, western England, northern Scotland and central Ireland. Top of the head is reddish-brown. Black bib beneath the bill. White area on the cheeks below the eyes extends back around the neck and is broken by central black patches. Grey chest. The wings are light brown and black, broken by a white wing bar edged by black. Sexes are alike.

Black-crowned waxbill (Blackcap waxbill, *Estrilda nonnula*): 12cm (4½in)
From Nigeria to Sudan and south to Dem. Rep. Congo in the west and Tanzania in the east. Black cap. Upperparts white, except for red on the flanks. Greyish back and wings with fine barring. Red rump and black tail. Bill reddish with dark markings. Black legs. Hens greyish-brown, with reduced red on the flanks. Young birds are buffer overall, with black bills.

Blue-breasted cordon bleu (blue waxbill, *Uraeginthus angolensis*): 13cm (5in)
Rep. Congo east to southern Kenya, south to Angola, Botswana, Zambia and Zimbabwe, extending to northern Namibia and to Natal and neighbouring parts of South Africa. Sky blue plumage from the bill down over the sides of the face and chest to the flanks. Upperparts and wings dark brown. Sky blue tail. Lighter fawn from the centre of the abdomen to the vent. Bill blackish, legs and feet pinkish. Blue plumage is restricted to the breast in hens. Young birds resemble hens, with paler blue coloration.

Golden song sparrow

Passer luteus

In spite of their name, these birds are not talented songsters, uttering little more than a series of chirping notes, even during the breeding season. Cocks undergo an unusual change at this time, however, as their bills are transformed from a pinkish shade to black. The depth of their yellow coloration can also vary, in some cases being paler, often reflecting slight regional variations. Although golden song sparrows tend not to feed in towns, they frequently roost there in large flocks. They are often nomadic when not breeding, with flocks typically of more than 100 birds wandering widely in search of favourable conditions. They breed communally too, and the young are reared primarily on invertebrates.

Identification:
Yellow head and underparts. Chestnut-coloured feathering runs over the back and wings, merging with black. Hens are a dull brown and have paler, more buff-coloured underparts.

Distribution: Extends in a broad band from Mauritania in western Africa eastwards right across the continent to northern parts of Sudan and Ethiopia.
Size: 13cm (5in).
Habitat: Scrub, cropland and urban areas.
Nest: Bulky.
Eggs: 3–6, off-white with darker irregular markings.
Food: Seeds and some invertebrates.

Red-cheeked cordon bleu

Uraeginthus bengalus

Distribution: Ranges across Africa south of the Sahara Desert, extending to eastern Angola, Zambia and southern parts of the Dem. Rep. Congo. Also thought to be in existence on the Cape Verde Islands.
Size: 13cm (5in).
Habitat: Villages, gardens and grasslands.
Nest: Bulky, usually an oval or spherical structure.
Eggs: 4–5, white.
Food: Seeds, invertebrates.

The depth of this species' sky blue coloration varies through its range, particularly among males. These colourful finches have adapted well to the spread of human settlement, and can often be sighted in villages. They seek their food primarily on the ground, hopping along in search of seeds as well as invertebrates, which are used to feed chicks in the nest. These so-called blue waxbills are also sufficiently agile to catch flying ants. Pairs are relatively solitary when nesting, but once the breeding season is over they will reunite to form quite large flocks. The red-cheeked cordon bleu's natural environment is open country, and although they may wander through their range they are unlikely to be encountered in the more densely forested areas.

Identification: Greyish-brown plumage extends from the top of the bill down over the back and wings. The plumage from around the eyes down on to the chest and flanks is sky blue, and the abdomen is light buff. Sexes are similar, except hens lack the dark red ear coverts and have less blue on their underparts.

BULLFINCHES, CANARIES AND BULBULS

While bullfinches are birds of northern climates, canaries as a group have a more southern range,
reaching right to the tip of Africa. Caged canaries are of course known for their attractive song, the
result of a domestication process that began about 500 years ago. Although less well known, bulbuls are
also talented songsters and are common garden visitors in Africa.

Common bullfinch

Pyrrhula pyrrhula

Distribution: Ranges widely across Europe, except the far north of Scandinavia and the southern half of the Iberian Peninsula, and extending eastwards through Asia. Also present on the Azores.
Size: 16cm (6.25in).
Habitat: Woodland areas.
Nest: Cup-shaped, made from vegetation.
Eggs: 4–6, greenish-blue with dark brownish markings.
Food: Seeds, invertebrates

These birds are unmistakable thanks to their stocky appearance and the bright pink coloration of the males. They are often seen in gardens but may also be encountered in woodland. Bullfinches are regarded as a potential pest by fruit farmers since they will eat the emerging buds in the early spring. Tree seeds, such as those of ash and beech, form a significant part of their diet in the winter, and they can also be beneficial to farmers by eating a range of invertebrates, particularly when rearing their young. Breeding starts from mid-April onwards, with a pair constructing their nest using twigs and lining the interior with softer material. The hen sits alone, with incubation lasting 14 days, after which both adults feed their growing brood. The chicks leave the nest when about 2¹/₂ weeks old.

Identification: Cock has a black face and top to the head, with deep rosy-pink underparts, lighter around the vent. Grey back, black wings and tail with a white area on the rump. The bill, legs and feet are all black. Hen is similar but with brownish rather than pink underparts. Young birds lack the black cap seen in hens, and show brownish coloration on the wing coverts.

Canary

Island canary, *Serinus canaria*

These small and relatively plain finches are the original ancestors of the millions of domestic canaries now kept throughout the world by bird-fanciers. Domestication has affected not just the canary's appearance but also its singing prowess. Wild canaries lack their domestic counterparts' vocal range, but the song of the cock bird is still most likely to be heard through the breeding period, from spring onwards. They are often observed in open country, sometimes associating in large flocks during the winter alongside *Carduelis* species, such as linnets (*C. cannabina*). The hen constructs a tidy nest using a variety of vegetation, usually choosing a location in a tree or bush, and incubates the eggs on her own for two weeks. She may not begin sitting immediately, which effectively extends the incubation period of those eggs laid first. This results in the chicks hatching closer together, improving the chances of survival of the youngest.

Identification: Yellowish sides to the face extending to the throat, and also on the rump and the lower underparts, merging into greyer plumage especially on the chest. Head is greyish with streaking, which becomes more prominent over the wings. Hens are similar but less yellow. Young birds are browner.

Distribution: Restricted to the western Canary Islands, off the north-west coast of Africa, Madeira and the Azores. Also introduced to the islands of Bermuda, Puerto Rico and Midway, part of the Hawaiian group.
Size: 12.5cm (5in).
Habitat: Open country.
Nest: Cup-shaped, made from vegetation.
Eggs: 3–5, bluish with reddish-brown markings.
Food: Mainly seeds.

Common bulbul

Pycnonotus barbatus

Common bulbuls range widely over much of the continent, and the southern population is sometimes recognized as a separate species (known as the black-eyed bulbul, *P. tricolor*) thanks to its yellow undertail coverts. They are noisy birds, congregating in groups as dusk falls and calling loudly to each other, although they do not form true flocks. They are agile in flight, able to catch flying insects, and may also venture on to lawns to search for invertebrates. Fruit also figures prominently in their diet, and they can cause serious damage in fruit-growing areas. Their nests sometimes attract the attentions of Jacobin's cuckoo (*Clamator jacobinus*), which adds an egg alongside those of the bulbuls. Instead of throwing out the eggs or young chicks the cuckoo chick suffocates its companions, and, with calls mimicking theirs, the intruder is reared by its foster parents.

Identification: Relatively dull brown coloration, darker on the head and becoming paler on the underparts, with white undertail coverts. Back and wings are brown. Young birds may have shorter tail feathers. Sexes alike.

Distribution: Ranges in a broad band across Africa, south of the Sahara, widely distributed throughout western Africa south as far as Rep. Congo. In the east, extends from Egypt down as far as South Africa. Also present in north-west Africa.
Size: 22cm (8¹/₂in).
Habitat: Areas with trees.
Nest: Cup-shaped, made from vegetation.
Eggs: 2–4, pinkish-white with darker markings.
Food: Fruit and invertebrates.

Black-headed canary (*Serinus alario*): 15cm (6in)
Namibia, Botswana and South Africa. Cock has a black head and chest (broken by white in *S. a. leucolaema*), with a white area around the nape extending over the underparts. Brownish and black markings on the flanks. Back and tail are chestnut. Black flight feathers. Hens are greyish on the head, with streaking extending back over the head. Underparts paler, with chestnut and black areas on the wings. Young birds similar to hens, but paler with streaking on the underparts.

Cape canary (yellow-crowned canary, *Serinus canicollis*): 12cm (5in)
Sporadic, parts of eastern Africa to South Africa, with a population in central Angola. Cock has yellowish-green underparts with a greyish crown and mantle. Some races are more yellow than others. Hens have prominent streaking on their head and back, with duller underparts. Young birds have more prominent streaking overall, with less yellow coloration.

African citril (*Serinus citrinelloides*): 12cm (4.75in)
From Ethiopia south to Zimbabwe and northern Mozambique. Cock has a black mask around the bill, encompassing the eyes. The underparts are otherwise yellowish, with slight streaking on the flanks. Yellow streak above each eye, upperparts otherwise greenish with darker streaking and two narrow yellow wing bars. Hens much duller, with prominent streaking on the underparts. Young birds resemble hens but are greyer, with brownish-buff rather than yellow wing bars.

African red-eyed bulbul

Pycnonotus nigricans

Bold and lively birds, with a small crest on their heads, which is usually raised when singing. They often sing from a conspicuous branch soon after sunrise, making them easy to observe. They are not easily intimidated, even by predators such as smaller birds of prey, which they may mob. Breeding is from September to March, with the nest located in a tree and protected by thorns, as high as 3.65m (12ft). The female incubates alone and the chicks hatch after about 12 days, leaving the nest after a similar interval. Red-eyed bulbuls feed mainly off the ground, seeking insects such as grasshoppers, particularly when chicks are being reared, as well as plucking fruits and berries off the branches. They will also probe flowers for nectar, but can easily be attracted to bird tables.

Distribution: Present in south-western Africa. Occurs through Namibia and in Botswana and South Africa, extending north as far as southern Angola
Size: 21cm (8in).
Habitat: Open country.
Nest: Cup-shaped, made from vegetation.
Eggs: 3, pinkish-white with darker markings.
Food: Fruit, invertebrates.

Identification: Black head. Bare red skin encircles the eyes. Dark brown back and wings. Upper breast greyish-brown, underparts turning whitish. Undertail coverts yellow. Bill, legs and feet black. Young have a paler eye ring. Sexes alike.

SMALL INSECT-EATERS AND MOUSEBIRDS

The presence of neighbouring trees greatly increases the variety of birds likely to be spotted in a garden. Shrubs, too, can be of benefit, providing cover, food and nesting opportunities. Many avian visitors are relatively small in size, but they can be quite bold by nature, as shown by the chiffchaff and the various sunbirds that can be encountered in these surroundings.

Chiffchaff

Phylloscopus collybita

The chiffchaff is a lively warbler, generally common through its range and often seen in gardens, particularly those with trees nearby. There are regional differences in appearance, with individuals found in western and central areas having brighter yellow coloration than those birds occurring further north and east. Its unusual name reflects its common two-note song pattern. Pairs are likely to start nesting from April onwards, with the female building the nest on her own. This is positioned relatively close to the ground in a suitable bush or shrub that provides good cover, typically an evergreen such as rhododendron, or sometimes in among brambles, offering protection against predators. The chiffchaffs slip in and out of the nest itself via a side entrance. The hen undertakes the incubation on her own, and this lasts for about 13 days, with the young chicks subsequently fledging after a similar interval. Chiffchaffs may rear two broods during the course of the summer.

Identification: Yellowish stripe above each eye, with a black stripe passing through the centre. Underparts whitish, with variable yellow on the sides of the face and flanks. Rest of the upperparts dark brownish-green. Pointed bill is dark. Legs and feet are black. Sexes are alike.

Distribution: Occurs through most of Europe during the summer but absent from parts of northern Scandinavia and Scotland. Resident in parts of southern Britain and Ireland and further south, near the Mediterranean. Overwinters in northern Africa and south of the Sahara. Also found in Asia.
Size: 12cm (4in).
Habitat: Wooded areas.
Nest: Dome-shaped, made from vegetation.
Eggs: 6, white in colour with brownish spotting.
Food: Invertebrates.

Goldcrest

Regulus regulus

These warblers are the smallest birds in Europe and are surprisingly bold, drawing attention to themselves with their high-pitched calls and the way they jerkily flit from branch to branch. They can be easily distinguished from the slightly larger firecrest (*R. ignicapillus*) by the absence of a white streak above the eyes. Goldcrests associate in groups both of their own kind and also with other small birds such as tits, seeking food relatively high up in the branches rather than at ground level. Pairs split off to breed in the early spring, with both sexes collecting moss and other material to construct their nest. This may be hung off a conifer branch, up to 12m (40ft) off the ground, although it may also be concealed among ivy or similar vegetation. Cobwebs act as thread to anchor the nest together, and the interior is lined with feathers. The young will have fledged by three weeks old, and the adults may nest again soon afterwards and rear a second brood.

Distribution: Resident through much of Europe, except for northern Scotland and northern Scandinavia, where pairs spend the summer. Often moves south to the Mediterranean for the winter. Range also extends eastwards into Asia.
Size: 8.5cm (3¹/₄in).
Habitat: Wooded areas.
Nest: Suspended basket made of moss.
Eggs: 7–8, buffy-white with brown markings.
Food: Mainly invertebrates.

Identification: Dumpy appearance, with cock birds having an orange streak (yellow in hens) running down the centre of the head, bordered by black stripes on each side. Prominent area of white encircling the eyes, with much of the rest of the head pale grey. White wing bars. The plumage on the back is greyish-green. Underparts are paler in colour. Bill is black, legs and feet greyish. Young birds have greyish heads and pale bills.

Eastern double-collared sunbird

Cinnyris mediocris

There are a number different species of double-collared sunbird, and their distributions overlap. For this reason it can be difficult to tell them apart, though much depends on the altitude at which sightings are made. The eastern double-collared sunbird is seen only at relatively high altitudes, above 1,500m (5,000ft), hence it is quite locally distributed through its range. Like other sunbirds, this species allows a relatively close approach when feeding, especially in flower gardens, which they visit regularly. Red flowers hold a particular attraction for them, especially the blooms of red hot pokers (*Kniphofia* species), which are native to Africa.

Identification: Iridescent green plumage on the head, chest and back. The rump is blue. Lower chest is scarlet, with yellow edging of longer feathers (known as pectoral tufts). Remainder of the underparts are olive. Wings and tail black. Bill is relatively short and narrow, curving down at its tip. Hens are a dusky shade of olive-green overall.

Distribution: Eastern side of Africa, ranging through parts of Kenya and Tanzania southwards into Malawi and Zambia.
Size: 10cm (4in).
Habitat: Forest and gardens.
Nest: Bulky, built off a branch.
Eggs: 2.
Food: Mostly nectar and small invertebrates.

Scarlet-chested sunbird (*Chalcomitra senegalensis*): 15cm (6in)
Widely distributed through western Africa, ranging from Senegal and The Gambia eastwards to Cameroon and the Central African Republic. Iridescent green crown and chin, with scarlet-red plumage on the throat and breast. Remainder of the plumage is blackish-brown, often a lighter shade on the wings. Hens are duller, having a mottled dark brown throat with yellowish underparts, and brown elsewhere.

White-backed mousebird (*Colius colius*): 33cm (13in)
Restricted to southern Africa, with a range extending from Namibia and Botswana down to western parts of South Africa. Predominantly ashy-grey in colour over the head and back. The rump area is maroon and the underparts are more of a buffy shade. Rufous on the breast. A distinctive white stripe runs down the back. The bill is grey with a black tip. Young birds have more evenly-coloured buffy underparts. Sexes are alike.

Red-faced cisticola (*Cisticola erythrops*): 13cm (5¹/₂in)
These African warblers have a wide distribution in western parts of the continent, and are also present on the eastern side, extending here down as far as northern parts of South Africa. Orange-brown facial coloration, with a brown crown, back and wings. More of an olive-grey shade in the summer, compared with the winter plumage. The underparts are a creamy shade, and the flanks are browner. Young birds resemble adults in winter plumage, but have a more yellowish suffusion. The upper bill is dark, yellower beneath, and the legs and feet are pinkish-grey. Sexes are alike, but cocks are slightly larger.

Red-faced mousebird

Urocolius indicus

Occurring only in Africa, mousebirds take their name not only from their coloration and narrow tails but also from the way they move through vegetation, climbing in a similar fashion to mice. Yet they can also fly strongly, in a straight line rather than the undulating flight pattern of many birds. Typical representatives of their group, red-faced mousebirds are highly social by nature and usually observed in groups consisting of up to 10 individuals. They will often come down to the ground in order to dust bathe, which helps to keep their plumage in good condition and free from parasites. Unfortunately, the young are not as agile as the adults. They will leave the nest when about 17 days old, before they are able to fly properly, and will often fall straight to the ground. Unable to clamber back up to the nest, they face starvation. The number of chicks that are reared successfully by these mousebirds is correspondingly low, with just one in four on average surviving to become independent.

Distribution: Confined to southern parts of Africa, extending up the coast of Angola in the west. An isolated population exists along the coast of Mozambique, extending as far as Tanzania.
Size: 33cm (13in).
Habitat: Prefers relatively open country.
Nest: Cup-shaped, made from vegetation.
Eggs: 3–5, whitish-coloured with red markings.
Food: Largely berries and other fruit.

Identification: Prominent red area of skin around the eyes, extending to the top of the bill. Brownish-grey overall, with a greenish suffusion. Crest on the head. Long tail feathers. Young birds greener on the face. Sexes are alike.

PIGEONS AND DOVES

The columbiformes have adapted well to living in close association with people, although their presence is frequently unwelcome. Large flocks of feral pigeons can cause serious damage to buildings in urban areas, not just with their droppings but also by pecking at the mortar, which is a source of calcium. Their adaptability is demonstrated by their readiness to breed throughout much of the year.

Rock dove

Columba livia

True rock doves have a localized range and favour cliffs and ruined buildings on which to breed. In the past, rock doves were kept and bred by monastic communities, where the young doves (known as squabs) were highly valued as a source of meat. Inevitably, some birds escaped from their dovecotes and reverted to the wild, and their offspring gave rise to today's feral pigeons, which are a common sight in almost every town and city, scavenging whatever they can from our leftovers. Colour mutations have also occurred, and as well as the so-called "blue" form there are now red and even mainly white individuals today.

Identification: Dark bluish-grey head, slight green iridescence on the neck. Light grey wings with two characteristic black bars across each wing. Feral pigeons often have longer wings than rock doves. Reddish-purple coloration on the sides of the upper chest. Remainder of the plumage is grey with a black band at the tip of the tail feathers. Sexes are alike.

Distribution: Rock dove occurs naturally in northern areas of Scotland and nearby islands, and in western Ireland. Also found around the Mediterranean. The feral pigeon's range extends throughout Europe and southern Africa, as well as to other continents.
Size: 35cm (14in).
Habitat: Originally cliffs and mountainous areas.
Nest: Loose pile of twigs or similar material.
Eggs: 2, white.
Food: Mainly seeds.

Above: The rock dove nests on loose twigs.

Wood pigeon

Columba palumbus

Distribution: Throughout most of Europe except for northern Scandinavia and Iceland, ranging eastwards into Asia. Also present in north-western Africa.
Size: 43cm (17in).
Habitat: Areas with tall trees.
Nest: Platform of twigs.
Eggs: 2, white.
Food: Seeds, plant matter and invertebrates.

Identification: Grey head, with a reflective metallic-green area at the nape of the neck and characteristic white patches on the sides. Bill is reddish at the base, becoming yellow towards the top. Purplish breast becoming paler on the underparts. Tip of tail is black. White edging to the wings most evident in flight, forming a distinct band. Sexes alike.

These pigeons can be significant agricultural pests in arable farming areas. In towns they will often frequent parks with established stands of trees, descending into nearby gardens and allotments to raid growing crops. However, they also occasionally eat potential crop pests such as snails. Pairs sometimes nest on buildings, although they usually prefer a suitable tree fork. Their calls are surprisingly loud and are often uttered soon after dawn. Outside the breeding season these birds will often congregate in large numbers. If danger threatens, they can appear quite clumsy when taking off thanks to their relatively large size.

Collared dove

Streptopelia decaocto

The westerly spread of these doves during the second half of the 20th century was one of the most dramatic examples of the changing patterns of distribution among bird species. In this case, the triggers for the distribution change are unclear. Collared doves had been recorded in Hungary in the 1930s, and they moved rapidly over the next decade across Austria and Germany to France, and also headed north to the Netherlands and Denmark. The species was first sighted in eastern England during 1952, and a pair bred there three years later. The earliest Irish record was reported in 1959, and by the mid-1960s the collared dove had colonized almost all of the UK. No other bird species has spread so far and so rapidly in recent times, to the extent that the collared dove's range now extends right across Europe and Asia.

Above: The collared dove is a frequent visitor to towns and will happily build its nest on the roof tops.

Identification: Pale greyish-fawn with a narrow black half-collar around the back of the neck. Dark flight feathers, with white along the leading edges of the wings. White tips to tail feathers, visible when spread. Depth of individual coloration can vary. Sexes are alike.

Distribution: Across much of Europe but not including the far north of Scandinavia and the Alps, ranging eastwards into Asia. More localized on the Iberian Peninsula and in northern Africa particularly.
Size: 34cm (13in).
Habitat: Parks and gardens.
Nest: Platform of twigs.
Eggs: 2, white.
Food: Mostly eats seeds and plant matter.

Laughing dove

Streptopelia senegalensis

These very adaptable doves are often seen in urban habitats, particularly in areas where they are expanding their range. In Australia, for example, bird-table offerings have afforded them a constant supply of suitable food, allowing them to become established here well away from their natural range. In northern Africa, these doves are frequently encountered near oases, which has led to them becoming known as palm doves. Their fast breeding cycle, with chicks hatching and leaving the nest within a month of the eggs being laid, means that they can rapidly increase their numbers under favourable conditions. Pairs may also attempt to breed throughout much of the year, rather than having a prescribed breeding period like most bird species, particularly those occurring outside the tropics.

Distribution: Ranges widely throughout most of Africa, both north and south of the Sahara Desert, although is absent from western-central parts. Also extends through the Middle East into Asia. Has been introduced to Western Australia.
Size: 26cm (10in).
Habitat: Acacia woodland, oases and open country.
Nest: Loose platform made from twigs.
Eggs: 2, white.
Food: Mainly seeds and invertebrates.

Identification: Reddish-brown, with a brown-and-black speckled collar under the neck. Grey bar on the leading edges of the wings. Underparts are pale. Long, relatively dark tail. Sexes are alike.

Stock pigeon (stock dove, *Columba oenas*): 32cm (12½in)
Throughout Europe, but absent from much of Scotland, northern Scandinavia and most of the mountainous central region. Range extends to north-western Africa and east to Asia. Grey head with green iridescence on the neck. The wings are dark grey with black markings. Black band across the tips of the tail feathers. Pale grey rump and lower underparts. The chest is pinkish-grey.

European turtle dove (*Streptopelia turtur*): 27cm (10½in)
Much of Europe but not common in Ireland, Scotland or Scandinavia. Present in northern Africa. More brightly coloured on the wings than its East Asian cousin, having orange-brown feathers with darker centres. Black-and-white barring on the sides of the neck. Head is greyish. Underparts are pale with a slight pinkish hue. White edge to the tail feathers.

Cape dove (Namaqua dove, *Oena capensis*): 26cm (10in)
Found in Africa south of the Sahara, including Madagascar. Also present in southern Israel and Arabia. Black area from the forehead down on to the chest, with bluish-grey behind. Long, narrow tail. Dark flight feathers and black markings on the wings, with rufous underwing areas. Upperparts are light grey, whiter on the underparts. Hens lack the black area on the face, displaying only a narrow stripe extending from the bill to the eye.

STARLINGS

Starlings are well represented in Europe and Africa, although they display greater diversity on the latter continent. Generally quite distinctive, sometimes with spectacular plumage, many starlings, including even the common starling, have an attractive metallic iridescence which gives them a sleek, attractive appearance that changes according to the light.

Common starling

European starling *Sturnus vulgaris*

These frequently sighted birds are resident in a vast range of areas. However, some populations of the common starling, especially in the more northerly part of their range, will undertake seasonal migrations. This prompts the sudden arrival of hundreds of birds in urban areas, especially where there are groups of trees suitable for roosting. They often prove noisy in these surroundings, even singing after dusk if the area is well lit. In flight, large flocks are adept at avoiding pursuing predators, such as hawks, by weaving back and forth in a tight formation. Small groups of starlings regularly visit bird tables, and may drive away other visitors. They are equally adept at seeking food on the ground, picking up seeds and probing for invertebrates. When breeding, a pair will often adopt the nest of a woodpecker, but in areas where nesting sites are in short supply, starlings may even tunnel into a suitable bank to create a nesting cavity. The young birds subsequently leave the nest at about three weeks after hatching.

Identification: Glossy. Purplish-black head with a greenish hue on the body, overlaid with spots. Dark brown wings and tail. Hens are similar, but spotting is larger and base of the tail is pinkish rather than blue, as in breeding males. Young birds are duller, brownish and lack iridescence.

Distribution: Range extends throughout Europe and north Africa, with Scandinavian and eastern European populations migrating further south for the winter. Also present further east into Asia, and has been introduced to North America and Australia.
Size: 22cm (8¹/₂in).
Habitat: By houses and buildings.
Nest: In a tree hole or birdhouse.
Eggs: 2–9, white to pale blue or green.
Food: Invertebrates, berries, birdfeeder fare.

Spotless starling

Sturnus unicolor

Pairs of spotless starlings may breed close to people, beneath roof tiles or in a suitable hole in a wall. They may also adopt nest cavities constructed by other birds, such as green woodpeckers (*Picus viridis*). The nest is built from dried grasses and other items including yellow flowers, and both members of the pair collect material to line the chamber. Spotless starlings seek food on the ground and in trees and bushes. Small amphibians such as young frogs may be eaten, and during the breeding period earthworms and caterpillars feature more prominently. In autumn and winter, fruits and seeds are eaten, and they may cause damage to ripening crops such as grapes. At this time of year they are more likely to be observed in mixed flocks with common starlings (*Sturnus vulgaris*), with roosts numbering as many as 100,000 individuals.

Identification: Predominantly glossy black with long feathers on the throat when in breeding plumage. In the winter, fine white spotting is evident over the head and extending down on to the chest. Bill is yellow, becoming darker in the winter, when the plumage is greyer overall. Young birds are relatively dark brown overall. Hens resemble cocks in breeding plumage, but have shorter neck feathers and less iridescence.

Distribution: Ranges through the Iberian Peninsula and adjacent areas of northern Africa. Also found on the Mediterranean islands of Sicily, Corsica and Sardinia.
Size: 22cm (8¹/₂in).
Habitat: Open woodland.
Nest: Hole or cavity lined with vegetation.
Eggs: 2–9, pale blue.
Food: Invertebrates and fruit.

Purple glossy starling

Lamprotornis purpureus

Like many of its relatives, the purple glossy starling is a very adaptable bird, able to feed both in trees and on the ground. They will descend to search for food in the aftermath of a grassland fire, and have even been known to grab invertebrates that are retreating from the flames. Although the starlings' traditional nest site is a tree hole, they have adapted to nesting under the roofs of buildings and may even use drainpipes. The hen incubates alone, but the cock bird helps to rear the chicks, which are fed mainly on invertebrates in the early stages after hatching. Invertebrates in the diet help to meet the chicks' need for protein in order to grow rapidly. Outside the breeding season in particular, these starlings can be seen in large groups, made up of as many as several thousand individuals. In such numbers, they readily drive off solitary birds of prey which are drawn to the colony.

Identification: Upperparts are bluish-green. Sides of the face and the underparts are a deep purple. Iridescence is most marked on the wings and in the vicinity of the neck. Tail feathers are purple. Iris is bright yellow in adults, but grey in young birds. Sexes are alike.

Distribution: Extends across Africa south of the Sahara, from Senegal in the west eastwards to parts of Sudan, Kenya and Uganda.
Size: 27cm (10¹/₂in).
Habitat: Light woodland and parkland areas.
Nest: Sticks in a tree hole.
Eggs: 3–4, blue-green with darker markings.
Food: Invertebrates, also fruit and berries.

African pied starling (*Spreo bicolor*): 25cm (10in)
Present through most of South Africa except for the north-west. Predominantly black, with white plumage restricted to the lower underparts, extending to the undertail coverts. Dark upper bill, with a mainly yellow lower bill and gape. White iris. Young birds are duller and have dark irides and gape. Sexes are alike.

White-crowned starling (*Spreo albicapillus*): 23cm (9in)
Present in eastern Africa, ranging from northern parts of Kenya up into southern Ethiopia and western Somalia. Prominent whitish cap extends right across the top of the head. Back and wings are bronzy-black, with white evident on the flight feathers. Underparts are dark grey with white streaking, and the lower underparts are white. Iris is yellow. Bill, legs and feet are black. Young birds are duller overall, with greyish-white plumage on the crown and dark irides. Sexes are alike.

Red-winged starling (*Onychognathus morio*): 30cm (12in)
Widely distributed through East Africa, from eastern Sudan and Ethiopia right down to the southern tip of South Africa. Cock bird is metallic black overall, with black bill, legs and feet. Flight feathers are reddish and the iris is red. Hens have evident greyish coloration over the head, nape and upper chest. Young birds resemble adult males but have dark irides and are less glossy overall.

Splendid starling

Superb starling *Spreo superbus*

Like other birds from this part of Africa, splendid starlings roost quietly during the heat of the day, which means they are hard to spot in spite of their bright coloration. They are most easily observed either early in the morning or late in the afternoon, often near water. Splendid starlings have recognized that tourists are a likely source of food, so in some areas they will frequent safari camps. Few birds are more adaptable when it comes to selecting a nest site. Pairs may build in the thatched roofs of village huts or take over the nests of weaver birds, often with the addition of thorny branches around the entrance hole to give protection from predators while the nest is occupied.

Distribution: Occurs on the eastern side of Africa, from northern Ethiopia southwards to Kenya, Somalia, western Uganda and Tanzania.
Size: 18cm (7in).
Habitat: Open country.
Nest: Variable, self-built or lines a tree hole.
Eggs: 4, dark blue.
Food: Invertebrates, fruits and berries.

Identification: Glossy black head merging into shiny blue nape and breast. Distinctive white band extends across breast. Belly is chestnut, and vent and undertail coverts are white. Wings are metallic bluish-green. Pale yellowish-white iris. Sexes are alike.

THRUSHES

Although overall not brightly coloured, some members of this group are excellent songsters. Their long, powerful bills enable them to prey on a range of invertebrates, and they also feed on berries and fruit. Some thrushes are migratory, either moving within Europe or flying further afield when the weather becomes unfavourable, often descending in large numbers.

Robin

Erithacus rubecula

The robin's colourful appearance belies its strong aggressive streak, for these birds are highly territorial. In the garden, robins can become very tame, regularly hopping down alongside the gardener's fork or spade to snatch invertebrates such as earthworms that come to the surface. Young, recently-fledged robins look very different from mature individuals – they are almost entirely brown, with dense spotting on the head and chest. Robins are not musical birds, and their calls consist largely of a tick-like note which is often drawn-out and repeated, particularly when they are alarmed by the presence of a nearby predator such as a cat. Since robins usually feed on the ground, they can be very vulnerable to these predators.

Identification: Bright orange extends from just above the bill, around the eyes and down over virtually the entire breast. The lower underparts are whitish-grey, becoming browner on the flanks. Top of the head and the wings are brown. Pale wing bar. Sexes are alike.

Distribution: Resident in the British Isles, western Europe and parts of northern Africa. Scandinavian and eastern European populations winter further south.
Size: 14cm (5½in).
Habitat: Gardens, parks and woodland areas.
Nest: Under cover, often near the ground.
Eggs: 5–7, bluish-white with red markings.
Food: Invertebrates, berries, fruit and seeds.

Song thrush

Turdus philomelos

Identification: Brown back and wings, with some black areas evident, and a yellow-buff area across the chest. Dark markings that extend over the chest and abdomen are shaped like arrows, rather than circular. Sexes are alike. Young birds have smaller spots, which are likely to be less numerous on their underparts.

The song of these thrushes is both powerful and musical. It can be heard particularly in the spring at the start of the breeding season, and is usually uttered from a relatively high branch. Song thrushes are welcomed by gardeners as they readily hunt and eat snails and other pests on the ground. Having grabbed a snail, the birds choose a special site known as an anvil where they smash it against a rock to break the shell and dislodge the mollusc within. These thrushes are excellent runners, and this allows them to pursue quarry such as leatherjackets (the larvae of certain species of crane fly, *Tipula* species). When breeding, song thrushes build a typical cup-shaped nest, which the hen is mainly or even solely responsible for constructing.

Distribution: Ranges widely throughout the whole of Europe. Eastern populations head to the Mediterranean region for the winter. Also present in northern Africa, even as far south as the Sudan.
Size: 22cm (8½in).
Habitat: Woodland areas, parks and gardens.
Nest: Cup-shaped.
Eggs: 5–6, greenish-blue with reddish-brown markings.
Food: Invertebrates, berries.

Common blackbird

Turdus merula

Blackbirds frequently descend on lawns to search for invertebrates. Earthworms, which feature prominently in their diet, are most likely to be drawn to the surface after rain, and slugs and snails also emerge in wet conditions. In the 19th century, blackbirds were rarely seen in gardens, but today they have become commonplace. They are quite vocal and have a variety of calls. Cocks are talented songsters, and both sexes will utter an urgent, harsh alarm call. Although blackbirds do not associate in flocks, pairs can be seen foraging together. As with other thrushes, their tails are surprisingly flexible and can be raised or lowered at will. It is not unusual to see pied blackbirds, with variable amounts of white among the black plumage. The majority of these birds, especially those with the most extensive white areas, are cocks.

Identification: Jet black plumage contrasts with the bright yellow bill, which becomes a deeper yellow during the winter. Hens are drab in comparison, brownish overall with some streaking, notably on the breast, and have a darker bill.

Left: The hen alone is usually responsible for incubating the eggs, although very occasionally the cock may share the task.

Distribution: Resident throughout virtually the whole of Europe, except the far north of Scandinavia. Also present in northern Africa. The majority of Scandinavian and eastern European populations are migratory.
Size: 29cm (11¹/₂in).
Habitat: Woodland, gardens and parkland.
Nest: Cup-shaped, hidden in a bush or tree.
Eggs: 3–5, greenish-blue with reddish-brown markings.
Food: Invertebrates, fruit and berries.

Karoo thrush (*Turdus smithi*): 22cm (9in)
Occurs in much of South Africa, apart from the east and southern coastal areas. Greyish-brown overall, darker over the wings and lighter on the underparts. Throat displays black rows of spots, but is otherwise whitish. A restricted area of rufous coloration is evident on the belly. The bill is yellowish, becoming redder at the tip. Legs and feet are pinkish. Sexes are alike. Young tend to display black spotting on their underparts, and red speckling on their upperparts.

Mistle thrush (*Turdus viscivorus*): 29cm (11¹/₂in)
Resident throughout most of western Europe south to northern Africa. Breeds as far north as Scandinavia and also further east. Relatively large thrush. White underparts, often smudged with an area of grey on the upper breast, and displaying a variable black spotted patterning. Pale sides to the head. Back and wings are grey. Sexes are alike.

Fieldfare (*Turdus pilaris*): 27cm (10¹/₂in)
Occurs in central parts of Europe, overwintering in the British Isles and south to the northern Mediterranean. White eye stripe and grey on the sides of the head. Brown band joins the wings across the back. The rump is grey. Rusty-yellow band across the breast with darker markings, especially on the flanks. Underparts otherwise white. Sexes are alike.

Common nightingale

Luscinia megarhynchos

The arrival of the common nightingale in Europe is seen as heralding the start of spring. However, these birds are often difficult to spot, since they utter their musical calls towards dusk and even after dark on moonlit nights. Their relatively large eyes indicate that these members of the thrush family are crepuscular, becoming active around dusk. Their drab, subdued coloration enables them to blend easily into the dense shrubbery or woodland vegetation that they favour. The common nightingale is only present in Europe from April to September, when it breeds, before it once again heads back to Africa for the winter.

Identification: Brown plumage extends from above the bill down over the back of the head and wings, becoming reddish-brown on the rump and tail. A sandy-buff area extends across the breast, while the lower underparts are whitish. The large eyes are dark and highlighted by a light eye ring. Sexes are alike.

Distribution: From southern England and mainland Europe on a similar latitude south to north-western Africa. Over-winters further south in Africa.
Size: 16cm (6in).
Habitat: Woodlands, gardens.
Nest: Cup-shaped.
Eggs: 4–5, greyish-green to reddish-buff.
Food: Mainly invertebrates.

GARDEN PREDATORS

A diverse range of birds may be encountered in the confines of a garden, preying on invertebrates and other vertebrates. Their hunting strategies may vary but they are all to some extent opportunistic, adapting to the prevailing conditions and the availability of food. The same applies to their breeding habits, with a number of these species often nesting in buildings.

Eurasian green woodpecker

Picus viridis

Distribution: Range extends across most of Europe, although absent from much of Scandinavia, Ireland, Scotland and various islands in the Mediterranean. Also present in parts of north-western Africa.
Size: 33cm (13in).
Habitat: Open woodland.
Nest: Tree hole.
Eggs: 5–8, white.
Food: Mainly invertebrates.

Unlike many of its kind, green woodpeckers hunt for food mainly on the ground, using their powerful bills and long tongues to break open ants' nests. They are equally equipped to prey on earthworms, which are drawn to the surface of lawns after rain, and may catch small creatures such as lizards. In the autumn, fruit forms a more significant part of their diet, but they avoid seeds, and so are not drawn to bird feeders. Pairing begins during the winter, with excavation of the nesting chamber taking two weeks to a month to complete. Unlike many woodpeckers they do not drum loudly with their bills to advertise their presence, but pairs can be quite vocal. Incubation is shared, with the hen sitting during the day. Hatching takes just over a fortnight, with the young fledging when a month old.

Identification: Red crown, with red below the eyes and blackish in between. Regional variations. Underparts greyish to green. Back and wings darker green, with yellow spotting. Yellowish rump. Hens often have black rather than red stripes below the eyes. Young are heavily spotted and barred, with a greyer crown.

Little owl

Athene noctua

Little owls can be seen resting during the daytime, on telegraph poles and similar perches in the open. Introduced to Britain in the 1800s, they have since spread right across southern England. They hover in flight, but are rather ungainly when walking on the ground. One factor which has assisted their spread is their adaptability in choosing a nest site – disused factories and even rabbit warrens may be used. The hen sits alone for the incubation, which lasts 24 days. Both adults feed the young, who fledge after five weeks. They will be independent within a further two months.

Identification: White spotting on the head, white above the eyes and a whitish moustache. Heavy brown streaking on a white chest. Larger whiter spots on the wings, barring on the flight feathers and banding across the tail. Whitish legs and feet. Bill yellowish, irides yellow. Young lack white spotting on the forehead. Sexes are alike, but hens usually larger.

Distribution: Range extends from southern Britain and throughout most of Europe at a similar latitude (not as far as Scandinavia) eastwards into Asia. Also present in northern parts of Africa, extending to parts of the Middle East.
Size: 25cm (10in).
Habitat: Prefers relatively open country.
Nest: Tree hole or a cliff hole.
Eggs: 3–5, white.
Food: Invertebrates and small vertebrates.

Thick-billed raven (*Corvus crassirostris*):
64cm (25in)
Restricted largely to the highland areas of
Ethiopia. An unmistakable corvid – the largest
member of the family – which is predominantly
glossy black in colour, except for a small white
patch at the back of the head. The glossy sheen
is most marked over the back and wings. The
black bill is greatly enlarged, with a raised ridge
running down the centre of the curved upper
bill. The bill also has a paler tip. Legs and feet
are black. Young birds have a slightly browner
hue to their plumage. Sexes are alike, but cocks
are slightly larger.

Bokmakierie (*Telophorus zeylonus*) 22.5cm (9in)
This bush shrike ranges from the western coast
of southern Angola, spreading out across
southern Namibia and into South Africa. Isolated
population exists in eastern Zimbabwe. Greyish
head and neck, with a yellow stripe above the
eyes and a black area beneath, which extends
downwards to form a bib on the lower chest.
Upper chest is bright yellow, with the remainder
of the underparts orangish-yellow. Greyish on
the flanks. Back, wings and tail are olive-green.
Sexes are alike. Young birds lack black markings.

Rock kestrel (*Falco rupicolus*): 33cm (13in)
Restricted to southern Africa, extending north as
far as Tanzania, although absent from much of
the eastern coast. Cock birds have a greyish
head with a yellowish throat. The wings are
brown with black markings, and the flight
feathers are black. The rump is grey, as is the
tail, which is barred with black markings and
ends in a white tip. Underparts are paler and
more rufous on the wings, with variable black
markings. White undersides of the wings display
grey markings. Young birds have rufous heads.
Hens have more heavily barred tails.

Jackdaw

Eurasian jackdaw *Corvus monedula*

These corvids are very adaptable birds, just
as likely to be seen foraging on rubbish
dumps as visiting garden bird tables. When
ants swarm on warm summer days, they are
sufficiently agile to catch these flying insects
on the wing. In agricultural areas, jackdaws
soon learn to pull ticks off the backs of
grazing animals such as sheep, as well as
stealing their wool, which they use to line
their nests. Pairs rarely nest in the open,
however, preferring instead the relative
security of an enclosed area, often utilising
buildings or even chimneys or church
steeples. The hen incubates the eggs alone,
and hatching takes
place after about
19 days. The
young chicks are
ready to leave the
nest after a further
five weeks. Relatively
social at all times,
jackdaws will often
associate in large groups
during the winter months,
not infrequently being seen
in the company of rooks
(*Corvus frugilegus*) in
agricultural areas.
Jackdaws are also to
be found in coastal
areas, and will even
breed on cliffs.

Distribution: Resident
throughout virtually the
whole of Europe, although
absent from large parts of
Scandinavia. Range extends
eastwards into Asia. Also
occurs in various parts of
north-western Africa.
Size: 39cm (15¼in).
Habitat: Prefers relatively
open country.
Nest: Made from sticks, sited
in a hole.
Eggs: 3–8, pale bluish-green
with darker markings.
Food: Omnivorous.

Identification: Glossy blackish
overall, darker on the
crown, around the eyes
and down on to the
throat. Back of the
head and neck are
lighter, almost silvery,
depending on the
race. Black bill,
legs and feet.
Distinctive
pale bluish
irides. Young
birds have blackish
irides and darker, less
glossy feathering.

Magpie

Common magpie *Pica pica*

Bold and garrulous, magpies are a common
sight throughout much of their wide range.
They are often blamed for the decline of
songbirds because of their habit of raiding
the nests of other birds. Magpies are usually
seen in small groups, although pairs will nest
on their own. If a predator such as a cat
ventures close to the nest there will be a
considerable commotion, and the nesting
magpies will be joined by others in the
neighbourhood to harry the unfortunate
feline. Magpies sometimes take an equally direct approach
when seeking food, chasing other birds – gulls in particular
– to make them drop their food. Magpies are quite agile
when walking, holding their long tails up as they move.

Identification: Black head, upper
breast, back, rump and tail, with
a broad white patch around the
abdomen. Broad white wing
stripe and dark blue areas
evident below on folded
wings. Depending on the
light, there may
be a green gloss
to the black plumage.
Sexes are alike, but
the cock may have a
longer tail.

Distribution: Virtually the
whole of Europe south to
north Africa. Present in parts
of Asia and North America.
Size: 51cm (20in).
Habitat: Open and lightly
wooded areas.
Nest: Dome-shaped stick pile.
Eggs: 2–8, bluish-green with
darker markings.
Food: Omnivorous.

CLASSIFICATION

The way in which different birds are grouped is known as classification. This is not only helpful in terms of distinguishing individual species and those that are closely related, but it also enables wider assessments of relationships between larger groups to be made.

Interest in how best to group birds into distinct categories is nothing new. It dates back nearly 2,500 years to the ancient Greeks, when an early method of classification was developed by the philosopher Aristotle. He sought to group living creatures on the basis of differences in their lifestyles, rather than on the basis of anatomical distinctions, which are favoured today. The first modern attempt to trace relationships between birds was made by Sir Francis Willoughby, in a book entitled *Ornithologia,* which was published in 1676. Willoughby saw the need for what was essentially an identification key that would enable readers to find an unknown bird by means of special tables devised for this purpose.

Willoughby's work concentrated solely on birds, but it was actually a Swedish botanist, Carl von Linné (also known as Linnaeus), who devised the universal system of classification that

Above: The so-called nominate subspecies of the African grey parrot – Psittacus erithacus erithacus.

Below: This is the timneh subspecies of the grey parrot, known scientifically as Psittacus erithacus timneh.

is now known as the Linnean System. Linné relied primarily on the physical similarities between living organisms as the basis for grouping them, laying the foundations for the science of classification, which is now known as systematics. He refined this approach through a series of new editions of his classic work *Systema Naturae,* which was originally published in 1735.

Linné's system operates through a series of ranks, creating what is sometimes described as a hierarchal method. Starting from a very general base, the ranks become increasingly specific, splitting into smaller groups, until finally, individual types of birds can be identified. One advantage of this system is that when a new species is discovered, it can be fitted easily into this existing framework.

New advances

While Linné and successive generations of taxonomists relied on physical similarities, the use of DNA analysis is currently transforming our understanding of the natural world. By comparing sequences of the genetic material DNA, it is possible for ornithologists to investigate which birds share DNA sequences that suggest a close relationship. This method of study is set to revolutionize taxonomy and is already leading to numerous revisions of the existing classification of birds.

How the system works

Birds, as animals, belong to the kingdom Animalia, and, having backbones, they are members of the phylum Chordata, which includes all vertebrates. The class Aves is the first division at which birds are separated from other vertebrates such as mammals. Birds alone comprise this major grouping, which is subdivided into smaller categories called orders.

Above: This is the African race of ring-necked parakeet (Psittacula krameri krameri). The plumage is of a more yellowish shade than its Indian relative, and the bill is darker.

It is then a matter of tracking an individual species down through the various ranks of classification. For example, the classificatory breakdown of the grey parrot is as follows:
Order: Psittaciformes
Family: Psittacidae
Genus: *Psittacus*
Species: *Psittacus erithacus*
Subspecies: *Psittacus erithacus erithacus, Psittacus erithacus timneh*
If you are unsure where you are in the ranking, the way in which the names are written gives a clear indication. The names of orders end in "-formes", while family names terminate with "-idae". At or below genus level, all names are italicized, with the genus comprising one or more species. The scientific name of a species always consists of two descriptions, with the genus names being written first. Species are the basic fundamental level in the taxonomic tree, enabling particular types of birds to be named individually. Members of a particular species generally identify with each

other and do not normally interbreed with other species. However, if interbreeding does occur, the resulting offspring are known as hybrids.

At the most specific level of the taxonomic tree are subspecies: closely related forms of the same species that are nevertheless distinctive enough to be identified separately. These are often defined on the basis of their size, although also because of distinct differences in coloration. In the case of the grey parrot (*Psittacus erithacus*) given above, the so-called nominate form, which is the first form to have been recognized, is *Psittacus erithacus erithacus*, as indicated by a repetition of the so-called trivial name *erithacus*. The subspecies timneh (which can be written in an abbreviated form *P. e. timneh* in the context of the nominate subspecies) is recognizable in this instance because of its smaller size, significantly darker grey coloration and maroon rather than red tail feathers.

It was Linné himself who devised this method of distinguishing between such closely related individuals, first describing it in 1758. His method is sometimes known as the trinomial

system, thanks to its use of three names in these cases.

What's in a name?

Even the choice of scientific names is not random. They can give an insight into a bird's appearance or distribution, often based on Latin. The name *flavinucha,* for example, indicates yellow plumage around the neck; the description *peruviana* in the case of the parrot-billed seed-eater (*Sporophila peruviana*) indicates the bird's distribution in South America. In a few instances, the species' description features a person's name, for example *Chloebia gouldiae* – the Gouldian finch – which the noted naturalist and explorer John Gould named after his wife Elizabeth, because of its beauty. In order to be recognized as a species, an example of the bird concerned, known as the "type specimen", has to be held in a museum collection, enabling a detailed description to be written up as part of the identification process.

Below: Subtle but consistent differences in appearance allow the various races, or "subspecies," to be distinguished. The Indian race of ring-necked parakeet (Psittacula krameri manillensis) is seen here. It has a bright red bill and greener overall plumage.

GLOSSARY

avifauna: The birds of a specified region or period of time.

breeding plumage: The often brightly coloured plumage that the cock birds of some species adopt before the breeding season. Also known as summer or alternate plumage.

carpal: The area of plumage at the top of the leading edge of the wings.

carrion-eaters: Birds such as vultures that feed on the carcasses of dead creatures that they themselves have not killed.

cere: The fleshy area encompassing the nostrils located above the bill. Often especially prominent in parrots.

cline: A gradual change in a characteristic of a species, such as size, or the frequency of a characteristic, over a geographical area.

clumping: The way in which small birds, such as the common wren (*Troglodytes troglodytes*) roost collectively as a means of retaining body heat.

cob: A male swan.

columbiforms: The group of birds that comprises doves and pigeons.

contour feathers: The smaller feathers covering the head and body.

corvid: A member of the Corvidae family, such as crows, ravens and jays.

coverts: The specific contour feathers covering the wings, and also present at the base of the tail.

cryptic: Refers to coloration or formation that conceals or camouflages.

culmen: The central ridge of the bill.

down: Plumage that primarily serves to conserve body heat, and has a loose texture.

eclipse plumage: A transitional plumage seen, for example, in the drakes of some species of duck, occurring after they have moulted their breeding plumage; usually much duller and resembling that of a female. Also seen in some finches and other birds.

frugivore: A species that eats mainly fruit.

irides: The coloured area around the pupil, corresponding to the iris.

irruption: An unpredictable movement of

Above: Red-throated diver pair (Gavia stellata).

large numbers of birds, typically in search of food outside their normal range.

lek: An area where the male birds of certain species, such as the capercaillie (*Tetrao urogallus*), gather to perform courtship rituals.

lores: The area between the bill and the eyes, on each side of the face.

mantle: The plumage on the back and folded wings of certain birds when it is the same colour.

melanistic: A dominance of black pigment in the plumage, such as in a particular colour phase of some species.

migrant: A bird that undertakes regular seasonal movements, breeding in one location and overwintering in another.

moustachial: An area of plumage, usually a stripe, running from the bill under the eye, resembling a moustache in appearance. Displayed by birds such as the bittern (*Botaurus stellaris*).

nidicolous: Refers to the chicks of species that remain in the nest for some time after hatching.

nidifugous: Indicates the chicks of species that leave the nest almost immediately after hatching.

nuchal: The plumage at the nape of the neck.

orbital: The skin around the eye.

pectoral: Of or located on the breast.

precocial: Refers to newly hatched young that are covered with down and fully active, able to run around at this stage.

race: A geographically isolated population below the level of species, which differs slightly, typically in size or colour, from other races of the same species group. Also referred to as subspecies.

racket/racquet: Enlargements at the tips of otherwise bare shafts of tail feathers, as seen in species such as the racket-tailed roller (*Coracias spatulatus*).

raptor: A bird of prey that actively hunts its food.

ratite: Any of the large, flightless birds, such as the ostrich (*Struthio camelus*), that have a flat breastbone without the keel-like ridge of flying birds.

scapular: Of or on the shoulder.

spatule: Spoon-shaped or spatula-shaped feathers, on the wing or the tail.

speculum: A distinctive patch of colour evident in the flight feathers of certain birds, particularly ducks and parrots.

syrinx: The voice organ of birds, located at the base of the trachea (windpipe).

tarsal: Refers to the area at or below the ankle in birds, as in tarsal spur.

torpidity: A state of dormancy, usually undertaken to conserve energy and combat possible starvation in the face of adverse environmental conditions.

tousling: Territorial, and aggressive, behaviour adopted by pairs during the breeding period, as seen for example in coots (*Fulica atra*). The pair attacks the chicks of other birds, or even their own offspring, if they venture too close. Chicks may then feign death to secure release.

vagrant: A species or population seen far from its normal range.

wattle: A wrinkled, fleshy, often brightly coloured piece of skin that hangs from the throat or chin of certain birds, such as the cock common pheasant (*Phasianus colchicus*), or which may be present elsewhere on the head.

zygodactyl: The 2:2 perching grip, with two toes holding the perch at the front and two at the back.

Below: Parrots have a zygodactyl perching grip.

SELECTED BIBLIOGRAPHY

Alderton, David (1992) *Parrots*, Whittet Books, London, UK.

Bannerman, D.A. (1928–1951) *The Birds of Tropical West Africa*, 8 vols, Oliver & Boyd, Edinburgh, UK.

Bannerman, D.A. & Lodge, G.E. (1957–63) *The Birds of the British Isles*, 12 vols, Oliver & Boyd, Edinburgh, UK.

Benson, C.W. & Benson, F. M. (1977) *The Birds of Malawi*, Montfort Press, Limbe, Malawi.

Borrow, Nik & Demey, Ron (2002) *Birds of Western Africa*, Princeton University Press, Princeton, USA.

Brewer, David (2001) *Wrens, Dippers and Thrashers*, Christopher Helm, London UK.

Brown, Leslie H., Urban, Emil K., & Newman, Kenneth B. (eds) (1982) *The Birds of Africa*, vol 1, Academic Press, London, UK.

Clark, W.S (1999) *A Field Guide to the Raptors of Europe, the Middle East and North Africa*, Oxford University Press, Oxford, UK.

Cramp, S. et al (1977–1994) *Birds of the Western Palearctic*, vols 1–9, Oxford University Press, Oxford, UK.

Dorst, Jean (1974) *The Life of Birds*, two vols, Weidenfeld & Nicolson, London, UK.

Etchecopar, R.D. & Hue, F. (1967) *The Birds of North Africa*, Oliver & Boyd, Edinburgh, UK.

Ferguson-Lees, James & Christie, David A. (2001) *Raptors of the World*, Christopher Helm, London, UK.

Forshaw, Joseph & Cooper, William T. (1989) *Parrots of the World*, Blandford Press, London, UK.

Fry, C. Hilary; Keith, Stuart & Urban, Emil K. (eds) (1986–2004) *The Birds of Africa*, vols 2–7, Academic Press, London, UK.

Fry, C. Hilary; Fry, Kathie & Harris, Alan (1992) *Kingfishers, Bee-eaters & Rollers*, Christopher Helm, London, UK.

Gibbs, David; Barnes, Eustace & Cox, John

(2001) *Pigeons and Doves*, Pica Press, Robertsbridge, East Sussex, UK.

Ginn, P.J.; McIlleron, W.G. & Milstein, P. le S. (1989) *The Complete Book of South African Birds*, Struik Winchester, Cape Town, South Africa.

Gooders, J. & Boyer, T. (1986) *Ducks of Britain and the Northern Hemisphere*, Dragon's World, London, UK.

Goodman, S.M. & Meininger, P.L. (eds) *The Birds of Egypt*, Oxford University Press, Oxford, UK.

Goodwin, Derek (1982) Estrildid *Finches of the World*, British Museum (Natural History), London, UK.

Harrap, Simon & Quinn, David (1996) *Tits, Nuthatches & Treecreepers*, Christopher Helm, London, UK.

Hayman, Peter; Marchant, John & Prater, Tony (1986) *Shorebirds*, Christopher Helm, London, UK.

Holyoak, D.T. (2001) *Nightjars and their Allies*, Oxford University Press, Oxford, UK.

Hoyo, Josep del; Elliott, Andrew & Sargatal, Jordi (eds) (1992–) *Handbook of Birds of the World*, vols 1–8, Lynx Edicions, Barcelona, Spain.

Kemp, A. (1995) *The Hornbills*, Oxford University Press, Oxford, UK.

Mackworth-Praed, C. W. & Grant, C. H. B. (1952–1973) *African Handbook of Birds* series 1–3, 6 vols, Longmans, London, UK.

Madge, Steve & Burn, Hilary (1988) *Wildfowl*, Christopher Helm, London, UK.

Madge, Steve & McGowan, Phil (2002) *Pheasants, Partridges & Grouse*, Christopher Helm, London, UK.

Mullarney, K.; Svensson, L.; Zetterstrom, D. & Grant, P.J. (1999) *Collins Bird Guide*, Harper Collins, London, UK.

Ogilvie, Malcolm & Ogilvie, Carol (1986)

Above: Great painted snipe (Rostratula benghalensis).

Flamingos, Alan Sutton Publishing, Gloucester, UK.

Penny, Malcolm (1974) *The Birds of the Seychelles and the Outlying Islands*, Collins, London.

Pforr, M. & Limbrunner, A. (1981–2) *The Breeding Birds of Europe*, two vols., Croom Helm, London, UK.

Serle, W. et al (1992) *A Field Guide to the Birds of West Africa*, Collins, London, UK.

Sinclair, Ian (1984) *Field Guide to the Birds of Southern Africa*, Collins, London, UK.

Sinclair, Ian & Ryan, Peter (2003) *Birds of Africa, South of the Sahara*, Struik Publishers, Cape Town, South Africa.

Sparks, John & Soper, Tony (1987) *Penguins*, David & Charles, Devon, UK.

Williams, J.G. & Arlott, N. (1980) *A Field Guide to the Birds of East Africa*, Collins, London, UK.

Williams, T.D. (1995) *The Penguins*, Oxford University Press, Oxford, UK.

Zimmerman, Dale A., Turner, Don A. & Pearson David J. (1996) *Birds of Kenya and Northern Tanzania*, Princeton University Press, Princeton, USA.

WEBSITES OF INTEREST

UK ORGANIZATIONS

British Bird Rarities Committee
http://www.bbrc.org.uk

British Ornithologists' Union
http://www.bou.org.uk

British Trust for Ornithology
http://www.bto.org

Hawk and Owl Trust
http://www.hawkandowl.org

Rare Birds Breeding Panel
http://www.rbbp.org.uk

Royal Society for the Protection of Birds
http://www.rspb.org.uk

Wildfowl and Wetlands Trust
http://www.wwt.org.uk

INTERNATIONAL BIRDING

African Bird Club
http://www.africanbirdclub.org

BirdLife International
http://www.birdlife.net/

Disabled Birders Association (UK)
http://www.disabledbirdersassociation.org.uk/DBAindex.htm

European Ornithologists' Union
http://www.eou.at/

Global Ringing and Banding Internet Links Database
http://www.birdsinthe.net/

Ornithological Society of the Middle East
http://www.osme.org

Pacific Seabird Group
http://www.pacificseabirdgroup.org

Rare Birds of the World
http://www.geocities.com/RainForest/Vines/2408/critical.html

INDEX

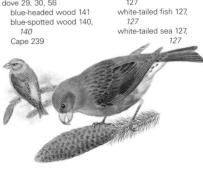

PICTURE ACKNOWLEDGEMENTS

The Publisher would like to thank
the following picture agencies for
granting permission to use their
photographs in this book:

Key: l = left, r = right, t = top,
m = middle, b = bottom

David Alderton: 29t, 58b.

Ardea: 6t, 13br, 14r, 15t, 18b, 19m, 19b,
20t, 21br, 23tr, 23b, 24b, 25b, 26t, 27t,
27b, 29b, 31t, 31m, 31b, 33m, 35b, 36t,
36b, 37t, 37m, 37b, 38t, 39t, 39m, 40t,
50tl, 50tr, 54t, 58m, 60t, 62t, 63tr, 66tl.

Dennis Avon: 13ml, 13br, 13bl, 15m, 22bl,
23tl, 26bl, 27t, 27b, 32t, 50b, 52tr, 52b,
56t, 56b, 60b, 62b, 246b, 247t, 247b.

Oxford Scientific Films: 6b, 8/9, 11, 13tl,
13tr, 13mr, 14l, 16t, 18b, 24t, 25tl, 25tr,
26br, 28bl, 30t, 33tr, 35t, 39b, 40b, 41t,
41b, 43t, 43b, 44t, 44m, 44b, 46t, 46m,
48t, 48br, 54b, 58t, 63tl, 63b, 246t,
endpaper.

**The artworks appearing in this book
were principally supplied by Peter
Barrett, with additional thanks to the
following illustrators for contributing**

their work: Anna Childs, Studio
Galante, Martin Knowelden,
Andrew Robinson, Tim Thackeray.

**All locations maps were drawn by
Anthony Duke, with the exception of
the migratory routes map on page 34,
which was supplied by Peter Barrett.**

NOTES

NOTES

NOTES

NOTES

NOTES

NOTES